Founding the Fatimid State

The Institute of Ismaili Studies
Ismaili Texts and Translations Series, 6

Previously published titles:

1. Ibn al-Haytham, *The Advent of the Fatimids: A Contemporary Shiʿi Witness.* An Edition and English Translation of Ibn al-Haytham's *Kitāb al-Munāẓarāt*, by Wilferd Madelung and Paul E. Walker (2000).
2. al-Shahrastānī, Muḥammad b. ʿAbd al-Karīm. *Struggling with the Philosopher: A Refutation of Avicenna's Metaphysics.* A New Arabic Edition and English Translation of al-Shahrastānī's *Kitāb al-Muṣāraʿa*, by Wilferd Madelung and Toby Mayer (2001).
3. Jaʿfar b. Manṣūr al-Yaman, *The Master and the Disciple: An Early Islamic Spiritual Dialogue.* Arabic Edition and English Translation of Jaʿfar b. Manṣūr al-Yaman's *Kitāb al-ʿĀlim wa'l-ghulām*, by James W. Morris (2001).
4. Idrīs ʿImād al-Dīn, *The Fatimids and their Successors in Yaman: The History of an Islamic Community.* Arabic Edition and English Summary of Idrīs ʿImād al-Dīn's *ʿUyūn al-akhbār*, vol. 7, by Ayman Fu'ād Sayyid, in collaboration with Paul E. Walker and Maurice A. Pomerantz (2002).
5. Naṣīr al-Dīn Ṭūsī, *Paradise of Submission: A Medieval Treatise on Ismaili Thought.* A New Persian Edition and English Translation of Naṣīr al-Dīn Ṭūsī's *Rawḍa-yi taslīm*, by S. J. Badakhchani with an introduction by Hermann Landolt and a philosophical commentary by Christian Jambet (2005).

Founding the Fatimid State:

The Rise of an Early Islamic Empire

An annotated English translation of
al-Qāḍī al-Nuʿmān's
Iftitāḥ al-Daʿwa

by

Hamid Haji

I.B.Tauris *Publishers*
LONDON • NEW YORK
in association with
The Institute of Ismaili Studies
LONDON

Published in 2006 by I.B.Tauris & Co Ltd
6 Salem Rd, London W2 4BU
175 Fifth Avenue, New York NY 10010
www.ibtauris.com

in association with The Institute of Ismaili Studies
42–44 Grosvenor Gardens, London SW1W 0EB
www.iis.ac.uk

In the United States of America and in Canada distributed by
St Martin's Press, 175 Fifth Avenue, New York NY 10010

ISBN 10: 1 85043 885 4
ISBN 13: 978 1 85043 885 4

A full CIP record for this book is available from the British Library
A full CIP record for this book is available from the Library of Congress

Library of Congress catalog card: available

Typeset in Minion Tra for The Institute of Ismaili Studies

Printed and bound in Great Britain by TJ International Ltd, Padstow, Cornwall

The Institute of Ismaili Studies

The Institute of Ismaili Studies was established in 1977 with the object of promoting scholarship and learning on Islam, in the historical as well as contemporary contexts, and a better understanding of its relationship with other societies and faiths.

The Institute's programmes encourage a perspective which is not confined to the theological and religious heritage of Islam, but seeks to explore the relationship of religious ideas to broader dimensions of society and culture. The programmes thus encourage an interdisciplinary approach to the materials of Islamic history and thought. Particular attention is also given to issues of modernity that arise as Muslims seek to relate their heritage to the contemporary situation.

Within the Islamic tradition, the Institute's programmes promote research on those areas which have, to date, received relatively little attention from scholars. These include the intellectual and literary expressions of Shiʿism in general, and Ismailism in particular.

In the context of Islamic societies, the Institute's programmes are informed by the full range and diversity of cultures in which Islam is practised today, from the Middle East, South and Central Asia, and Africa to the industrialised societies of the West, thus taking into consideration the variety of contexts which shape the ideals, beliefs and practices of the faith.

These objectives are realised through concrete programmes and activities organised and implemented by various departments of the Institute. The Institute also collaborates periodically, on a programme-specific basis, with other institutions of learning in the United Kingdom and abroad.

The Institute's academic publications fall into a number of interrelated categories:

1. Occasional papers or essays addressing broad themes of the relationship between religion and society, with special reference to Islam.
2. Monographs exploring specific aspects of Islamic faith and culture, or the contributions of individual Muslim thinkers or writers.
3. Editions or translations of significant primary or secondary texts.
4. Translations of poetic or literary texts which illustrate the rich heritage of spiritual, devotional and symbolic expressions in Muslim history.
5. Works on Ismaili history and thought, and the relationship of the Ismailis to other traditions, communities and schools of thought in Islam.
6. Proceedings of conferences and seminars sponsored by the Institute.
7. Bibliographical works and catalogues which document manuscripts, printed texts and other source materials.

This book falls into category three listed above.

In facilitating these and other publications, the Institute's sole aim is to encourage original research and analysis of relevant issues. While every effort is made to ensure that the publications are of a high academic standard, there is naturally bound to be a diversity of views, ideas and interpretations. As such, the opinions expressed in these publications must be understood as belonging to their authors alone.

To the memory of
Aliya

Table of Contents

Maps and Tables

Maps

Tables

Acknowledgements

I would like to express my profound gratitude to Dr Farhad Daftary, Head of Department of Academic Research and Publications at The Institute of Ismaili Studies, London, for inviting me to undertake this project as well as for his support during the course of my work. I am grateful to the staff of the library of the Institute for providing access to its rich collections of manuscripts and printed materials indispensable for my project.

I am particularly indebted to Professor Wilferd Madelung for going meticulously through the entire manuscript of my work. His corrections and invaluable comments have ameliorated the quality of my translation. I am also most thankful to Marzuki Haji of the Cartographic Resources Unit at the University of Plymouth for his invaluable assistance in drawing a master map of the area studied. Finally, I would like to thank Kutub Kassam for his painstaking editorial review of my manuscript.

Chronology

145/762	The Shīʿī *dāʿī*s Abū Sufyān and al-Ḥulwānī arrive in the Maghrib.
184/800	The Aghlabid residence al-Qaṣr al-Qadīm (al-ʿAbbāsiyya) founded by Ibrāhīm b. al-Aghlab, founder of the Aghlabid dynasty.
263/876	Raqqāda founded by the Aghlabid emir Ibrāhīm b. Aḥmad.
266/880	ʿAlī b. al-Faḍl's pilgrimage and conversion to the Ismaili cause.
268/881	The *dāʿī*s Ibn Ḥawshab and ʿAlī b. al-Faḍl arrive in the Yemen.
270/883	Their mission becomes manifest in the Yemen.
279/892	Abū ʿAbd Allāh meets Kutāma pilgrims in Makka.
280/893	Abū ʿAbd Allāh arrives in Kutāma territory on 14 Rabīʿ I/4 June.
289/902	Rajab/June–July: al-Mahdī departs from Salamiya.
289/902	Abū ʿAbd Allāh's conquest of Mīla.
289/902	Dhū al-Qaʿda/October: First Aghlabid expedition under Abū Ḥawāl sets out to Kutāma territory.
290/903	Second Aghlabid expedition commanded by Abū Ḥawāl sets out against Abū ʿAbd Allāh.
290/903	28 Shaʿbān/27 July: The Aghlabid emir Abū al-ʿAbbās ʿAbd Allāh is murdered.
290/903	Ramaḍān/July–August: The Aghlabid emir Ziyādat Allāh executes his brother Abū Ḥawāl, his paternal uncles and his brothers.
291/904	Abū ʿAbd Allāh's conquest of Saṭīf.

291/904	Aghlabid counter-offensive under the command of Ibn Ḥabashī.
293–296/ 906–909	Abū ʿAbd Allāh conquers Ṭubna, Billizma, Tījis and Bāghāya. He defeats the Aghlabid army near Dār Madyan, and takes Qasṭīliya and Qafṣa.
295/907	Ziyādat Allāh leaves for al-Urbus, gathers his troops there and entrusts the command of the army to Ibrāhīm b. Abī al-Aghlab.
296/909	1 Jumādā II/25 February: Abū ʿAbd Allāh begins his march from Īkjān against Ibn Abī al-Aghlab in al-Urbus.
296/909	21 Jumādā II/17 March: Abū ʿAbd Allāh sends a detachment of horsemen to Manyūla, and the following day to Shaqbanāriya.
296/909	23 Jumādā II/19 March: Abū ʿAbd Allāh disposes his troops for battle, and takes al-Urbus. Ziyādat Allāh escapes from Raqqāda. End of Aghlabid rule.
296/909	1 Rajab/25 March: Abū ʿAbd Allāh enters Raqqāda.
296/909	1 Ramaḍān/24 May: Abū ʿAbd Allāh appoints al-Marwadhī *qaḍī*.
296/909	Ramaḍān/June: Abū ʿAbd Allāh leaves for Sijilmāsa, leaving his brother Abū al-ʿAbbās and Abū Zākī in charge of government.
297/910	20 Rabīʿ II/6 January: al-Mahdī arrives in Ifrīqiya; he enters Raqqāda triumphantly and confers high honours on Abū ʿAbd Allāh and Abū al-ʿAbbās.
297/910	21 Rabīʿ II/7 January: al-Mahdī is proclaimed caliph at Raqqāda, al-Qayrawān and al-Qaṣr al-Qadīm.
298/911	15 Jumādā II/18 February: Abū ʿAbd Allāh, Abū al-ʿAbbās and Abū Zākī are executed.
301–302/ 913–914	First Fatimid expedition against Egypt commanded by Ḥubāsa b. Yūsuf.
303/916	al-Mahdī lays the foundations of the city of al-Mahdiyya.
306/918	Second Fatimid expedition against Egypt commanded by the future al-Qāʾim.

306/918–19	The construction of al-Mahdiyya is completed.
308/921	Shawwāl/February–March: al-Mahdī moves to al-Mahdiyya.
312/924	al-Nuʿmān enters the service of al-Mahdī.
322/934	14 Rabīʿ I/4 March: Death of al-Mahdī.
322/934	On 10 Jumādā II/28 May, al-Mahdī's death is announced.
332/943	The Kharijite Abū Yazīd begins his rebellion.
334/946	13 Shawwāl/18 May: Death of al-Qā'im.
336/947	Abū Yazīd is defeated by al-Manṣūr.
337/948	al-Manṣūr invests al-Nuʿmān with the highest judicial office of the Fatimid state.
341/953	29 Shawwāl/19 March: Death of al-Manṣūr. Beginning of the reign of al-Muʿizz.
344/955	Fatimid fleet raids Almeria in Andalusia.
346/957	al-Muḥarram/April: al-Qāḍī al-Nuʿmān completes the *Iftitāḥ al-daʿwa*.
347/958	Jawhar's campaign in the Maghrib to re-establish Fatimid authority.
358/969	Jawhar's conquest of Egypt for the Fatimids.
362/973	al-Muʿizz moves to Egypt accompanied by al-Qāḍī al-Nuʿmān.
363/974	End of Jumāda II/27 March: Death of al-Qāḍī al-Nuʿmān in Cairo.

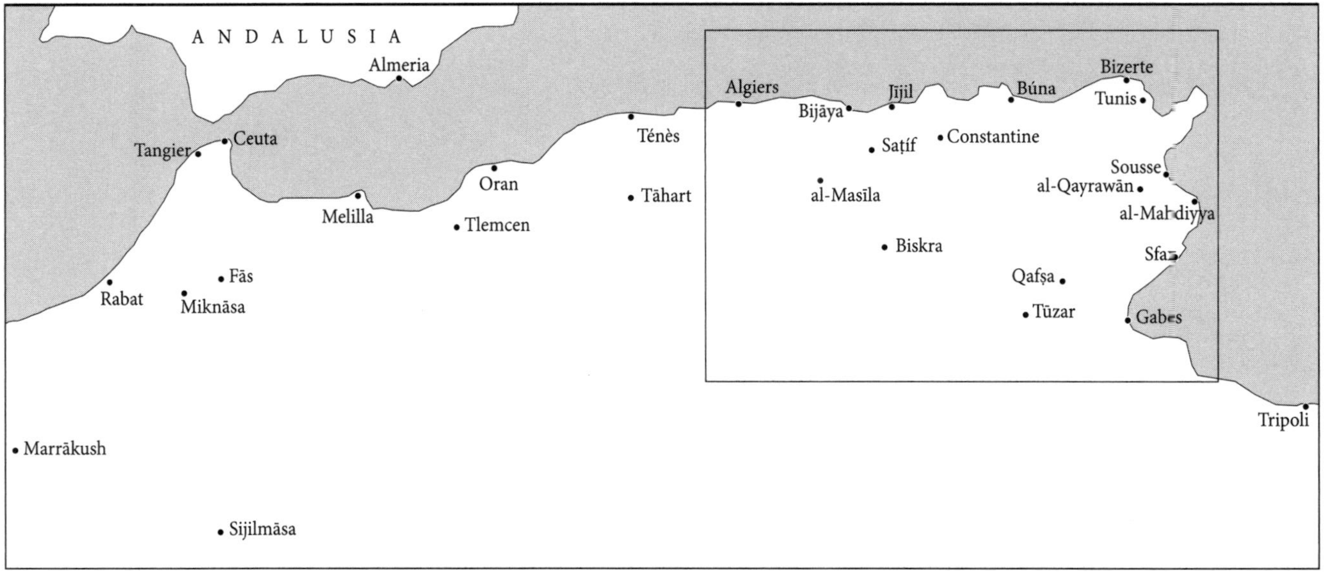

Map 1: The Maghrib

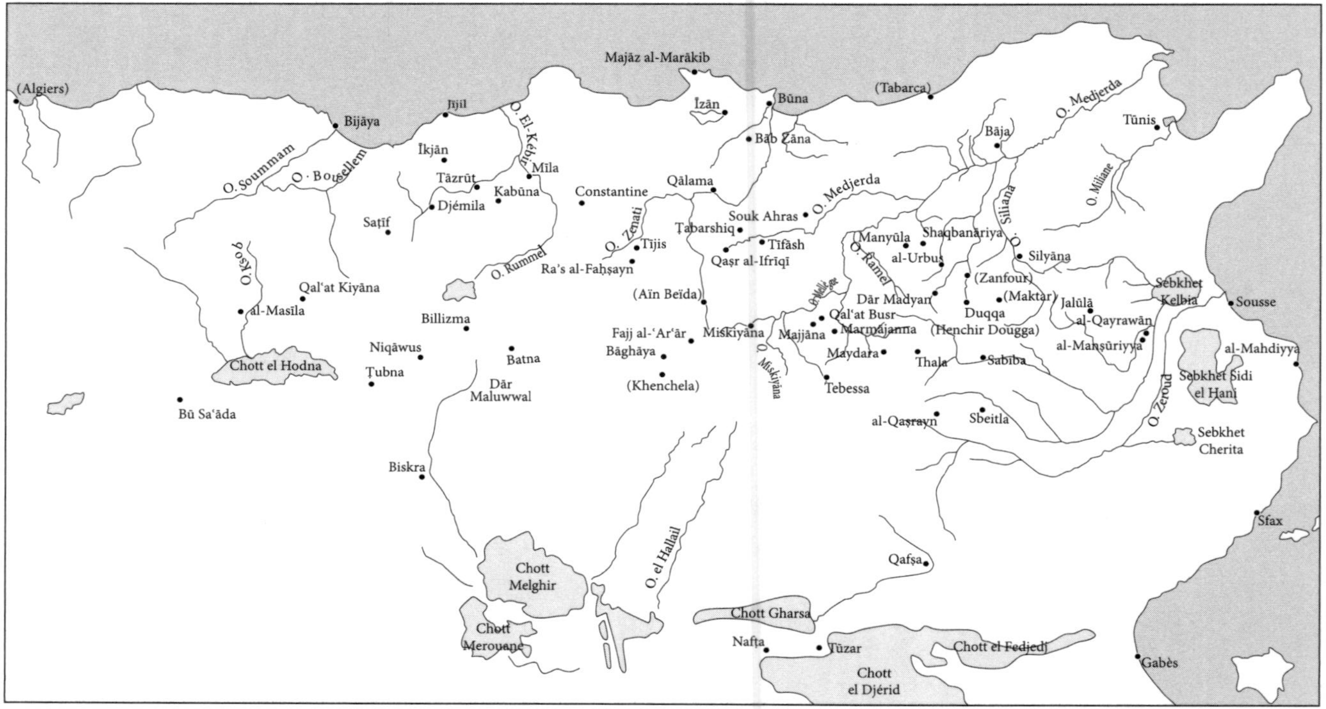

Map 2: The Eastern Maghrib

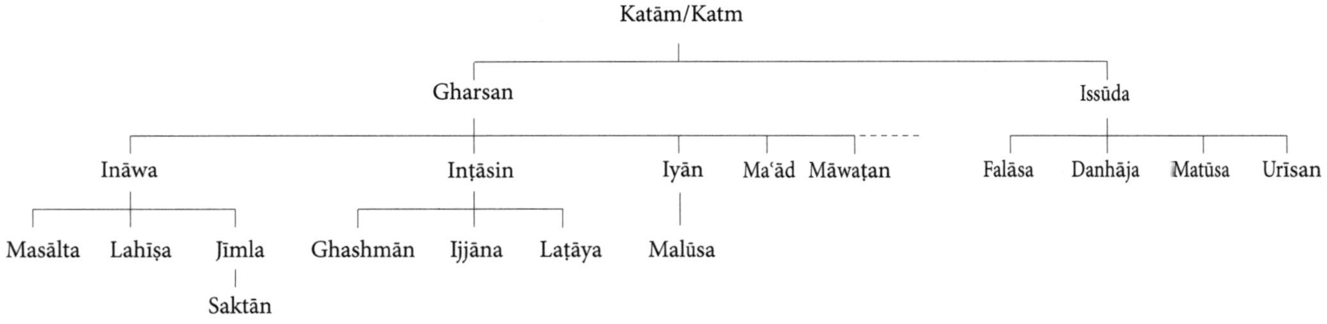

Table 1: Kutāma Clans and their Lineage

- al-Aghlab
  - (1) Ibrāhīm I (184/800)
    - (2) ʿAbd Allāh I (Abū al-ʿAbbās)
    - (3) Ziyādat Allāh I (Abū Muḥammad)
    - (4) al-Aghlab (Abū ʿIqāl)
      - Muḥammad (d. 233/847–848) (Governor of Tripoli)
        - (6) Aḥmad (Abū Ibrāhīm) (242/856)
          - (8) Muḥammad II (Abū ʿAbd Allāh Abū al-Gharāniq) (250/863)
          - (9) Ibrāhīm II (Abū Isḥāq) (261/875)
            - (10) ʿAbd Allāh II (Abū al-ʿAbbās) (289/902)
              - (11) Ziyādat Allāh III (Abū Muḍar) (290–296/903–909)
              - Muḥammad (Abū Ḥawāl)
            - Abū al-Aghlab (ascetic)
              - Ibrāhīm
        - (7) Ziyādat Allāh II (Abū Muḥammad) (249/863)
      - (5) Muḥammad I (Abū al-ʿAbbås) (226/841)
      - Aḥmad (Abū Jaʿfar)

Table 2: The Aghlabids

Introduction

The Author

The author of *Iftitāḥ al-daʿwa*, Abū Ḥanīfa al-Nuʿmān b. Muḥammad b. Manṣūr b. Aḥmad b. Ḥayyūn al-Tamīmī, generally called al-Qāḍī al-Nuʿmān (d. 363/974), was the most eminent exponent of Fatimid jurisprudence and an official historian of the Fatimids. His works, all written in Arabic, cover various other subjects, including Qurʾanic exegesis (*taʾwīl*) and etiquette.[1] He entered the service of the first Fatimid caliph-imam al-Mahdī bi-llāh (r. 297–322/909–934) in about 312/924 in Ifrīqiya (present-day Tunisia and eastern Algeria), and served the first four caliph-imams of the Fatimid dynasty in various capacities for almost fifty years until his death.

On the eve of the advent of the Fatimids, Ismaili jurisprudence had not yet developed, while the Muslim population of Ifrīqiya mostly belonged to two recognised Sunni schools of jurisprudence: the school of Mālik b. Anas (d. 179/796),[2] followed by the popular majority, and the school of Abū Ḥanīfa (d. 150/767), which was usually favoured by the deposed Aghlabid dynasty. The new rulers imposed the application of Ismaili ritual and law in some specific matters, and sought to win adherents. Those who readily joined the Ismaili cause were members of old-established Shīʿī families as well as Ḥanafī scholars deprived of patronage. Among the few Mālikī

1. Ismail K. Poonawala, *Biobibliography of Ismāʿīlī Literature* (Malibu, Calif., 1977), pp. 51–68, gives a complete list of al-Nuʿmān's works, including those attributed to him, numbering sixty-two works.

2. On the significance of Mālikism in Ifrīqiya during the period, see Hussain Monès, 'Le malékisme et l'échec des Fatimides en Ifriqiya', in *Etudes d'orientalisme dédiées à la mémoire de Lévi-Provençal* (Paris, 1962), vol. 1, pp. 197–220.

scholars of al-Qayrawān to embrace the Ismaili faith was al-Nuʿmān's father, and it is most likely that al-Nuʿmān was brought up as an Ismaili. Already in his youth he was assiduous in collecting and transcribing books. At al-Mahdī's suggestion, al-Nuʿmān undertook the collection and classification of a vast number of legal traditions narrated on the authority of the family of the Prophet (*ahl al-bayt*). This endeavour resulted in his voluminous first work, entitled *Kitāb al-Īḍāḥ* (*The Book of Elucidation*), of which only a small fragment has survived. Fortunately, some of his several abridgements of the work, including an easy-to-memorise versified version composed during the reign of the second Fatimid caliph-imam al-Qāʾim bi-amr Allāh (r. 322–334/934–946), have survived. These as well as his subsequent works on jurisprudence represent a development of his thought towards consolidating the legal practices with a view to the codification of Ismaili jurisprudence.

In his several polemical works refuting the principles and methods adopted by the Sunni schools of jurisprudence and their founders, al-Nuʿmān established as authorities of jurisprudence, apart from the Qurʾan and the sunna, the rulings of the imams from the family of the Prophet, including the reigning imam. In one of the earliest Fatimid treatise on the imamate entitled *al-Urjūza al-mukhtāra* (*The Exquisite Poem*), composed during the reign al-Qāʾim, he defended zealously the rights of the Fatimids to the imamate. This legitimist doctrine was seriously challenged by the Kharijites who comprised the indigenous Berbers. Their rebellion led by Abū Yazīd (d. 336/947) rattled the Fatimid state during the last two years of al-Qāʾim's reign and the early part of the reign of his successor al-Manṣūr bi-llāh (r. 334–341/946–953). After crushing the rebellion al-Manṣūr founded, near al-Qayrawān, his new residential capital al-Manṣūriyya to mark his victory. The caliph summoned al-Nuʿmān from Tripoli, where he had appointed him as a judge shortly after his accession to the caliphate, and invested him with the judgeship of al-Manṣūriyya, al-Mahdiyya, al-Qayrawān as well as all the other towns and provinces of Ifrīqiya.

Al-Nuʿmān reached the height of his career during the glorious reign of al-Muʿizz li-dīn Allāh (r. 341–365/953–975) when he was invested with absolute judicial authority to investigate complaints (*maẓālim*) brought before him from the subjects. He was also authorised to hold sessions of wisdom (*majālis al-ḥikma*), in the royal palace, to instruct the congregation in the Ismaili religious doctrines. Under the close supervision of the caliph he composed his *Daʿāʾim al-Islām* (*The Pillars of Islam*) which represents a culmination of more than thirty years of his effort to codify Fatimid jurisprudence. It was proclaimed as the official code of the Fatimid state, and continues to be one of the primary sources of Ismaili law up to the present day.[3]

When al-Muʿizz moved to Egypt in 362/973 after the Fatimid conquest of that country, al-Nuʿmān, together with members of his family, accompanied the caliph. Fatimid law, as codified by al-Nuʿmān, began to be applied and taught in Egypt. He continued to serve al-Muʿizz and died in Cairo at the end of Jumādā II 363/27 March 974. His sons and grandsons continued to teach his works and serve the Fatimids in the judiciary for nearly half a century.

Al-Nuʿmān is also rightly regarded as the founder of Fatimid historiography. His major historical work, *Iftitāḥ al-daʿwa*[4] (*Commencement of the Mission*), completed during the reign of al-Muʿizz, relates in detail the exploits of the Ismaili mission (*daʿwa*), first in the Yemen and then in Ifrīqiya among the Kutāma Berbers, which eventually succeeded in establishing a long-awaited Shīʿī state under the supreme authority of a hereditary imam from the *ahl al-bayt*.

Importance of the Work

The *Iftitāḥ* is the most important primary source containing a detailed narrative account of the establishment of Fatimid dominion in

3. For a detailed account of al-Qāḍī al-Nuʿmān's role in the codification of Ismaili jurisprudence, see Ismaili K. Poonawala, 'Al-Qāḍī al-Nuʿmān and Ismaʿili Jurisprudence', in F. Daftary, ed., *Mediaeval Ismaʿili History and Thought* (Cambridge, 1996), pp. 117–143.

4. This form of the title is found in all but one of the manuscripts consulted, which gives the longer title *Iftitāḥ al-daʿwa wa-ibtidāʾ al-dawla*, retained by Wladimir Ivanov in his *Ismaili Literature: A Bibliographical Survey* (Tehran, 1963), p. 34; Carl Brocklemann, *Geschichte der arabischen Litteratur (GAL)* (Leiden, 1996), SI, p. 325; and Poonawala, *Biobibliography*, p. 58. The word *kitāb*, which precedes both forms of the title in the manuscripts, is not considered to be part of the title. For extant manuscripts and variant forms of the title, see Poonawala, *Biobibliography*, p. 59.

North Africa. It relates the successive phases of the Ismaili *daʿwa*: its rise in the Yemen under the direction of the *dāʿī* Ibn Ḥawshab, the *dāʿī* Abū ʿAbd Allāh al-Shīʿī's initial training under him, his mission among the Kutāma Berbers, his military campaigns, the fall of the Aghlabids, and the advent of al-Mahdī in Ifrīqiya. The author relates these events, using biographical and archival sources readily accessible to him. It appears from comparing texts of subsequent narratives of the rise of the Fatimids in Ifrīqiya that most of their information is derived eventually from the *Iftitāḥ* through the lost chronicles of two eminent historians of Ifrīqiya.[5] The *Iftitāḥ* was also used by later Ismaili writers, particularly the Yemenite *dāʿī* Idrīs ʿImād al-Dīn (d. 872/1468) who quotes extensively from it in his voluminous work on the history of the *daʿwa* and the imams, *ʿUyūn al-akhbār*.

The *Iftitāḥ* devotes a few pages to al-Mahdī's emigration to the Maghrib and his captivity in Sijilmāsa. The author retraces briefly successive stops of al-Mahdī's journey, which allows us to verify the account of another early Ismaili text *Sīrat al-Ḥājib Jaʿfar*[6] whose version of al-Mahdī's emigration is more detailed. The *Iftitāḥ* specifies the historical context of his emigration and elucidates the choice of his destination which was determined especially by the rising fortunes of Abū ʿAbd Allāh. It relates the reasons which inclined al-Mahdī to avoid the Yemen, his intended destination, after his hasty escape from

---

5. One of them, a young contemporary of al-Qāḍī al-Nuʿmān, Abū Isḥāq Ibrāhīm al-Raqīq (d. after 418/1027), was superintendent of the chancery under the Zīrids. He was sent in 388/998 by the Zīrid emir Bādīs on a diplomatic mission to the Fatimid Caliph al-Ḥākim. On him see Taqī al-Dīn Abū al-ʿAbbās Aḥmad b. ʿAlī al-Maqrīzī, *Kitāb al-Muqaffā al-kabīr*, ed. Muḥammad al-Yaʿlāwī (Beirut, 1987), pp. 426–428; and Mohamed Talbi, 'Ibn al-Raḳīḳ', *EI*[2], vol. 3, pp. 902–903. The other historian, Abū Muḥammad ʿAbd al-ʿAzīz b. Shaddād (d. 590/1194), was a member of the Zīrid family. On him see Mohamed Talbi, 'Ibn Shaddād', *EI*[2], vol. 3, p. 933.

6. Muḥammad b. Muḥammad al-Yamānī, *Sīrat al-Ḥājib Jaʿfar b. ʿAlī wa-khurūj al-Mahdī min Salamiya wa-wuṣūluh ilā Sijilmāsa wa-khurūjuh minhā ilā Raqqāda*, ed. W. Ivanow, in *Bulletin of the Faculty of Arts*, University of Egypt, vol. 4 (1936), pp. 107–133; tr. Wladimir Ivanow, *Ismaili Tradition Concerning the Rise of the Fatimids* (London, etc., 1942), pp. 184–223; French tr. Marius Canard, 'L'autobiographie d'un chambellan du Mahdî ʿObeidallâh le Fâṭimide', *Hespéris*, 39 (1952), pp. 279–329, reprinted in his *Miscellanea Orientalia* (London, 1973), article V. See also Albert Gateau, 'La Sīrat Jaʿfar al-Ḥājib: contribution à l'histoire des Fatimides', *Hespéris*, 34 (1947), pp. 375–396.

Salamiya to Egypt, in 289/902, shortly before the capture of the town by the Qarmatians. The mission in the Yemen assigned to the two *dāʿīs* Ibn Ḥawshab and ʿAlī b. al-Faḍl was compromised by the treachery of the latter and the chief *dāʿī* Fīrūz. Moreover, the Yemen did not offer to al-Mahdī's ambitions so many advantages as the Maghrib. After arriving in the district of Qasṭīliya, in what is now Djerid in south-western Tunisia, al-Mahdī abandoned his plan to reach Abū ʿAbd Allāh among the Kutāma and instead proceeded farther west to Sijilmāsa. The *Iftitāḥ* connects this more clearly than the *Sīra* to the arrest, in al-Qayrawān, of the brother of Abū ʿAbd Allāh, Abū al-ʿAbbās, whom al-Mahdī had sent, after his arrival in Tripoli, probably on a spying mission. Abū al-ʿAbbās was thrown in prison in Raqqāda, and it is in order not to endanger his life, asserts al-Nuʿmān, that al-Mahdī, instead of going to Abū ʿAbd Allāh's headquarters in Īkjān as anticipated, proceeded to Sijilmāsa. The *Iftitāḥ* appears to indicate that this turn-around of al-Mahdī was determined by political reasons. Undoubtedly, the military power of the Aghlabids was seriously shaken, but still considerable, and the arrival of al-Mahdī in Ifrīqiya coincided with a new Aghlabid offensive under the command of Ibn Ḥabashī, in the beginning of the autumn of the year 291/904. Evidently al-Mahdī preferred not to proceed to Īkjān in such unfavourable conditions.

The *Iftitāḥ* provides valuable information on some Aghlabid emirs, particularly the last of them, Ziyādat Allāh (r. 290–296/903–909), as well as officials who exercised military and civil functions in the Aghlabid state, complementing information found in other sources. More significantly, it highlights the activity of some supporters of Abū ʿAbd Allāh who played a major role in his mission but about whom only sketchy information has been preserved in the sources. They were Kutāma tribesmen who adhered to the *daʿwa* very early and became pillars of his administration. Distinguished among them were his two main officials, Abū Zākī Tammām b. Muʿārik and Ghazwiyya b. Yūsuf. Abū Zākī, from the Kutāma clan of Ijjāna, distinguished himself by his dedication and bravery. He became Abū ʿAbd Allāh's most faithful companion to whom the latter entrusted the government of Ifrīqiya during his expedition to Sijilmāsa in 296/909. Two years later Abū Zākī was one of the organisers of a plot against al-Mahdī. It was at Abū Zākī's house that the conspirators held their meetings. After his arrest, al-Mahdī sent him to Tripoli to have him executed by his uncle, who was then governor of the city. Ghazwiyya, from the Kutāma clan of Malūsa, distinguished himself by his bravery in Abū ʿAbd Allāh's military campaigns and conquests, and then particularly in the defence of the strategically important town of Bāghāya from Aghlabid attacks. He led the advance guard which preceded Abū ʿAbd Allāh to Raqqāda after the flight of the last Aghlabid emir. Unlike Abū Zākī, Ghazwiyya remained faithful to al-Mahdī and disowned Abū ʿAbd Allāh because of the plot against him. He kept al-Mahdī informed on the conspirators and became Abū ʿAbd Allāh's killer. Soon, however, he met the same fate as his victim, when he also turned against al-Mahdī after the caliph ordered, in 302/915, the arrest of his brother Ḥubāsa, with whom he had been colluding. Ḥubāsa, not mentioned by name in the *Iftitāḥ*, had commanded the Fatimid fleet during the first campaign to Egypt, when he became disaffected with his master.[7]

The *Iftitāḥ* is equally important for the social and political history of Ifrīqiya at the advent of the Fatimids. It relates in detail the conditions among the Kutāma where the *daʿwa* was established. Their territory was a remote, mountainous region where the Aghlabids exercised only nominal authority. The Kutāma represented several clans which did not recognise any authority other than their chiefs. Their situation afforded a favourable terrain to Abū ʿAbd Allāh's mission. However, Abū ʿAbd Allāh was not able at first to rally all the Kutāma to his cause. Some tribes offered him their strong and immediate support while others, led by chiefs jealous of their authority, rose against him. About this turbulent phase of the *daʿwa* among the Kutāma, the *Iftitāḥ* presents details of Abū ʿAbd Allāh's struggles against a hostile tribal coalition which eventually turned in his favour, allowing him to establish his authority over all the Kutāma, who then became instrumental in his military campaigns which led to the establishment of Fatimid dominion in North Africa.

---

7. On these events see Abū al-ʿAbbās Aḥmad b. Muḥammad Ibn ʿIdhārī al-Marrākushī, *Kitāb al-Bayān al-mughrib fī akhbār al-Andalus wa-al-Maghrib*, ed. G. S. Colin and E. Lévi-Provençal (Leiden, 1948), vol. 1, pp. 170–172. On Ḥubāsa see also al-Maqrīzī, *al-Muqaffā*, pp. 39–42.

The Mission in the Yemen and Ifrīqiya

The *Iftitāḥ* contains forty-two chapters of unequal length which follow a definite chronological order. The first five chapters give a detailed account of the initial stage of the *daʿwa* in the Yemen. The imam appointed Ibn Ḥawshab to conduct the Ismaili *daʿwa* there together with a Yemenite, ʿAlī b. al-Faḍl. The two *dāʿīs* arrived in the Yemen in 268/881, and their joint effort resulted in the firm establishment of the *daʿwa* in the Yemen, from where *dāʿīs* were sent to other countries. Abū ʿAbd Allāh was sent to the Yemen to be trained for his mission. He remained close to Ibn Ḥawshab for about a year, attending his teaching sessions (*majālis*) and accompanying him on military expeditions. This prepared him for his mission in North Africa where Shiʿism had already gained a foothold with the coming of two *dāʿīs*, Abū Sufyān and al-Ḥulwānī, about 135 years before him. North Africa appeared to be a favourable terrain for his assignment, and Abū ʿAbd Allāh proceeded there after a pilgrimage to Makka. Among the pilgrims he met some Kutāma Berber tribesmen from Ifrīqiya, who were impressed by his personality, eloquence and knowledge. Abū ʿAbd Allāh accepted their invitation to accompany them on their return journey. On their way he inquired about the circumstances of their country to determine whether it was suitable for launching his mission. The information they gave him convinced him that the Kutāma offered an excellent opportunity for spreading his mission. He therefore accompanied them to their land and settled in a fortified place in the mountainous region of Īkjān which became the headquarters of his mission. Abū ʿAbd Allāh's sincerity and dedication to his work and his ability to inspire this dedication in others gave impetus to his mission.

Emergence of supporters

The next eight chapters relate Abū ʿAbd Allāh's establishment in Kutāma territory and the emergence of a local community of supporters. Abū ʿAbd Allāh assumed the role of a teacher among the Kutāma, and spent about seven years spreading the doctrine about the merits of ʿAlī b. Abī Ṭālib and the imams from his progeny. Abū

ʿAbd Allāh's teaching was confidential and addressed to individuals who were ready to receive it. He set out to create a community based on norms of conduct applicable to all its members. He endowed the emergent community with the appropriate structure before confronting Aghlabid armies. He reorganised the politico-social structure of the Kutāma by dividing them into seven sections which constituted military divisions, and he appointed for each section a body of responsible commanders and *dāʿīs* to consolidate his government. He imposed acts of worship on all his companions, and enacted various regulations to curb offences and encourage charity and piety. He treated everybody with justice and equity, and punished severely anyone who deserved to be punished. Al-Nuʿmān highlights the righteousness and piety of Abū ʿAbd Allāh and the community of his Kutāma supporters. This new order is contrasted with the debauchery of the last Aghlabid emir and a laxity of morals among his boon companions.

The author often makes comparisons of the situation in Ifrīqiya before the coming of Abū ʿAbd Allāh and al-Mahdī with the situation in Arabia before the advent of the Prophet.[8] Abū ʿAbd Allāh considered his supporters to be extraordinary, likening them to the community of the first Muslims who supported the Prophet and fought his battles. He called them true believers (*muʾminūn*) and his opponents disbelievers (*kāfirūn*). Just as the Prophet emigrated with his supporters from Makka to Madina, Abū ʿAbd Allāh emigrated with his supporters from Īkjān to Tāzrūt and called it 'the abode of emigration' (*dār al-hijra*), one of the names of Madina. Hypocrites (*munāfiqūn*) were denounced but tolerated just as they were in the city of the Prophet. This emergent community, based on a new authority over and above the authority of the elders of the tribes, was perceived as a threat not only by the Aghlabid rulers of Ifrīqiya but also by the prevalent tribal order among the Kutāma and other Berber tribes. Clashes erupted between Kutāma clans supporting Abū ʿAbd Allāh and those opposing him. An alliance between the

8. See James E. Lindsay, 'Prophetic Parallels in Abu ʿAbd Allah al-Shiʿi's Mission among the Kutama Berbers, 893–910', *International Journal of Middle East Studies*, 24 (1992), pp. 39–56.

rulers of Mīla, Saṭīf and Billizma and the leaders of the Kutāma tried to break his ranks, but their alliance fell apart, and Abū 'Abd Allāh was able to extend his hold among the Kutāma, including those who had not adhered to the *da'wa*. Having united the Kutāma under his authority, Abū 'Abd Allāh was now ready for the inevitable military confrontation with those who resisted him. Alarmed at the growing influence of the Ismaili *dā'ī*, the Aghlabid emir, Ibrāhīm b. Aḥmad (r. 261–289/857–902), tried to tempt him with worldly reward in exchange for abandoning his mission, and threatened to attack him if he did not accept his offer. Abū 'Abd Allāh was not intimidated. He rejected the emir's offer and in turn spelled out boldly the objectives of his mission, summoning the emir to obey God, to conform to His book, and to submit to the Imam al-Mahdī from the progeny of His Messenger in order to secure his salvation. At the same time he expressed his readiness to fight the emir until the eventual victory of his mission.

Military confrontation

The next nineteen chapters, with the exception of an intervening chapter on al-Mahdī's emigration, describe military expeditions and Abū 'Abd Allāh's conquests until his final victory and the fall of the Aghlabids. Having established his authority over the Kutāma, Abū 'Abd Allāh launched his first attack on the fortress town of Mīla which he captured in the summer of 289/902. The fall of Mīla alarmed the Aghlabid emir Abū al-'Abbās 'Abd Allāh (r. 289–290/902–903) who immediately launched his first expedition against Abū 'Abd Allāh, under the command of his son Abū Ḥawāl. The author praises the strategy of the Aghlabid general and highlights his military superiority. He took Mīla, devastated Tāzrūt, which had been evacuated by Abū 'Abd Allāh and threatened Īkjān. However, after an unfavourable engagement Abū Ḥawāl retreated and returned to Ifrīqiya because of severe winter conditions. The second Aghlabid expedition (290/903), again commanded by Abū Ḥawāl, also ended in failure. The author explains Abū Ḥawāl's retreat by the deterioration of the situation in the Aghlabid capital Raqqāda. The emir 'Abd Allāh had been assassinated, and his son Ziyādat Allāh, who is said to have instigated the murder, had succeeded him. He promptly recalled his brother Abū Ḥawāl and had him executed.

It appears from al-Nuʿmān's account that while conducting his military operations, Abū ʿAbd Allāh carefully assessed the situation of his supporters in face of their enemies. Most of the time, the Kutāma had to confront armies far superior to them in numbers and equipment. This situation forced Abū ʿAbd Allāh to use varying tactics in the battles against the Aghlabids and others who stood in his way. He drew all possible advantage from the terrain to safeguard his forces from enemy attacks. He dispatched scouting parties to gather intelligence on enemy troops. He conducted intermittent raids, striking the same place time after time until the enemy was overwhelmed. He avoided getting embroiled in large-scale battles with the enemy when such confrontations were unnecessary or uncertain of victory. He controlled the timing of his attacks to confuse the enemy. He also accepted peace and granted amnesty to those who wished to submit. He impressed favourably upon the population by his magnanimity, expecting his troops to conduct themselves irreproachably. Many other factors worked together to ensure his final victory which subdued vast regions of the Maghrib as well as the former Aghlabid domains in Sicily. The most important factor was the morale of the Kutāma. Abū ʿAbd Allāh participated with them throughout the struggle, refusing to avoid danger. He encouraged them continuously to fight for the ultimate objective of establishing an ideal state under the sovereignty of al-Mahdī, and to attack the Aghlabids and the Abbasids, confident of achieving eventual victory. No doubt, the corruption at the court of Ziyādat Allāh and his lack of resolve to fight worked in favour of Abū ʿAbd Allāh.

The third Aghlabid expedition (291/904–5), commanded by Ibn Ḥabashī, took place after Abū ʿAbd Allāh's conquest of Saṭīf. Ibn Ḥabashī was a prominent member of the Aghlabid family and close adviser of Ziyādat Allāh, but he was inexperienced in military matters. Abū ʿAbd Allāh's military success is narrated in detail. His offensive, from 293/906, in the Awrās mountains captured one by one the Aghlabid fortresses which lacked supplies. These included Ṭubna, Billizma, Tījis and Bāghāya. He then launched Kutāma contingents towards Qasṭīliya, gaining a foothold in this prosperous region, and thereby threatening al-Qayrawān from the south-west. He triumphed finally in 296/909 at al-Urbus over his adversary Ibrāhīm b. Abī al-Aghlab and entered the Aghlabid capital from where the last emir, Ziyādat Allāh, abandoned his throne and fled to Tripoli by night.

Consolidation

The last ten chapters give an account of the advent of the Fatimids, the reign of al-Mahdī bi-llāh and a general survey of events until the year 346/957 when the work was completed. Abū ʿAbd Allāh's mission entered its conclusive phase when he entered Raqqāda in 296/909. He remained in the Aghlabid capital for about two months until the situation became stable. During this short period, he introduced administrative and political measures to reflect the new order. Having granted safety to the populace, including those who had served the Aghlabids, he outlined the behaviour he expected from the people and intensified the search for opponents of his orders to bring them to justice. Changes introduced in the call to prayer and sermons began to reflect the Shiʿi ritual. A Shiʿi *qāḍī* appointed by him was authorised to appoint judges and arbitrators in the other towns. Abū ʿAbd Allāh himself remained modest, in spite of having amassed everything that had belonged to the Aghlabids. The most important of these possessions for him were horses, weapons and implements which enabled him to conduct warfare. Having appointed his brother Abū al-ʿAbbās and Abū Zākī as his deputies to govern Ifrīqiya, he set out on a military campaign to free al-Mahdī from captivity in Sijilmāsa. On this arduous westward march to the remote regions of the Maghrib, Abū ʿAbd Allāh attacked and subdued Berber tribes that he came across on his way. Having secured the release of al-Mahdī and his son, after conquering Sijilmāsa, Abū ʿAbd Allāh returned to al-Qayrawān with al-Mahdī who formally assumed supreme authority.[9]

9. For the ten month's rule of Abū ʿAbd Allāh and his brother Abū al-ʿAbbās in Raqqāda and al-Qayrawān, before the arrival of al-Mahdī, we have a contemporary account by an Ismaili *dāʿī*, reporting at first hand the thoughts and activities of the two brothers and his own experiences: Abū ʿAbd Allāh Jaʿfar b. Aḥmad Ibn al-Haytham, *Kitāb al-Munāẓarāt*, ed.

The basis of the nascent state rested on al-Mahdī's sovereignty as imam from the progeny of the Prophet. Anyone rebelling against the imam would have to be fought.[10] The *Iftitāḥ* elucidates the circumstances that led to the execution of Abū ʿAbd Allāh, his brother Abū al-ʿAbbās and several others. Al-Nuʿmān informs us on the cause of Abū ʿAbd Allāh's downfall and the plot against al-Mahdī just two years after his advent. He names the conspirators, their motives, the place of their secret meetings, and reveals the measures taken by al-Mahdī to thwart the conspiracy. Abū al-ʿAbbās, ambitious brother of Abū ʿAbd Allāh, appears as the leader of the plot who exerts his influence on his younger brother. Abū al-ʿAbbās had mastery of Ismaili doctrines and demonstrated his talent during controversies with the scholars of al-Qayrawān.[11] Having exercised power until al-Mahdī's arrival in Raqqāda, he expressed his resentment when al-Mahdī assumed the responsibilities of the state without intending to share his authority. He incited some Berber chiefs against al-Mahdī until they dared to express openly their suspicions on the imam's impeccability and even question the authenticity of his imamate. Abū ʿAbd Allāh eventually succumbed to the instigation of his brother and asked al-Mahdī openly to reign without governing and let him exercise power in his name. Al-Nuʿmān presents in detail how al-Mahdī, well informed

---

and tr. W. Madelung and P. E. Walker as *The Advent of the Fatimids: A Contemporary Shiʿi Witness* (London, 2000).

10. See the author's exposition on fighting those who rebel: al-Qāḍī al-Nuʿmān b. Muḥammad, *Daʿāʾim al-islām*, ed. A. A. A. Fyzee (Cairo, 1951–1960), vol. 1, pp. 388–395; tr. A. A. A. Fyzee, rev. I. K. H. Poonawala, *The Pillars of Islam* (New Delhi, 2002), vol. 1, pp. 479–489. For an analysis of al-Nuʿmān's position on rebellion, see Khaled Abou El Fadl, *Rebellion and Violence in Islamic Law* (Cambridge, 2001), pp. 226–229.

11. On these controversies see Abū ʿAbd Allāh Muḥammad b. Ḥārith b. Asad al-Khushanī, *ʿUlamāʾ Ifrīqiya*, ed. ʿIzzat al-ʿAṭṭār al-Ḥusaynī (Cairo, 1953), pp. 258–275; Hady Roger Idris, 'Contribution à l'histoire de l'Ifriḳiya. Tableau littéraire de la vie intellectuelle et administrative à Kairouan sous les Aglabites et les Fatimites (4 premiers siècle de l'Hégire), d'après le Riyāḍ En nufūs de Abū Bakr El Mālikī', *Revue des études islamiques*, 9 (1935), pp. 148–150; al-Qāḍī Abū al-Faḍl ʿIyāḍ, *Tartīb al-madārik wa-taqrīb al-masālik li-maʿrifat aʿlām madhhab Mālik*, selections ed. Muḥammad al-Ṭālibī as *Tarājim Aghlabiyya mustakhraja min Madārik al-Qāḍī ʿIyāḍ* (Tunis, 1968), pp. 354–358; Abū al-Qāsim b. ʿĪsā Ibn Nājī al-Tanūkhī, *Maʿālim al-īmān fī maʿrifat ahl al-Qayrawān* (Cairo, 1968–1972), vol. 2, pp. 298–309; and Ibn al-Haytham, *Kitāb al-Munāẓarāt*, index.

of the intentions of the conspirators, exploited their hesitations and thwarted the conspiracy. The author names the killers of Abū ʿAbd Allāh and his brother, but is careful not to implicate al-Mahdī directly in their execution. Al-Nuʿmān throws all responsibility for this conspiracy on Abū al-ʿAbbās, without tarnishing the memory of Abū ʿAbd Allāh, whose merit was recognised by al-Mahdī. Having eliminated the conspirators, al-Mahdī sent armies to the outlying regions to suppress rebellions. This situation continued during the reign of his son and successor al-Qāʾim bi-amr Allāh and his grandson al-Manṣūr bi-llāh. The *Iftitāḥ al-daʿwa* was completed during the reign of al-Muʿizz li-dīn Allāh, in 346/957, twelve years before the Fatimid conquest of Egypt. The author deals briefly with these later events because his aim was only to portray the stages of the establishment of the *daʿwa* itself to preserve its history for posterity.

Editions and manuscripts

It was due to the pioneering efforts of Wladimir Ivanow that Arabic Ismaili texts relating to the rise of the Fatimids were first edited and translated into English, including some fragments of the *Iftitāḥ*. These fragments give an account of al-Mahdī's emigration from his residence in Salamiya in Syria, his arrival in Sijilmāsa in the remote Maghrib, and Abū ʿAbd Allāh's successful campaign to liberate him from captivity.[12] These fragments were largely translated into French by Marius Canard in an appendix to his translation of the memoirs of al-Mahdī's chamberlain, *Sīrat al-Ḥājib Jaʿfar*.[13] It was not until 1970 that the integral text of the *Iftitāḥ*, edited by Wadād al-Qāḍī, was first published in Beirut. It is based on three manuscripts: two from the American University in Beirut,[14] and one from the Hamdani Collection from its photocopy in the Egyptian National Library (Dār

12. Ivanow, *Rise*, Arabic text pp. 40–46 (tr. pp. 224–231). Cf. below pp. 121–126 and pp. 196–198.

13. Canard, 'L'autobiographie', pp. 324–328.

14. MS/297.8: N 97 aAC.1, dated 1280/[1863], and MS/297.8: N 97 aAC. 2. For codicological details of these manuscripts, see Yūsuf Q. Khūrī, *al-Makhṭūṭāt al-ʿArabiyya al-mawjūda fī Maktabat al-Jāmiʿa al-Amrīkiyya fī Bayrūt* (Beirut, 1985), p. 132.

al-Kutub al-Miṣriyya).[15] This latter manuscript was also used as a basis by Farhat Dachraoui, together with one manuscript of Indian origin, copied in 1350/[1931], from the collection of Louis Massignon. Farhat Dachraoui's integral edition, already completed in 1961, was published in Tunis only in 1975.[16] Massignon's manuscript was also used by Mohamed Talbi for his monograph on the Aghlabids, particularly for the chapter on the fall of the dynasty,[17] and his critical review of Wadād al-Qāḍī's edition.[18] Besides the manuscripts used by the editors, several other manuscripts of the *Iftitāḥ* are held in private libraries of Ismaili communities in Yemen, India and Pakistan, some of which are now preserved in the West. The Institute of Ismaili Studies in London has seven copies in its collection of manuscripts.[19] I have compared these copies with the editions, where necessary, for producing this first integral translation of the work into any language.

The translation of the *Iftitāḥ* allows non-Arabist readers to access this important primary source. I have attempted to be as close to the

15. The copy was completed on Friday 7 Shaʿbān 1315 [31 December 1897]. It is composed of 143 folios (17 x 9 cm), executed in clear handwriting.

16. In the meantime Farhat Dachraoui published two important studies based on the *Iftitāḥ*: 'Contribution à l'histoire des Fāṭimides en Ifrīqiya', *Arabica*, 8 (1961), pp. 189–203, and 'Les commencements de la prédication ismaʿilienne en Ifriqiya', *Studia Islamica*, 20 (1964), pp. 89–102. There followed his doctoral dissertation, a monograph on the Fatimids in the Maghrib, in which the *Iftitāḥ* is used as the main source: *Le califat fatimide au Maghreb (295–365 H./909–975 JC.): histoire politique et institutions* (Tunis, 1981). Based on Dachraoui's edition, two short chapters were translated into English: James E. Lindsay, 'Kitāb Iftitāḥ al-daʿwa by al-Qāḍī al-Nuʿmān: Section II, Chapters VIII and IX', *Al-ʿArabiyya*, 22 (1989), pp. 157–168.

17. Mohamed Talbi, *L'émirat aghlabide 184–296/800–909, histoire politique* (Paris, 1966), pp. 538–699.

18. M. Ṭalbi, [Review of Wadād al-Qāḍī's edition of the *Iftitāḥ*], *Ḥawliyyāt al-Jāmiʿa al-Tūnisiyya*, 7 (1970), pp. 273–277.

19. MS 78, MS 79, MS 254, MS 934, MS 1001, MS 1147, and MS 1242. For details of these manuscripts see Adam Gacek, *Catalogue of Arabic Manuscripts in the Library of The Institute of Ismaili Studies* (London, 1984–1985), vol. 1, pp. 29–30; Delia Cortese, *Ismaili and Other Arabic Manuscripts: A Descriptive Catalogue of Manuscripts in the Library of The Institute of Ismaili Studies* (London, 2000), pp. 50–51; Delia Cortese, *Arabic Ismaili Manuscripts: The Zāhid ʿAlī Collection in the Library of The Institute of Ismaili Studies* (London, 2003), pp. 49–50.

original Arabic text as possible, but at the same time made allowance for modern English idiom and expressions. The translation of verses from the Qurʾan draws upon Yusuf Ali's and Pickthall's translations with some adaptation. Several toponyms, names of individuals and tribes and events need to be explained, and for which I have supplied ample footnotes with references wherever necessary for further reading. The material has been organised in numbered chapters and subdivisions introduced into some chapters to make the text more readable and accessible. The publication includes genealogical charts, maps of Ifrīqiya and eastern Maghrib, as well as a chronology summarising the complex chain of events and battles that gave rise to the Fatimid state.

Hamid Haji

Translation of
Iftitāḥ al-daʿwa
Commencement of the Mission

Praise be to God, Supporter of the truth and Helper of its adherents. He triumphs over falsehood and subdues its party. He, the most truthful speaker, says: *It is the party of God that must certainly triumph* (5:56); *And that Our forces – they surely must conquer* (37:173); *My righteous servants shall inherit the earth* (21:105). He sealed the prophethood of the prophets and the messengership of the messengers with the prophethood and messengership of Muḥammad. He caused the imamate to abide in his descendants and offspring until the Day of Judgement, to honour him and safeguard His religion from being superseded by any religion or abrogated by any law (*sharīʿa*). He guaranteed to his people victory, investiture, assistance, support and protection. He has not left the earth without an imam on it for the community (*umma*), who states the truth and who serves as the proof (*ḥujja*), even if those who get the upper hand triumph on (earth), and the entrusted imams go into seclusion as a precaution.

Indeed, they have on every 'island' (*jazīra*)[1] on earth a missionary (*dāʿī*) on their behalf, and in every region of (the earth) a guide to them. If we were to enumerate every imam among them, may God's blessings be upon them, and everyone who conducted the mission on his behalf and carried out his command, the book would become lengthy with their account. Instead, we have preferred to narrate the activity of the *daʿwa* in the land of the Maghrib until the time of al-Mahdī,[2] may God's blessings be upon him. We shall relate the

1. Literally 'island', of which there were twelve, *jazīra* (plural *jazāʾir*) refers to provinces of the Muslim world where the Ismaili *daʿwa* was active. See Ivanow, *Rise*, pp. 20–21; Jaʿfar b. Manṣūr al-Yaman, *Asrār al-nutaqāʾ*, ed. Muṣṭafā Ghālib (Beirut, 1984), p. 59. On the organisation of the *daʿwa*, see Wladimir Ivanow, 'The Organization of the Fāṭimid Propaganda', *Journal of the Bombay Branch of the Royal Asiatic Society*, new series, 15 (1939), pp. 1–35; and Farhad Daftary, 'The Ismaili *daʿwa* outside the Fatimid *dawla*', in M. Barrucand, ed., *L'Égypte fatimide: son art et son histoire* (Paris, 1999), pp. 29–43.

2. On al-Mahdī see al-Maqrīzī, *al-Muqaffā*, pp. 53–99; French tr. Edmond Fagnan, 'Traduction de la biographie d'ʿObeyd Allâh contenue dans le « Moḳaffa » de Maḳrīzī', in *Centenario della nascita di Michele Amari* (Palermo, 1910), vol. 2, pp. 35–85; Farhat Dachraoui,

beginning of the *da'wa* there, al-Mahdī's emigration to that land, his advent and manifestation, and his taking control of it, so that this account may remain recorded, and continue to be remembered and transmitted with the passage of time for all times and days. We have already devoted another book exclusively to the signs of the Mahdī (*Ma'ālim al-Mahdī*),[3] may God's blessings be upon him, giving an account of his description, his advent and his reign, together with the relevant traditions reported from the Messenger of God, may God's blessings be upon him and his progeny, and giving the glad tidings about him.

1

The account of the beginning of the mission (*da'wa*) in the Yemen, the [*dā'ī*] in charge of it, and the factors which allowed him to accomplish his mission.

We begin with the account of this blessed mission since it was the basis of the mission about which we intend to relate. It was to that mission that the *dā'ī*[4] was sent and it is from the Yemen that he was dispatched to the Maghrib. He received instruction from the head of its *da'wa* and followed his moral example. The head of the *da'wa* in the Yemen was Abū al-Qāsim al-Ḥasan b. Faraḥ b. Ḥawshab b. Zādān

'al-Mahdī 'Ubayd Allāh', *EI*², vol. 5, pp. 1242–1244; J. Walker, 'al-Mahdī 'Ubaid Allāh', *EI*, vol. 5, pp. 119–121; Ḥasan Ibrāhīm Ḥasan and Ṭāhā Aḥmad Sharaf, *'Ubayd Allāh al-Mahdī: Imām al-Shī'a al-Ismā'iliyya wa-mu'assis al-dawla al-Fāṭimiyya fī bilād al-Maghrib* (Cairo, 1947); Samuel M. Stern, *Studies in Early Ismā'īlism* (Jerusalem-Leiden, 1983), p. 96–145; and Heinz Halm, *The Empire of the Mahdi: The Rise of the Fatimids* (Leiden, 1996).

3. In his *Sharḥ al-akhbār fī faḍā'il al-a'imma al-aṭhār*, ed. al-Sayyid Muḥammad al-Ḥusaynī al-Jalālī (Qumm, n.d.) vol. 3, pp. 355ff., al-Qāḍī al-Nu'mān gives a gist of this work. See also Poonawala, *Biobibliography*, p. 58.

4. He is the *dā'ī* Abū 'Abd Allāh al-Shī'ī, for whom the *Iftitāḥ* is our main source. See also Shihāb al-Dīn Aḥmad b. 'Abd al-Wahhāb al-Nuwayrī, *Nihāyat al-arab fī funūn al-adab*, selections ed. Muṣṭafā Abū Ḍayf Aḥmad as *Nihāyat al-arab fī funūn al-adab: al-dawla al-Fāṭimiyya bi-bilād al-Maghrib (296–361h/909–972m)* (Casablanca, 1988), pp. 23–49; al-Maqrīzī, *al-Muqaffā*, pp. 25–35; and Samuel M. Stern, 'Abū 'Abd Allāh al-Shī'ī', *EI*², vol. 1, pp. 103–104.

al-Kūfī.[5] He was called al-Manṣūr (the victorious) in the Yemen because of the victory which he was granted. However, when people called him thus, he would tell them, 'Al-Manṣūr is one of the imams from the progeny of Muḥammad, may God bless him and grant him salvation. Have you not heard the saying of the poet:

> When al-Manṣūr from the progeny of Aḥmad becomes manifest,
> Tell the sons of al-ʿAbbās to arise on a foot!'

Traditions referring to al-Manṣūr, peace be upon him, are numerous. It is related on the authority of Jaʿfar b. Muḥammad, may God's blessings be upon him, that he said, 'From us is al-Mahdī and from us is al-Manṣūr.' In another tradition it is reported: 'Rejoice, for the days of the oppressors are about to come to an end. The restorer will come, through whom God will restore the community of Muḥammad. He is al-Mahdī and then al-Manṣūr, through whom God will cause religion to triumph.'

The origin of Abū al-Qāsim, head of the mission in the Yemen, according to what men of knowledge and trust from among his associates have informed us, is that he was an inhabitant of al-Kūfa from a learned Shiʿi family. He had read the Qurʾan and implemented it (*qawwamahu*).[6] He had studied traditions (*ḥadīth*) and religious sciences (*fiqh*). He was among the adherents of Twelver Imami Shiʿism who follow Muḥammad b. al-Ḥasan b. ʿAlī b. Muḥammad b. ʿAlī b. Mūsā b. Jaʿfar b. Muḥammad.[7] They believed that he was the Mahdī,

---

5. On him see also Wilferd Madelung, 'Manṣūr al-Yaman', *EI*², vol. 6, pp. 438–439; Taqī al-Dīn Abū al-ʿAbbās Aḥmad b. ʿAlī al-Maqrīzī, *Ittiʿāẓ al-ḥunafā bi-akhbār al-aʾimma al-Fāṭimiyyīn al-khulafā*, ed. J. al-Shayyāl et al. (Cairo, 1967–1973), vol. 1, pp. 40–41; Henry Cassels Kay, *Yaman: Its Early Mediaeval History* (London, 1892), Arabic text of al-Janadī, *Kitāb al-Sulūk*, pp. 139–150 (tr. pp. 191–209); Cornelis van Arendonk, *Les débuts de l'imāmat zaidite au Yémen*, tr. J. Ryckmans (Leiden, 1960), pp. 119–125, 237, 239–243; and Heinz Halm, 'Die Sīrat Ibn Ḥaušab: die ismailitische *daʿwa* im Jemen und die Fatimiden', *Die Welt des Orients*, 12 (1981), pp. 107–135.

6. Instead of *qawwamahu* three manuscripts have *ḥafiẓahu* (learnt it by heart): MS 254, fol. 2b; MS 934, fol. 3a; MS 1242, fol. 2b.

7. The twelfth Imam according to the Ithnāʿashariyya. On him see Jasim M. Hussain, *The Occultation of the Twelfth Imam: A Historical Background* (London, 1982); and Abdulaziz A. Sachedina, *Islamic Messianism: The Idea of Mahdi in Twelver Shiʿism* (Albany, 1981).

who would become manifest, and that it would come to pass what is related about him in traditions reported from the Prophet, may God's blessings be upon him. They falsely attributed that [status] to him and adopted him as a protector. However, they did not see him, so they alleged that he had hidden himself from them. Then that became void among them. There are lengthy stories about him and amazing nonsense.

Abū al-Qāsim related that one day, while he was thinking about this matter, he remembered the verses of the poet al-Fihrī:[8]

O party (*shīʿa*) of truth, men of faith and piety,
Has not God's help descended upon you against fright and rebuke?
Therefore, do not summon to claimants, transgressors and traitors
When the tenth [imam] disappears or one is added to the ten.[9]
The league of patience will overcome the wrongdoers.
So in ninety-six,[10] allegation and denial will be settled.
About what people say that the pearl has been sold for dung,
The treasured stone has become worthless.
The orphan who lay [hidden] behind the door has pounced upon the nest.

His mentioning the orphan here points to al-Mahdī, may God's blessings be upon him. Thus it happened as happened with the Messenger of God, may God bless him and grant him salvation. God says: *Did He not find thee an orphan and give thee shelter*? (93:6).

Abū al-Qāsim said [continuing the narration]: I realised that the time referred to by al-Fihrī had come close. This went through my mind and I became preoccupied with this thought. So I went out to the Euphrates, or the Tigris. As I was walking on [the bank of] the

8. Dachraoui thinks that he is probably the Arab poet of Madina Ibrāhīm b. ʿAlī b. Salma b. Harma al-Fihrī (d. *ca.* 176/792), who was known for his Shiʿi leanings. On him see Charles Pellat, 'Ibn Harma', *EI*², vol. 3, p. 786. See also Muḥammad al-Yaʿlāwī, *al-Adab bi-Ifrīqiya fi al-ʿahd al-Fāṭimī* (Beirut, 1986), pp. 21–22.

9. Al-Mahdī is the addition to the first ten Ismaili imams, the tenth being Imam al-Ḥusayn b. Aḥmad. See Idrīs ʿImād al-Dīn, *ʿUyūn al-akhbār wa-funūn al-āthār fī faḍāʾil al-aʾimma al-aṭhār*, ed. M. Ghālib, (Beirut, 1973–1984), vol. 4, p. 397.

10. That is, in the year 296/909 when al-Mahdī assumed power after the fall of the Aghlabids.

river, it was time for prayer. I performed ablution and prayed, and sat reflecting upon my situation. Then I began reciting the Qur'an. I started with the *Sūrat al-Kahf*.[11] While I was reciting it, suddenly an old man, accompanied by another man, approached me. And by God, never before had my eyes gazed upon anyone who filled my heart with greater reverence than that old man. He alighted at a spot and the man sat down in front of him, both at a distance from me. I interrupted the recitation out of respect for him and remained looking at him. Suddenly a young man approached walking haughtily. He came near me. Out of respect for the old man I ignored him, but he did not heed me, so I asked, 'Who are you?'

He replied, 'A descendant of al-Ḥusayn.'

I shed tears and said, 'By my father, al-Ḥusayn, may God's blessings be upon him, the one stained with blood, to whom this water was denied.'[12]

I saw then that the old man looked at me. The man who was sitting in front of him said something which I did not understand. Then the man told me, 'Come near us. May God have mercy upon you!'

So I went to him and sat before the old man. I noticed his tears flowing on his beard. I think it was upon my mentioning al-Ḥusayn, may God's blessings be upon him. He asked me, 'Who are you who mention al-Ḥusayn in what you said?'

I replied, 'A man from the Shīʿa.'

He asked, 'What is your name?'

I replied, 'al-Ḥasan b. Faraḥ b. Ḥawshab.'

He said, 'I know your father adhered to the Twelver Shīʿa.'

I said, 'Indeed.'

He asked, 'Do you follow the same way?'

I remained quiet. He said, 'Speak, for I am one of your brothers.'

I said, 'I used to be a follower of that way until it turned out to be

---

11. *Sūrat al-Kahf* (no. 18) takes its title from the story of the Companions of the Cave related in it. On them see Arent J. Wensinck, 'Aṣḥāb al-Kahf', *EI*, vol. 1, pp. 478–479; and Rudi Paret, 'Aṣḥāb al-Kahf', *EI²*, vol. 1, p. 691.

12. Cf. Muḥammad b. Mālik al-Ḥammādī, *Kashf asrār al-Bāṭiniyya wa-akhbār al-Qarāmiṭa*, ed. Muḥammad Zāhid b. Ḥasan al-Kawtharī (Cairo, 1939), p. 21, where similar words are attributed to ʿAlī b. al-Faḍl at the mausoleum of al-Ḥusayn. On the bloody battle here alluded to, see E. Honnigmann, 'Karbalāʾ', *EI²*, vol. 4, pp. 637–639.

false. I am out here in this place only because of my distress about this matter.'

Then I related to him what had happened to me. He said, 'I see in you alertness, for I listened to you while you were reciting. Why did you interrupt the recitation?'

I replied, 'By God, may God support you, only reverence for you silenced me.'

He said, 'Recite, just as you had been reciting.'

So I continued from where I had stopped until I reached [the verse] *Then they proceeded until, when they met a young man, he slew him* (18:74).[13] Then he signalled to me with his hand to be quiet, and I became quiet. He then asked, 'Are you a believer in the Justice and Unity of God?'[14]

I replied, 'Yes, that is my creed.'

He asked, 'What justice is there in slaying an innocent soul who had slain none except for His word: *and we feared that he would grieve them by obstinate rebellion and ingratitude*' (18:80).

I remained silent. He said, 'Speak!'

I asked, 'What shall I say? By God, it is as if I had never read the verse. I lack the knowledge thereof, so if you consider explaining the matter to me, then do so.'

He said, 'Before accomplishing that, one must deal with a thin veil.'

I said, 'Would you remove the veil for me? May I be made your ransom!'

He said, 'That will happen when it is possible, if God, the Exalted, wills.'

Then he began [to talk about] something else until, when he came

---

13. The rest of the verse: *Moses said, 'Hast thou slain an innocent person who had slain none? Truly a foul (unheard of) thing hast thou done!'* The story of Moses and the unnamed sage related in the *sūra* (verses 60–82) deals with the theme of spiritual awakening and search after ultimate truths. The sage is called al-Khaḍir/al-Khiḍr by the majority of the commentators. See, for example, Muḥammad b. Ismāʿīl al-Bukhārī, *Ṣaḥīḥ al-Bukhārī*:, tr. M. M. Khan (New Delhi, 1987), vol. 6, pp. 210–224; and Arent J. Wensinck, 'al-Khaḍir', *EI*, vol. 4, pp. 861–865.

14. 'Justice and Unity of God' refers to two of the five principles of Muʿtazilī theology. See Henrik S. Nyberg, 'al-Muʿtazila', *EI*, vol. 6, pp. 787–793; and Daniel Gimaret, 'Muʿtazila', *EI*², vol. 7, pp. 783–793.

to the place where its answer was to be found, he began [to talk about] something else. Meanwhile, I kept on asking him for the answer to it, but he would say something similar to what he had said [earlier]. Then he moved to rise, so I said, 'O my master, I would like to know the stopping place.'

He asked, 'Why?'

I replied, 'So that your promise be fulfilled.'

He smiled, and said, 'Perhaps we shall meet right here tomorrow, if God, the Exalted, wills.'

He departed, leaving me. Then, when he disappeared from my sight, I regretted that I did not follow him so as to know his place of residence. The purport of what he said greatly impressed upon my heart and my mind became preoccupied with what I had heard. The following day I returned to the spot and stayed there till nightfall, but I saw no one. Similarly, I came and went for several days. I cannot describe how saddened I was that he had slipped from me. I was on the brink of despair because of this until the man who was with the old man passed by me. I stood up, greeted him and asked, 'What has become of the old man? May God preserve him. He had promised me to meet the day after I met him here with you. I have been visiting this spot frequently ever since that day as he had promised to meet me.'

He replied, 'If he had promised you, then he would not have let you down, but in his conversation there was no expression of a firm promise.'

I asked, 'Where can I see him? By God, my heart is preoccupied with what I heard from him.'

The man told me, 'Sit down. Let us talk a little.'

We sat down, and the man turned out to have a lot of knowledge. I implored him, but he wanted to rise and depart. I said, 'By God, I will not leave you until you reveal to me the matter.'

We persisted until he administered the oath of allegiance[15] to me and informed me that the old man was indeed the imam of the time (*imām al-zamān*).[16] He disclosed to me a lot of information and let

15. On this practice see Heinz Halm, 'The Isma'ili Oath of Allegiance (*'ahd*) and the 'Sessions of Wisdom' (*majālis al-ḥikma*) in Fatimid Times', in Daftary, ed., *Mediaeval Isma'ili History*, pp. 91–115.

16. On the imams of the period of occultation (*satr*) after Muḥammad b. Ismā'īl up to the

me know the whereabouts of the imam and united me with him. (The imam) bestowed upon me special honours, allowed me proximity and indicated that the matter was imminent and the time was approaching. In many of his conversations he would say, 'The House (sanctuary in Makka) is Yemenite, the corner of the Kaʿba (*rukn*) is Yemenite, the religion is Yemenite, and the Kaʿba is Yemenite. This religion will not rise and triumph except from the Yemen.'

(Abū al-Qāsim) said [continuing the narration]: Then one day (the imam) said to me, 'O Abū al-Qāsim, would you like to go away from your homeland for the sake of God?'

I said, 'O my master, it is up to you to command, for whatever you order me to do, I shall obey.'

He said, 'Be firm! I am under the impression that a man from the Yemen has just come to me, for only you are suitable for the Yemen.'[17]

I said, 'I seek God's help for whatever pleases you.'

The man [in question] was an inhabitant of Jayshān,[18] a town in the Yemen. He was a handsome young man from a well-to-do, prosperous Shiʿi family. He was called Abū al-Ḥasan ʿAlī b. al-Faḍl.[19] He had gone on pilgrimage from Jayshān with a group of its inhabitants with the group of Yemenites in the year 266/880. Having accomplished his pilgrimage, he set out to visit the mausoleum of al-Ḥusayn, may God's blessings be upon him, with a group of Yemenites and other [pilgrims] from among the Shīʿa who were there during the season of

---

advent of al-Mahdī, see Farhad Daftary, 'A Major Schism in the Early Ismaʿili Movement', *Studia Islamica*, 77 (1993), pp. 123–139. For al-Mahdī's statement on his genealogy see Ḥusayn F. al-Hamdānī, *On the Genealogy of Fatimid Caliphs* (Cairo, 1958); and Abbas Hamdani and François de Blois, 'A Re-examination of al-Mahdī's Letter to the Yemenites on the Genealogy of the Fatimid Caliphs', *Journal of the Royal Asiatic Society* (1983), pp. 173–207.

17. In al-Maqrīzī, *al-Muqaffā*, p. 62: 'Be firm! I am under the impression that a man will come from the Yemen.'

18. On this Yemenite town see Yāqūt b. ʿAbd Allāh al-Ḥamawī, *Muʿjam al-buldān* (Beirut, 1955–1957), vol. 2, p. 200.

19. His name is ʿAlī (also Muḥammad in some sources) b. al-Faḍl al-Jadanī (d. 303/915). On him see also Ibn al-Athīr, *al-Kāmil fī al-taʾrīkh* (Beirut, 1967), vol. 6, p. 126; al-Ḥammādī, *Kashf*, pp. 21–22; Kay, *Yaman*, Arabic text of al-Janadī, *Kitāb al-Sulūk*, pp. 139–150 (tr. pp. 191–207); and Farhad Daftary, *The Ismāʿīlis: Their History and Doctrines* (Cambridge, 1990), pp. 118, 131–132, and 134.

the pilgrimage. When they arrived at the mausoleum, they found it full of Shiʿis. This ʿAlī b. al-Faḍl began to weep and wail at the mausoleum. He would relate the virtues of al-Ḥusayn, may God's blessings be upon him, and declare his excellence. One of the *dāʿīs*[20] observed him every day while he was acting in this way, and having seen his intention and diligence remained alone with him and comforted him. He disclosed to him some knowledge and asked him some questions. ʿAlī b. al-Faḍl trusted him and kept company with him and sought to find out what he knew. Then one day during his conversation the man asked him, 'Tell me, if you had attained the occupant of this mausoleum at which you weep and whose excellence you declare, what would you have done for him?'

He replied, 'By God, I would have placed my cheek and kissed the ground which he trod. I would have sought blessings from the surplus [of water] of his ablution and, had I witnessed his death, I would have been the first to be slain in front of him.'

(The man) asked, 'You have missed him. Now what is left for you?'

(ʿAlī b. al-Faḍl) said, 'What you see of sorrow and grief for him.'

He said, 'You seem to assume that God, the Exalted and Glorified, has cut off his cause with his death, and removed His proof (*ḥujja*) from His creation with his death.'

He replied, 'Certainly not! But how can I act about it?'

The man remained silent and ʿAlī b. al-Faḍl implored him, saying, 'By God, you would not have spoken to me thus about him without having some trace of him, so direct me to him.'

(ʿAlī b. al-Faḍl) began to frequent him, while he avoided him, and he implored him, while he shut himself off, until the time came for the departure of his companions and he bid them farewell, and wrote to his family, and failed to depart. The man withdrew to his place and he followed him, so he asked him, 'Where are you heading?'

(ʿAlī) replied, '[I am coming] with you. By God, I will not leave you until you lead me to the one you referred to.'

---

20. He is identified as Maymūn al-Qaddāḥ in anti-Ismaili sources, which is obviously chronologically impossible. See al-Ḥammādī, *Kashf*, p. 21. On Maymūn al-Qaddāḥ see Wilferd Madelung, 'Maymūn al-Ḳaddāḥ', *EI*², vol. 6, p. 917.

He set out with him, and when he entered the city in which the imam had been residing, he took him to the mosque and told him, 'Sit in this place until I come back to you.'

He sat [there] and (the man) went away without him and stayed away for forty days while 'Alī remained in that mosque without leaving the place except for the need of nature. Meanwhile, the man was observing him without being seen. Having seen the strength of his resolve and his intention, he returned to him. When ('Alī) saw him he rushed towards him and said, 'O my master, what is [the meaning of] this action? You broke off with me, abandoning me.'

He replied, 'And were you here all along?'

He replied, 'Where else would I go? You had asked me to sit in this place until you came back to me.'

He asked, 'What would you have done if I had not returned?'

He replied, 'By God, I would not have left until I died and faced God, forgiven.'

(The man) took ('Alī) to his place and administered an oath of allegiance to him and led him to the imam. Having seen ('Alī) and inquired into his situation, (the imam) told Abū al-Qāsim, 'O Abū al-Qāsim, this is the one we had been waiting for. How do you feel about what I advised you regarding the Yemen?'

(Abū al-Qāsim) replied, 'O my lord, it is as I have told you; it is up to you to command.'

(The imam) said, 'Resolve, in the name of God, for by God, indeed God will cause you to triumph and *dā'īs* will indeed proceed from you to the remotest parts of the earth.'

(The imam) summoned 'Alī b. al-Faḍl and questioned him about the Yemen, its state of affairs and rulers. ('Alī) gave him the information he required on the matter. Then (the imam) asked, 'Do you know 'Adan Lā'a?'

('Alī) replied, 'O my lord, perhaps you mean 'Adan Abyan?'[21]

(The imam) said, 'No, it is indeed 'Adan Lā'a.'

---

21. On 'Adan Lā'a (in the country of Lā'a, north-west of Ṣan'ā') and 'Adan Abyan see Yāqūt, *Mu'jam*, vol. 4, p. 89; al-Ḥammādī, *Kashf*, pp. 24–25; and Abū al-Fidā', *Kitāb Taqwīm al-buldān*, ed. J. T. Reinaud and W. Mac Guckin de Slane (Paris, 1840), pp. 90–91. Present-day Abyan is a small locality about eighteen kilometres to the north-east of Aden. See Oscar Löfgren, 'Abyan', *EI*², vol. 1, p. 169, and ''Adan', *EI*², vol. 1, pp. 180–182.

(ʿAlī) said, 'I do not know it.'

(The imam) said to Abū al-Qāsim, 'Proceed to ʿAdan Lāʿa, and count on it, for our cause will become manifest from there, our dominion will become strong therein, and our *dāʿīs* will disperse from there.'

(The imam) said to ʿAlī b. al-Faḍl, 'I am dispatching this brother of yours as a *dāʿī* to the Yemen and you will accompany him.' Then to each one of them he commissioned a [particular] region and gave directives. (The imam) gave to Abū al-Qāsim a letter containing principles and indications which began as follows:

> In the name of God, the Compassionate, the Merciful. From the Father of the Muslims, the Commander of the Faithful, the Inheritor of the inheritors, the Sky of those who travel by night, the Sun of those who contemplate, the Moon of those who seek light, the Direction of those who pray, the Security of those who fear, the Slayer of the cursed devil, the Pillar of Islam, the Banner of banners, the Pen of pens, the Day of days, the Light of completeness. Thus is the message of a poor servant who since years endeavours in the ocean, hoping that his ark will escape sinking and that the passengers will escape perdition.

Then (the imam) revealed the communication whose principles he had established and ideas which he wanted to express. While making recommendations to him he said, 'If you meet someone smarter than you in the art of controversy, drown him in the esoteric.'

(The *dāʿī*) asked, 'How am I to do so?'

(The imam) replied, 'You will interrupt the discussion and show him that the reply that you want to give covers an esoteric aspect which you cannot reveal. Keep this from him until he loses the argument.'[22]

Then (the imam) urged (Abū al-Qāsim) to take good care of ʿAlī b. al-Faḍl, saying, 'He is a young man, inexperienced in the matter. Watch how you deal with him.'

He commissioned to ʿAlī a [particular] region and gave him directives and told him, 'This man whom we are dispatching with you is a sea of knowledge. Watch how you accompany him.'

---

22. On the etiquette of Ismaili *dāʿīs* and the procedure they should adopt with their followers, see al-Qāḍī al-Nuʿmān, *Kitāb al-Himma fī ādāb atbāʿ al-aʾimma*, ed. Muḥammad Kāmil Ḥusayn (Cairo, [1948]), pp. 54–55, 136–140.

(The imam) bade farewell to them both and prayed for them. They both withdrew from him, heading for the Yemen.

Abū al-Qāsim said [continuing the narration]: After bidding farewell to the family and loved ones, and filled with a longing to withdraw from going away from home, I set off. When I departed from al-Qādisiyya,[23] I became apprehensive personally. I paid attention to a good omen which I heard. I listened to a camel driver saying:

O driver of fine camels,
Skilful at driving away,
Give glad tidings to your mounts
Of the light of dawn.

(Abū al-Qāsim) said [continuing the narration]: I liked it and found that good omen appropriate when I heard it. I arrived in Makka at the time of the arrival of the pilgrim caravan from the Yemen, and I heard that Muḥammad b. Yuʿfir,[24] the hereditary ruler of Ṣanʿāʾ, had shown penitence and asceticism and had relinquished sovereignty. He returned to the people what he had appropriated from them, and dealt equitably with grievances. This is because he was aware of predictions made before him that his power would cease from his hand and that the *dāʿī* of the Mahdī would defeat him. He therefore relinquished power of his own accord and refrained from it, distributing wealth. It is said that he gave away in a single day one million [dirhams],[25] so that one of the poets[26] from his household stood up while they had come together and said in a long *rajaz* meter poem:

---

23. A station south-south-west from al-Kūfa on the pilgrim road from Baghdad to Makka. See Laura Veccia Vaglerii, 'al-Ḳādisiyya', *EI*², vol. 4, pp. 384–387.

24. The reign of Muḥammad b. Yuʿfir, assassinated in 269/882, was marked by an upsurge of the Ismaili *daʿwa*. See al-Ḥammādī, *Kashf*, pp. 25–26. The Yuʿfirids (232–387/847–997) were the first local Yemenite dynasty to emerge in Islamic times. On them see Clifford E. Bosworth, *The New Islamic Dynasties: A Chronological and Genealogical Manual* (Edinburgh, 1996), p. 100; Rudolf Strothmann, 'Yaʿfur', *EI*, vol. 8, p. 1145; and Gerald Rex Smith, 'Yuʿfirids', *EI*², vol. 11, p. 342.

25. al-Ḥammādī, *Kashf*, p. 23, has 1,000 dinars.

26. The poet is named Ibrāhīm by al-Ḥammādī, *Kashf*, p. 23.

O Dhū Ḥiwāl,[27] lamps of the horizon,
Bestowers of gifts which pour forth
Of pure gold, leafy and of silver,
Watch your dominion lest it will disintegrate.
Then you will seek to repair that which cannot be repaired
Except with the ends of lances,[28]
While the people are in anarchy and souls are wiped out,
Like the sheep [attacked by] the wolf are made to swallow blood.
For the head is useful only with the neck,
A foot will not stand on a slippery place,
Fine wheat is unlike ordinary wheat,
Nor are kings of subjects like the common people.
This Abū Yuʿfir amongst you has joined,
Like the high mountain and precipitous lion;
So whichever of you rises will precede.[29]

Then his nephew rose and tried to restore the reign, but it had become weak and most of it had been dissipated and the kingdom had become fragmented. This was the doing of God, the Mighty, the Glorious, for the sake of His friends.[30] The pilgrims accomplished the pilgrimage and departed for the Yemen. Abū al-Qāsim and Abū al-Ḥasan went with them and both arrived in the Yemen at the beginning of the year 268/881. The two resided in the Yemen for two years, and carried on preaching covertly. Then the mission became manifest in the Yemen in the year 270/883.

Abū al-Qāsim said [continuing the narration]: I asked every Yemenite I met about ʿAdan Lāʿa, but they all said that Lāʿa itself was a

27. The Yuʿfirids were of Dhū Ḥiwāl, a tribe from Shibām-Kawkabān some 40 kilometres north-west of Ṣanʿāʾ. Hence they are also referred to as Ḥiwālids.

28. Literally, 'branches of lofty date palms'.

29. Cf. Idrīs ʿImād al-Dīn, *ʿUyūn al-akhbār*, ed. Ghālib, vol. 5, p. 32, and selections ed. Muḥammad al-Yaʿlāwī as *Taʾrīkh al-khulafāʾ al-Fāṭimiyyīn bi-al-Maghrib: al-qism al-khāṣṣ min kitāb ʿUyūn al-akhbār* (Beirut, 1985), p. 61.

30. The expression 'friends of God' (*awliyāʾ Allāh*, singular *walī Allāh*) is used by Shiʿis for their imams and by Sufis for their saints. The Arabic root WLY combines the meaning of being in close proximity and of having protection, sanctity and authority (*walāya*) from that closeness. On the Ismaili concept of *walāya*, see also note 173 below. On the word *awliyāʾ* see note 144 below.

well-known place but they did not know ʿAdan Lāʿa. They only knew ʿAdan Abyan. Hence I proceeded to ʿAdan Abyan, since I could not find anyone able to inform me about ʿAdan Lāʿa, where I had been commissioned to go. In ʿAdan Abyan, I came across a group of Shiʿis known as the Banū Mūsā. This ʿAdan is the seaport for India and the chief town in the country. I enquired as to what is imported to that locality before going there. I was advised to take cotton, so I bought some cotton and placed it as a disguise so that anyone would see that I was a merchant. I entered [the place] with my companion. We asked where we could sell the cotton and we were directed to the place. We rented a shop in its market and sat in there to sell (the cotton). One day, while I was sitting, suddenly it began to rain heavily. While I remained in this position, I noticed men in front of me standing in a row looking at me and passing remarks. Then one of them came up to me, stood facing me and said, 'Would you enter with us inside the shop?'

So I stood with them, and (the man) said, 'I do not think this is the face of a cotton (*ʿuṭb*) merchant.' [*ʿUṭb*] meaning cotton, as they call it.

I asked, 'How is that?'

He asked, 'Do you have any knowledge of the progeny of Muḥammad?'

I replied, 'I am a merchant.'

He said, 'Don't tell me that! Perhaps you have heard of the Banū Mūsā?'

I said, 'Yes.'

He said, 'We are of them. We are Shiʿis and at this time we are expecting the *dāʿī* of the Mahdī to come to us. Indeed we find that you respond to his description. Therefore, convey to us what you have, for we are your brethren.'

He did not let up on me until I disclosed to him the matter, and he did not depart until I administered to him the oath of allegiance. Then he rose and brought his companions to me, and I administered [the oath of allegiance] to them. They took me to their residence and I lived among them. They said, 'We have some brothers among the Shiʿis in ʿAdan Lāʿa. What do you say if we send someone to inform them?'

I asked, 'Is there [such a place as] ʿAdan Lāʿa?'

They replied, 'Indeed.'

I said, 'I was sent to that place, but I did not find anyone who could inform me about it.'

So they sent them word, and men from among them came. I administered [the oath of allegiance] to them, travelled with them and found a residence of Shi'is. They informed me about a man from among them called Aḥmad b. 'Abd Allāh b. Khalī', who had knowledge among them. He had been expecting my arrival and had said that I would come that year. He had prepared weapons for the purpose which they brought to me. His activities came to the attention of Ibn Yu'fir who apprehended him and imprisoned him. He died in the prison not long ago. They lodged me in one of his houses.

Afterwards, Abū al-Qāsim married the daughter of this deceased Aḥmad, and later sent his nephew al-Haytham as a *dā'ī* to the land of Sind.[31] There a lot of people responded to his preaching, and today his mission is widespread in Sind.

Abū al-Qāsim said [continuing the narration]: I wrote to the imam informing him of my progress, and I received his letters in reply. We remained in an uneasy situation until we received the letter announcing the designation of al-Mahdī, may God's blessings be upon him, and directing us to exact allegiance in his favour. Our circumstances then became orderly and God gave us victory. I sent the reply to that letter together with a lot of money and some exquisite objects and embroidered robes from the Yemen. It is said that when the imam received those things, he summoned al-Mahdī, whom he had already designated, and handed over the same to him, saying, 'This is the first fruit of your reign and a blessing of your dominion.'

He read out the letter to him announcing what God had set aside for him, and greeted him citing these appropriate lines of poetry:

God has given you eminence unsurpassed.
Many wished to deny you it and withhold it from you,
But God willed to convey it to you,
So they put its necklace around your neck.[32]

31. On the beginning of the Ismaili *da'wa* in Sind see Samuel M. Stern, 'Ismā'īlī Propaganda and Fatimid Rule in Sind', *Islamic Culture*, 23 (1949), pp. 298–307, reprinted in his *Studies in Early Ismā'īlism* (Jerusalem, 1983), pp. 177–188.

32. These lines were uttered by the poet 'Abd Allāh b. Hammām al-Salūlī (d. after 96/715),

The *daʿwa* spread in the Yemen, and its activities became manifest. Abū al-Qāsim sought permission to wage war and he was allowed to do so. He constructed a stronghold in the mountain of Lāʿa (Jabal Lāʿa), and recruited armies. He conquered towns in the Yemen and gained control of Ṣanʿāʾ[33] from where he drove away the Yuʿfirids (Banū Yuʿfir). He dispatched *dāʿī*s in the regions of the Yemen as well as to other countries, to al-Yamāma,[34] al-Baḥrayn, Sind, India (al-Hind), and towards Egypt, and the Maghrib. He had several exploits whose account would be too long to relate. It is not our intention to do so and investigate them at length. However, we must relate something about them, God willing.

2

Anecdotes about Abū al-Qāsim, head of the *daʿwa* in the Yemen.

The trustworthy companions of Abū al-Qāsim, may God's mercy be upon him, have reported to us about him that he said: The matter of the Mahdī, peace be upon him, and the glad tidings became clear to me in the Yemen more than ever before. Hardly did I pass through or enter a place without coming across some report about him or something pointing to him.[35] One day, while I was travelling through a desert in the Yemen, the strap of my sandal snapped, so I walked briskly to a boulder and sat on it to repair it. While I was doing this,

---

when he became the first to pledge allegiance to the Umayyad caliph al-Walīd b. ʿAbd al-Malik in 86/705. See ʿImād al-Dīn Ismāʿīl Ibn Kathīr, *al-Bidāya wa-al-nihāya* (Beirut, 1974), vol. 9, p. 70. The lines have been attributed to Kuthayyir (d. 105/723). See Kuthayyir ʿAzza, *Dīwān Kuthayyir ʿAzza*, ed. Iḥsān ʿAbbās (Beirut, 1971), p. 533.

33. On the part played by ʿAlī b. al-Faḍl in the conquests made by the *daʿwa* in the Yemen, see al-Ḥammādī, *Kashf*, pp. 30–32, 210–211; Kay, *Yaman*, Arabic text of al-Janadī, *Kitāb al-Sulūk*, pp. 143–144 (tr. pp. 198–199); and Ḥusayn F. al-Hamdānī, *al-Ṣulayḥiyyūn wa-al-ḥaraka al-Fāṭimiyya fī al-Yaman* (Cairo, 1955), pp. 35–37.

34. A district in Central Arabia. Adolf Grohmann, 'al-Yamāma', *EI*, vol. 8, pp. 1154–1155; and Abū al-Fidāʾ, *Taqwīm*, pp. 96–97.

35. On the idea of the awaited Mahdī, restorer of religion and justice, and predictions about his advent see Wilferd Madelung, 'al-Mahdī', *EI*², vol. 5, pp. 1230–1238.

an old man, tired and out of breath, approached me and asked me, 'Who are you?'

I replied, 'A stranger.'

He asked, 'Do you know anything about the Mahdī?'

I asked, 'Who is the Mahdī?'

He said, 'If you do not know him, then perhaps this incident has happened just by chance.'

I asked, 'And what is that?'

He replied, 'I came upon in this very place an old man from among the ulema of the Shīʿa who said, "The messenger of the Mahdī will enter this village, and the strap of his sandal will snap near this boulder. He will sit on it to repair it. Perhaps some of you will live to see that day".'

I said, 'The Shīʿa have many sayings.'

He said, 'Yes, indeed they do.'

However, I did not find acceptance with the old man. He turned away from me and went away.

(Abū al-Qāsim) said [continuing the narration]: The first time I arrived in the Yemen, I entered the mosque of Ṣanʿāʾ and prayed two units (*rakʿatayn*) near a column. I was tired. Then I folded up my cloak and placed it under my head. I lay down on my back, placing one foot on the other. While I was in this position, an old man stopped in front of me and kicked me. He asked me to get up and scolded me.

I got up and asked, 'O shaykh, why am I being singled out, whereas many people are lying down in the mosque?'

He replied, 'I am not reproaching you for lying down, but this is a column about which it is related that when the *dāʿī* of the Mahdī enters Ṣanʿāʾ, he will come to this column, pray two units and lie on his back near it, placing one foot on the other. I am only reproaching you for simulating him.'

I asked, 'What have I got to do with this?'

Someone who heard him, spoke to him, saying, 'How amazing what you are saying, as if this man were indeed the *dāʿī* of the Mahdī.'

He said, 'He is not that man, but I disdain that anyone else should compare himself to him.'

I got up and slipped away. It was as if they believed that this would happen when (the *dāʿī*) appeared among them and made it possible.

A companion of (Abū al-Qāsim) has reported to us about him that he heard a tradition narrated by the Shīʿa in the Yemen, that three Yemenites came to Abū ʿAbd Allāh Jaʿfar b. Muḥammad, may God's blessings be upon him. He asked one of them, 'Which Yemen are you from?'

(The man) replied, 'From al-Mudhaykhira.'[36]

(The imam) remarked, 'It is a town whose characteristics are such and such,' and he described to him its features.

(The man) said, 'Indeed, may God make me your ransom! It is as if the town were in front of you.'

(The imam) said, 'Indeed, there will always be therein one enemy of ours.'

He asked the other man, 'Which Yemen are you from?'

(The man) replied, 'From a town called al-Janad.'[37]

(The imam) remarked, 'It is a town whose characteristics are such and such,' and he described to him its features.

(The man) said, 'It is indeed as you say. May God make me your ransom! It is as if you were beholding the town.'

(The imam) said, 'How different it is from al-Mudhaykhira! There will always be in al-Janad a friend of ours as long as it exists.'

(The imam) asked the third man, 'Which Yemen are you from?'

(The man) replied, 'From Jayshān.'

(The imam) remarked, 'It is a town whose characteristics are such and such, and he described to him its features.'

(The man) said, 'Indeed!'

(The imam) said, 'On its heights is a lotus tree and on its lower ground is a lotus tree.'

(The man) said, 'Indeed!'

---

36. On al-Mudhaykhira, located in the mountainous region of south-western Yemen, see Kay, *Yaman*, pp. 221–223, 231–232; Yāqūt, *Muʿjam*, vol. 5, pp. 90–91; and al-Hamdānī, *al-Ṣulayḥiyyūn*, pp. 36–37.

37. Town situated at six days' march, 58 parasangs (*farsakh*), south of Ṣanʿāʾ. See Yāqūt, *Muʿjam*, vol. 2, pp. 169–170; and Abū al-Fidāʾ, *Taqwīm*, pp. 90–91.

(The imam) continued, 'Between the two lotus trees there is a treasure belonging to Muḥammad, may God bless him and his progeny.'

When he heard this tradition, Abū al-Qāsim said, 'By God, I extracted that treasure.'

He was asked what it was. He replied, 'Seventy men whom I counted among the inhabitants of (Jayshān). They became the most prominent *dā'īs*. They were the instrument of religion and the most trustworthy believers.'

'Alī b. al-Faḍl, whose account we have given, was from there. He was the instrument of the *da'wa*. We have already given his account. The poet Ibn Jīrān[38] was from there. He adhered to Shi'ism and so did his brothers.

(Abū al-Qāsim) said [continuing the narration]: As for al-Mudhaykhira, it is still as Ja'far b. Muḥammad, may God's blessings be upon him, had said. I know in (al-Mudhaykhira) an enemy of the progeny of Muḥammad. I have paid much attention to it, and it is still like that up to now, just as you know.

As for al-Janad, I came across there some Shi'is who acknowledged that (tradition) as being right in former times. God confirmed the veracity of their account and gave victory to their argument through me.

He was asked as to how that happened, and he replied: I entered (the town) incognito and went straightaway to the main mosque. There I prayed the midday, the afternoon and the sunset prayers. Then I asked someone who was there, 'Can one spend the night here? I am a foreigner. I would like to spend the night in the mosque.'

He replied, 'Indeed! All foreigners that you see in (the mosque) will spend the night here.'

So I sat down, and when we had prayed the night prayer, they formed two circles and began to debate with each other about knowledge. I sat between the two circles. One of the circles was made up of Shi'is and the other of Ḥashwiyya.[39] They spent an hour of the night

38. Abū Muḥammad al-Ḥasan b. Aḥmad al-Hamdānī, *Ṣifat Jazīrat al-'Arab*, ed. Muḥammad b. 'Alī al-Akwa' (3rd ed., Ṣan'ā', 1983), p. 202, names the poet as Ibn Jibrān.

39. A pejorative term applied to traditionists who took anthropomorphic descriptions literally. See 'Ḥashwiyya', *EI²*, vol. 3, p. 269.

debating with each other. Then the Shiʿis left and the others prepared to leave. However, a man among them told them to sit down for a while, so they sat down. He then began to look at the Shiʿis who were leaving until the last of them left. Then he turned towards his companions and said, 'Do you know the tradition relating to this night?'

They responded, 'What is the tradition relating to it?'

He said, 'Is it not such and such night of such and such month of such and such year?'

They replied, 'Indeed it is so.'

Then he took out a book from his sleeve and asked, 'Is this not a book transmitted by so-and-so from these rascals (*faʿala*)?', meaning the Shiʿis.'

They looked at the book and said, 'That is so. It is well known among them.'

He selected a tradition from the book and read it out to them, which related that an imam, peace be upon him, had told the author of the book, 'Whoever among the people of your country lives to such and such year should look for the *dāʿī* of the Mahdī on such and such night of that year, that particular night, for he will spend the night in its mosque.'

They said, 'We have already heard this tradition.'

He said, 'You see that they left, without any of them remembering or knowing this matter. Come on, let us nullify their saying and prove them wrong. Let us drive out all those who are in the mosque tonight, so that no one will spend the night in the mosque and thereby nullify their prediction.'

They agreed and one of them got up and said, 'O assembly of foreigners, go away! None of you should spend the night in this mosque under any circumstances, the reason being that there is a story to this effect which makes it impossible for you to do so.'

Abū al-Qāsim said: I saw all of them gathering their belongings and leaving. I did not know where to go, so I made for a corner of the mosque and sat there, hoping that anyone who evicted me would take me to his house. They became dispersed ejecting the people and putting out the lamps. Then a man from among them came to me when most of the lamps had been put out. He asked me to get up. I got up and said, 'I am a stranger. I don't know where to go. Perhaps you can take me with you for the night and accommodate me at your place.'

He said, 'By God, I have no room.'

I said, 'God be praised! You are evicting me from God's house, and denying me your house!'

He appeared to be embarrassed and saw that the people had gone out, so he departed and left me alone. They closed the door of the mosque, and I spent a long night, fearing that the mosque would be searched the following morning, but this did not happen. They returned in the morning, opened the doors and people came inside and prayed, without suspecting me of anything.

Abū al-Qāsim said: I set out from al-Janad bound for a region. One day, while I was travelling, suddenly I saw a large body of troops approaching. People were saying, 'These are the troops of Ibn Yuʿfir. They want to wage war against Jaʿfar b. Ibrāhīm,[40] ruler of al-Mudhaykhira.'

They dispersed in gorges in a mountain out of fear of the troops. I was among those who were dispersed there. I saw a cave and went inside. While I was sitting in the cave, suddenly a man came in, greeted me and sat down. He asked me, 'Where are you from?'

I replied, 'I am from this group of travellers. We saw the troops approaching, so we dispersed in this gorge until they pass.'

He wished me well, talked to me politely and asked me questions about the permissible (*ḥalāl*) and the forbidden (*ḥarām*). Abū al-Qāsim mentioned these, saying that he replied to him on those questions, and he reported the replies. (Abū al-Qāsim) said: I looked at the man. His eyes were filled because of me and he shed tears. Then he stood near me and began to kiss my head, my hands and my feet, and said, 'O my master, the Messenger of God has sent me to you so that you may deliver me, hold my hand and save me.'

I asked him how that would be, and he said, 'I was a man, seeing in my dream the Messenger of God, may God bless him and grant him

---

40. The lord of al-Mudhaykhira Jaʿfar b. Ibrāhīm al-Manākhī, who was defeated and killed by ʿAlī b. al-Faḍl in 294/908. See al-Ḥammādī, *Kashf*, pp. 29–30.

salvation, on a particular night every year. I would be prepared for that night and not be deprived of my vision. However, this year I did not see it, and some time passed. I was very much distressed at this, but when I retired last night I saw (the Messenger of God), may God bless him and grant him salvation, as well as his progeny. I began to ask, 'O Messenger of God, how I longed to see you. You deprived me of what you had habituated me.'

He said, 'I am giving you glad tidings and informing you that the *dā'ī* of the Mahdī is in your country and amongst your people, so hasten to him and take your share from him.'

I said, 'O Messenger of God, how can I contact him?'

He said, 'You will find him tomorrow in such and such cave.' And he mentioned this cave. I said, 'I fear that I might find someone else, so he described your features to me, and said, 'However, ask him about such and such,' and he mentioned to me these questions, [and said], 'If he answers you [by saying] such and such, and he mentioned to me your answer, then he is the right person.'

Abū al-Qāsim said: I was overcome with fear and tears, and said, 'What can I say to the one sent to me by the Messenger of God, may God's blessings be upon him?' I conversed with him and explained the situation to him and administered [the oath of allegiance] to him. This man was well known in the Yemen, and reported this matter and related it.

A companion of Abū al-Qāsim has reported to us about Abū Muḥammad 'Abd Allāh b. 'Abbās,[41] who was one of the most distinguished Yemenite *dā'īs* of Abū al-Qāsim, and whom he appointed as his successor to the *da'wa* after him, that he said, 'Abū al-Qāsim sent me to Egypt to preach. I arrived in an Arab quarter, and came across them in their group, smearing their camels with tar.[42] When they saw

41. He was a Yemenite from the Shāwir branch of the Hamdān who was personally known to al-Mahdī. He succeeded Ibn Ḥawshab after his death in 302/914 on al-Mahdī's approval. He was killed by a disappointed son of Ibn Ḥawshab, Abū al-Ḥasan. See al-Ḥammādī, *Kashf*, pp. 28–30; Kay, *Yaman*, Arabic text of al-Janadī, *Kitāb al-Sulūk*, pp. 150–151 (tr. pp. 208–209); and al-Hamdānī, *al-Ṣulayḥiyyūn*, pp. 49–51.

42. This treatment is used as a remedy for, or preservative against, the mange or scab. See A. J. Higgins, 'Common Ectoparasites of the Camel and their Control,' in A. Higgins, ed.,

me approaching, they stopped what they were doing, approached me and asked, "Who are you?"

I replied, 'A stranger.'

They asked, 'What do you want of us?'

I replied, 'I want to teach.'

They said, 'You are welcome!'

An old man from among them took me by the hand, escorted me to his house and lodged me at his place. He vacated for me a tent and provided a bed for me. He brought me food and I ate. Then at night, he conversed with me at length. After a part of the night had past, he said, 'I implore you by God. You have not really revealed to me who you are and why you are here.'

I said, 'Did I not inform you that I am a teacher?'

He said, 'I do not think so.'

But I did not reveal to him anything. He came to me next morning and persisted for days and nights, investigating me and asking me questions as someone with knowledge, while I persisted with him in saying what I had said at the beginning that I was a teacher. Then he gathered for me the boys of the locality and I sat to teach them. During that time, when he was alone with me, he would say to me the same thing as before. He did not let up on me until I disclosed to him the matter and administered [the oath of allegiance] to him. He turned out to be among the finest to whom I preached. I conducted the *daʿwa* in that place extensively. Afterwards he would tell me, 'By God, it is as if God bestowed reverence and majesty for you in my heart. Indeed, it was only for this reason that you came. I had prior knowledge about it.' Abū Muḥammad said, 'I did not ask him regarding that knowledge, nor did he mention it to me.'

3

Forerunners sent to the Maghrib before the *dāʿī's* arrival there.

In the year 145/762–63 two men from the east arrived in the Maghrib. It is said that Abū ʿAbd Allāh Jaʿfar b. Muḥammad, may God's

---

The Camel in Health and Disease (London, 1986), pp. 75–76.

blessings be upon him, sent them, instructing them to spread the exoteric (*ẓāhir*) knowledge of the imams from the progeny of Muḥammad, may God's blessings be upon them, and proclaim their excellence. He instructed them to go beyond Ifrīqiya to the frontiers of the Berbers, and then each one to proceed separately to a region. When the two arrived at Marmājanna,[43] one of them, named Abū Sufyān, settled there at a place called Tālā.[44] He constructed a mosque, married a woman, and bought a slave-girl and a slave. It is said that he worked with his slave and ordered his wife to work with her slave-girl. He had such integrity, piety and reputation in the region that he became renowned there. The inhabitants of those regions would come to him to hear him relate the virtues of the *ahl al-bayt*, may God's blessings be upon them. They learned these from him, and those of the inhabitants of Marmājanna who adhered to Shiʿism did so through him. (Marmājanna) is a centre of Shiʿism (*dār shīʿa*), and it was due to him that they adhered to Shiʿism. The same is true of the inhabitants of al-Urbus,[45] and it is said that due to him the inhabitants of Nafṭa[46] also adhered to Shiʿism. The reason for this is that some of them used to come frequently to that region, bringing with them

---

43. Marmājanna was one stage to the west of Sabība (S'biba) on the route from al-Qayrawān to Tāhart and Fās. See Ibn Ḥawqal, *Kitāb Ṣūrat al-arḍ* (Beirut, 1979), p. 84; Abū ʿUbayd al-Bakrī, *al-Masālik wa-al-mamālik*, ed. and French tr. W. Mac Guckin de Slane (Paris, 1965), p. 145 (tr. p. 278); and Abū ʿAbd Allāh Muḥammad al-Idrīsī, *Kitāb Nuzhat al-mushtāq fī ikhtirāq al-āfāq*, ed. and French tr. R. Dozy and M. J. de Goeje (Leiden, 1986), pp. 118–119 (tr. pp. 137, 139).

44. The ancient town of Thala, in present-day Tunisia, to the north-east of Tebessa, on El Kef to Kasserine route. On it see Charles J. Tissot, *Géographie comparée de la province romaine d'Afrique* (Paris, 1884–1888), vol. 2, pp. 633–635; and Talbi, *L'émirat aghlabide*, p. 575, note 2.

45. Ancient Lares or Laribus, now Lorbeus, located to the south-east of El Kef, was a vital base for the Aghlabid army to the north-west of al-Qayrawān. See Ibn Ḥawqal, *Ṣūrat al-arḍ*, p. 86; al-Idrīsī, *Nuzha*, p. 117 (tr. pp. 136–137); al-Bakrī, *al-Masālik*, pp. 46, 53 (tr. pp. 99, 114); and Yāqūt, *Muʿjam*, vol. 1, p. 136. On Abū ʿAbd Allāh's conquest of the town see below pp. 165ff.

46. Ancient Nepta, located in the rich region of Qasṭīliya. Nafṭa was called 'the Little Kūfa' (*al-Kūfa al-Ṣughrā*) because of its significant Shiʿi cell. See Georges Marçais, 'Nefṭa', *EI*, vol. 6, p. 900; Georges Marçais and Djilali Sari, 'Nafṭa', *EI²*, vol. 7, pp. 890–891; al-Bakrī, *al-Masālik*, p. 48 (tr. p. 102), pp. 74–75 (tr. pp. 152–153); al-Idrīsī, *Nuzha*, p. 105 (tr. p. 123).

dry dates, which they exchanged for wheat. They would come to (Abū Sufyān) to hear and learn from him. It is said that one of them had a camel which perished. (Abū Sufyān) saw him crying, had pity for him, and said, 'I will lend you a camel, and if you wish, sell it to you on deferment (*nuẓiru*).'

He replied, 'Rather, sell it to me on deferment until I reach my town, and bring you its price.'

He was not among his companions who had learned from him, so (Abū Sufyān) asked him, 'Can you find a guarantor?'

He replied, 'Indeed.'

He said, 'Then look for him.'

He said, 'God is my guarantor to you.'

He said, 'I agree.'

(Abū Sufyān) handed over the camel to him, and when (the man) reached his town, he continued to use it and went with it frequently to Bāghāya[47] He continued doing this for a long time. Then the camel became detached from the file of camels in the night and wandered towards Marmājanna. While Abū Sufyān was in his mosque, suddenly the camel loaded with dry dates arrived in the courtyard of the mosque and halted. (Abū Sufyān) looked at it. He recognised it and said, 'The guarantor has paid fully for you.'

He wrote to the place, giving him this information. Its owner came to (Abū Sufyān) with the price, so (Abū Sufyān) handed (the camel) over to him with its load. (The man) set about to apologise to him, but he cut him short and received him hospitably until he had exchanged his dry dates for wheat and left. Anecdotes about (Abū Sufyān) relating his virtue and piety are many.

The other man, known as al-Ḥulwānī, advanced until he arrived at Sūjmār[48] where he settled in a place called al-Nāẓūr.[49] He constructed

---

47. Bāghāya was a strategically important fortified town at the foot of the Awrās (Aurès). See Ibn Ḥawqal, *Ṣūrat al-arḍ*, pp. 84–85; al-Bakrī, *al-Masālik*, pp. 50, 144–145 (tr. pp. 277–278); al-Idrīsī, *Nuzha*, p. 103 (tr. p. 121); and Yāqūt, *Muʿjam*, vol. 1, p. 325. On Abū ʿAbd Allāh's conquest of the town see below pp. 150ff.

48. The author locates Sūjmār in the territory of the Sumāta, which lay on the eastern edge of Kutāma territory and to the north-west of Qasṭīliya.

49. Talbi, *L'émirat aghlabide*, p. 576, identifies al-Nāẓūr with Nador, between Guelma (Qālama) and Duvivier.

a mosque, married a woman, and bought a slave and a slave-girl. He gained such high reputation in that locality by his piety, virtue and knowledge that he became famous. People from different tribes came to him and many elements of the Kutāma,[50] Nafza,[51] and Sumāta[52] adopted Shiʿism through him. He would tell them, 'We have been sent, Abū Sufyān and myself, and we have been told, "Go to the Maghrib! You will come to a waste land. Plough it, labour it, and tread it until the sower comes to it, and finds it ready to sow his seeds".'

Between their coming to the Maghrib and the coming of the sower, that is Abū ʿAbd Allāh, 135 years elapsed. Abū Sufyān died at Marmājanna, where the location of his tomb and his mosque is still known today. Al-Ḥulwānī outlived him a long time, such that his disciples lived on to the time of Abū ʿAbd Allāh. He left behind him a daughter called Umm Mūsā and died at al-Nāẓūr in the district of Sūjmār, where his tomb and his mosque are to be found.

Among (al-Ḥulwānī's) disciples who lived on to the time of Abū ʿAbd Allāh was Abū Ḥayyūn, better known by his *kunya* Abū al-Mufattish. While still young, he received basic education from (al-Ḥulwānī). Later he learned from his disciples (*rijāl*) and lived on to the time of Abū ʿAbd Allāh. We shall relate his dealings with him when we give his account in the appropriate place, if God, the Most High, wills.

---

50. On the Kutāma, who were central to the establishment of Fatimid dominion, the *Iftitāḥ* is our main source. See also Mūsā Luqbāl, *Dawr Kutāma fī tārīkh al-khilāfa al-Fāṭimiyya mundh ta'sīsihā ilā muntaṣaf al-qarn al-khāmis al-hijrī (11m)* (Algiers, 1979); René Basset, 'Ketāma', 'Kutāma', *EI²*, vol. 5, p. 540; ʿAbd Al-Raḥmān b. Muḥammad Ibn Khaldūn, *Kitāb al-ʿIbar wa-al-dīwān al-mubtada' wa-al-khabar fī ayyām al-ʿarab wa-al-ʿajam wa-al-barbar wa-man ʿāṣarahum min dhawī al-ṣulṭān al-akbar* (Beirut, 1956–1961), vol. 6, pp. 301–309, partial French tr. W. Mac Guckin de Slane, *Histoire des Berères et les dynasties musulmanes de l'Afrique septentrionale* (Paris, 1978), vol. 1, pp. 291–299; and Talbi, *L'émirat aghlabide*, pp. 589–598.

51. The Nafza (Nefza) belong to the Butr branch of the Berbers. They had settled over a large area along the coast between Ifrīqiya and Fās. See 'Nafza', *EI²*, vol. 7, p. 896. According to Ibn Ḥawqal, *Ṣūrat al-arḍ*, p. 102, the Nafza descend from the Zanāta.

52. The Sumāta were a branch of the Nafzāwa (Nafzaoua). See Ibn Ḥazm, *Jamharat ansāb al-ʿArab*, ed. ʿAbd al-Salām Muḥammad Hārūn (Cairo, 1971), p. 497; Ibn Khaldūn, *al-ʿIbar*, vol. 6, pp. 231, 234 (tr. *Berbères*, vol. 1, pp. 230–231). The name also applies to their territory cited in Ibn Khaldūn, *al-ʿIbar*, vol. 4, p. 66 (tr. *Berbères*, vol. 2, p. 510). The territory of the Sumāta was located to the north-west of Qasṭīliya. See al-Bakrī, *al-Masālik*, p. 74 (tr. p. 152).

4

The arrival of Abū ʿAbd Allāh, *dāʿī* of the Maghrib, to the head of the *daʿwa* in the Yemen and his departure from there on his behalf.

The said Abū ʿAbd Allāh was from al-Kūfa. His name was al-Ḥusayn b. Aḥmad b. Muḥammad b. Zakariyā. He was learned, intelligent, religious, pious, honest and respectable. He was most proficient in the esoteric, and had some limited competence in the knowledge of the exoteric. When the *daʿwa* was firmly established in the Yemen, and when its power became manifest, the imam sent Abū ʿAbd Allāh to Abū al-Qāsim, *dāʿī* of the Yemen. He wrote to him instructing him to enlighten (Abū ʿAbd Allāh), guide him and instruct him. Abū ʿAbd Allāh was directed to imitate his conduct, observe the procedure of his deeds and the manners of his actions, to imitate them, conform to them and act diligently upon them. Then he could go to conduct the mission wherever he wished. It is [also] said rather, that he was specifically assigned the Maghrib and sent to Kutāma territory, which is more reliable of the two reports.

Abū ʿAbd Allāh thus came to Abū al-Qāsim, head of the *daʿwa* in the Yemen. The latter put him up at his place, allowed him proximity, honoured him, and he had known him before. (Abū ʿAbd Allāh) stayed with him from the time of departure of pilgrims from Makka to the Yemen until the time of their setting out for the pilgrimage in the following year. During this time he attended his instructional sessions (*majālis*) and set out with him on his military expeditions without leaving him. Then, when it was time for the Yemenites to set out for the pilgrimage to Makka, Abū ʿAbd Allāh set out with them to Makka.[53] Abū al-Qāsim dispatched with (Abū ʿAbd Allāh) a man on his own behalf to escort him and support him according to the custom of the *dāʿī*s, just as ʿAlī b. al-Faḍl had accompanied him, so as to avoid any misadventure befalling him, and that there should be someone with him to succeed him until the order of the imam, peace be upon him, would arrive.

---

53. This was in the year 278/891–892. See Yaḥyā b. Saʿīd al-Anṭākī, *Taʾrīkh al-Dhayl*, ed. and tr. I. Kratchkovsky and A. Vasiliev as *Histoire de Yahya-ibn-Saʿïd d'Antioche: continuateur de Saʿïd-ibn-Bitriq* in *Patrologia Orientalis*, 18 (1924), p. 749.

The man whom (Abū al-Qāsim) dispatched was called ʿAbd Allāh b. Abī al-Malāḥif.[54] He accompanied (Abū ʿAbd Allāh) until he arrived in Kutāma territory and consolidated his position. Whenever he dispatched a man for some reason in this manner, he would not inform any of his family or children, or near or distant relative about his travel, or where he was heading or travelling. The same happened with Abū ʿAbd Allāh and his companions from among the Kutāma. ʿAbd Allāh b. Abī al-Malāḥif had a mother who lost her reason when she missed him, and became disturbed. Abū al-Qāsim had pity for her, so he dispatched to Abū ʿAbd Allāh a Yemenite man called Ibrāhīm b. Isḥāq al-Zabīdī[55] to remain with him instead of Ibn Abī al-Malāḥif. He wrote to Abū ʿAbd Allāh instructing him that he send Ibn Abī al-Malāḥif back to him, and he complied.

Abū ʿAbd Allāh was styled *al-Sayyid* (the Master) among the Kutāma, just as the Arabs call *al-Sayyid* anyone who holds authority among them or is of a noble descent. Abū ʿAbd Allāh introduced this custom according to tradition prevalent in the east. He called the said Ibrāhīm, when the latter came to him, *al-Sayyid al-Ṣaghīr* (the Little Master). (Ibrāhīm) was also known as al-Hawwārī.[56] The reason for this is that, before his mission became manifest, he made (Ibrāhīm) stay with a Kutāma shaykh, and he was asked who this man was. He replied that he was a Hawwārī, and from then this name was applied to him. This Ibrāhīm was not of commendable conduct, and likewise was Ibn Abī al-Malāḥif. When he returned to the Yemen, he joined with those who caused dissension there.[57] We shall narrate about him.

---

54. He is also mentioned in al-Yamānī, *Sīrat al-Ḥājib Jaʿfar*, p. 125 (tr. Ivanow, *Rise*, p. 211); and Ibn al-Athīr, *al-Kāmil*, vol. 6, p. 127; see also al-Yaʿlāwī's note on him in al-Maqrīzī, *al-Muqaffā*, p. 24.

55. He was appointed governor of Tāhart in association with Dawwās b. Ṣūlat al-Lahīṣī after the fall of the Rustamids. See Ibn ʿIdhārī, *al-Bayān*, vol. 1, p. 153.

56. Meaning from the Berber tribe of Hawwāra, whom legends give a Yemenite origin. On them see note 237 below. The *nisba* al-Hawwārī is also formed from a toponym. See al-Ḥasan Ibn Rashīq al-Qayrawānī, *Unmūdhaj al-zamān fī shuʿarāʾ al-Qayrawān*, ed. Muḥammad al-ʿArūsī al-Maṭwī and Bashīr al-Bakkūsh (Tunis, 1986), p. 419.

57. This is an allusion to the treachery of the chief *dāʿī* Fīrūz, who deserted al-Mahdī in Egypt and joined forces with the dissenter ʿAlī b. al-Faḍl. See p.122 below. On Fīrūz see al-Yamānī, *Sīrat al-Ḥājib Jaʿfar*, pp. 114–115 (tr. Ivanow, *Rise*, pp. 195–197); and Canard, 'L'autobiographie', pp. 293–294.

When Abū ʿAbd Allāh advanced from the Yemen towards Ifrīqiya he proclaimed among the Kutāma that he was from Ṣanʿāʾ. This designation was used to curse him from the pulpits of mosques of the Aghlabids. It was proclaimed, 'O God! If the insolence of this infidel from Ṣanʿāʾ has become base and his pasture has become tasty, while he rejects Your favours, alters Your religion, and opposes Your book, then O God, curse him severely, disgrace him for long, relieve Your servants of him, and cleanse Your earth and land from him.'[58]

When Abū ʿAbd Allāh came to know of this, he would say, 'What they say about me is similar to what the idolaters among the Arabs were saying about the Messenger of God, may God's blessings be upon him, when they were insulting him, "O God, do such and such to Mudhammam (blameworthy)" so as to avoid glorifying him by saying 'Muḥammad' (praiseworthy). The Messenger of God, may God's blessings be upon him, would say, "Do you not see how God has dispelled their evil? They are insulting Mudhammam, whereas I am Muḥammad".'[59]

When Abū ʿAbd Allāh left Abū al-Qāsim from ʿAdan Lāʿa with the one he had commissioned with him, he sent with them some men to escort them to the limit of where he was obeyed in the Yemen, and wrote to those with whom he corresponded for the subsequent route to Makka, giving recommendation for them both. Then Abū ʿAbd Allāh left him. I was informed by someone who was in (Abū al-Qāsim's) presence on the day he said farewell to (Abū ʿAbd Allāh) from Lāʿa while (the informant) was in a sitting room of his overlooking the mountain, that (Abū al-Qāsim) looked at (Abū ʿAbd Allāh) high on the mountain in front of him and began to scratch the ground with his finger in his direction and said, 'With him indeed lies the salvation of many people.'

---

58. Cf. p. 140 below.

59. Cf. ʿAbd al-Malik Ibn Hishām, *al-Sīra al-nabawiyya*, ed. ʿUmar ʿAbd al-Salām Tadmurī (Beirut, 1993), vol. 2, p. 10, tr. A. Guillaume, *The Life of Muhammad* (Karachi, 1982), pp. 161–162. By drawing a parallel from this prophetic tradition, al-Qāḍī al-Nuʿmān confirms that Abū ʿAbd Allāh was not originally form Ṣanʿāʾ as mentioned in some sources.

5

Abū ʿAbd Allāh's meeting with Kutāma tribesmen in Makka and his arrival with them in Kutāma territory.

Abū ʿAbd Allāh arrived in Makka with the group of Yemenite pilgrims. When the pilgrims had accomplished their pilgrimage, and stayed at Minā, Abū ʿAbd Allāh began to walk about at Minā, and passed by a party of Kutāma tribesmen among those who performed the pilgrimage that year. They were in their camps, and among them there were two men of the Shīʿa who had adopted Shiʿism through al-Ḥulwānī: Ḥurayth al-Jīmalī and Mūsā b. Makārima. Abū ʿAbd Allāh heard them relating to their companions the virtues of ʿAlī, peace be upon him. He sat with the two men to relate something on the same subject with them. They all came close to him and he talked with them at length. As he prepared to rise, they rose with him. They walked with him, saying that they wanted to know where his camp was, and he walked with them to it. Then, the following day, they came to him and he talked to them at length. They became more fond of him and eager to meet with him. He began to ask them about their country and they informed him. When it was time to depart from Minā, they asked him, 'Where are you heading?'

He replied, 'For Egypt.'

They were pleased with his reply and departed with him. They began to walk around him as he travelled, and camped near him when he camped, serving him and glorifying him. When they halted at the first watering place, they bought for him a sheep and slaughtered it. They prepared food for him, camped with him and brought him food.

He asked, 'What is this?'

They replied, 'This is our custom with guests, for you are a guest among us.'

He declined to accept it and adjured them not to do so, but they said, 'We are along the way.'

He began to respond kindly to them in that regard and grew in their esteem everyday. Everyday they heard from him something new, the like of which they had not heard. They sought his opinion and he gave it to them. Their hearts leaned towards him. All the Kutāma who performed the pilgrimage that year came to see him and walked around him when he walked, and if he dismounted for any need, they would halt and someone among them dismounted with him to serve him until he would fulfil his need, and hold his mount until he rode again. If they passed by water, they would bring water for him. If he prepared to set out, they would not set out for themselves until his luggage would leave and they would carry it. If he dismounted at a halting place, they would be around him, serving him and trying to satisfy his needs in his presence. The same is the case with the Kutāma today. They glorify and give precedence to whoever has the slightest amount of knowledge. Even a teacher among them who does not know well anything other than the recitation of the Qurʾan has esteem, position and dignity among them.

During his conversation Abū ʿAbd Allāh would ask them about their country, and the situation of its inhabitants. They gave him information from which he gathered that it was the place for achieving what he wanted. Among the questions he asked them about (their country) are the following:

He asked them, 'How is your obedience to the ruler and his authority over you?'

They replied, 'He does not have our obedience or any authority over us other than we say that he is a ruler.'

He asked them, 'How far is it between you and his residence?'

They replied, 'Ten days' journey.'

He asked them, 'Are there any towns near to you?'

They replied, 'Yes.' They mentioned Mīla,[60] Saṭīf,[61] and Billizma,[62]

---

60. The fortified town of Mīla, ancient Mileu, in present Algeria. Its fortress dominated Kutāma territory and was noted for its impregnable nature. See Aḥmad b. Abī Yaʿqūb al-Yaʿqūbī, *Kitāb al-Buldān*, ed. A. W. T. Juynboll (Leiden, 1861), pp. 11–12; French tr. G. Wiet, *Les pays* (Cairo, 1937), p. 214; al-Idrīsī, *Nuzha*, p. 94 (tr. p. 110); al-Bakrī, *al-Masālik*, pp. 63–64 (tr. pp. 132–134). On Abū ʿAbd Allāh's conquest of Mīla see below pp. 110ff.

61. The town of Saṭīf (Sétif), ancient Sitifis, in present Algeria. See al-Yaʿqūbī, *Kitāb al-Buldān*, p. 12 (tr. p. 214); al-Idrīsī, *Nuzha*, p. 98 (tr. p. 115); al-Bakrī, *al-Masālik*, p. 76 (tr. pp. 154–155); Yāqūt, *Muʿjam*, vol. 3, p. 220; Abū al-Fidāʾ, *Taqwīm*, pp. 140–141. On Abū ʿAbd Allāh's conquest of Saṭīf see below pp. 126ff.

62. Billizma, now Ksar Belezma in Algeria, was a fortified town in Kutāma territory. See

saying, 'These are within our frontiers.'

He asked, 'Does the ruler of Ifrīqiya have governors there?'

They replied, 'No, but there are only notables who rule these towns and who give (the ruler) no more [recognition] than proclaiming [his name] from the pulpits of mosques, while they obey him in disobedience.'

He asked, 'Do you owe them obedience?'

They replied, 'No, rather they flatter those of us who live near them, and we have power over them.'

He asked, 'To whom do you owe allegiance?'

They replied, 'Every man among us in his self is powerful. We have chiefs among us in every tribe. We have those who have acquired some science, and teachers whose opinion we seek in what relates to our religion. We seek their arbitration in matters that arise among us, and whoever they condemn abides by the judgement that they impose, and if he deviates from it, the assembly of chiefs (*jamāʿa*) turns against him. We ourselves set aside whatever tithe (*ʿushr*) and alms (*ṣadaqa*) are due from our property, and distribute them to those who are needy amongst us.'

He asked, 'Does the ruler have no say over you in this matter?'

They replied, 'No.'

He asked, 'What is the extent of your territory?'

They replied, 'A distance of five days' journey in length by three days in width.'

He asked, 'Are you one tribe?'

They replied, 'The name Kutāma applies to us all. Then we are divided into tribes, clans and families.'

He asked, 'Do you live far apart from each other?'

They replied, 'No, there is no great distance between us.'

He asked, 'Are you united then?'

They replied, 'No, we wage war against each other. After killing, we are reconciled. One group among us makes peace with another while waging war against others. Such is our custom.'

---

al-Yaʿqūbī, *Kitāb al-Buldān*, p. 12 (tr. p. 214); Ibn Ḥawqal, *Ṣūrat al-arḍ*, pp. 91–92; al-Idrīsī, *Nuzha*, p. 99 (tr. p. 116); al-Bakrī, *al-Masālik*, p. 50 (tr. pp. 107–108). On Abū ʿAbd Allāh's conquest of Billizma see below pp. 134ff.

He asked, 'If outsiders suddenly attack you, do you join forces?'

They replied, 'No one has ever wished to do that to us.'

He asked, 'Why?'

They replied, 'Because of our large numbers and the inaccessibility of our territory.'

He asked, 'How many do you number?'

They replied, 'None of us or any outsider has ever counted that as far as we know.'

He asked, 'Do you have horses and weapons?'

They replied, 'That is our greatest possession in which we take pride and which we make ready for our need in warfare among us.'

(Abū 'Abd Allāh) asked them all these and similar questions during his conversation. He kept these in mind and remembered the situation of the territories and the tribes. He asked them everything and carried it out as a conversation without purpose, while becoming aware of this from them. He sought from them the information needed for his purpose and what he was hoping for from them, while they were not aware of what he wanted. They did not realise that he was only conducting this as a conversation in accordance with what they saw of him, while he was pleased with what he heard to that effect and saw that the purpose would be served through them.

Now when they arrived in Egypt, he declared to them that he wanted to remain there. They expressed sadness for his separation and said, 'What makes you stay here? We see that you have no trading to conduct, nor is this your country.'

He replied, 'I want to teach.'

They were delighted at his reply, and said, 'We do not think you will find a country more advantageous for you to practise teaching than our country.' They began to inform him of the money spent for (teaching) among them and the high regard in which the inhabitants of their country hold those who teach among them, and said, 'If you wish, consider what you might expect to earn by teaching each year. We shall add to that according to your expectation and award you that of our own accord. We shall pay some of it to you now if you want the wages for the year and two years or whatever you like.'

He showed them that he had not decided either way. They became more interested in him and discussed the matter relating to him among themselves and asked him until he agreed to set out with them. They were very happy at this and said to each other, 'Indeed, we have something to be proud of, for we are taking to the land of the Kutāma something which no one has brought before us.'

They began to request him further, saying, 'A lot of your brothers among us hold the opinions that you hold, and if they saw you and the people saw you, they would be satisfied with you for their elders rather than their boys, for we do not bring the like of you for teaching boys, and whatever you wish for the sake of teaching you will find many times that in our wealth.' He praised them.

When they saw that he had resolved to travel with them, they gathered together and said, 'We will collect for him dinars which we will pay him to strengthen his resolve, and we will carry his provisions.'

They collected dinars which they brought to him, but he refused to take these from them. They tried everything to change his mind, but he refused, saying, 'There was nothing on our part that would require this. If it were, we would accept it from you.'

They replied, 'Then do us a favour by accepting this, for it will be a good deed on your part among us.'

He refused to accept it politely with thanks. This ennobled him in their eyes, and their respect for him grew in their hearts.

Then they set out from Egypt. They wanted to carry his provision, but he did not allow them to do so, and travelled along with them discreetly as he had done. He became more majestic in their eyes. Their route was from Tripoli to Qasṭīliya,[63] because it was the main highway, without entering Ifrīqiya. When eventually they arrived at Sūjmār in the territory of the Sumāta, they were met by the local people who lodged them among them. Abū al-Mufattish,[64] Abū al-Qāsim

63. The name Qasṭīliya refers to the district, and sometimes to its administrative centre Tūzar or Tawzar, ancient Thusuros, now Tozeur, in the region of Djerid in south-western Tunisia. See Mohamed Talbi, 'Ḳasṭīliya', *EI*², vol. 4, pp. 739–741; Georges Yver, 'Tūzer', *EI*, vol. 8, pp. 983–984; Taoufik Bachrouch, 'Tūzar', *EI*², vol. 10, pp. 759–760; and Jean Despois, 'Djarīd (Bilād al-)', *EI*², vol. 2, pp. 462–464. On Abū ʿAbd Allāh's conquest of the town see p. 163 below.

64. He was a former pupil of al-Ḥulwānī, and also known as Abū Ḥayyūn. See p. 44 above.

al-Warfajūmī[65] and Abū ʿAbd Allāh al-Andalusī,[66] who adhered to Shiʿism, met Ḥurayth and Mūsā, their companions. These two informed them about Abū ʿAbd Allāh. The Sumāta observed the honour with which all the Kutāma treated him. So each one of them wanted him to stay at his place. Eventually they drew lots. (Abū ʿAbd Allāh's) lot fell to Abū ʿAbd Allāh al-Andalusī, so (Abū ʿAbd Allāh) stayed with him, while Ḥurayth stayed with Abū al-Mufattish and Mūsā stayed with Abū al-Qāsim. The Sumāta lodged each of the Kutāma with one of their men according to their custom with guests of the community when they stay with the group. Each one slaughtered a sheep for his guest, and attended to him with kindness and hospitality.

Abū ʿAbd Allāh observed the truth of their situation which they had described. Abū al-Mufattish and Abū al-Qāsim al-Warfajūmī together with Ḥurayth and Mūsā came to (Abū ʿAbd Allāh) in the night and conversed with him for long. Abū ʿAbd Allāh saw a people who had more knowledge and understanding than the ones whom he had seen and accompanied. He found among them a strong basis of the knowledge of the Shīʿa and the excellence of the *ahl al-bayt*, so he talked with them at length and brought them clarification. At the end of the instructional session (*majlis*), when they were about to rise, Abū al-Mufattish looked at (Abū ʿAbd Allāh) and said, 'By God, I do think that you are the sower announced by al-Ḥulwānī.' He informed him about (al-Ḥulwānī) and rose. Abū ʿAbd Allāh said to Abū ʿAbd Allāh al-Andalusī, referring to Abū al-Mufattish, '[What] a fine shaykh!'

When Abū al-Mufattish went out, he told his companions, 'If it were not for one thing which al-Ḥulwānī used to say, I would not have doubted that this is the man whose glad tidings al-Ḥulwānī had announced.'

---

65. He is referred to as being among the four Kutāma pilgrims whom Abū ʿAbd Allāh met in Makka. See Ibn Khaldūn, *al-ʿIbar*, vol. 4, p. 66 (tr. *Berbères*, vol. 2, p. 510).

66. He is referred to in Ibn Khaldūn, *al-ʿIbar*, vol. 4, p. 66 (tr. *Berbères*, vol. 2, p. 510) as Muḥammad b. Ḥamdūn b. Simāk al-Andalusī, from the family of Banū Ḥamdūn which held important functions in the Fatimid and Spanish Umayyad administrations. See Marius Canard, 'Une famille de partisans, puis d'adversaires, des Fatimides en Afrique du Nord', in *Mélanges d'histoire et d'archéologie de l'Occident musulman II: Hommage à Georges Marçais* (Algiers, 1957), pp. 33–49.

They asked, 'O Abū Ḥayyūn, what is it?'

He replied, 'When (al-Ḥulwānī) described him, he said that there would be a finger in his mouth.'

When Abū 'Abd Allāh came to know about this, he smiled and said, 'This is not so.'

Then afterwards, when he administered the oath of allegiance to those who had heard this from Abū al-Mufattish and imposed secrecy, he placed his finger on his mouth and said, 'This is the finger that al-Ḥulwānī was talking about. I command you silence and secrecy, and as for there being a finger in the mouth of a man, that cannot be.'

They said, 'It is indeed so, by God!'

Testimony for this was thus established among them.

When the group retired from him Abū 'Abd Allāh al-Andalusī remained with him. He had understanding, acuteness and knowledge. He had been a teacher in the locality. Then he settled there and rose to the rank of the learned of the place and adopted Shiʿism. Abū 'Abd Allāh continued to converse with him and found in him what he wanted. Eventually he revealed to him the matter and administered to him the oath of allegiance on that same night. It is related that they both prayed the dawn prayer in the state of ritual purity from the night prayer. Abū ʿAbd Allāh then went to sleep after the prayer, and Abū 'Abd Allāh al-Andalusī rose and slaughtered many sheep. He went to the Kutāma who were about to depart and adjured them to stay with him that day. This was difficult for them because of the proximity of their country. He told them, 'This guest who is with you stayed awake in the night and slept after praying, and I fear that if he travels today, he might become weak.'

They replied to him, 'If that is the case, we will stay, for if we were able to protect him with our lives, we would do so.'

(Abū 'Abd Allāh al-Andalusī) offered them hospitality and began to make preparations for travel. Abū al-Mufattish and Abū al-Qāsim al-Warfajūmī saw him doing this and asked, 'What is this provision that we see you making?'

He told Abū al-Mufattish, 'I think that [after] what you said about this man being the sower as you did say, I considered accompanying him so as to become acquainted with what he bears.'

Abū al-Qāsim said, 'By God, I will do so as well.'

Abū al-Mufattish who was old and weak physically said, 'I also, by God, were I able to travel, I would be with you. However, when you two become informed about his matter you shall write to me, and I will be carried to him.'

Mūsā and Ḥurayth perceived much liking of their companions for him that their happiness at him and joy at their coming with him was increased by it. The group spent the night and departed in the morning.

6

Abū ʿAbd Allāh's arrival in Kutāma territory and the beginning of his mission there.

The group travelled and entered the frontier of Kutāma territory on Thursday, middle of Rabīʿ I 280/4 June 893. They were accompanied by Abū ʿAbd Allāh al-Andalusī and Abū al-Qāsim al-Warfajūmī. Everyone of the Kutāma argued with the other about Abū ʿAbd Allāh, each wanting to take him to his own locality out of devotion for him. This resulted in disputing and tussling. Eventually they let him choose where among them he wished to proceed, and they came to that agreement. (Abū ʿAbd Allāh) asked them, 'In which locality among you is a ravine called Fajj al-Akhyār (the Ravine of the Righteous)?'

They looked at each other as if they understood that he already knew the place, and they replied, 'It is in the territory of the Banū Saktān,[67] and their route from this locality passes through it.'

He said, 'Then let us proceed there, so that, God willing, we will go to every group from among you in their localities, and visit them in their houses, so as not to favour any one of you with a share of myself to the exclusion of others.'

They were satisfied with this, and every group from among them travelled to its own direction. Abū ʿAbd Allāh set out with Ḥurayth,

67. The Saktān were a branch of the Jīmla, one of the main clans of the Kutāma. See Ibn Khaldūn, *al-ʿIbar*, vol. 4, p. 66 (tr. *Berbères*, vol. 2, p. 510).

Mūsā, Abū al-Qāsim al-Warfajūmī and Abū ʿAbd Allāh al-Andalusī for Īkjān,[68] the locality of Mūsā and Ḥurayth of the Banū Saktān.

When he arrived at Fajj al-Akhyār, he asked them, 'Is this Fajj al-Akhyār?'

They replied, 'Indeed it is.'

Then Mūsā and Ḥurayth said to him, 'By God, we do not remember having mentioned to you this ravine, so from where did you learn its name? We see that you already knew it without our having acquainted you with it.'

He replied, 'Lands can be described and mentioned to the people even if they have not seen them.'

Afterwards he would say, 'By God, this ravine has only been named after you, for it has been reported in the traditions that the Mahdī will emigrate far away from his fatherland, at a time of vicissitudes and troubles, during which his defenders will be the best of men whose name will derive from *kitmān* (secrecy), and you Kutāma are the ones referred to, because you originate from this ravine which is called Fajj al-Akhyār (the Ravine of the Righteous).'

Abū ʿAbd Allāh stopped at Īkjān and settled there. All the Kutāma pilgrims who had travelled with him set out from there towards their respective localities. They informed their companions whom they came across about him, and described to them his knowledge and position. Then people came to visit him from every region and he became known among them. He held instructional sessions (*majālis*) with them, informing them about the distinct virtues of ʿAlī b. Abī Ṭālib, may God's blessings be upon him and upon the imams from his descendants, peace be upon them. When he noticed that they had each retained his teachings and when he felt that one of them was well disposed to what he wanted out of him, he would then gradually initiate him until he responded. Then he would administer the oath of allegiance to him. Previously, (Abū ʿAbd Allāh) had administered the oath of allegiance to Abū al-Qāsim al-Warfajūmī, Ḥurayth and Mūsā.

68. The exact position of Īkjān is difficult to establish. See Talbi, *L'émirat aghlabide*, pp. 600–601, note 4. Information in the *Iftitāḥ* allows us to locate Īkjān to the north of Saṭīf and Mīla nearer the latter; al-Idrīsī, *Nuzha*, p. 98 (tr. p. 115), and Abū al-Fidā', *Taqwīm*, p. 141, locate Īkjān near Saṭīf; Ibn Khaldūn, *al-ʿIbar*, vol. 4, p. 67 (tr. *Berbères*, vol. 2, p. 511), states that it was located in the territory of the Banū Saktān, hence between Saṭīf and Mīla.

Ḥurayth exclaimed, 'How long was our journey with you and yet we were unaware of something like this proceeding from you!'

Hārūn b. Yūnus b. Mūsā al-Masāltī[69] who was known as the chief of elders (*shaykh al-mashāyikh*), a member of the Masālta,[70] came to him. (Abū 'Abd Allah) initiated him in the mission. Al-Ḥasan b. Hārūn al-Ghashmī,[71] member of the Ghashmān[72] of Tāzrūt[73] came to him. He initiated him in the mission. He was a young, intelligent, graceful man, of noble character, from the fortunate society of easy means. He had accomplished good actions and gained a high reputation. Among the Ijjāna,[74] Abū Yūsuf Māknūn b. Ḍubāra[75] and his nephew Tammām b. Muʿārik Abū Zākī,[76] who was still young, came to receive Abū ʿAbd Allāh. He initiated both of them in the mission. He noticed in Abū Zākī energy, vivacity of spirit, ardour in his occupations, flexibility as well as a strong desire to have the qualities and the zeal to obtain them. Abū Zākī joined his service and was his

69. Abū Mūsā Hārūn b. Yūnus al-Azāyī al-Masāltī became a staunch supporter of Abū ʿAbd Allāh from the very beginning. His title, 'chief of elders', denotes a high rank among the Kutāma. Later, Abū Mūsā dared to question publicly the imamate of al-Mahdī. See p. 216 below. On Abū Mūsā see also Ibn al-Haytham, *Kitāb al-Munāẓarāt*, index.

70. The Masālta were a branch of the Kutāma. They occupied the region to the west of the mountain of Īkjān, north of Saṭīf. See Ibn Khaldūn, *al-ʿIbar*, vol. 6, p. 302 (tr. *Berbères*, vol. 1, p. 292).

71. He was a chief of the Ghashmān and a staunch supporter of Abū ʿAbd Allāh in his fight against his opponents.

72. The Ghashmān were a branch of the Kutāma. See Ibn Khaldūn, *al-ʿIbar*, vol. 6, p. 302 (tr. *Berbères*, vol. 1, p. 292).

73. The *Iftitāḥ* allows us to situate Tāzrūt approximately between Īkjān and Mīla. See also *Berbères*, vol. 2, p. 512, note 2, and vol. 4, p. 531.

74. The Ijjāna were a branch of the Kutāma. See Ibn Khaldūn, *al-ʿIbar*, vol. 6, p. 302 (tr. *Berbères*, vol. 1, p. 292). They were neighbours of the Jīmla, occupying the region to the south of Īkjān.

75. Abū Yūsuf was appointed governor of Mīla after Abū ʿAbd Allāh's conquest of the town. See below, p. 111; and Ibn Khaldūn, *al-ʿIbar*, vol. 4, p. 69 (tr. *Berbères*, vol. 2, p. 513). Later, under the reign of al-Mahdī, he was governor of Tripoli. See below, p. 220; and Ibn ʿIdhārī, *al-Bayān*, vol. 1, p. 164.

76. Abū ʿAbd Allāh appointed Abū Zākī to govern Ifrīqiya jointly with Abū al-ʿAbbās while he was away to free al-Mahdī from captivity. See p. 195 below. Abū Zākī was among those later accused of treason and executed on the orders of al-Mahdī. See p. 220 below. On Abū Zākī see also Ibn al-Haytham, *Kitāb al-Munāẓarāt*, index.

close companion. The mission of Abū ʿAbd Allāh became well known and he carried it out openly.

Then (Abū ʿAbd Allāh) was struck with an illness of a stone which afflicted him severely. They told him, 'If only you could reach a bath.' He was told that the bath was nearby in Mīla.[77] So he set out with a man from the Banū Saktān. When he arrived in Mīla, he proceeded to an inn there which belonged to Farjūn, a client of the lord of Mīla, Mūsā b. ʿAbbās,[78] and stayed there. A man approached Mūsā b. ʿAbbās and told him, 'The man from the east whom you know resides in Īkjān and whom the Kutāma visit has arrived in Mīla. He is staying at Farjūn's inn and Farjūn stands before him.'

(Farjūn) was one of (Mūsā b. ʿAbbās's) important slaves. His son resides today in Mīla in opulence with a large family. It is related that he died leaving behind twenty male children, all of whom rode behind him when he rode. He was noble, ambitious and honourable.

(Farjūn's) master Mūsā said to him, 'Go and bring me this man from your inn. You must not neglect the matter regarding someone like him.'

So (Farjūn) set out to bring him and considered himself responsible for him. This is because (Abū ʿAbd Allāh) had become his guest by staying at his inn. He feared lest Mūsā did something odious to him, and that would be a blemish on him. So he dispatched someone secretly to warn him and ordered him to leave, and moved back and forth until he knew that he had left. Then he came to the inn and inquired about (Abū ʿAbd Allāh). He was told that he had left, so he began to look for him. Then he returned to Mūsā to inform him that he found out that (Abū ʿAbd Allāh) had already left. Then he avoided mentioning him, and God protected him from his mischief. The chamber of this inn in which (Abū ʿAbd Allāh) stayed is known for his stay until today.

---

77. A water-spring in Mīla was noted for its healing properties. See al-Bakrī, *al-Masālik*, p. 64 (tr. p. 134).

78. He is Mūsā b. ʿAbbās b. ʿAbd al-Ṣamad whose family, from the Arab tribe of Sulaym, seems to have provided the Aghlabids, under the reign of Ibrāhīm b. Aḥmad, useful commanders in Sicily. See al-Yaʿqūbī, *Kitāb al-Buldān*, p. 351 (tr. p. 214); and Ibn Khaldūn, *al-ʿIbar*, vol. 4, pp. 67, 69 (tr. *Berbères*, vol. 2, pp. 511, 513).

It is related that (Abū ʿAbd Allāh) arrived on the back of a piebald she-mule which had been with him for a long time during which he rode it. He returned to Īkjān. Mūsā b. ʿAbbās's search for him was reported and stories about him spread among the Kutāma who rushed to see him from every region. It became widely known among the people that he preached a secret doctrine which they did not know, and that anyone who accepted that doctrine would not reveal anything about it. When people closest to him, or his relatives, or those dearest to him, asked into what he had been initiated, and what he was told, he would reply, 'Seek to attain and you will find certitude.'

This was an expression which Abū ʿAbd Allāh had taught them, and which they regularly repeated when asked. He called them 'brothers' (*ikhwān*), and when he called them, he would say 'O our brother.' This is how they addressed each other.

Abū ʿAbd Allāh's cause became famous and he became known by the appellation of 'al-Mashriqī' (the Easterner).[79] Anyone who adhered to his *daʿwa*, embraced his cause and was associated with him, it was said that he was an Easterner (Mashriqī), and consequently they were called 'al-Mashāriqa' (Easterners). The family of those who had adhered to his preaching observed their dedication to prayer, fasting, doing works of charity and deeds of piety, and their avoidance of sins, and their sound state. They were encouraged to join their cause and came to (Abū ʿAbd Allāh) from every region. (Abū ʿAbd Allāh) initiated in the mission each one who came to see him. He returned to his own land, locality and family, and came back frequently to him to listen to him. Some of them settled in Īkjān, wishing to be close to him.

(Abū ʿAbd Allāh) conducted the mission among a group of Banū Saktān. They vacated for him a place to sit to listen to instruction (*samāʿ*). They offered hospitality to anyone who came to him and reached him. The believers brought him provisions and expended on this, wishing to gain reward and proximity to God, the Mighty, the Glorious, through doing charity. This was the first expense on his behalf which he specified and charged them with. Those who adhered to the *daʿwa* in their group became like stars, exemplary in

79. This nickname denoted Abū ʿAbd Allāh's origin. See p. 77 below.

works of charity. People were amazed at their evil condition before adhering to the *da'wa* and how they changed thereafter. Those whose vile self could not give up sins and leadership of the world began to insinuate about them, accusing them of impiety and leaving the community, saying, 'If this doctrine had any good in it, it would not be secret, rather it is totally contrary to the religion of Islam. What they are pretending is merely hypocrisy by which they seek to attract the people.' Such things were said increasingly in every region.

This matter and (Abū 'Abd Allāh's) prestige came to the attention of Mūsā b. 'Abbās, ruler of Mīla. He asked the Banū Saktān to dispatch Abū 'Abd Allāh so that he might investigate his situation, and bring about a confrontation between (Abū 'Abd Allāh) and the ulema at Mīla in front of him. They scornfully refused to do so, saying, 'We are not of those who will hand over their guest to you.' He tried to persuade them to do so and sent them back the envoy, and coaxed them, warning them of the consequences that if news of (Abū 'Abd Allāh) reached Ibrāhīm b. Aḥmad,[80] he would dispatch troops to them, which would bring them unpleasant consequences. They replied bluntly, 'We are not of those who will hand him over, nor forsake him, nor let anyone lay a hand on him while he is our guest and amongst us.' When (Mūsā b. 'Abbās) failed to persuade them and realised that they would not comply with his demand, he tried to harm them through other Kutāma, but they disdained to lend him a hand against members of their own families.

Ibrāhīm b. Aḥmad, ruler of Ifrīqiya, came to know about Abū 'Abd Allāh and wrote to Mūsā b. 'Abbās asking about him. Mūsā b. 'Abbās described the situation of (Abū 'Abd Allāh) as weak, and feared the coming of Ibrāhīm b. Aḥmad, lest he come and attack him and remove him, because he did not trust him. However, he wrote to him to beguile him, relating to him in his letter the overall information about (Abū 'Abd Allāh). Ibrāhīm b. Aḥmad understood well the position of Mūsā b. 'Abbās with regard to the matter.

80. The Aghlabid emir Abū Isḥāq Ibrāhīm b. Aḥmad b. Muḥammad b. al-Aghlab (r. 261–289/857–902). On him and other emirs of the dynasty, see Georges Marçais and Joseph Schacht, 'Aghlabids', *EI*[2], vol. 1, pp. 247–250; and Talbi, *L'émirat aghlabide*, pp. 271–322.

7

Ibrāhīm b. Aḥmad's reply to Mūsā b. ʿAbbās conveyed by an envoy from him and his message to Abū ʿAbd Allāh.

(The narrator) said: When Ibrāhīm b. Aḥmad understood the reply of Mūsā b. ʿAbbās and realised his purpose, he wrote to him a letter and sent to him the astrologer Ibn al-Muʿtaṣim,[81] ordering him to use subtle means to be conveyed to Abū ʿAbd Allāh. He ordered him to investigate (Abū ʿAbd Allāh's) situation and return with the correct information about him. He gave him orders for (Abū ʿAbd Allāh) and asked him to convey these to him. (The envoy) reached Mūsā b. ʿAbbās, and Mūsā sent (someone) to one of the Banū Saktān informing him that Ibrāhīm b. Aḥmad had sent a man to Abū ʿAbd Allāh to meet with him and asking him to convey the matter to (Abū ʿAbd Allāh). He submitted the matter to Abū ʿAbd Allāh who accepted the offer. Then Mūsā b. ʿAbbās dispatched Ibn al-Muʿtaṣim secretly to Abū ʿAbd Allāh as Ibrāhīm had commanded him to do, and he sent him to the man to whom he had written about the matter, and who brought them together. Abū ʿAbd Allāh allowed him to approach him and gave attention to him. Ibn al-Muʿtaṣim told him, 'The emir Ibrāhīm b. Aḥmad has sent me to you and instructed me to convey a message from him. I am his messenger, and if you allow me to convey to you the message, I will convey it to you.'

Abū ʿAbd Allāh told him, 'Convey your message, for the messenger has only to convey the message.'

He asked, 'Will I be safe?'

(Abū ʿAbd Allāh) replied, 'You are safe by God's protection. Tell me everything that he has told you.'

He said, 'The emir asks you, "What has incited you to incur my displeasure, violate my kingdom, corrupt my subjects and revolt against me? If you seek any worldly dignity, then that is what you will find with me. If you redress yourself, give up transgression, and then come to me, you will be safe. Then if you wish to stay in my country, you may do so, and if you like to retire to the place from where you

---

81. Ibrāhīm b. Aḥmad had a penchant for astrologers and soothsayers. See Ibn ʿIdhārī, *al-Bayān*, vol. 1, pp. 122–123.

came, you may do so. If your purpose is that of those whose self entices them to oppose the imams and to seek to corrupt the ignorant of the community, then perhaps you know that those who are enticed by their self with your wish, and what your self has enticed you with, will result in immediate perdition before an evil outcome in the Hereafter. Let not the apparent enthusiasm of these riffraff for following you deceive you, for if I turned my face towards you they would abandon you and dissociate from you. Therefore, know that I only wished to be discharged from you by showing the case against you. This is my first and last communication to you. After this, I will not accept repentance from you, nor any false step from you. My only response to you will be that I myself will attack you with all my brave men and supporters of my dominion and all the people of my kingdom. Then you will regret it, if you are now defiant in your transgression. Then regret will be of no avail to you, nor will repentance be accepted from you. If you understand this today for tomorrow, then *the one who warned you is discharged from you*".'[82]

Abū ʿAbd Allāh replied, 'You have spoken. Now listen! You have conveyed the message. Now communicate! Tell him, "As for the threats and menace that you have made, I am not the one to be frightened by menace, nor scared by thunderous threats. As for your frightening me with the supporters of your reign and the men of your kingdom, the children of the vanities of this world who covet it, who are frightened of every thunderbolt, and who respond to every caller and screamer, I am with the supporters of religion and protectors of the believers who are not frightened of the multitude of supporters of the unjust, according to the saying of God, the Mighty, the Glorious, who is the most truthful sayer: *How oft, by God's will, hath a small force vanquished a big one? God is with those who steadfastly persevere* (2:249). As for Ibrāhīm tempting me with his world and offering me its cream and vanities, I am not among the greedy to incline towards him, nor do I want what he has so that I would come

82. Cf. Arabic proverb '*Qad aʿdhara man andhara*', explained in Muḥammad b. al-Qāsim Ibn al-Anbārī, *Kitāb al-Aḍdād*, ed. Muḥammad Abū al-Faḍl Ibrāhīm (Kuwait, 1960), p. 321. The text of the emir's message and Abū ʿAbd Allāh's reply is largely preserved in Lisān al-Dīn Ibn al-Khaṭīb, *Aʿmāl al-aʿlām*, part 3, ed. Aḥmad Mukhtār al-ʿAbbādī and Muḥammad Ibrāhīm al-Kattānī (Casablanca, 1964), pp. 38–39.

to him. I have only been sent as a messenger for a matter decreed and approaching, and for fulfilling a prior promise of God, for God does not fail in His promise, nor does He wrong any human being except him who wrongs himself. So if his self entices him to what he is threatening, and invites him to it, then he will know that God is after him and no group will be of avail to him *however numerous they be, and know that God is with the believers*" (8:19). This is the reply to the message you brought, so convey it, and then carry my letter to him. Convey from me what I have entrusted you to do. I summon him to God, the Mighty, the Glorious, to His book, and to the Imam al-Mahdī from the progeny of His Messenger. My summons is from one who brings him irrefutable proof, and who wishes to save him. Now if he accepts this from me, he will gain his rectitude, but if he is stubborn, then my justification has come to him in advance. Even if he were my companion, I would hasten to march to fight him. However, he and those who come after him have a provision for a while until the appointed time comes, until the term approaches. *Those who do wrong will come to know by what a (great) reverse they will be overturned*' (26:227).

Then Abū ʿAbd Allāh dismissed the messenger in the best condition. (The messenger) conveyed to Ibrāhīm his message. He asked him about (Abū ʿAbd Allāh's) description and he described him to him most vividly. Thereupon Ibrāhīm became pale and deemed Abū ʿAbd Allāh to be too dangerous and news of him alarming. He avoided mentioning him and knew that he was the one who would put an end to his dynasty. (Ibrāhīm) had a liking for the science of predictions and future events.[83] He had only sent [the messenger] to him to investigate his matter. Thus, when he learnt the fact and it turned out to be true, he was bewildered. When (Abū ʿAbd Allāh) was mentioned to him in public, he would show indifference towards him and lack of concern about him. However, when he was mentioned to him in private and with his dignitaries, he would say, 'By God, if he came to me, to this city, through one gate, I would

83. On the science of predictions see Toufic Fahd, *La divination arabe* (Paris, 1987), pp. 219–228; Toufic Fahd, 'Malḥama', *EI*², vol. 8, p. 247, and 'Djafr', *EI*², vol. 2, pp. 375–377; 'Malāḥim', *EI*², vol. 6, p. 216.

go out before him through another gate. By God, it seems as if I see the garments of his companions spread out on the balconies of this palace of mine.'

(Ibrāhīm) had a penchant for Shiʿism, and so did several members of his household, the elite among whom were the Sālimis (al-Sālimiyyūn).[84] A group among them were afflicted with leprosy. That is why the poet Ibn Ḥasan[85] lampooned one of them saying:

If you were cut to pieces by leprosy or followed the cause of ʿAlī
You would not be a genuine Sālimī among the Sālimīs.

Ibrāhīm appointed ʿAlī b. Abī Ḥajar[86] governor of Qafṣa[87] and Qasṭīliya and made recommendations to him when he was preparing to set out, saying, 'Adopt with (the governed) the conduct of the two ʿUmars.'[88]

'No,' he replied. 'I will only adopt with them the conduct of ʿAlī b. Abī Ṭālib, peace be upon him, if you agree to this, or else I will return your diploma of investiture.'

(ʿAlī b. Abī Ḥajar) was one of the members of his family who had

84. The Sālimīs (al-Sālimiyyūn) were a collateral branch of the ruling Aghlabid family. They were partisans of Sālim b. Ghalbūn, governor of al-Zāb, who rebelled in 233/847 against his cousin, the emir Muḥammad b. al-Aghlab (r. 226–242/841–856). See Ibn ʿIdhārī, *al-Bayān*, vol. 1, pp. 109–110; Talbi, *L'émirat aghlabide*, pp. 240–242.

85. Dachraoui, in his edition, p. 56, states that he is Abū ʿIqāl Ghalbūn b. al-Ḥasan b. Ghalbūn, nephew of Sālim b. Ghalbūn. A biographical notice on him and extracts of his poems are given in Abū Bakr al-Mālikī, *Kitāb Riyāḍ al-nufūs fī ṭabaqāt ʿulamāʾ al-Qayrawān wa-Ifrīqiya*, ed. Bashīr al-Bakkūsh (Beirut, 1994), vol. 1, pp. 527–545; and Ibn Nājī, *Maʿālim*, vol. 2, pp. 214–231.

86. Abū al-Ḥasan ʿAlī b. Abī Ḥajar was one of the three envoys sent by Ziyādat Allāh b. ʿAbd Allāh to the court of the Byzantine emperor in 294/908. See Ibn ʿIdhārī, *al-Bayān*, vol. 1, p. 144. His family provided high officials to the Aghlabid state. ʿAlī's father, Abū Ḥajar Jaʿfar b. Muḥammad (d. 264/878), was governor of Sicily under Ibrāhīm b. Aḥmad. See Ibn ʿIdhārī, *al-Bayān*, vol. 1, p. 117; and Ibn al-Khaṭīb, *Aʿmāl*, pp. 115–116.

87. Gafsa, ancient Capsa, 146 miles south of al-Qayrawān. On the importance of the town in the Middle Ages see Georges Yver, 'Gafṣa', *EI*, vol. 3, pp. 126–129; and Mohamed Talbi, 'Ḳafẓa', *EI²*, vol. 4, pp. 414–416. On Abū ʿAbd Allāh's conquest of the town see p. 163 below.

88. The expression 'the two ʿUmars' (*al-ʿUmarān*) refers to Abū Bakr and ʿUmar b. al-Khaṭṭāb. See Abū ʿAbd Allāh Muḥammad b. Aḥmad al-Qurṭubī, *al-Jāmiʿ li-aḥkām al-qurʾān* (Beirut, [1952]-1967), vol. 5, p. 68, and vol. 16, p. 91.

adopted Shiʿism. Ibrāhīm told him, 'By God, it is the most virtuous conduct. Adopt it, but I do not think that you will.'

Muḥammad b. al-Aghlab[89] had designated Saḥnūn b. Saʿīd,[90] who was a Mālikī, to the judgeship. This was in order to satisfy the populace of al-Qayrawān because of what came to pass between him and his brother Aḥmad,[91] so they supported him. However, the members of his family rebuked him for this. Then when Saḥnūn died, his disciples gathered and arranged with his son Muḥammad,[92] to come to Muḥammad b. al-Aghlab and inform him of the death of his father and tell him that he had recommended him to pray for him. They said, 'He will not be able to object to this. Then when he comes and prays, we shall talk to him about you so that he might appoint you as judge.'[93]

They arranged with a group of people that when that happened they should shout and talk. Hence Muḥammad b. Saḥnūn came to Muḥammad b. al-Aghlab for this purpose and arranged to be with him at the time of the late afternoon prayer. The bier of Saḥnūn was brought out to al-Sabkha,[94] near his house. Muḥammad b. al-Aghlab

---

89. The Aghlabid emir Abū al-ʿAbbās Muḥammad b. al-Aghlab (r. 226–242/841–856).

90. Saḥnūn (d. 240/855) was appointed *qāḍī* in 234/849 by the emir a year after he regained power from his brother Abū Jaʿfar Aḥmad. On him see Mohamed Talbi, 'Saḥnūn', *EI*², vol. 8, pp. 843–845; Fritz Krenkow, 'Saḥnūn', *EI*, vol. 7, pp. 64–65; Abū al-ʿArab Muḥammad b. Aḥmad b. Tamīm al-Qayrawānī, *Ṭabaqāt ʿulamāʾ Ifrīqiya wa-Tūnis*, ed. ʿAlī al-Shabbī and Naʿīm Ḥasan al-Yāfī (Tunis, 1968), pp. 184–187, 233–236; al-Mālikī, *Riyāḍ al-nufūs*, vol. 1, pp. 345–375; ʿIyāḍ, *Madārik*, pp. 86–136.

91. Abū Jaʿfar Aḥmad b. al-Aghlab who, in 231/846, rebelled against his brother and seized power. See Ibn ʿIdhārī, *al-Bayān*, vol. 1, pp. 108–109; Ibn al-Khaṭīb, *Aʿmāl*, pp. 21–22; Talbi, *L'émirat aghlabide*, pp. 222–231.

92. Muḥammad b. Saḥnūn (d. 256/870), who became leader of the Mālikī school after the death of his father. On him see al-Mālikī, *Riyāḍ al-nufūs*, vol. 1, pp. 443–458; al-Khushanī, *ʿUlamāʾ Ifrīqiya*, pp. 178–182, 256; ʿIyāḍ, *Madārik*, pp. 170–188; Gérard Lecomte, 'Muḥammad b. Saḥnūn', *EI*², vol. 7, p. 409.

93. In fact the Ḥanafī Sulaymān b. ʿImrān (d. 270/883) succeeded Saḥnūn. See al-Khushanī, *ʿUlamāʾ Ifrīqiya*, pp. 179, 236–240; Ibn Nājī, *Maʿālim*, vol. 2, p. 152.

94. *Sabkha* is a flat, salt-encrusted depression, usually just above the water-table, that is subject to periodic flooding and evaporation. See Georges Yver, 'Sebkha', *EI*, vol. 7, p. 202, and 'Sabkha', *EI*², vol. 8, p. 685. Apparently al-Sabkha referred to here was close to Bāb Nāfiʿ to the east of al-Qayrawān, because the emir prayed near this gate for Saḥnūn, and where

came out accompanied by a group of members of his family and his entourage from al-Qaṣr al-Qadīm.[95] When they reached al-Hārūniyya,[96] they halted there. He stopped before them and asked, 'What caused you to halt?'

They replied, 'You have come out to pray for Saḥnūn, so we could not stay away from you. You know the alienation between us and him. He considered us to be disbelievers and we considered him to be a disbeliever. Now if we pray for him, the people will think that we agree with his situation.'

He asked, 'Then what do you want?'

They replied, 'That you excuse us from praying for him.'

He said, 'I excuse you.'

They said, 'We shall stay here because if we come with you near the coffin, the people will think that we are praying for him.'

He said, 'Do so.'

So they stayed at al-Hārūniyya, and mats were spread for them and they sat down.[97] Muḥammad b. al-Aghlab advanced, leading his black guards[98] and prayed for Saḥnūn. The people of al-Qayrawān were informed about them, and this absolved them from what they agreed and had said in what they had been arranging. Muḥammad paid no attention to them and left.

Because of this Shiʿi leaning among them, they reported accounts of the Mahdī, peace be upon him, and what is reported on the

---

Saḥnūn's grave is located. See al-Mālikī, *Riyāḍ al-nufūs*, vol. 1, p. 347; and Ibn Nājī, *Maʿālim*, vol. 2, pp. 101, 104.

95. This Aghlabid residence, also known by the name of Qaṣr al-Aghāliba, was located about three miles south-east of al-Qayrawān. It was founded in 184/800 by Ibrāhīm b. al-Aghlab (r. 184–196/800–812), founder of the Aghlabid dynasty, who named it 'al-ʿAbbāsiyya' in honour of the Abbasids. See Hassan Hosni Abdul-Wahab, 'al-ʿAbbāsiyya', *EI*², vol. 1, p. 24; and Georges Marçais, *L'architecture musulmane d'Occident* (Paris, 1954), pp. 26–27.

96. Apparently al-Hārūniyya was located between al-Qaṣr al-Qadīm and Bāb Nāfiʿ, in the suburbs south of al-Qayrawān.

97. The emir's companions were hostile towards Saḥnūn and Mālikism because Saḥnūn had denounced their Muʿtazilī leanings. See Ibn Nājī, *Maʿālim*, vol. 2, p. 102.

98. Black slaves (*ʿabīd*) formed part of the Aghlabid guards since Ibrāhīm b. al-Aghlab. Their role was more important than that of white slaves (*mawālī*). See Madeleine Vonderheyden, *La Berbérie orientale sous la dynastie de Benoû'l-Aṛlab 800–909* (Paris, 1927), pp. 197–199. On al-Mahdī's use of these groups see p. 212 below.

authority of the Prophet, peace and blessings of God be upon him, and studied books of predictions and tales of future events. Ibrāhīm understood all this and pursued it. He came to know about an old man in one of the villages of Tunis, Qaryat al-Khirbatayn, that he was well versed in the science of predictions and was a poet.[99] (Ibrāhīm) ordered him, who was senile, to be brought before him and questioned him. He made excuses because of his advanced age, and the fact that he had forgotten most of this knowledge. (Ibrāhīm) cajoled him and gave him presents saying, 'You must relate to me whatever you have retained.'

So he related to him poetry about (the Mahdī) which was widespread, and which people related and recited. He alluded to (the Mahdī) in it without expressing clearly. It is the poem which begins thus:

I say, as I have abandoned poetry to those who are qualified for it,
And I have lived a long time and in the best that is drawing near:
Shall I, after ninety years I count
And four after that in order,
Vie with the people of poetry in composing Rajaz?
God refuses this after my withers have been cut.
Rather, I hope for forgiveness from God,
With the return of one whose innermost heart is trustworthy and
who is repentant.
I long for forgiveness through recitation,
Which I will repeat by night with the thought of one turning back.
I have turned my affairs to the One whose slave I am,
My God, Lord of the throne, Bestower of needs.
During my life I shall only implore the Owner of loftiness,
If not, then let the joints of my fingers of my right hand be cut.
Surely, oh trustee of God and son of His trustee,
And the tenth of the lords of the Aghlabid kings,[100]
I found a book from ancient time,

99. The poet in question is a certain al-Ḥarbī, also referred to as al-Tūnisī, and his two poems are cited in al-Qāḍī al-Nuʿmān, *Sharḥ al-akhbār*, (*juz'* 15), vol. 3, pp. 420–421; Idrīs ʿImād al-Dīn, *ʿUyūn al-akhbār*, ed. al-Yaʿlāwī, pp. 52–54, ed. Ghālib, vol. 5, pp. 28–29; and al-Yaʿlāwī, *al-Adab bi-Ifrīqiya*, pp. 13–16.

100. Ibrāhīm b. Aḥmad (r. 261–289/875–902) is reckoned to be the ninth Aghlabid ruler, not tenth.

The narration of noble elders,
Narration of Wahb[101] on the authority of Saṭīḥ[102] and Daniel,[103]
Elders of true knowledge, without falsehood:
Seven banners will follow each other from the east
To the west, black, with fluttering strands,
With them will move (men) with eyes looking askance,
you will see them,
Their mouths a string of pearls and long moustaches.

In it he also says:

The governors of the Abbasids are twenty governors,
The lands of the west obey them against their will,
But in ninety-six[104] a banner will come down
From the west in an assembly of massive processions,
Their gathering will split asunder the land of the Berbers.
With cavalry like swarms of sand grouses,
The sun of God will rise from the west,
Then repentance will not be anticipated for any repentant.
From the sons of Fāṭima will come forth a man,
Pious and pure in honour endowed with abundant gifts,
The namesake of the Prophet of God and the son of
his sincere friend,
The most noble offspring and the most honourable claimant.
He will fill God's earth with justice and mercy,
With days of sincerity and beneficial attainments,
But by the one-eyed Deceiver (*al-dajjāl*)[105] his assembled legions
will be demolished,
Except for a band rising in the mountain high and stable.

---

101. The story-teller Wahb b. Munabbih (d. 114/732) who was well versed in Jewish and Christian traditions. On him see Raif Georges Khoury, 'Wahb b. Munabbih', *EI*², vol. 11, pp. 34–36.

102. The legendary diviner of pre-Islamic Arabia Saṭīḥ b. Rabīʿa. On him see Georges Lévi Della Vida and Toufic Fahd, 'Saṭīḥ b. Rabīʿa', *EI*², vol. 9, pp. 84–85.

103. The prophet Daniel, on whom see Georges Vajda, 'Dāniyāl', *EI*², vol. 2, pp. 112–113.

104. See note 10 above.

105. On the Deceiver (*al-dajjāl*), an apocalyptic figure similar to the Antichrist, see Armand Abel, 'Dadjdjāl', *EI*², vol. 2, pp. 76–77. Fatimid writers identify the Kharijite rebel Abū Yazīd Makhlad b. Kaydād with the Deceiver.

Then Jesus son of Mary will slay (the Deceiver),
With the power of a Lord who has no conqueror.
Then the son of Mary will die, returning to God,
According to an inescapable decree from God.

He alluded to (the Mahdī) in it without declaring clearly, separating its verses, making cryptic allusions to him. People used to narrate and recite them. They also recited the poetry of Ibn ʿAqib,[106] in which he says:

I said when sleep flew away from me,
Until when will this night without a morning continue?
Sorrow and sleeplessness have been tormenting me,
Both pledging not to cease.
How can someone not be sad who does not see,
O Misṭaḥ, that he will attain
An age wherein he will see the imam of guidance,
By God in the Maghrib conquering
And constructing al-Bayḍāʾ[107] in a green deep sea,
In which will swim its whale.
Its inhabitants will be saved from horrors,
From it the whole earth will be conquered.
If my life span were to be extended to his age,
I would be in the epoch which will prosper.
But how far is life from what I see?
In what I see (now) death holds authority.

In it he also says:[108]

Listen to the truth and stop playing.
Here is a true statement without a lie.
When the star shows the extended tail,

---

106. The unknown poet is also cited in al-Qāḍī al-Nuʿmān, *Sharḥ al-akhbār*, (*juzʾ* 15), vol. 3, pp. 423–424, where his name appears as Ibn Aʿqab. Idrīs ʿImād al-Dīn, *ʿUyūn al-akhbār*, ed. al-Yaʿlāwī, p. 54, ed. Ghālib, vol. 5, p. 29, gives the poet's name as Ibn ʿUqba. See also Wilferd Madelung, 'The Sufyānī between Tradition and History', *Studia Islamica*, 63 (1986), pp. 39–40; and al-Yaʿlāwī, *al-Adab bi-Ifrīqiya*, pp. 18–20.

107. The new Fatimid capital of al-Mahdiyya is referred to as al-Bayḍāʾ on p. 228 below.

108. The poem is cited in al-Qāḍī al-Nuʿmān, *Sharḥ al-akhbār*, (*juzʾ* 15), vol. 3, p. 424; and Idrīs ʿImād al-Dīn, *ʿUyūn al-akhbār*, ed. al-Yaʿlāwī, p. 54, ed. Ghālib, vol. 5, p. 29.

Then an evident event has approached,
In ninety-six will come to you wonder.
After the completion of 200 years in Rajab,
From Jījil[109] will surge forward a tumultuous army,
More effective than brightly burning embers
Of Berbers marching on every hill,
Cavalry and infantry who are not wearied by fatigue.
They have filled the east with fear and terror.
Have inflicted in the west humiliation and exhaustion.
Ninety thousand [invaders] between head and tail,
Their mark is rancour and show of anger.
Among them is a mingling of Quraysh and Arabs
With every cutting sword as it strikes,
Until they pass ascent and descent.
In every army is a banner of headbands
Which the rider inserts in the wooden part of the horse's bridle,
Led by a mature man learned in the books (of prophesies),
Seeking refuge in determination when the situation
 becomes troubled,
Taking the far-away matter from near.
The reign will change when it changes,
To that of the Mahdī according to the text of the books
Related by Daniel and Saṭīḥ among the Arabs.

When Abū 'Abd Allāh entered Raqqāda,[110] the poet Abū al-Yusr[111]

---

109. Ancient Igilgili, coastal town of Djidjelli in present-day Algeria, fifty miles east of Bijāya (Bougie), from where rise the Kutāma mountains. See al-Idrīsī, *Nuzha*, pp. 97–98, 102 (tr. pp. 114–115, 120); Georges Yver, 'Djijelli', *EI*², vol. 2, pp. 537–538.

110. Founded in 263/876 by the Aghlabid emir Ibrāhīm b. Aḥmad, Raqqāda, about six miles south of al-Qayrawān, became the centre of Aghlabid dominion, replacing al-'Abbāsiyya. On Raqqāda see Georges Marçais, 'Raḳḳāda', *EI*², vol. 8, pp. 414–415.

111. Originating from Baghdad, Abū al-Yusr Ibrāhīm b. Muḥammad al-Baghdādī al-Shaybānī al-Qayrawānī al-Riyāḍī (d. 298/911) sought fortune in Andalusia, before settling in al-Qayrawān. He served the Aghlabids until the fall of the dynasty, and then the Fatimids from the time of Abū 'Abd Allāh's arrival in Raqqāda. Soon he became one of Abū 'Abd Allāh's courtiers, and accompanied him during his expedition to Sijilmāsa. Subsequently al-Mahdī, upon his installation in Raqqāda, entrusted to him the charge of secretary of the chancellery. See Ibn 'Idhārī, *al-Bayān*, vol. 1, pp. 152–153, 159, 162–163; and Mohamed Mokhtar Labidi, 'al-Shaybānī', *EI*², vol. 9, p. 396.

recited to him this poem, and told him, 'We used to relate it "in the year ninety,[112] wonder will come to you". However, we see that this is impossible, and that its correct version is "in ninety-six", and thus it was related in what has been cited above, that it is "in the year ninety"'.

Its impossibility remained unknown until Abū 'Abd Allāh's coming to Ifrīqiya in the year [2]96, when it became known. If it was (correctly) in the year ninety, in that year Abū 'Abd Allāh's mission became complete, strong and firm. When Abū al-Yusr recited this poem to Abū 'Abd Allāh, in the presence of the jurists of the inhabitants of al-Qayrawān, Ibn 'Abdūn[113] said, 'We have never heard any prediction more correct than this one.'

Ibrāhīm b. Aḥmad had detained in his prison a man, an inhabitant of Bāghāya, called Karīm b. Zurzūr because of a grudge he held against him. He escaped from his prison and came to the Banū Mālik[114] of Billizma seeking refuge with them from Ibrāhīm b. Aḥmad. They granted him asylum. This happened long before the time of Abū 'Abd Allāh. Ibrāhīm sent [someone] to pursue him, but they defended him. Then he set out himself at the head of troops, but he could not subdue them. So he withdrew from them and displayed forgiveness and pardon towards them until a group of them came to him. He presented them garments and gifts, and was charitable to them, granting them official posts. They came to him from everywhere. He continued to act in this manner with them until about 1,000 men of them gathered.

---

112. The year 290.

113. Abū al-'Abbās Muḥammad b. 'Abd Allāh b. 'Abdūn b. Abī Thawr al-Ru'aynī (d. 297/910) was a prominent Ḥanafī jurist with Mu'tazilī leanings. He was appointed to the office of *qāḍī*, and then dismissed after about thirty months in office by Ibrāhīm b. Aḥmad. See al-Khushanī, *'Ulamā' Ifrīqiya*, pp. 242–245, 307; Ibn 'Idhārī, *al-Bayān*, vol. 1, pp. 121, 161; and Ibn Nājī, *Ma'ālim*, vol. 2, pp. 273–276.

114. The Banū Mālik were a branch of the Tamīmī Arabs settled in Billizma. While respecting the Kutāma, the Banū Tamīm and their clients were hostile to the Aghlabids. In 280/893 Ibrāhīm b. Aḥmad attempted to crush them. See al-Ya'qūbī, *Kitāb al-Buldān*, p. 12 (tr. p. 214); Ibn 'Idhārī, *al-Bayān*, vol. 1, p. 123; and al-Nuwayrī, *Nihāya*, vol. 24, ed. Ḥusayn Naṣṣār (Cairo, 1983), p. 131 (partial French tr. W. Mac Guckin de Slane, *Berères*, vol. 1, pp. 427–428).

He had made them stay in Raqqāda in a place which he surrounded with a wall and installed a gate to it which was near the inn of the people of Billizma. Then when they gathered and he was sure that no one else would come there, he locked them in by night and surrounded them with his black guards, who killed all of them.

In Billizma there was a man from Nafṭa who was a Shiʿi and who used to foretell the end of the dominion of the Aghlabids. He was pursued, so he went to Billizma. He was a poet called Muḥammad b. Ramaḍān who sought protection with the Banū Mālik. He used to eulogise them, and they protected and defended him. They learned of Ibrāhīm's killing of the inhabitants of Billizma, while (the poet) was residing with them, and he composed a poem about this event:[115]

Great is the calamity if what they mention is true,
In the news and information that has come to us,
About one thousand men most marvellous like lions
who have been killed,
Betrayed in an hour of the dark of the night.
Had the lions' assailant by night awakened them,
Misfortune and alternation from them would have befallen him.
Tell Ibrāhīm son of Aḥmad in a message
From the one well informed about what he will do
and what he will leave.
From the fugitive for the sake of his love of the imams from
The progeny of the Prophet and the best of mankind
to be mentioned,
Know that the most unfortunate of mankind will have the longest
Hand in the affliction they mete out one day when they
become powerful,
Especially the guest, the foreign (*gharīb*)[116] neighbour and those
To whom they give their word of honour before they
protected them.
What is your excuse for (this) disgrace and shameful act,

---

115. The poem of Muḥammad b. Ramaḍān is cited in al-Qāḍī al-Nuʿmān, *Sharḥ al-akhbār*, (*juz*ʾ 15), vol. 3, p. 426; and Idrīs ʿImād al-Dīn, *ʿUyūn al-akhbār*, ed. al-Yaʿlāwī, pp. 55–56, ed. Ghālib, vol. 5, p. 30. See also the text of the poem established by al-Yaʿlāwī, *al-Adab bi-Ifrīqiya*, pp. 23–26

116. Near (*qarīb*) in al-Qāḍī al-Nuʿmān, *Sharḥ al-akhbār*, (*juz*ʾ 15), vol. 3, p. 426.

Which you perpetrated deliberately when an excuse stands up?
You have given your guest a glass to drink which you shall drink, for
Soon, the order of God is expected.
The dominion of the Qā'im, the Mahdī,
Its days have approached and what has been announced
in traditions
From the Prophet. In them is mentioned the end of your age,
O offspring of Aghlab, people of treachery! So restrain yourselves.
After you the dominion of the sons of al-ʿAbbās will be cut,
And so will the dominion of the sons of Marwān since
they were haughty.

It is said that when this poem came to Ibrāhīm's knowledge, he inquired about its composer and was informed about him. He said, 'May God curse the one who pursued him and drove him away. Such a person should not be harmed. If he were to come to us, we would pardon him and be charitable towards him. He is staunch in loyalty to those who have granted him asylum and been kind to him. Good deeds thrive in such a person. His adherence to Shiʿism will not be held against him, rather it will bring him close to us and make him dear to us. Convey this to him on our behalf. Then if he wishes to come to us, he will be safe. He will have dignity and honour at our court.'

His declaration came to the knowledge of Muḥammad b. Ramaḍān, who realised that he only wished to lure him. Someone told him something else. Thereupon he composed the following verses:

If I did not see him hunting with his grain, I would pick his grain.
Who is cheated by a treacherous man who does not fear
God his lord?

This Muḥammad b. Ramaḍān often used to mention the Mahdī in his poems. On him he says:[117]

Ask the female gazelle of the hunter where her dwelling is,
For her listlessness and fatigue aroused me.
Perhaps she is one whose folks have strayed from her,

117. Cf. al-Qāḍī al-Nuʿmān, *Sharḥ al-akhbār*, (*juz'* 15), vol. 3, p. 426; Idrīs ʿImād al-Dīn, *ʿUyūn al-akhbār*, ed. al-Yaʿlāwī, p. 56, ed. Ghālib, vol. 5, p. 30.

So her abodes have disappeared and her wandering has lasted long.
I stayed awake after her tribe went to sleep.
The separated young of the gazelles are the beautiful ones.
Pass by the abode whose folks have gone away
And disregard how after decay its state has become.
This is the hour of truth whose time has come,
The moment has come for the reign of the unjust to fall.
Already I see the sun of the earth rising
From the west, together with the crescent.
He will fill God's earth with equity and justice,
The entire earth, valleys and mountains.
I will feel secure in it and protected from what I fear
I will gain closeness (to God) through him and I will attain it.

This Muḥammad b. Ramaḍān lived up to the time of al-Mahdī, peace be upon him, when he had become senile. (Al-Mahdī) appointed him judge of Mīla where he lived and died while he was its judge. May God have mercy upon him.

Yaʿqūb b. al-Maḍā[118] was a member of the Aghlabid family. He owned estates in the region of Jamma.[119] When he went there he would come to the island on which al-Mahdiyya is built. He would halt there, walk round it, look at it, and say, 'This is the description of the island about which it has been said that the Mahdī will build his city upon it. By God, I do not know any site on the coast of Ifrīqiya which resembles the description more than this place.'

Accounts and poems on this subject are numerous. They fall outside the scope of this book. The Shiʿis narrate and report them. There are several accounts and reports about (the city), announcing

118. He is Yaʿqūb b. al-Maḍāʾ Sawāda b. Sufyān (brother of al-Aghlab) b. Sālim b. ʿIqāl. He shunned political life and was devoted to asceticism. See Muḥammad b. ʿAbd Allāh Ibn al-Abbār, *Kitāb al-Ḥulla al-siyarāʾ*, ed. Ḥusayn Muʾnis (Cairo, 1963), vol. 1, p. 182.

119. Jamma refers to the peninsula on which al-Mahdiyya was founded. See Ibn ʿIdhārī, *al-Bayān*, vol. 1, pp. 169, 187; ʿAbd Allāh b. Muḥammad al-Tijānī, *Riḥlat al-Tijānī*, ed. Ḥasan Ḥusnī ʿAbd al-Wahhāb (Tunis, 1958), pp. 368, 371, 376–378; Abū ʿAbd Allāh Muḥammad b. ʿAlī Ibn Ḥammād, *Akhbār mulūk Banī ʿUbayd wa-sīratuhum*, ed. and tr. M. Vonderheyden (Algiers-Paris, 1927), p. 9 (tr. p. 21). On the topography of al-Mahdiyya and its suburbs see Néji Djelloul, 'Histoire topographique de Mahdia et de ses environs au Moyen Âge', *Les cahiers de Tunisie*, 162–163 (1992–1993), pp. 71–103 + 5 plates.

it just as there were reports about the sending of the Messenger of God, may God's blessings be upon him and his progeny, before he was sent. These accounts were related and reported by several Arabs in poetry and stories, such as Umayya b. Abī al-Ṣalt,[120] Waraqa b. Nawfal,[121] Zayd b. 'Amr,[122] As'ad Abū Karib,[123] Quss b. Sā'ida,[124] Khālid b. Sinān,[125] and others.

When Abū 'Abd Allāh's activities gained strength and became manifest, Ibrāhīm b. Aḥmad acted like Muḥammad b. Yu'fir, king of the Yemen whose account we have related above. He abdicated power, showed repentance and returned most of what he had appropriated.[126] He distributed wealth to the people, wore wool and displayed asceticism. He set out to attack the king of the Byzantines, designating his son Abū al-'Abbās[127] to rule. We shall relate his account.

Ibrāhīm b. Aḥmad left Ifrīqiya and set out at sea in the Rajab of the year 289/June 902. At the approach of the year [2]90/902–3 in which the events are reported, he reached Sicily and from there set out for

---

120. On Umayya b. Abī al-Ṣalt, poet of the Thaqīf see James E. Montgomery, 'Umaiya b. Abī 'l-Ṣalt', *EI*^{2}, vol. 10, p. 839.

121. On Waraqa b. Nawfal, a cousin of the Prophet's wife Khadīja, see C. F. Robinson, 'Waraḳa b. Nawfal', *EI*^{2}, vol. 11, pp. 142–143.

122. Zayd b. 'Amr was a Makkan who followed monotheism before the mission of the Prophet. On him see Michael Lecker, 'Zayd b. 'Amr', *EI*^{2}, vol. 11, pp. 474–475.

123. He is Tubbān/Tibbān As'ad Abū Karib (Tubba' II), King of the Yemen, who during an expedition to Yathrib and Makka embraced monotheism. On him see Ibn Hishām, *al-Sīra al-nabawiyya*, vol. 1, pp. 35–42 (tr. pp. 7–12).

124. On Quss b. Sā'ida, the orator and sage of pre-Islamic Arabia, see Charles Pellat, 'Ḳuss b. Sā'ida', *EI*^{2}, vol. 5, pp. 528–529.

125. Khālid b. Sinān was a diviner who foretold the coming of the Prophet Muḥammad. On him see Charles Pellat, 'Khālid b. Sinān', *EI*^{2}, vol. 4, p. 928.

126. Ibrāhīm's abdication was apparently decided by the Abbasid caliph al-Mu'taḍid bi-llāh, following complaints about his cruelty from the inhabitants of Tunis. See Ibn 'Idhārī, *al-Bayān*, vol. 1, pp. 131–133; and al-Nuwayrī, *Nihāya*, vol. 24, p. 135 (tr. *Berbères*, vol. 1, pp. 431–432).

127. He is Abū al-'Abbās 'Abd Allāh b. Ibrāhīm (r. 289–290/902–903), who was recalled from Sicily where he had been sent by his father to restore order. He was assassinated probably at the instigation of his son Ziyādat Allāh. See p. 117 below.

Taormina (Ṭabrmīn),[128] which he conquered on Sunday 22 Shaʿbān/1 August of the same year [289/902].[129] When he wanted to set out to sea, he granted twenty dinars to every horseman, and ten dinars to every foot-soldier. A large body of troops assembled under him. He would say that he would never return to Ifrīqiya. From Taormina he advanced to Cosenza (Kusantah)[130] and laid siege to it. During the siege, he became ill with colic (*ʿillat al-baṭn*), and died on the night of Saturday 13 Dhū al-Qaʿda of the year.[131] There was a shower of shooting stars for five nights before his death, on the eighth night of this month.[132] It was the tenth night of Tishrīn I, which is October.[133] His reign, from the time he assumed office until his death, lasted for twenty-eight years, six months and a few days. The troops withdrew to Sicily where Ibrāhīm's body was brought and buried.[134] Then Ziyādat Allāh proceeded with the army to his father Abū al-ʿAbbās. It came to (Abū al-ʿAbbās's) knowledge that (Ziyādat Allāh) wanted to attack him, so he arrested him and detained him. We shall give his account subsequently.[135]

---

128. A town in eastern Sicily which was the last remaining Byzantine stronghold on the island.

129. On this expedition see Talbi, *L'émirat aghlabide*, pp. 519–528.

130. Cosenza, a town in Calabria in southern Italy.

131. Some uncertainty about the exact day of Ibrāhīm's death is found in most sources. It is most likely that he died on Saturday 17 Dhū al-Qaʿda 289/23 October 902. See Talbi, *L'émirat aghlabide*, pp. 526–527, note 4.

132. This celestial phenomena was observed in al-Ramla in the east by al-Mahdī and his entourage from the terrace of the governor's house. See al-Yamānī, *Sīrat al-Ḥājib Jaʿfar*, p. 112 (tr. Ivanow, *Rise*, pp. 192–193); and Canard, 'L'autobiographie', pp. 289–290.

133. The 8th of Dhū al-Qaʿda 289 corresponds to the 14th of October 902, not the 10th.

134. According to al-Nuwayrī, *Nihāya*, vol. 24, p. 138 (tr. *Berbères*, vol. 1, p. 434) and Ibn al-Khaṭīb, *Aʿmāl*, p. 36, Ibrāhīm was buried in Palermo; but according to Ibn al-Athīr, *al-Kāmil*, vol. 6, p. 6, the body was taken to al-Qayrawān for burial.

135. See p. 118 below.

8

The uprising of the coalition of Kutāma against Abū ʿAbd Allāh to seize him in Īkjān.

The cause of Abū ʿAbd Allāh spread in Kutāma territory, and he was called 'al-Mashriqī' (the Easterner) because he came from the east. Then all those who swore allegiance to him and adhered to his *daʿwa* were associated with him and called 'Easterners' (al-Mashāriqa). When one of them swore allegiance, it was said that he had become an Easterner. People saw the excellence of the situation of those who adhered to his mission, their abstinence from corruption for which they had been known, and their dedication to prayer, fasting and pious deeds. This persuaded them to adhere to that cause. People came to him from everywhere, and he admitted in the mission those from among the tribes that he approved. When the chiefs of the tribes and the governors of the towns observed this, and did not see any effort on the part of Ibrāhīm b. Aḥmad to deal with him, they feared the extinction of their leadership from their hands, and the coming to power of those whom they considered to be below them who advanced and rushed to his cause. So they wrote to each other about the matter, rallied together, exchanged correspondence and formed a coalition.

Among those who formed the coalition for this purpose were Mūsā b. ʿAbbās, lord of Mīla, ʿAlī b. ʿUslūja,[136] lord of Saṭīf, and Ḥayy b. Tamīm, lord of Billizma. These commanders had the equipment, bravery, the men (*ʿadad*) and strength, and they had a lot of wealth. Among the chiefs and elders of the tribes of the Kutāma and governors of their affairs were Fatḥ b. Yaḥyā al-Masāltī, who was called the commander (*al-amīr*), Mahdī b. Abī Kināwa, chief of the Lahīṣa,[137] Faraḥ b. Jīrān, chief of the Ijjāna, Abū Tamīm Faḥl

136. He is referred to as ʿAlī b. Ḥafṣ b. ʿUslūja in Ibn Khaldūn, *al-ʿIbar*, vol. 4, p. 67 (tr. *Berbères*, vol. 2, p. 511). He was better known as Ibn ʿUslūja from his mother's name. See p. 126 below.

137. The Lahīṣa were a branch of the Kutāma. See Ibn Khaldūn, *al-ʿIbar*, vol. 6, p. 302 (tr. *Berbères*, vol. 1, p. 292).

b. Nūḥ,[138] chief of the Laṭāya,[139] and Ziyāda al-Matūsī,[140] chief of the Matūsa.[141] These in addition to their leadership and precedence were heroes, each one of them equalling a battalion. They devised stratagems and made plans to seize Abū ʿAbd Allāh. They did not consider that they would be able to seize him by force from the hands of the Banū Saktān, because (the plotters) did not doubt that they were protecting him, and if they were protecting him, then all the Jīmla[142] and the Kutāma tribes near them would stand up in anger with them. They feared that if (the tribes) did so, it would lead to them becoming his supporters and all the Kutāma would be divided into two factions, and they would not be safe from harmful consequences in the matter. They agreed to approach in his matter Bayān b. Ṣaqlān,[143] one of the most distinguished notables of the Banū Saktān, who at that time had not sided with Abū ʿAbd Allāh. They said, 'Let us approach (Bayān) in (Abū ʿAbd Allāh's) regard, and win him over by giving him gifts. Then if he responds favourably, the Banū Saktān will be divided and we will be able to achieve our objective.'

When Abū ʿAbd Allāh came to know of this he went into hiding. No one had any knowledge of him or knew of his whereabouts except those who were among the believers. The enemy sent a party from among them to Bayān with four mares and 100 sheep as present, saying, 'This man has altered religion and divided the people. He has

138. The text here has 'Tamīm b. Faḥl' which must be corrected on the basis of subsequent mention of him in the *Iftitāḥ*. Also, Ibn Khaldūn, *al-ʿIbar*, vol. 4, p. 68 (tr. *Berbères*, vol. 2, pp. 512–513), gives 'Faḥl b. Nūḥ' without mentioning the *kunya*.

139. The Laṭāya or Laṭāna were a branch of the Kutāma. See Ibn Khaldūn, *al-ʿIbar*, vol. 4, p. 68 (tr. *Berbères*, vol. 2, p. 513).

140. Ibn Khaldūn does not mention al-Matūsī among the chiefs who formed the coalition. The other chiefs are mentioned, with some orthographical variations. See Ibn Khaldūn, *al-ʿIbar*, vol. 4, p. 67 (tr. *Berbères*, vol. 2, pp. 511–512).

141. The Matūsa were a branch of the Kutāma. See Ibn Khaldūn, *al-ʿIbar*, vol. 6, p. 301 (tr. *Berbères*, vol. 1, p. 291); al-Idrīsī, *Nuzha*, p. 98 (tr. p. 115), locates the village of Matūsa at twelve miles to the east of Bijāya (Bougie).

142. The Jīmla were a branch of the Kutāma. See Ibn Khaldūn, *al-ʿIbar*, vol. 6, p. 302 (tr. *Berbères*, vol. 1, p. 292). They occupied the territory to the south of Īkjān.

143. He is referred to as the chief (*raʾīs*) of the Banū Saktān in Ibn Khaldūn, *al-ʿIbar*, vol. 4, p. 67 (tr. *Berbères*, vol. 2, p. 512).

caused disunity and division among relatives. We have called upon you about him and hope you will stand up to rid us of this villain by seizing this man and expelling him from our land if you are averse to killing him and by banishing him from us. After you have done so we shall grant you supreme authority over all the Kutama and Arabs, which will bring you glory and honour in this world, and reward and compensation in the Hereafter. You will remove a discomfort from your household and rid them of evil, for if they continue to have him in their midst, people will not leave them in peace and they will not be safe from the ruler's military action against them. If they then hand him over to him, they will do so under duress. If they protect him, they will not be safe from harmful consequences, and will lose comfort and incur expenses for him and for those of his supporters who seek refuge with them.'

Bayān replied to them, 'This man is residing amongst us and has become our guest. How can we act like this towards him?'

They said, 'Expel him from your frontiers. Then if someone else accepts him, the discomfort will be amongst them and not you. If he wishes to leave for his country or wherever he wants to proceed outside Kutāma territory, we shall let him go without hindering him.'

Bayān b. Ṣaqlān replied to them, 'Our expelling him and driving him away would also be a defect on our part and a disgrace. However, the opinion is that we gather the ulema and he should come out to meet them and debate with them. If he is right, then we as well as you are the most worthy to support what is true and follow it, and if he is following falsehood, those who follow him will know it and will turn away from him. Then we shall be able to expel him.'

They tried to persuade him to change, but they were unable. So they returned to their companions and informed them of what had happened with him. It did not meet with their approval for they feared that (Abū ʿAbd Allāh) would win the argument. His position would become strong and their leadership would come to an end because of him. What they had feared because of him would happen to them. By acting in this manner they only aimed at establishing their worldly interests. They did not seek to establish any truth or eliminate falsehood. They considered carefully their situation and agreed to withdraw with a body of troops and weapons and make it appear that they were bringing the ulema. Then when (Abū ʿAbd Allāh) came out towards them, they would seize him, kill him and withdraw to a secure place.

They got together and set out in a large body of troops, cavalry and infantry and seized the area between Tākūt and Wādī al-Najāt. When the Banū Saktān saw them, they gave the battle-cry. They rode their horses and brought out their infantry and weapons. They confronted them and the two sides met in battle. They told Bayān, 'We have come to you because of the differences between us and you.'

(Bayān) asked, 'What is there between me and you that you have come to us, advancing with weapons? We said that the ulema could be brought to debate with the man, but we see you coming to us in multitude, intending to remove him by force.'

They argued loudly among themselves. A party of followers (*awliyā'*)[144] who had infiltrated among (the opponents) attacked them and gave battle and fierce fighting ensued. The Jīmla were rallied together in battle in which the followers played a distinguished part not seen before. The assembled men were defeated and fled. The Banū Saktān turned away from them. The enemy left in disarray and defeated. The position of the followers became firm and strengthened. Abū ʿAbd Allāh remained in hiding. The followers feared for him if he were to appear.

The coalition withdrew and thought out their plan. They could only consider going back to Bayān. So they sent a message to him, saying, 'We made a mistake by coming with a crowd. This was not done deliberately on our part. People heard from each other about us and followed us. We plead with you for the well-being of our community. We prefer you over us all. We have chosen you for ourselves to preserve our blood and bring together our authority which is crumbling, and that you bring together our unity which has been shattered. Because of this man, brother has turned against brother, father against son, and kin against kin, regarding each other as enemies. Those who have accepted him consider those who stay away from him as

144. The term *awliyā'* refers to staunch supporters of Abū ʿAbd Allāh's mission who fought his battles. The translation of *awliyā'* as 'followers' renders only one of the meanings of the word which generally also means protectors, patrons, clients, defenders, partisans, officers, companions and friends. Cf. note 30 above.

disbelievers. This is the beginning of dissension and emergence of apostasy. You are the most deserving to gain its reward, to reject from himself and his family dishonour and evil, directing them aright. He is a man from the people of the east who, as you know, are devils. Our ulema are Berbers, a people who do not have that intelligence. If they were to debate, he would win the argument against them, and they will find no argument against him. This will increase the seduction through him and strengthen his cause. Do you think that we and our fathers and the people of the east and the west are in error and this man alone amongst all the people holds right guidance and truth? Can anyone be taken in by this, especially when his doctrine is secret, and what he is preaching is unknown? If it were true and sound he would set it forth openly, not hide it.'

They kept repeating to (Bayān) the supreme authority and glory which they had promised him.

(Bayān) listened to them and promised them that he would endeavour amiably to expel (Abū ʿAbd Allāh). He began to talk about the matter, reasoned with his kin and frightened them of the consequences saying, 'There was one war in which you gained victory. War can at times bring victory and at times defeat, and you cannot be sure that another war will not bring defeat. Therefore, expel this man from among your midst without any harm to him or you, while you retain your might, and before he and you are defeated.'

9

Abū ʿAbd Allāh's departure from Īkjān and his journey to Tāzrūt.

When Bayān b. Ṣaqlān's words came to the knowledge of Abū ʿAbd Allāh and the community of believers, those of them who belonged to the Banū Saktān went to see Bayān and related to him what they had heard he was saying. They told him that he would bring dishonour upon himself and them if they drove away their guest and gave up their protégé. Thereupon (Bayān) began to reiterate to them what they had heard he was saying and warned them of the consequences of their action.

This information came to the knowledge of al-Ḥasan b. Hārūn al-Ghashmī, who had converted to the faith. He was one of the best believers and a man of intelligence, etiquette and good character. He was generous and prosperous, and was obeyed among his people. He lived in Tāzrūt. He came to see Abū ʿAbd Allāh and related to him what had come to his knowledge. He requested him and expressed his wish for him to move to his place. He promised him that he himself, his people and wealth would defend and protect him. (Abū ʿAbd Allāh) consulted the followers on this matter. They advised him to accept the offer, except those of them who belonged to the Banū Saktān, who found this unbearable and detestable. They said, 'We shall protect you ourselves until we are all killed so that you remain safe.'

(Abū ʿAbd Allāh) thanked them for what they had expressed. The community of believers were of the opinion that his residing with al-Ḥasan b. Hārūn was better for strengthening the faith, and more secure for him as well as the believers.

So Abū ʿAbd Allāh proceeded to (the place of al-Ḥasan b. Hārūn). Those of the Banū Saktān who were able to leave with him, as well as those believers who were able to emigrate migrated. He appointed as his deputy al-Ḥakam b. Nāsib to administer the affairs of the believers who were weak as well as those who were unable to travel with him. Al-Ḥasan b. Hārūn travelled with him to Tāzrūt. He was received there by those who were believers as well as others. Those who were travelling with him offered to stay with them, while al-Ḥasan b. Hārūn lodged him at his own residence. The Ghashmān provided for the needs of the believers. They shared with them their wealth and allowed them their place in it, displaying towards them happiness and joy which pleased them. As believers from every region came to them, each one of them began to bring with him whatever he could to strengthen and lodge the believers. From there, they began to send some of it to the weak believers who had remained in Īkjān, even when sometimes it was difficult for them to transport it, they would ride their horses, each man carrying in his saddle-bag[145] under him on his saddle the amount of food he could, bringing it to them, giving

145. Reading *khurj* rather than *khurūj* as in the text.

it to them, and returning. Thus al-Ḥasan b. Hārūn expended some of his wealth as well as the wealth of close members of his family, with which he increased the means of subsistence of the believers.

Abū ʿAbd Allāh came to be situated near the territory of the Ijjāna, the Malūsa,[146] the Lahīṣa, the Laṭaya and the Jīmla. People came to him from everywhere, and his cause became manifest and his ranks swelled. The Ghashmān rallied to assist and protect him. A multitude of believers from all the Kutāma tribes gathered around him. They stayed among them as a garrison with Abū ʿAbd Allāh, ready to fight for him and protect him from those who wanted to harm him.

Bayān b. Ṣaqlān repented for what he had done to (Abū ʿAbd Allāh) and joined the *daʿwa*, and with him the strength of the believers grew in Īkjān. The importance of al-Ḥasan b. Hārūn grew because of his involvement in this. He was praised and thanked because of his feat and his wealth which he expended. This news reached the regions of the Kutāma and among the notables of their people.

Now al-Ḥasan b. Hārūn had an elder brother called Maḥmūd who became jealous of this. He could not bear the prestige of his brother, because formerly he had enjoyed seniority over him owing to his age, and he had also been obeyed in his family. Then the notables gave attention to his brother because of what he had accomplished. This was difficult for him, and he spoke about it and it was divulged from him. However, al-Ḥasan flattered him, gave him precedence, showed his piety and sought his sympathy, fearing that he might divide the clan of Ghashmān or bring divisions among them.

When Abū ʿAbd Allāh became established at Tāzrūt and news of this reached those who had formed a coalition against him, they were upset. His situation was hard for them to bear, and their worry about him increased.

---

146. The Malūsa were a branch of the Kutāma occupying the territory to the south-east of Īkjān. See Ibn Khaldūn, *al-ʿIbar*, vol. 6, p. 302 (tr. *Berbères*, vol. 1, p. 292). Certain elements of them, including Ghazwiyya, were staunch supporters of Abū ʿAbd Allāh from the very beginning of his mission.

10

Meeting of the coalition to find a way to resolve the case of Abū ʿAbd Allāh.

When the coalition came to know of Maḥmūd b. Hārūn's jealousy of his brother al-Ḥasan, they hoped thereby to attain what they wanted with regard to Abū ʿAbd Allāh. They rallied around Mahdī b. Abī Kināwa al-Lahīṣī, one of the members of the coalition. They reported to him what they had come to know about Maḥmūd, and said to him, 'He is your neighbour and your friend. Perhaps you will be able to win him over and divide the clan of Ghashmān, and we shall be able to achieve our objective.'

So Mahdī [b. Abī Kināwa] rode out to Maḥmūd and lodged at his place. He told him that the Kutāma notables had rallied around him, and sent him to meet with him. They were aware of the [closeness] between himself and (Maḥmūd) and they were telling (Maḥmūd), 'Your brother has harmed himself and members of his family. He has brought upon the Ghashmān an affliction from which the Banū Saktān have recovered. They have got rid of its evil and then he has brought it upon them.'

(Mahdī) began to warn him of the harmful consequences. He related to him matters about Abū ʿAbd Allāh similar to those which the people related to Bayān, and sought to win (Maḥmūd) over by the coalition agreeing upon him, and their hope that an end would be put to what had befallen them through his effort. He promised him on their part supreme authority, chiefship and command over themselves. This, coupled with his envy and jealousy of his brother, won him over.

(Maḥmūd) replied to him, 'It is indeed as you say. I am only grieved by (Abū ʿAbd Allāh's) affair, but he is firmly established and strong, and his followers have become numerous. Now he is no longer like he used to be when he was among the Banū Saktān. The majority of Ghashmān and many Kutāma tribes have responded to him. They have moved to him and remain around him. They protect him and fight for him against anyone who wants to harm him. If I invite those of the Ghashmān who obey me to seize him, we shall be divided into two factions. Either of the defeated side will be among us and we will annihilate each other. My view about him is the same as Bayān's view, that we bring the ulema for them to debate with him. Then if he loses the argument, we shall be able to find a way to deal with him; and if it is otherwise, we shall make alternative plans about him.'

Mahdī [b. Abī Kināwa] went to the people, and informed them of what had happened. They told him, 'Who from among our ulema will debate with him? You can see that if anyone of our ignorant men joins his cause and debates with them, he silences them. How then if he himself would debate with them?'

Mahdī [b. Abī Kināwa] told them, 'I saw that Maḥmūd has the urge to kill him and an inclination to the supreme authority which we promised him, besides being filled with envy for his brother. I did not find his position any different when I left him. We only have to provide the ulema, and when they bring (Abū 'Abd Allāh) out, we shall attack him and kill him. If we do this, then it could be that we put an end to the cause of the disease.'

They were in agreement with this view. They sent to look for ulema from every region, and selected some of their valiant men and battle heroes to go to (Abū 'Abd Allāh) with the ulema, saying, 'We shall not come in large numbers any more like we did with the Banū Saktān, which could result in the like of what happened.'

Their news reached al-Ḥasan b. Hārūn and Abū 'Abd Allāh. Abū 'Abd Allāh told them, 'Let the Ghashmān rally around Maḥmūd, treat him kindly and report to him what they have come to know about him. They should warn him of the shame, dishonour and harmful consequences that this will bring. Let them make him leader over them and raise his importance as much as they can, and see what he does. They did so, and al-Ḥasan as well as some Ghashmān came to (Maḥmūd) and related to him what they had come to know about him and the coalition. They told him, 'We are members of your family and your tribe, and you are our chief and commander. This man is your guest and our guest, and we have honoured him. You have seen what dishonour was brought upon the Banū Saktān for expelling him, which they now regret, and that Bayān has accepted his mission, and attempted to bring him back to him in order to put right the wrong he had done to himself, but he did not respond to him in this [matter], so do not bring shame and dishonour upon us. They brought to him an exemplar of the Qur'an and took an oath by it before him. They made him leader over themselves and this won him over. He gathered those of the Ghashmān who inclined towards him and informed them of the pact which the coalition had made to assassinate Abū ʿAbd Allāh.

The coalition embarked upon what they had contracted. When Maḥmūd learnt that they had come near Tāzrūt, he mounted with the bulk of Ghashmān with weapons and in military order. Abū ʿAbd Allāh told the community of believers, 'Ride with them, and if you are able to provoke war, then do so.'

When they met, (the coalition) told Maḥmūd, 'These are the ulema whom we have brought,' and they removed (the ulema) aside.

Maḥmūd told (the coalition), 'Withdraw, and call (the ulema) before us so that we bring them and the man together with ten of your notables and distinguished men in a session, and see what happens to them and him.'

Thus, what (the coalition) had contracted fell apart in their hands, and they said, 'Don't you care to bring (Abū ʿAbd Allāh) out here so that everyone present can witness what happens between him and the ulema, and that this becomes more widely known to the people and more decisive for the matter?'

Maḥmūd replied to them, 'That is not the intent of the debate, nor have you come for that purpose. Indeed, it has come to our knowledge that you have contracted something.'

His brother al-Ḥasan spoke, saying [about him], 'Here comes the one who is covetous of us, and wishes to remove our guest from our hands by overpowering us.'

(The coalition) refused (Maḥmūd). So he attacked them and so did the followers. Fighting broke out. Maḥmūd was angry and fought fiercely, and the followers fought like never before. Maḥmūd was wounded. Then they disengaged and Maḥmūd died from his wounds. His death gladdened his brother, as well as Abū ʿAbd Allāh and the followers. They proclaimed to avenge his blood. The Ghashmān were united and rallied together. Most of them adhered to the *daʿwa*. The leadership of al-Ḥasan became firmly established, and Abū ʿAbd

Allāh handed to him the reins of the cavalry and appointed him chief of all the believers.

War broke out between the Ghashmān and the Lahīṣa because of Maḥmūd's death. The Malūsa rallied around Abū ʿAbd Allāh together with most of the tribes. Abū ʿAbd Allāh appeared in public. He would witness the war and participate in it. All the believers were supporters of the Ghashmān, while the opponents were supporters of the Lahīṣa. Their leader was Mahdī b. Abī Kināwa. His brother Abū Madīnī,[147] had joined the *daʿwa* and emigrated to Abū ʿAbd Allāh. He was intelligent, sincere and brave. His brother Mahdī was the strongest horseman of his time. He was of a most frightening appearance. It is related that his body was entirely covered with hair and looked awful. He struck [his enemies] hard. It is related that the followers used a stratagem against him in one of the battles, when he marched against them and the battle had joined. At the site of the battle, there was a fenced graveyard with graves. They stationed for him in that enclosure the strongest infantrymen that they could find, and sent a rider to allure him to them. (The rider) insulted him and enraged him, so he attacked him. The rider then led him on to the place where the infantrymen were stationed. Mahdī threw his lance at (the rider) and struck him, piercing him. The lance fell in front of the rider, and people thought that he had missed him. They did not realise that he had struck him until they saw him falling off his mule. The infantrymen confronted Mahdī. They seized his bridle and surrounded him, while the cavalry attacked him. He struck at the infantrymen and dispersed them, and defended himself from the cavalry and escaped from them by force. As was proper to him, on that day he worked a miracle never seen before. Indeed, such things did happen. He was admired for shooting arrows, for when they penetrated the game animal, the dart would come out of it without there being any blood on it because of the force of the blow and the speed with which it came out. There is a tradition to this effect from the Prophet about

147. Abū Madīnī b. Abī Kināwa al-Lahīṣī was Abū ʿAbd Allāh's commander and continued to serve under the reign of al-Mahdī. He was left to govern Tripoli together with Ḥubāsa b. Yūsuf al-Malūsī after its revolt was crushed by the future al-Qā'im. See Idrīs ʿImād al-Dīn, *ʿUyūn al-akhbār*, ed. al-Yaʿlāwī, p. 192, ed. Ghālib, vol. 5, p. 125. Abū Madīnī must be identified with Abū Madyan who took Barqa in 304/916–917. See Ibn ʿIdhārī, *al-Bayān*, vol. 1, p. 175.

the Kharijites. He described them saying, 'They will stray from the religion as an arrow passes though the game's body.'[148] That is, they would go out without adhering to anything from it. The fact that such things were worked by Mahdī with a single blow from the palm of the hand with a long lance is something unheard of before him or after. This account is authentic.

Warfare prolonged between the two factions, each taking vengeance on the other. When Abū Madīnī looked at his brother Mahdī's persistence in his error and stubbornness, he was distressed by it and saddened. He would go to him and exhort him, and invite him to God. He sought to frighten him, and warned him of his punishment. However, this only increased his error and persistence. When (Abū Madīnī) realised that he would not refrain from this, he met a young man from the Lahīṣa who had accepted the *da'wa*, and emigrated to Tāzrūt together with the believers. He was called Lāwa b. Ṣūḥān. He was strong and brave. Abū Madīnī told him when he was alone with him, 'Woe unto you! Maybe you see the persistence of Mahdī and the shame he has brought upon us, and the disagreement and disobedience which he has provoked among the Lahīṣa. If God, the Most High, delivers us from him, the Lahīṣa will be divided and they will adhere to religion. I surmise that we should come together, you and I, when we meet together and approach him aside, as I have been doing, in order to admonish him and speak to him. Then if we can, we will both throw two lances at the same time. If he shields himself, perhaps he will protect himself against one of them, and perhaps God will deliver [us] from him and put an end to his influence.' They agreed on this plan, and reached a mutual agreement.

Then, when they met for battle, the two went aside and called (Mahdī). He approached them. His brother Abū Madīnī talked to him like he used to do until he had confidence in him. Then they both struck him a single blow together. Both their lances hit him one after the other, and he fell down. The followers attacked him, and the Lahīṣa attacked and rescued him and carried him away. He died from his wounds after reaching his place. After him, the Lahīṣa were

---

148. Cf. al-Bukhārī, *Ṣaḥīḥ*, vol. 5, pp. 448–449, and vol. 9, pp. 52–54; al-Qāḍī al-Nu'mān, *Da'ā'im*, vol. 1, p. 389 (tr. *Pillars*, vol. 1, p. 482), and *Sharḥ al-akhbār*, (*juz'* 15), vol. 3, p. 381.

divided and they accepted the *daʿwa*. The Ghashmān and the Lahīṣa made peace and became united through religion. Thus, the cause of the faithful became glorious, strong and firm. They waged war against their neighbouring tribes and made raids against those distant.

Their cavalry went out raiding the Mazāta,[149] whose chief at that time was Yūsuf al-Ghaṭṭāshī. He had gone to the court of Ibrāhīm b. Aḥmad, who gave him presents, garments and mounts, and offered him a priceless slave-girl. The believers made a raid against him while his companions were dispersed, tending their camels. The cavalry attacked him and seized all his belongings. They captured the slave-girl given to him by Ibrāhīm b. Aḥmad. He escaped only with his life by hiding in an underground granary. They killed those of his companions that they could and returned to Abū ʿAbd Allāh with booty. He chose the slave-girl for himself, who became his only maid servant to bear him a child.

11

Offensive by all the tribes against Abū ʿAbd Allāh and his victory over them.

When Abū ʿAbd Allāh's enemies saw the rise of his power, the fall of the dominion of the Lahīṣa over them, the murder of Mahdī, and that they had no alternative but to fight, they regrouped among themselves. They spread rumours among the tribes, called upon the populace to fight and devoted themselves entirely to warfare. They sent word to the Mazāta, who responded to them favourably because the followers had overthrown their chief. They agreed that every tribe should move with its household towards him and surround him from every side and besiege him from every direction until the Ghashmān hand him over or else they would attack them.

This information came to the knowledge of Abū ʿAbd Allāh, who ordered all the followers to move to Tāzrūt. So they moved

149. According to al-Bakrī, *al-Masālik*, p. 50 (tr. p. 107), these Mazāta were located to the north of Billizma. On the Mazāta see Tadeusz Lewicki, 'Mazāta', *EI*², vol. 6, pp. 943–948; and Ibn Khaldūn, *al-ʿIbar*, vol. 6, pp. 116–117 (tr. *Berbères*, vol. 1, p. 232).

to Tāzrūt from every region. The Kutāma came from its outskirts and surrounded him. The people of the towns stayed apart in one camp. The Ijjāna, the Laṭāya and all the tribes of the region of Mīla assembled in another camp, and the Kutāma elements of the region of Saṭīf gathered under Fatḥ b. Yaḥyā apart, and the Mazāta gathered apart. The nearest of them to besiege him were the Ijjāna and the Laṭāya. When Abū ʿAbd Allāh saw this situation, he emerged with those who were with him from Tāzrūt and set up camp in its environs and dug himself in for battle. The followers, the *dāʿī*s and the elders rallied around Abū ʿAbd Allāh and said, 'You are our pivot and we all gravitate towards you. You are a favour and grace from God. He guided us through you and acquainted us with whatever truth that He has done. Your survival is the survival of religion and the whole assembly of believers. We have an opinion to submit to you for you to consider. Do you allow us to mention it to you?'

He replied, 'Relate what seems appropriate to you.'

They said, 'You see the multitude that has amassed against us. We are a minority in their midst, and *war is deception*.[150] The enemy had expected to reach us through tricks, deception and subtle means, but they did not succeed and were incapable. God protected you, and defended you from them. So they have devoted themselves entirely to warfare, as you can see. We are not of those who surrender until God, the Mighty, the Glorious, grants us victory or we die to the last of us. If indeed victory comes to us in this, then that is what we ask from God. It will not harm us to have protected you with our hands and done so with determination and sound opinion about you. If it is the other way round and we are defeated, God forbid, then there is none amongst us who doubts that he will proceed to the mercy of God. Perhaps God will compensate you with others, and His cause will be made manifest at your hands through whoever of us or others that He wills. The evil intention of the enemy is only directed to you; they concern only you. We are of the opinion that we should remove

150. Arabic proverb *al-ḥarb khadʿa/khudʿa/khudaʿa*, explained in al-Maydānī, *Majmaʿ al-amthāl* (Cairo, 1955), vol. 1, p. 197. The expression is also found in prophetic traditions. See al-Bukhārī, *Ṣaḥīḥ*, vol. 4, pp. 166–167, 519; and Abū Dāwūd Sulaymān b. al-Ashʿath al-Sijistānī, *Sunan Abī Dāwūd*, ed. Muḥammad Muḥyī al-Dīn ʿAbd al-Ḥamīd ([Beirut], n.d.), vol. 3, p. 43, English tr. Ahmad Hasan (New Delhi, 1985), vol. 2, p. 728.

you from this place secretly and transfer you to an unnoticeable place where you would remain hidden with those who will protect you, guard you and watch over you. Then if we win, you shall return to us as you wish. However, if it goes against us, you shall be safe and will take care of others. We would not have caused you to bear this danger, and we will not confront with you this number, and shall not meet with you this [force of] large number and strength.'

Abū 'Abd Allāh thanked them and praised them. He incited them to struggle (*jihād*) and have patience. He recited to them the word of God: '*How often has a small force vanquished a big one by God's leave? God is with those who steadfastly persevere*' (2:249). He exhorted them at length in a session (*majlis*) of great blessing, disclosing to them a lot of wisdom. He assured them that the cause of God would be accomplished. It would triumph over its enemies, and he was convinced that God's promise to His friend would be fulfilled and that His cause would be accomplished through him. He told them, 'I am not of those who deem themselves more important than you, nor those who seek to avoid the *jihād* together with you. Therefore keep your faith in God. '*And fall into no disputes, lest you lose heart and your power depart*' (8:46). Let the strong among you provide for the weak among you, and the rich among you provide for the poor among you. Put your trust in God, your Lord, and have confidence in His help to you.' He revived them with these words and their morale was raised. He raised their vision and increased their resolve.

On hearing this and seeing the believers, Abū 'Abd Allāh al-Andalusī rose on his feet with delight, saying, 'By God! The cause of God is firm in you, just like this is firm in this.' He pointed with his hand to his ear and his head. 'By God! If you confronted these mountains with this resolve, you would bring them down.'

They left Abū 'Abd Allāh, and every one of them brought out whatever resources, horses and weapons he had. They gave horses to those of the infantry who knew well how to ride, and they gave weapons to those who had no weapons. They distributed among themselves whatever they had until they were equal in military array, resources and weapons. The troops were reviewed. They numbered 700 horsemen, no more no less. Their foot-soldiers numbered about

2,000, after leaving behind all those among them who were weak, as well as those unable to wage war. They remained people of strength and bravery in this number. They set up camp and dug in on the bank of Wādī Tāfrant not far from the Laṭāya troops led by their chief Faḥl b. Nūḥ.[151]

Abū ʿAbd Allāh called the elders and told them, 'I think it would be in your interest to send a man from among you who has some connection with Faḥl b. Nūḥ, so that he would be friendly towards him and call him to peace. It may be that we shall be able to divide this coalition.'

They replied, 'Sahl b. Birkās is related to him by marriage and he associates with him. (Abū ʿAbd Allāh) advised (Sahl b. Birkās) as to what to tell him, and sent him to (Faḥl b. Nūḥ). So Sahl set out until he stopped near the halting place of the Laṭāya, and cried out to Faḥl, who came out towards him, greeted him and asked him how he was. Then (Sahl) said, 'O Abū Tamīm! You are our chief, our commander, and son of our commander, and our in-law. Would you then accept for your sisters that the Berbers, that is the Mazāta, take them into captivity, and that your brothers and cousins be slain at their hands?'

Abū Tamīm replied to him, 'By God! I would not want it, nor would I accept it, for there is nothing between us and you which would make this necessary. Our only demand before you is this man who has altered religion and has planted this discord among us. Hand him over to us, or expel him from our land and he will be removed from our midst.'

He replied, 'Praise be to God! O Abū Tamīm! Would you yourself accept it if he were at your place, had sought your hospitality and been under your protection? Is it acceptable for you to do to him what you are ordering us to do?'

Faḥl remained silent.

Sahl told him, 'By God! You would not accept such a thing, nor would you act thus towards him. So do not wish for us what you would not wish for yourself, for we are your brothers, your tribe, your cousins and your brothers-in-law.'

---

151. He was one of the organisers of the resistance in Mīla and died while defending the town under attack by Abū ʿAbd Allāh. See p. 111 below.

Faḥl replied, 'What should I do with the community of these people?'

Sahl replied to him, 'You are their support and their pivot. If you followed something, they would not contradict you about it.' Thus he began to magnify him and raise his importance.

Faḥl said to him, 'Then what shall we do?'

Sahl told him, 'We shall make peace with you and you shall make peace with us. We shall make an agreement with you and you shall make an agreement with us. We shall swear before you and you shall swear before us to cease warfare between us. Every tribe shall return to its locality and we shall be like adherents of one of the schools (*madhāhib*) of Muslims. Whoever among you wishes to join our school, can do so, and whoever from us wishes to revert to what you hold, can do so. No one would be compelled to do so, nor will anyone be censured for this, just as happens among the adherents of the schools in the towns, in every respect and place. Then what necessitates war with us and not with them, and why is it allowed to shed our blood among them?'

Faḥl replied to him, 'Let me meet with our companions and come back to you.'

He said, 'Do so.'

Faḥl departed and sent word to Faraḥ b. Jīrān and all the notables of the tribes who were present, and they got together. He then informed them of what Sahl had said without omitting anything. Faraḥ b. Jīrān turned pale and began to scratch the ground with his lance, squinting at it. This happened while they were mounted on their horses. When Faḥl finished what he wanted to say, Faraḥ b. Jīrān told him, 'O Abū Tamīm! This is a stratagem and beguilement of this disbeliever. By God! These people have no covenant, no protection, no religion and no trust. They only want to free themselves from our hands, having seen that they are in our grip. No! By God! We are not of those who shall let them go until they hand this man over to us, or God will judge between us and them.'

All those who were present spoke in similar terms as Faraḥ b. Jīrān. Then Faḥl b. Nūḥ told them, 'I have only conveyed to you the words that the man brought. However, if you have already made up your mind, then I will only follow your opinion and say what you say.' Thereupon they praised him.

The messenger withdrew to Sahl to give him the news. Sahl returned to Abū ʿAbd Allāh and informed him of the matter in the presence of the elders. Abū ʿAbd Allāh said, 'By God! This is the proof of [God's] help to you, and the cause of favour to you; so seek God's help and fight against the enemy immediately before they amass against you.'

All the Mazāta were stationed in the region of the territory of the Malūsa, and all [the inhabitants of] the towns, the Kutāma and Saṭīf in the region of the Masālta were in the region bordering the Malūsa. Abū ʿAbd Allāh mobilised those who were with him and marched towards the Kutāma and Mīla, namely the Ijjāna, the Laṭāya, the Jīmla, the Malūsa, the Danhāja,[152] the Ghashmān of Sajjā,[153] the Ūrissa[154] and the inhabitants of Mīla. They fought them and one of the horsemen of the coalition, who was the strongest among them, was killed, and the battle became dispersed. None of the followers was hit. Their hearts were strengthened when they saw that they had resisted them.

On the following day, they returned to resume fighting. A large number of the coalition were killed, while the followers remained unharmed, and they dispersed. This increased their trust in God, the Mighty, the Glorious, and in His help, and their hearts were strengthened.

On the third day, they returned to resume fighting at daybreak. Fighting between them continued till the time for the midday prayer. It became heated and intense, and some fighters overpowered others. On that day, the bravery of Ghazwiyya[155] came to light, for he proved

152. The Danhāja were a branch of the Kutāma. See Ibn Khaldūn, *al-ʿIbar*, vol. 6, p. 301 (tr. *Berbères*, vol. 1, p. 291); al-Bakrī, *al-Masālik*, p. 110 (tr. p. 216); al-Idrīsī, *Nuzha*, p. 78 (tr. p. 89) and p. 169 (tr. p. 202).

153. Apparently a locality. The Ghashmān of Sajjā must be distinguished from those of Tāzrūt who adhered to the *daʿwa*.

154. The Ūrissa were a branch of the Kutāma. See Ibn Khaldūn, *al-ʿIbar*, vol. 6, p. 301: Warīsan (tr. *Berbères*, vol. 1, p. 291: Ourîcen). Other variants of Ūrissa in the MSS and sources: Ūrisha, Ūrīshiya, Ūrīsa, Ūrissa, Ūrishiya. The Ūrissa were among the Kutāma who revolted after the execution of Abū ʿAbd Allāh, and installed a Mahdī of their own. See pp. 226–227 below.

155. He is Ghazwiyya b. Yūsuf al-Malūsī whose name frequently appears in the sources as ʿArūba. See Ibn ʿIdhārī, *al-Bayān*, vol. 1, pp. 149–150, as Gharawayh b. Yūsuf al-Malūsī, and pp. 162 and 164 as ʿArūba b. Yūsuf al-Malūsī; Ibn Khaldūn, *al-ʿIbar*, vol. 4, p. 68 (tr. *Berbères*, vol. 2, p. 513) has ʿArūba b. Yūsuf al-Malūshī; Ibn al-Athīr, *al-Kāmil*, vol. 6, p. 135, has ʿArūba.

himself very courageous in the infantry. Ghazwiyya b. Yūsuf was wounded. The wound caused him to lose his voice. However, when the shadow shifted from west to east, and the sun declined, Ghazwiyya struck and killed a man from the infantry of the coalition who was most brave in battle. The followers attacked, and the coalition attempted to retrieve the man's body, but were unable to do so. The followers intensified their attack on them, routing them completely. They pursued them, killing them, setting fire to their camps, and plundering their wealth, until they were obstructed by darkness. They did not pay attention to any slave-girl or any free woman, nor did they unveil any private part. They retired to their halting places, their hands full of booty. Those troops dispersed. Some of them entered Mīla and some of the tribes returned to their locality.

The next morning, Abū ʿAbd Allāh and the followers came across the troops of the region of Saṭīf and fought them. God put them to flight before them, making them able to attack from behind. They killed them rapidly and plundered their wealth. On the fourth day, they launched an offensive against the Mazāta and fought them. They fled before them. The followers seized their storehouse of provisions as well as all their wealth and belongings. After having pursued them, they killed them and annihilated them, acquiring all their wealth and belongings. Then on that day twenty camels were sold for a dinar and a camel for five onions. As for sheep and goats, possessions and wealth, they were unable to carry them, nor did they know how to drive their livestock. They plundered an uncountable number of horses. The followers came into possession of an uncountable number of livestock and wealth, and they pulled back to Tāzrūt. Thus God dispersed the troops that had banded together against them and caused all of them to be killed at their hands. He caused them to inherit their wealth, livestock, possessions, horses and weapons. They acquired an uncountable number of such wealth of the cities as saddles, bridles, adornment, horses, booty, robes, wealth, weapons, banners and drums.

12

Abū ʿAbd Allāh's founding at Tāzrūt a place of refuge and a base from which to wage war against the tribes.

Abū ʿAbd Allāh constructed a castle at Tāzrūt in which he lived by himself, and allocated houses around it to the followers. The believers emigrated there from every region. They built [houses], lived there, settled there and grew in strength. Several tribes sought safety with them. They waged war against neighbouring tribes which resisted them, and launched raids against distant tribes. Hardly a day passed without them having gained some land somewhere and settling in foreign territory. Most people submitted to them and began to seek to adhere to the *daʿwa* willingly or out of fear. All the Ghashmān of Tāzrūt, the Malūsa and the Lahīṣa supported Abū ʿAbd Allāh, and they became united in the faith, and all the Ijjāna people agreed to that. The chief of the [Ijjānī] believers at that time was Abū Yūsuf Māknūn b. Ḍubāra. Abū Yūsuf's nephew Abū Zākī Tammām b. Muʿārik, who was then a young man, remained steadfast and drew near to Abū ʿAbd Allāh. Faraḥ b. Jīrān feared for himself, and so did a group of Ijjāna chiefs that the masses would overpower them. So they departed to Mīla. Among those who departed together with them were Faraḥ b. Jīrān, Yūsuf b. Maḥmūd[156] and Wazra b. Naṣr. When they settled in Mīla, all the Ijjāna adhered to Abū ʿAbd Allāh. Faḥl b. Nūḥ reached Mīla with a group of Laṭāya. The rest of them rallied to Abū ʿAbd Allāh. His authority and mission spread among these tribes and his power became well established.

Fatḥ b. Yaḥyā gathered around himself those of the Masālta and others who obeyed him, and he remained with them. Those of the Masālta who obeyed him were members of his household, those near to them and their relations, and the Banū ʿIfnīt, because they of old adhered to the Ibāḍī school. They were the only ones among the Kutāma to adhere to that (school).[157] They were brave among

156. He was one of the organisers of the resistance in Mīla and was executed together with the other Berber chiefs after the conquest of the town by Abū ʿAbd Allāh. See below pp. 111ff.

157. Before the establishment of Shiʿism among the Kutāma, they were probably inclined

the Masālta. They detested the power of Abū ʿAbd Allāh. The Azāya among the Masālta, who were members of the household of Abū Mūsā Hārūn b. Yūnus, and their supporters separated from (Fatḥ b. Yaḥyā) and adhered to the *daʿwa*. Abū ʿAbd Allāh came to know about him. He waged war against (Fatḥ b. Yaḥyā) and defeated him, and killed many of his partisans. (Fatḥ b. Yaḥyā) fled with some members of his household towards Saṭīf. Then he wrote to Abū ʿAbd Allāh asking for pardon. He sought to join his cause after all the Masālta had surrendered to Abū ʿAbd Allāh, and he found no place to seek refuge. Abū ʿAbd Allāh ordered Hārūn b. Yūnus to write to him, granting him pardon and asking him to present himself. So he came to him, and Abū ʿAbd Allāh received him and pardoned him. He ordered Abū Mūsā to take from (Fatḥ b. Yaḥyā) the oath of allegiance and summon him. However, Abū Mūsā began to delay this. He examined him and treated him harshly, saying, 'You killed a group of followers; you must pay their blood-money.'

It is said that (Abū Mūsā) detested (Fatḥ b. Yaḥyā's) acquaintance with Abū ʿAbd Allāh because of his position of leadership and his previous renown, and because he, in addition to this, was obeyed in his tribe, strong in spirit, valiant with his hand and a well-known knight among his people. (Abū Mūsā) feared that he might rise above him and gain influence with Abū ʿAbd Allāh so as to become his equal. This matter about (Abū Mūsā) came to the knowledge of Fatḥ b. Yaḥyā who was frightened of his mischief and fled. He found refuge with the ʿAjīsa,[158] and gathered troops around himself from among them and others. Abū ʿAbd Allāh came to know about him. He proceeded with troops towards him, and passed by the region of Saṭīf, without touching those who were in the town. Fatḥ b. Yaḥyā and those with him protected themselves in a fortified fortress in the place where they gathered. The fortress was called Nūbar, which is

---

to Kharijite doctrines. Ibn ʿIdhārī, *al-Bayān*, vol. 1, p. 124, citing al-Warrāq, states that the shaykh of the Kutāma group whom Abū ʿAbd Allāh met during the pilgrimage was inclined to Ibāḍī doctrines.

158. According to Ibn Ḥazm, *Jamhara*, p. 495, the ʿAjīsa, like the Kutāma, the Ṣanhāja, the Masmūda, the Awraba, the Azdāja and the Awrigha, belonged to the Burnus branch of the Berbers. The ʿAjīsa occupied the mountainous region to the north of al-Masīla (M'sila). See Ibn Khaldūn, *al-ʿIbar*, vol. 6, pp. 295–296 (tr. *Berbères*, vol. 1, p. 285).

also called Wushnūk. The troops surrounded him in (the fortress), and they fought them on it. They threw huge rocks from above the fortress which echoed like thunder. Whenever Abū ʿAbd Allāh saw (a rock) approaching, he covered his face with his sleeve so as not to see the injuries it inflicted upon the followers. They continued until they conquered the fortress and killed most of those that were in it. Among those killed in it on that day was Taṣūlā b. Yaḥyā, brother of Fatḥ b. Yaḥyā. Fatḥ himself fled. The followers took from them a lot of booty. The ʿAjīsa and the Zuwāwa[159] submitted to Abū ʿAbd Allāh, as well as all the Kutāma of Majris.[160] (Abū ʿAbd Allāh) withdrew with the troops to Tāzrūt.

Fatḥ b. Yaḥyā reached Ifrīqiya, for he did not find any other place of refuge. He went before Abū al-ʿAbbās b. Ibrāhīm b. Aḥmad,[161] who was then in Tunis, his father Ibrāhīm being away on an expedition to Sicily. (Abū al-ʿAbbās) gave him presents, allowed him proximity, lodged him and honoured him. (Abū al-ʿAbbās) asked (Fatḥ b. Yaḥyā) information about Abū ʿAbd Allāh. (Fatḥ b. Yaḥyā) made (Abū ʿAbd Allāh's) situation appear weak before (Abū al-ʿAbbās), saying, 'If only you dispatched troops against him you could seize him.'

Abū al-ʿAbbās replied, 'Did you not gather together a large number of troops but were unable to defeat him?'

(Fatḥ b. Yaḥyā) replied, 'Our situation is not at all the same as your situation. We were fighting without a leader or adequate weapons. We were fought by the people of the land who knew us. However, if troops came from you, it would put awe in the people's hearts. Then they would have a leader. They would bring the weapons which we did not have, and the men whom the local people are not accustomed to;

159. The Zuwāwa occupied the region to the east of the Djurdjura, on the western edge of Kutāma territory. Ibn Ḥazm, *Jamhara*, p. 501, affirms their affiliation to the Kutāma. However, according to Berber genealogists the Zuwāwa descend from al-Abtar and are affiliated to the Zanāta. See Ibn Ḥazm, *Jamhara*, p. 496; Ibn Khaldūn tends to agree with the Zuwāwa's affiliation to the Kutāma. See Ibn Khaldūn, *al-ʿIbar*, vol. 6, pp. 261–263, 302, 308–309 (tr. *Berbères*, vol. 1, pp. 255–256, 292, 298–299).

160. A mountainous region to the north-west of Saṭīf which bears today the name of Djebel Megris. It was occupied by the Majris who are considered among the Hawwāra. See Ibn Khaldūn, *al-ʿIbar*, vol. 6, p. 284 (tr. *Berbères*, vol. 1, p. 275); al-Tijānī, *Riḥla*, p. 216.

161. The Aghlabid ruler ʿAbd Allāh b. Ibrāhīm (r. 289–290/902–903).

they would fight them with arms not known to them such as wooden arrows, lances and other things. The army of the sultan has prestige. If it entered the land of the Kutāma, most of those who have adhered to Abū ʿAbd Allāh would turn towards it.'

He extolled (Abū al-ʿAbbās) with this and enticed him, hoping to return to his land, his family and his children, and to regain his leadership. However, Abū al-ʿAbbās refrained from it after being tempted by what he had said.

His father Ibrāhīm b. Aḥmad had confided to him about Abū ʿAbd Allāh and forbidden him to wage war against him, saying, 'Be on guard against him. If you see him advancing to attack you, then leave before him and join me in Byzantine territory. You are unable to overpower him, for he is the one who will put an end to our dynasty.'

Abū al-ʿAbbās relied on this instruction, and returned property and estates which had been seized unlawfully. He remained weak and humble, expecting what his father had entrusted to him and presented to him. So when Fatḥ b. Yaḥyā reported to him what he did, he listened to him and inclined towards him, but kept aloof from him until the son[162] of Mūsā b. ʿAbbās came to him. We shall report what happened then in its place, God willing.

Abū ʿAbd Allāh's influence spread all over Kutāma territory. His *dāʿīs* appeared in all its regions, and his authority triumphed over it and became firmly established. Everyone in it without exception adhered to his *daʿwa*, either willingly or out of fear and abandoned, denying it in his heart and overcome by his misery, yet persisting in denying it and holding on to what he believed without defending anything, or attacking anyone of his people. All those who were like this came under the precepts of religion and the authority of the believers who governed their affairs. Their authority encompassed them from behind. This happened after Abū ʿAbd Allāh fought many battles with the Kutāma tribes, which are too long to narrate. He pursued fighting them for about two years after routing them all, and their reach diminished. He killed them and plundered their wealth until they responded to him and submitted to his authority,

162. He is Abū Ibrāhīm who was sent from Mīla by his father to see the Aghlabid emir and incite him to fight Abū ʿAbd Allāh. See p. 111 below.

willingly and wholeheartedly, or unwillingly and out of fear. Only the towns and their rulers, and those who rallied around them and adhered to them, withstood. They were those overcome by distress and who were, according to the foreknowledge of God, to be struck by calamity from among the chiefs of the tribes and the notables of the clans; those who disdained to join the *daʿwa* and to come under the authority of someone of their clan whom they considered as being under their command. There were also those fearful of their previous ill deeds. Satan beguiled them to persevere in their transgression and ignorance. Some elements of the tribes settled around towns associated with their inhabitants. Their rulers won them over by deceiving them, and they corresponded with them, while infiltrating among them secretly. Outwardly they professed obedience and overt submission to the *daʿwa*. They were tolerated as they were, just as the Messenger of God, peace be upon him and his progeny, tolerated the hypocrites in Madina.

13

Measures adopted by Abū ʿAbd Allāh among the Kutāma to reign over them and for which they submitted to him.

The reason for Abū ʿAbd Allāh's ascendancy was that God willed to manifest the power of His friends, strengthen His religion, and exalt His word. What we have related happened for reasons which cannot be understood except by His power and strength. So when God manifested His authority and strengthened His help, the *daʿwa* of Abū ʿAbd Allāh spread, and all sorts of people responded to his call and adhered to his cause. Among them were those who thereby wished to gain God's favour and reward, and were faithful to Him about it, and preferred what is with Him. There were those who wished thereby to attain piety as well as this world, and who pursued their portion of the Hereafter and this world. There were those who adhered to that, thereby seeking glory, honour, prestige and leadership. There were those who thereby wished to gain and benefit. There were those who were filled with envy and rivalry. There were those who adhered to him out of fear, dissimulation and deceit. Other reasons are too long to relate, but they amount to two things: the matter of this world and the matter of the Hereafter, just as was the case of those who lived before.

God has informed us about a people who lived during the time of the Messenger of God, may God's blessings be upon him and his progeny. He says: '*Among you are some that hanker after this world and some that desire the Hereafter*' (3:152). And He says: '*There are men who say, "Our Lord! Give us (Thy bounties) in this world," but they will have no portion in the Hereafter. And there are men who say, "Our Lord! Give us good in this world and good in the Hereafter, and defend us from the torment of the Fire"*' (2:200–201).

God supported Abū 'Abd Allāh with good fortune, for He willed to manifest His friends, and He supported him with His guidance. (Abū 'Abd Allāh) observed that the root upon which he could base his cause, and its pole upon which its pivot might rest, was religion, and what truth imposes, so that the affairs of mankind would be straightened out. So he relied upon it and made it the basis of his policy. He did not give precedence to anyone, or delay anyone, or praise anyone, or mention anyone, or reward, punish, abandon, or demand, or draw near, or turn away, or keep secret, or clarify, except what was imposed by religion and truthfulness, and what duty and right imposed as truth. He would not accept from anyone anything but this. He would only reward on its account and punish on its account. He would not allow any laxity in it.

People of all strata submitted to his policy according to their wish and intent towards him, either out of belief and good intention, or out of hypocrisy and reputation. Showing good out of hypocrisy brings well-being on the surface. However, God rewards and punishes according to the unseen. (Abū 'Abd Allāh) treated people according to their compliance with this policy, and would not be satisfied with them for anything else. Nor would he treat them softly in this matter. If he came to know that anyone had violated anything of it, he would punish him accordingly, without condoning or disregarding it, whoever it might be from among those who were known for their piety and adherence to the community of believers. He would remove him, reject him, expel him, send him away, and forbid the believers to approach him, go near him, sit with him or talk to him.

(The transgressor) would remain for a long time, for several days and months, aloof, abandoned, expelled and repulsed in his tribe, his family and his immediate circle, his children, and all those who see him and know him, until he would sincerely show repentance and do good deeds. He would be examined at length according to the offence he had committed and the error he had made. At that time, he would restore his situation and bring him close to his deeds. Then anyone liable to the legally prescribed punishment (*ḥadd*) would be so punished, and anyone liable to [other] punishment would be so punished. Whoever deserved a status would be raised to it and whoever fell short would be cast away.

People weighed their actions and remained careful, knowing that he would be watchful over them and would not disregard them. Their circumstances became settled and their condition became fine. Then he became harsh in punishing those who deserved harsh treatment. He disciplined them with the sword and punished them with fright. He would place (the punishment) in their hands, not entrusting it to anyone else, allowing no authority over them to anyone else. If he wished to kill anyone of them, he would order the person's brother, his father or his nearest relative to do so. He would consider it to be a mark of his obedience, and it would be easier for him than seeing someone else carrying it out, so that he would become angry. The search for him would be ended by his appointing him rather than someone else. In this there was benefit in several regards. Everyone refrained from offences and kept away from disgraceful acts out of fear, willingly, through dissimulation or alarm. They knew for certain that there was no laxity with regard to (offences), and that he would not pardon them. Their longing to commit them ceased. Corruption and treachery ceased, while piety, religion and honesty spread. That is why the forefathers have said that *authority is a market*,[163] and as long as people know what will sell well in (the market), they will bring it to it. This can only happen in accordance with what we have mentioned regarding desire and

163. Cf. Arabic saying *innamā al-sulṭān sūq*, attributed to ʿUmar b. ʿAbd al-ʿAzīz, explained in Ismāʿīl b. Muḥammad al-ʿAjlūnī al-Jarrāḥī, *Kashf al-khafāʾ wa-muzīl al-ilbās ʿammā ishtahara min al-aḥādīth ʿalā alsinat al-nās*, ed. Aḥmad al-Qalāsh (Aleppo, n.d.), vol. 2, p. 431.

fear and lack of hope for permission and laxity. God, the Mighty, the Glorious, knows His creation best. If He had known that they would act aright through any other way, He would not have ordained reward and punishment for them. If He had known that reward would work without punishment or punishment without reward, He would not have established the two together. But He knows that it is in the nature of human beings, the way they have been created, that only reward and punishment will redress them.

The supporters of Abū ʿAbd Allāh were living in such a virtuous situation and sound condition that a community like them had not been seen or known about. Merchants would travel with their belongings and evident wealth, passing alone and in twos, in the mountains, gorges, deserts, open country and isolated places. They would spend the night wherever they happened to walk, and go wherever they liked and wished to go, feeling as if they were in their own house or in their market. They would spend the night in safety and wake up safe in the morning. Indeed, an animal from the flock of sheep would get lost from its shepherds, and riding animals with their saddles and reins would roam in the open country and in populated regions, among men, women and children, none of whom would turn their attention to the animals, no one would covet them and no one would long to have them. They would remain thus for days and nights until their owner would come to look for them. Similarly, an item would be lost, falling to the ground, and it would remain there for a long time and for several days and nights, until its rightful owner or the person who had lost it would come and recover it.

People kept away from vices and abandoned differences of dogmas, and became single-minded. They were called 'brethren' (*ikhwān*) and formed bonds with each other, privately and publicly. If one of them called someone whose name he did not know, or whom he wished to call without naming him in his call or conversation, he would say, 'O our brother!' This expression was often repeated in their conversation and call. If two of their men got together, they would shake hands, embrace one another, and each one would kiss the hand of the other. The nobleman would not scorn the commoner, nor would the strong man seek to promote himself over the weak one. Abū ʿAbd Allāh would do the same to anyone who came to visit him. He would also call everyone, 'O our brother!' They learnt this expression from him and adopted his manners.

They knew of his abstinence, virtue and honesty towards them, and they esteemed him because of that. He resided among them for a long time without mentioning any woman or considering to mention one. They alluded to this and remarked about it, but he would not consider it until a slave-girl[164] fell to his lot after a long time. He chose her for himself. He would not accept for himself from anyone of them anything, however little or much. They tried hard but he would not do so, and would only spend what his Master gave to him and for which he had received written instruction from him to take. Sometimes this would be delayed and he would be in need, so he would resort to selling secretly something which he had and spend it, while there was a lot of wealth in his hand and which was licit for him to spend. He treated them with dignity and respect. He was not seen laughing among them or joking with them. Nor was he heard using obscene language, frivolous talk or falsehood. However, he was neither depressed nor cheerful, but he was between the two, not pleasing them so as to make them reckless. If he spoke, he pronounced with truth, rightness, correctness and wisdom; and if he remained silent, he did so with dignity, gentleness and respect. He was not withdrawn from them, making them lonely and scaring them away. He would consult them and see them in private. He would confide in them and allow them proximity to himself according to their position and merit. He would give precedence to people of religion and the pious among them who had seniority.

(Abū ʿAbd Allāh) divided the Kutāma into seven sections. He assigned troops for each section and appointed a commander over it. He appointed in every locality a *dāʿī*. He called the commanders and the *dāʿī*s 'elders' (*mashāyikh*), even those who had not attained old age. He entrusted to the elders the direction of the affairs of the believers and made them custodians of the part of the booty[165] which

164. This slave-girl was presented by Ibrāhīm b. Aḥmad to the chief of the Mazāta, Yūsuf al-Ghaṭṭāshī, and was subsequently taken captive by the followers along with the booty. See p. 89 above.

165. The author has a particular interpretation of the term *ghanīma* (booty) which he equates to *khums*. Hence, while defining the share to be set aside for the imam from the income of the believers, he gives to the term *ghanīma* an acceptation which covers, together with booty

was set aside for the Guardian of the Muslims (*walī al-muslimīn*). He himself never received any part of it, nor did he have access to it or see it. The elders retained the custody of it until the arrival of al-Mahdī when they handed it over to him. This led them to be corrupt, because they deemed that it would remain in their custody for ever.[166] However, Abū ʿAbd Allāh had only wished thereby to please them, for it did not belong to him that he could take it from their custody, and he judged that leaving it to them in trust was more prudent for its safe-keeping and better for them. Then it became difficult for them when they had to relinquish (the custody of the funds). Like the breaking of any custom, they disapproved change in this custom, as the poet says:

> Do not congratulate me after having been generous to me,
> For abolishing a custom is harsh.[167]

One of the ancients has said, 'Custom is nature and discontinuing it is an offence.'[168] This was not because of Abū ʿAbd Allāh's bad policy. The matter about it became corrupted on the part of the ill-judgement of those who refused to accept this and became corrupt for its sake. Abū ʿAbd Allāh did only what was required as we mentioned before. Error attaches only to one who changes what is sound, not one who originates it.

Among Abū ʿAbd Allāh's policies was also to put his companions to test in great trials. Then he would raise those of them with whose test he was satisfied according to their merit. This is why they did not consider any test to be unbearable, nor were they averse to it. Rather, they would rush to it, pursued it, and he would engage them to die and cause them to perish for the sake of religion, and they would accept it and rush to it.

---

strictly speaking, all the gains (*kasb*) made by every member of the community. See al-Qāḍī al-Nuʿmān, *Kitāb al-Himma fī ādāb atbāʿ al-aʾimma*, ed. Muḥammad Kāmil Ḥusayn (Cairo, [1948]), pp. 68–69.

166. On his way from Sijilmāsa to Raqqāda, al-Mahdī passed via Īkjān to take possession of these funds, whereupon the elders expressed their resentment. See p. 203 below.

167. Abū al-Aswad al-Duʾalī, *Dīwān*, ed. Muḥammad Ḥasan Āl Yāsīn (Beirut, 1974), p. 64.

168. Cf. al-Maydānī, *Majmaʿ al-amthāl*, vol. 2, p. 343.

He would send emissaries from them to the east before the emigration of al-Mahdī, and to Sijilmāsa[169] after he arrived there, and to faraway regions in whichever direction he wished. Whenever he chose someone for this task and had confided it to him, he would not inform anyone of his family or children about it. None of them would know where he had gone. He would be lost in their view until his return. (Abū ʿAbd Allāh) sent with them a lot of money which they conveyed. They would travel under cover in the condition of the poor and the pilgrims of the remote regions of the Maghrib in rags and worn out clothes until they had delivered to the imam what was sent with them. Then they would return in the same manner.[170]

He deliberated when God granted him most of the country while he was not able to reach Sijilmāsa by himself without first conquering Ifrīqiya. It came to his knowledge that Ziyādat Allāh had written to al-Yasaʿ b. Midrār,[171] ruler of Sijilmāsa, about al-Mahdī, stating that he was in his vicinity. He therefore feared for (al-Mahdī's) life and picked 100 men of the Kutāma and charged them to go to Sijilmāsa in the guise of travellers, and that when they reached there, they should attack and kill Ibn Midrār and deliver al-Mahdī. Each one resolved to face 100 combatants. Although they knew that there would not be in Sijilmāsa such a number, they made a deal with their right hands and made a covenant with God concerning this matter. They set out until, when they approached Tāhart,[172] their mission was uncovered.

---

169. The site of this ancient town lies in south-eastern Morocco in the oasis of the Tafilelt, immediately to the west of the modern town of Rissani. Sijilmāsa, famous for its wealth, was founded by the Miknāsa Berbers in 140/757. See al-Bakrī, *al-Masālik*, pp. 148–152 (tr. pp. 282–290); al-Idrīsī, *Nuzha*, pp. 60–61 (tr. pp. 69–70); Abū al-Fidāʾ, *Taqwīm*, pp. 136–137; Georges S. Colin, 'Sidjilmāsa', *EI*, vol. 7, pp. 404–405; M. Terrasse, 'Sidjilmāsa', *EI*², vol. 9, pp. 545–546. On Abū ʿAbd Allāh's conquest of Sijilmāsa see below, pp. 196ff.

170. Cf. al-Yamānī, *Sīrat al-Ḥājib Jaʿfar*, pp. 121–123 (tr. Ivanow, *Rise*, pp. 205–206, 209); al-Maqrīzī, *Ittiʿāẓ*, vol. 1, p. 60; Ibn ʿIdhārī, *al-Bayān*, vol. 1, p. 139.

171. The dynast al-Yasaʿ b. Maymūn b. Midrār b. al-Yasaʿ b. Samghūn b. Midlān al-Miknāsi (r. 270–296/882–909). On the Midrārids see Bosworth, *The New Islamic Dynasties*, pp. 29–30; Charles Pellat, 'Midrār', *EI*², vol. 6, pp. 1038–1042; and Ibn al-Khaṭīb, *Aʿmāl*, pp. 144–149.

172. On Tāhart, capital of the Kharijite kingdom of the Rustamids, see Mohamed Talbi, 'Tāhart', *EI*², vol. 10, pp. 99–101; Georges Marçais, *La Berbérie musulmane et l'Orient au Moyen Age* (Paris, 1946), pp. 101–116; and Ibn ʿIdhārī, *al-Bayān*, vol. 1, pp. 196–199. Abū ʿAbd Allāh captured the town in 296/909, on his way to Sijilmāsa. See note 346 below.

Having been recognised, they were unable to accomplish the mission and withdrew. They had these great intentions and astounding vision because of the way (Abū ʿAbd Allāh) had disciplined and formed them to accomplish their purpose. God, the Mighty, the Glorious, granted him success and guidance because of His will to fulfil His command and manifest His religion.

Among his policies was also to take great care to give them advice, remind them and repeat to them exhortation and wisdom. He would gather them for this purpose and hold sessions (*majālis*) for them most of his days. He would order the *dāʿī*s whom he dispatched to do the same and train them for this purpose. Most of their days were spent attending assemblies and listening to sermons. The people were either eager witnesses of these sermons or attended fearing loss through absence. Every one present must absorb something (of these sermons) in order to benefit from them. Their actions thus turned upon adherence to religion and hypocrisy. The past imams used to act according to this, so that someone said, while swearing by God, 'He had sought knowledge first not for the sake of God.'

They could see that Abū ʿAbd Allāh's conduct was marked by self-denial and rejection of this world, and not motivated by gain. He was frugal in food, drink, conveyance, dress and appearance. They imitated his conduct, investing their toil and diligence in spending for the sake of God, the Mighty, the Glorious, cooperating to this end and sharing this ideal. Since at the beginning they had only very little wealth which God granted them as booty, just like the early ancestors at the beginning of the mission of the Prophet, may God bless him, they did not, because of this, occupy themselves with what exceeded sufficiency and covered their basic needs.

Among his policies was also to incite them to act thus and recount to them its merit. He would elucidate to them the reward of mutual bonds between them, helping each other, cooperation, assisting each other, being constantly caring, offering food, and bonds of kinship of the people of religion and all the believers. They would hasten to do that and were happy with it and cooperated in that. None of them considered wealth for himself without his brother. Nor would anyone see merit and honour, except in what he received and the help he provided. Never had there been any community or generation behaving like they did. In this matter they held ranks according to their intentions and effort, their men as well as their womenfolk. There are many such accounts about them, which would be too long to relate exhaustively and explain clearly. They would fall outside the scope of this book.

We have recounted and shall mention a group of those who were renowned for this [conduct], and who expended their wealth for it, and about whom there are remarkable tales. One of them about whom such tales are related is Kuwayrit b. Qays al-Lahīṣī. Indeed, it is related that he spent his entire wealth on helping his brothers, feeding them and alleviating their plight. It was related that he would gather around him every wounded fighter and treat his wounds. He would treat him and attend to him until he was healed and recovered, in which case he would visit him and provide for him; or he died, in which case he would shroud him and bury him. It is related that he carried on tearing his clothes to wrap the wounds of the wounded until he and his sons were left without clothes. They would not go to the market to buy any. A group of wounded [fighters], whom he looked after, fed and treated, were in need of bandages for their wounds, but he did not have any. So he used up for this purpose all the clothes which he, his sons and his family had. One day he sent his son to a wife of his, who was a bride having clothes. He asked her to have (the clothes) and recompensed her for them with wealth, and removed her clothes from her and ripped them, making bandages with which he bandaged the wounds of his brothers. The book would become too long if it were related what he and others endured to feed the poor believers and attending to them.

There were women who accomplished such work and devoted themselves to it, seeking thereby to gain reward for it, such as the wife of Yaḥyā b. Yūsuf, known under the name of Ibn al-Aṣamm al-Ijjānī, who was a companion of al-Ḥulwānī whom we have mentioned before. He died long before the coming of Abū ʿAbd Allāh. When he was about to die, he presented his wealth to his wife who at that time was young whereas he was old. He had educated her and taught her Shīʿī doctrines and devotion to the imams (*walāya*).[173] He said

173. On the central Ismaili concept of *walāya* (devotion to the imam and recognition of

to her before he died, 'This is the money which I have been setting aside because we heard from al-Ḥulwānī regarding the Mahdī that he would tread upon our land. I have been setting this money aside to be presented for fighting (*jihād*) for the Mahdī or for his *dāʿī*. Let it remain with you in trust from God. When that time comes, donate this money and expend it for charity.'

After his death, his brother, Yāsīn b. Yūsuf, married her and she was still alive when Abū ʿAbd Allāh arrived. She adhered to the *daʿwa* and her conduct was good. She brought the money and presented it to him, informing him of the last wishes of her husband. She had money which she expended for fighting (*jihād*). She would prepare food with her own hands for fighters, for poor believers and for those of them who stopped by her family, to the extent that her hands would bleed from grinding and handling food for them. There were other women like her whose account would only lengthen this book. They attended instructional sessions (*majālis*) and listened to words of wisdom. There were some old women, who followed these sessions and rose to the rank of *dāʿī*s (*ḥadd al-daʿwa*). Among them were Umm Mūsā, daughter of al-Ḥulwānī whom we have mentioned before,[174] and other old women of the Kutāma. They also rendered services to the believers, looked after the sick and treated the wounded with devotion and insight, because these women, as well as the men whom we have mentioned before, listened to admonishment and wisdom, and were strengthened with education and right conduct.

Abū ʿAbd Allāh was a cause of well-being occasioned for them by God. He was a gate of blessing which God opened for them, and a source of happiness which He offered to them. Through him He opened their eyes, saved them from ignorance, and guided them from error. Through him He bestowed favours upon them.

---

his authority) see al-Qāḍī al-Nuʿmān, *Daʿāʾim*, vol. 1, pp. 3–98, (tr. vol. 1, pp. 18–122). Also Azim Nanji, 'An Ismāʿīlī Theory of *Walāyah* in the *Daʿāʾim al-Islām* of Qāḍī al-Nuʿmān', in *Essays on Islamic Civilization Presented to Niyazi Berkes*, ed. D. P. Little (Leiden, 1976), pp. 260–273. Cf. note 30 above.

174. See p. 44 above.

14

The conquest of the town of Mīla.

The Banū Abī Khinzīr were among the notables of Mīla. They were Arabs from the Rabīʿa,[175] known under the name of al-Sanājira, having originated from Sinjār,[176] a town of Diyār Rabīʿa.[177] Their chief at that time was Ḥasan b. Aḥmad.[178] He came to Abū ʿAbd Allāh secretly and adhered to the *daʿwa*. He informed Abū ʿAbd Allāh on the situation of the town. At that time Abū ʿAbd Allāh was waging war against them, while the chiefs of the tribes and all the Laṭāya joined them. He would march with troops against them and there would be fierce fighting between them. Then he would withdraw to Tāzrūt. At the same time, he waged war against the remaining groups of Kutāma until he defeated them and they submitted to his authority.

When the matter of the Kutāma was settled for Abū ʿAbd Allāh and he subdued those who had stubbornly resisted him, he gathered them and marched with them against Mīla. (His) troops surrounded them from every direction and besieged them. Mūsā b. ʿAbbās[179] and those Kutāma who had sought refuge with him, such as Faḥl b. Nūḥ, Faraḥ b. Jīrān, Yūsuf b. Maḥmūd and Wazra b. Naṣr[180] came out to

---

175. The Rabīʿa are Northern Arabs whose lineage goes back to Ishmael, son of Abraham, through Nizār, Maʿadd, and ʿAdnān. On them see H. Kindermann, 'Rabīʿa and Muḍar', *EI²*, vol. 8, pp. 352–354.

176. On Sinjār, a town to the west of al-Mawṣil, see C. P. Haase, 'Sindjār', *EI²*, vol. 9, pp. 643–644.

177. On Diyār Rabīʿa, the largest province of the Jazīra, see Marius Canard and Claude Cahen, 'Diyār Rabīʿa', *EI²*, vol. 2, pp. 348–349.

178. Ḥasan b. Aḥmad b. ʿAlī b. Kulayb b. Abī Khinzir became one of Abū ʿAbd Allāh's commanders who, together with Ghazwiyya, led the advance guard which preceded him to Raqqāda after the flight of the last Aghlabid emir. Abū ʿAbd Allāh then appointed him governor of al-Qayrawān, where he was retained by al-Mahdī. Subsequently, in 297/909–910, al-Mahdī appointed him governor of Sicily to restore order. The following year the populace rose against him and he was overthrown in 300/912–913. Then al-Mahdī sent him at the head of the Fatimid fleet against the rebel of Sicily, Ibn Qurhub, whose son Muḥammad defeated him and killed him in 301/913–914. See Ibn ʿIdhārī, *al-Bayān*, vol. 1, pp. 151, 159, 166, 168, 171; and Ibn Khaldūn, *al-ʿIbar*, vol. 4, pp. 442–443.

179. He was lord of Mīla. See p. 58 above.

180. These were the former chiefs of the coalition against Abū ʿAbd Allāh.

meet them. He fought them fiercely. Faḥl b. Nūḥ was killed in battle and Abū ʿAbd Allāh and his supporters captured the suburbs of Mīla. All those who were in the town entered the citadel and became confined there. When they saw that they were unable to resist them, Mūsā b. ʿAbbās summoned Ḥasan b. Aḥmad b. Abī Khinzīr, whom he knew to have adhered to (Abū ʿAbd Allāh's) cause. He sent him to Abū ʿAbd Allāh to seek from him guarantee of safety. Abū ʿAbd Allāh granted them safety, guaranteeing to spare their lives as long as they did not cause any mischief. They opened the gates of the town and the followers entered. The son of Mūsā b. ʿAbbās, Abū Ibrāhīm, escaped with a group of them by night and arrived in Ifrīqiya. It is related that Mūsā b. ʿAbbās and the Kutāma chiefs who were with him sent them away. When the Kutāma tribesmen entered [the town], they killed Faraḥ b. Jīrān as well as the two Ijjānī tribesmen, Yūsuf b. Maḥmūd and Wazra b. Naṣr. It is said that the one who instigated the killing was Abū Zākī, because they were the notables of the Ijjāna, and he feared they might become more powerful than him.

Abū ʿAbd Allāh released Mūsā b. ʿAbbās and wished him well. Abū ʿAbd Allāh appointed Abū Yūsuf Māknūn b. Ḍubāra al-Ijjānī governor of Mīla. He was the paternal uncle of Abū Zākī. (Abū ʿAbd Allāh) [then] returned to Tāzrūt at the head of his troops.

Abū Ibrāhīm and those who had escaped with him fled to Abū al-ʿAbbās b. Ibrāhīm b. Aḥmad, who was at the time in Tunis, and gave him the news. They described the cause of Abū ʿAbd Allāh as weak to him and incited him to dispatch troops with them against him, and guaranteed to him his authority. Fatḥ b. Yaḥyā al-Masāltī who had come previously to him joined with them in this. They informed him that if troops came to them, most people would stand with him. So he ordered mobilisation of troops, distributed gifts, assembled his notables and appointed as commander over them his son Muḥammad Abū ʿAbd Allāh, better known as Abū Ḥawāl.[181] He was a brave, strong, courageous horseman. He was not cross-eyed (*aḥwal*). It was only a nickname applied to him because sometimes

181. He is called Abū Khawāl in Ibn Khaldūn, *al-ʿIbar*, vol. 4, p. 69 (tr. *Berbères*, vol. 2, p. 514), and al-Aḥwal (cross-eyed) in al-Nuwayrī, *Nihāya*, vol. 24, p. 145 (tr. *Berbères*, vol. 1, p. 440).

he winked with his eye when he stared at something. A large number of troops gathered around him.

Abū ʿAbd Allāh came to know that it was Mūsā b. ʿAbbās who had sent his son for this purpose. So he ordered him to be detained and put under guard. Then, when this proved to be true and the troops approached him, he ordered him to be executed in captivity among the Banū Julāma, and his body was thrown in an underground granary in (the town). Abū ʿAbd Allāh gathered the troops around him and prepared to encounter Abū Ḥawāl.

15

Abū Ḥawāl's military expedition to Kutāma territory and his retreat from there.

This Muḥammad, well-known as Abū Ḥawāl, b. ʿAbd Allāh Abī al-ʿAbbās b. Ibrāhīm b. Aḥmad, was supported by 12,000 men, among them cavalry and infantry, whom he picked and chose. His father dispatched to him money, robes, weapons and equipment. He lavished gifts upon them and gave robes of honour and mounts to their notables. Among (the notables) whom he gave robes of honour and mounts were Fatḥ b. Yaḥyā and Abū Ibrāhīm b. Mūsā b. ʿAbbās. He presented to them, as well as to the Kutāma battle heroes who were with them, ornamented saddles and bridles. (Abū Ḥawāl) set out with the troops from the town of Tunis in the month of Dhū al-Qaʿda 289/October 902. He gave gifts, robes and pack animals to the notables of all the tribes whom he passed on the way. They hastened towards him and reinforced him. He approached Saṭīf and as he reached (the town) he doubled the number of his troops. The Banū ʿUslūja, rulers of Saṭīf, and the Banū Tamīm, rulers of Billizma, received him with those around them who had not adhered to Abū ʿAbd Allāh. They marched in a large number of troops. With them (Abū Ḥawāl) attacked those Kutāma inhabitants of Majris who had joined the party of Abū ʿAbd Allāh, and killed them wantonly. He plundered their wealth, and took their women and children captive. Then he proceeded in the direction of Tāzrūt to Abū ʿAbd Allāh.

Abū ʿAbd Allāh came to know of (the offensive) and came out towards him together with those who were with him. Abū Ḥawāl, since he set out from Bāghāya, had made his troops march in a state of alert, in formation for battle at every stage. When he halted, he would only spend the night in a trench dug around him from the moment of his halting and completed before sunset. He applied this arrangement to his men, stationing them at fixed measurement by a number of cubits, and arranged their halting according to fixed arrangement, so that every group knew its position. When night fell upon them guards stood at the entrance of the trench. The infantry went round inside it with shields and the cavalry patrolled by night beyond the infantry inside the trench. One thousand mounted troops would come out and patrol around (the guards) until morning. They proceeded with this arrangement during winter.

Abū ʿAbd Allāh advanced towards him. They met in the territory of the Malūsa and fierce fighting took place. Abū ʿAbd Allāh and his supporters were put to flight at the end of the day. Abū Ḥawāl pursued him until the approach of nightfall. Then he halted and dug in. The next morning he marched against them, who had been camping near to him. They fought and again the supporters of Abū ʿAbd Allāh were put to flight. Then heavy snow fell and intervened between them.

Abū ʿAbd Allāh and his supporters retreated to Tāzrūt, but did not consider that (the town) would protect them. They took whatever belongings they could and they all withdrew to Īkjān. The snowfall subsided and Abū Ḥawāl reached Tāzrūt. He found (the town) deserted, so he set it on fire and demolished the castle of Abū ʿAbd Allāh which he had built there. He marched until he reached Mīla, but here also he found that its inhabitants had deserted it and had withdrawn to Īkjān. He set up camp near it in a south-westerly direction (*dabūr al-qibla*), not far from Mīla, by the side of the grassland known by the name of Mūsā b. ʿAbbās, waiting to march on to Abū ʿAbd Allāh in Īkjān, and dug in at that place.

The following morning, Abū Ibrāhīm b. Mūsā b. ʿAbbās sought permission from (Abū Ḥawāl) to go to Kujārma to recover [the body of] his father and bury him. It was lying near to where he was killed. He allowed him to do so. (Abū Ibrāhīm) went with several horses until he reached Kujārma, which is in the territory of the Laṭāya not far from Mīla. He found (the town) deserted, its inhabitants having left with Abū ʿAbd Allāh. While he was recovering the body of his father, suddenly mounted troops approached with pack animals from the inhabitants of Kujārma bringing their supplies. They attacked Abū Ibrāhīm and those who were with him, who fought them back. Abū ʿIqāl b. Abī Ibrāhīm b. Mūsā b. ʿAbbās, who was a strong horseman, was killed. The battle-cry engaged the two sides and every side reinforced its supporters. They fought each other in close combat with reinforcements until nightfall, when Abū Ḥawāl's supporters were routed. The followers pursued them until they approached the camp [of Abū Ḥawāl]. However, night fell and they withdrew from them. Those in the camp were agitated and spent the night with Abū Ḥawāl. At night there was discord among them. They stormed the trench and struck their faces, every tribe moving to its station. Abū Ḥawāl tried to remedy this situation, but he was unable to do so. He then ordered to decamp. He lit torches and travelled by night. He proceeded towards the territory of the Jīmla heading for Ifrīqiya. Before morning he had left the frontiers of the Kutāma. Abū ʿAbd Allāh's supporters came to know of this, so they entered his encampment and plundered whatever was left there. A detachment of mounted troops in pursuit of (Abū Ḥawāl) lost trail of him and gave up the pursuit. Abū Ḥawāl travelled until he returned to his father in Tunis.[182] The Kutāma all returned to their regions and the inhabitants of Mīla returned to their town.

Then al-Ḥasan b. Hārūn fell ill and died at Īkjān. May God have mercy upon him. Bayān b. Ṣaqlān and Abū Jaʿfar Aḥmad b. Sulaymān al-Saktānī, who was called al-Jarrāra, had attained a worthy standing with Abū ʿAbd Allāh, and were of good conduct. They requested him, with a group of the Banū Saktān, to settle in Īkjān. He considered it to be the most appropriate place for him. So he settled there and constructed a castle there. People travelled to it and it became an abode of emigration for the believers.

182. Abū Ḥawāl's return to Tunis must also be linked with the death of his grandfather Ibrāhīm b. Aḥmad in Sicily and the attitude of revolt of his brother Ziyādat Allāh against their father Abū al-ʿAbbās who had just assumed officially the emirate in Dhū al-Qaʿda 289/November 902. See al-Maqrīzī, *Ittiʿāẓ*, vol. 1, pp. 58–59.

Abū ʿAbd Allāh despatched *dāʿīs* to the tribes and himself conducted instructional sessions (*majālis*), sitting in session every day for the believers, relating *ḥadīth* to them and giving them explanations. He ordered the *dāʿīs* to do the same. The believers became sincere in their intent, their understanding increased and their condition became sound.

(Abū ʿAbd Allāh) sent a group of spies to Ifrīqiya who gathered information for him ceaselessly. It is said that not a day passed without him getting reports from there. Then he received the news of Ibrāhīm b. Aḥmad's death. That day he conducted the public assembly with the elders gathered around him. They noticed that he was depressed and tense. He did not speak to them when they dispersed. After taking leave of him, they gathered among themselves saying, 'Some news he has received must be worrying him. We must not leave without knowing what it is. If we can think of a way to do it, we will use it.'

They stayed there and sent back one of them to him. He sought permission of (Abū ʿAbd Allāh) to be seen, and told him what they had said among themselves. (Abū ʿAbd Allāh) ordered him to call them back. Then he said, 'I have come to know that you were troubled by my distress, which is because of something preoccupying my thoughts.'

They asked, 'What is it? Acquaint us with it. It might be that we will be able to do something about it.'

He replied, 'God has taken the sinner Ibrāhīm b. Aḥmad unto Himself. He is dead.'

They praised and thanked God and rejoiced at this news, and said, 'Why does that sadden you?'

He replied, 'That does not sadden me, but when the sinner's son[183] heard of the death of his father Ibrāhīm, he made much show of piety and restored to the people everything that his father had seized from them. He acts justly towards them and is humble with them. He sits on a mat in the chief mosque with a whip near him to hear grievances just like judges do. Thereby he wins over the hearts of the common people.'

183. The Aghlabid emir Abū al-ʿAbbās ʿAbd Allāh (r. 289–290/902–903). On him see Talbi, *L'émirat aghlabide*, pp. 538ff.

They said, 'That will weaken him.'

He said, 'Do not say that! How can you deal with someone who faces you sitting on a mat with a whip, winning thereby the hearts of the common people? Be serious in what you do, and work hard!'

He had hardly finished talking to them and warning them when he received the news of the assassination of Abū al-'Abbās, and that his son, Ziyādat Allāh, had assumed power, and that it was he who had plotted to kill him.[184] (Ziyādat Allāh) committed forbidden acts and indulged in debauchery and drinking wine. He gave them this good news and said, 'What you had been expecting is no more. This [man] is now your companion and the last one to wage war against you. After him you will attain power, God willing.'

16

Abū Ḥawāl's second military expedition and his defeat.

When Abū Ḥawāl returned to his father (Abū al-'Abbās) he described to him his initial attack and conquest of the country, stating that his withdrawal was only because of something unexpected. All those Kutāma who were with him supported this statement of his. They described Abū 'Abd Allāh as weak. This tempted him and he prepared a second army which was larger in number than the first and provided with more weapons and supplies. He dispatched it with his son Abū Ḥawāl, who set out with (this army) in earnest, taking his first route. The tribes also joined him. He marched until he halted at Saṭīf just as he had done on his march the first time, in formation and on the lookout. He advanced from Saṭīf. Abū 'Abd Allāh who came to know of this, himself advanced from Īkjān with all those who were with him. He set up camp at Tāsadsut near the territory of the Lahīṣa. Abū Ḥawāl set up camp in the territory of the Malūsa.

Abū 'Abd Allāh dispatched the entire cavalry which was with him and set it ahead towards Abū Ḥawāl and himself remained at Tāsadsut. When the cavalry was in sight at a visible distance from Abū Ḥawāl, he emerged from his trench with all his companions.

184. On these events see Talbi, *L'émirat aghlabide*, pp. 542ff.

The troops fought a fierce battle. The companions of Abū ʿAbd Allāh overcame Abū Ḥawāl, forcing him and (his companions) to retreat in their trench. At nightfall they withdrew from (Abū Ḥawāl) and spent the night. The following morning they continued attacking. Abū Ḥawāl remained in the trench without coming out to attack them. He saw that his companions had been overcome. They watched over them till nightfall and returned to Abū ʿAbd Allāh and informed him of what had happened. They said to him, 'It is advisable to set out at once with all the troops and besiege them for they will most certainly flee by night.'

Abū ʿAbd Allāh replied, 'I do not think so. However, if they do flee, they will be damned.'

When night fell Abū Ḥawāl gathered his belongings. Then he lit torches and pulled back to return to Saṭīf. Many horsemen from Abū ʿAbd Allāh's army advanced when they were sure of Abū Ḥawāl's flight and got near to him. As he set out, they attacked his rear guard, killing some of his companions, and seizing a lot of booty from them. Abū ʿAbd Allāh's army came next morning and plundered everything which remained in Abū Ḥawāl's camp and returned to Īkjān with Abū ʿAbd Allāh. Abū Ḥawāl returned to Saṭīf with those who were with him.

Then Ziyādat Allāh Abū Muḍar b. ʿAbd Allāh Abī al-ʿAbbās, it is said, plotted to kill his father and bribed some eunuchs to this end. Rather it is said that the eunuchs did it to please him. Ziyādat Allāh at that time was imprisoned and in chains. The cause of his imprisonment is that Ibrāhīm b. Aḥmad, his grandfather, was furious at him because of his corruption and committing fornication while they were together in Byzantine territory. He therefore ordered him to be imprisoned in a desert tent (*khibāʾ*) under guard. Then when Ibrāhīm was about to die, he entrusted the commandment of those who were with him to his son Abū al-Aghlab and gave him his seal ring. Abū al-Aghlab was temperate and mild. Now when Ibrāhīm died, he feared that his brother Abū al-ʿAbbās would hate him because of his position. Therefore, he called Ziyādat Allāh and told him, 'Your father is the emir. Therefore, you have a greater right to this office than me.'

(Abū al-Aghlab) handed over to him the seal ring of Ibrāhīm and dissociated himself from his responsibilities. Ziyādat Allāh took command of the army. He had been besieging Cosenza and was about to conquer it. Ziyādat Allāh withdrew from (the town) and set out for Sicily intending to oppose his father from there. He distributed a lot of money to the leaders of the army and called upon them to rebel with him. This is because he knew from his father that he would punish him for what he had done. Those whom he called upon to rebel told him, 'Our children and family are in Ifrīqiya. If we rebel with you, they will not be safe from punishment. However, we are with you with our supporters (*jamāʿa*). Then when we arrive in Ifrīqiya, we shall rise with you and remove your father and appoint you.'

One of them wrote about this to his father. When they left with the fleet, Abū al-ʿAbbās ordered many horsemen and a great force. They were at sea. Then when Ziyādat Allāh disembarked, they arrested him and brought him to (his father).[185] He hit him hard with the staff, put him in chains and imprisoned him. Then (Ziyādat Allāh) plotted against (Abū al-ʿAbbās), or (the plot) was carried out for him. The eunuchs who used to enter (Abū al-ʿAbbās's) harem by night came to him while he was asleep, or it is related that he was drunk, and they killed him inside his palace in Tunis on the night of Wednesday 28 Shaʿbān 290/27 July 903. The duration of his reign since the departure of his father for Sicily until the night of his assassination was one year and fifty-two days.

Having murdered him, the eunuchs came to Ziyādat Allāh to give him the news. They brought a blacksmith to break his chains and acknowledged him as the emir. He refused any involvement, fearing that this was a scheme of his father against him. So they left and brought to him his head at night. When he saw that, he ordered his chains to be cut. He succeeded his father and seized his wealth. The next morning he displayed anger and executed the eunuchs who had assassinated his father. He arrested his brothers and his uncles and imprisoned them.[186] He wrote a letter to his brother Abū Ḥawāl in the

185. Ziyādat Allāh was arrested on his return from Sicily on 19 Jumādā II 290/20 May 903. See Ibn ʿIdhārī, *al-Bayān*, vol. 1, p. 134; and Ibn al-Athīr, *al-Kāmil*, vol. 6, p. 103.

186. There is no doubt that Ziyādat Allāh was implicated in the murder of his father. See Ibn ʿIdhārī, *al-Bayān*, vol. 1, p. 134; Ibn al-Athīr, *al-Kāmil*, vol. 6, p. 103; al-Nuwayrī, *Nihāya*, vol. 24, p. 144 (tr. *Berbères*, vol. 1, p. 439); Abū Bakr b. ʿAbd Allāh Ibn al-Dawādārī, *Kanz al-durar*

name of his father, instructing him to return to him to consolidate his position and gather troop reinforcements. He impressed on him to come urgently. Ziyādat Allāh feared his status.[187] He sent the letter with a messenger and urged him to hurry. He also wrote to the leaders of the armies announcing the death of his father and called for the arrest of Abū Ḥawāl if he failed to return. He ordered the messenger to hand over (the instructions) to them if he saw that he tarried. When Abū Ḥawāl received the letter, it agreed with his wishes. He did not like to stay, because he knew that he could not resist Abū ʿAbd Allāh and he saw his victory over him. He immediately summoned the leaders of the army, read out to them the letter and ordered them to prepare to leave. The people were happy with this order for they would return to their localities. Therefore, they hurried towards him and he departed [with them].

When (Abū Ḥawāl) arrived at Billizma, he came to know about the assassination of his father. It was Ḥayy b. Tamīm who gave him the news and said, 'If you wish to stay with us we shall protect you and defend you.'

(Abū Ḥawāl) refused and continued his journey. As he approached Bāghāya he was met by Ṣāliḥ b. al-Rūḥānī[188] at the head of troops who arrested him and shackled him. He dispatched him with the courier and took charge of the army, producing the letter of Ziyādat Allāh to this effect. He departed with (the army) and arrived in Tunis. Ziyādat Allāh executed his brother Abū Ḥawāl, his paternal uncles and his brothers in the month of Ramaḍān 290/July-August 903.[189] This was an act of God for His friends, and His will to put an end to the dynasty

---

wa-jāmiʿ al-ghurar, vol. 6, ed. Ṣalāḥ al-Dīn al-Munajjid (Cairo, 1961), pp. 39–40; and Ibn al-Khaṭīb, *Aʿmāl*, p. 37.

187. Ziyādat Allāh's decision, motivated probably by fear of a possible rebellion of his brother with the army, prevented Abū Ḥawāl from giving a decisive battle to Abū ʿAbd Allāh.

188. He is elsewhere named Futūḥ al-Rūmī, a commander dispatched by Ziyādat Allāh with fifty mounted troops, bearing instructions for Abū Ḥawāl to return. See Ibn ʿIdhārī, *al-Bayān*, vol. 1, p. 136, note 2 (variant MS); and al-Nuwayrī, *Nihāya*, vol. 24, p. 145 (tr. *Berbères*, vol. 1, p. 440).

189. The execution of twenty-nine members of his family took place on 3 Ramaḍān at Jazīrat al-Kurāth, twelve miles to the north of Tunis. See Ibn ʿIdhārī, *al-Bayān*, vol. 1. p. 135; al-Nuwayrī, *Nihāya*, vol. 24, p. 145 (tr. *Berbères*, vol. 1, p. 440); Ibn al-Khaṭīb, *Aʿmāl*, p. 38.

of the unjust. They killed each other. This weakened them and their power waned.

Abū al-ʿAbbās was interested in the science of rendering legal opinions. He adhered to the teachings and the school of Abū Ḥanīfa. He professed the doctrine of the created Qur'an. The commonalty (*ʿāmma*)[190] were hostile to him for this reason. When Ziyādat Allāh assumed power, he sought to gain popularity with them, so he dismissed the Ḥanafī *qāḍī* al-Ṣadīnī[191] from the judgeship and appointed in his place Ḥimās b. Marwān[192] who adhered to the school of Mālik. (Ziyādat Allāh) was designated as an adherent of the sunna. His banners were embroidered with the inscription: 'Triumph comes from God to the emir Ziyādat Allāh b. ʿAbd Allāh, who observes the sunna of the Messenger of God,' in spite of his debauchery, insolence, corruption and committing crimes against his father. Ordinary people paid no attention to that, nor did they heed him. It was divulged about him that he drank grape wine, which was unknown before him in Ifrīqiya. He introduced singing and musical instruments, and gathered pleasure-seekers, sissies and jesters. He would not desist from drinking wine and was almost always to be seen intoxicated. He preferred boon companions who slapped each other in front of him, making obscene remarks in his presence, and used

---

190. The term *ʿāmma* here also refers to Mālikī jurists.

191. Muḥammad b. Aswad b. Shuʿayb al-Ṣadīnī (d. 304/916–917), from the Berber tribe of Ṣadīna, was appointed *qāḍī* by Ibrāhīm b. Aḥmad before his departure for Sicily. He was maintained in his functions by his successor Abū al-ʿAbbās ʿAbd Allāh. The latter granted him the offices of *qāḍī* and governor of al-Qayrawān and appointed him also to watch over the conduct of government agents and tax collectors. See al-Nuwayrī, *Nihāya*, vol. 24, p. 144 (tr. *Berbères*, vol. 1, p. 439); al-Khushanī, *ʿUlamāʾ Ifrīqiya*, pp. 251–252; ʿIyāḍ, *Madārik*, pp. 285, 344, 390, 411; and Ibn ʿIdhārī, *al-Bayān*, vol. 1, p. 175.

192. On Abū al-Qāsim Ḥimās b. Marwān b. Simāk al-Hamdānī see al-Khushanī, *ʿUlamāʾ Ifrīqiya*, pp. 207, 309; al-Mālikī, *Riyāḍ al-nufūs*, vol. 1, pp. 118–122; ʿIyāḍ, *Madārik*, pp. 340–350; Ibn Nājī, *Maʿālim*, vol. 2, pp. 320–330; and Ibn ʿIdhārī, *al-Bayān*, vol. 1, p. 136. In a letter dispatched to al-Qayrawān announcing the dismissal of al-Ṣadīnī and appointment of his successor, Ziyādat Allāh states: 'I have dismissed this rude, stupid man, this heretic (*mubtadiʿ*) and deviator, who acts as your judge, and I appoint Ḥimās b. Marwān to the judgeship. He is compassionate, forbearing, pious and learned in the Book and the sunna.' See ʿIyāḍ, *Madārik*, p. 344; Ibn Nājī, *Maʿālim*, vol. 2, p. 327; and al-Nuwayrī, *Nihāya*, vol. 24, p. 145 (tr. *Berbères*, vol. 1, p. 440).

inappropriate speech and committed such acts. They used to take tied, inflated bladders of sheep for him and he placed them under his rug. Then as some eminent person of his men entered and sat down, they would clatter under him and he would laugh, and so would his companions in many [situations of] being foolish, jest, insolence and debauchery.[193] Abū ʿAbd Allāh would get reports about him and come to know of this. His men would talk about it. He would say, 'Rejoice, for this man will be the last one to fight you.'

Then Ziyādat Allāh moved from Tunis to Raqqāda and settled there. His grandfather, Ibrāhīm b. Aḥmad, had moved from (Raqqāda) when the people of Ifrīqiya rebelled against him, and resisted in Tunis. He advanced against them, defeated them, conquered (the town) and stayed there. Ziyādat Allāh considered (Tunis) to be isolated from al-Qayrawān, and he feared lest Abū ʿAbd Allāh reach Raqqāda and seize it. Therefore, he set out for (Raqqāda) and settled there. He constructed the ramparts of this town, for it did not have any ramparts in the days of Ibrāhīm b. Aḥmad. It was surrounded only by a moat and gates.[194]

17

Al-Mahdī's emigration from his residence in the east, and his arrival in Sijilmāsa.

Then the imamate came to al-Mahdī, and the imam before him who had designated him to succeed him died.[195] He used to say to him,

---

193. Cf. Muḥammad Ibn Shākir al-Kutubī, *Fawāt al-wafayāt wa-al-dhayl ʿalayhā*, ed. Iḥsān ʿAbbās (Beirut, 1973–1974), vol. 2, pp. 34–35; Ṣalāḥ al-Dīn Khalīl b. Aybak al-Ṣafadī, *al-Wāfī bi-al-wafayāt*, vol. 15 ed. B. Radtke (Wiesbaden, 1979), pp. 20–21.

194. On the disturbances of the year 280/893 which led Ibrāhīm b. Aḥmad to leave Raqqāda and settle in Tunis, see Ibn ʿIdhārī, *al-Bayān*, vol. 1, pp. 123–124; and al-Nuwayrī, *Nihāya*, vol. 24, p. 132–133 (tr. *Berbères*, vol. 1, pp. 428–429). This rebellion, which rattled the Aghlabids, coincided with the arrival of Abū ʿAbd Allāh in Ifrīqiya. The same year the emir constructed a moat around the town and erected iron gates. See Marçais, *L'architecture musulmane*, pp. 27–28.

195. It is worth noting that al-Nuʿmān does not reveal the name of the concealed imam or his relation to al-Mahdī.

'After my death you shall emigrate far away and encounter a severe ordeal.' So when God took him to Himself, and al-Mahdī assumed the imamate after him, rumours about him spread widely. Signs of his advent began to appear and prophecies concerning him became clear to everyone as about to be fulfilled. Al-Mahdī feared for his life from the Abbasids.[196] In this connection he had many adventures which would be too long to narrate and explain, and many ordeals as predicted to him by his predecessor. He himself left accompanied by his son, the imam who succeeded him, who at the time was a child, while al-Mahdī himself was a young man in the plenitude of his age,[197] until he reached Egypt.[198] He was expecting to proceed to the Yemen,[199] where one of his *dāʿīs* had preceded him, but (the *dāʿī*'s) resolve became corrupted. He went to see Abū al-Qāsim who was in charge of the *daʿwa* in the Yemen and sought to mislead him, but found him firm in his conviction. So he left him and went to ʿAlī b. al-Faḍl, the companion of (Abū al-Qāsim) who was residing in a district of the Yemen. He succeeded in winning him over and corrupted him. It was said at that time regarding this: 'An ʿIrāqī approached an ʿIrāqī seeking to beguile him. He was unable to do so. Then he approached a Yemenite and beguiled him.'

ʿAlī b. al-Faḍl renounced the cause of God and His friends, committed unlawful deeds, denied the exoteric and invited people to

---

196. By lavishing gifts upon the governors of Salamiya, al-Mahdī gained their support and escaped being hunted by the Abbasids. See al-Yamānī, *Sīrat al-Ḥājib Jaʿfar*, pp. 108–109 (tr. Ivanow, *Rise*, pp. 186–188).

197. At the time of his his departure from Salamiya in 289/902, al-Mahdī was twenty-eight or twenty-nine years old. He was born in 259/873 or 260/874. See Idrīs ʿImād al-Dīn, *ʿUyūn al-akhbār*, ed. Ghālib, vol. 5, p. 89. On al-Mahdī's son, see note 206 below.

198. After his departure from Salamiya, al-Mahdī stayed briefly in Damascus. Then he passed through Tiberias, without entering the town. He proceeded to al-Ramla, whose governor was his follower. He stayed in al-Ramla, and from there proceeded to Egypt. See al-Yamānī, *Sīrat al-Ḥājib Jaʿfar*, pp. 111–113 (tr. Ivanow, *Rise*, pp. 190–193). In any case, al-Mahdī arrived in Egypt only after the failure of the Qarmatian insurrection and the capture of its chief by the Abbasids in 291/904.

199. Ever since his departure from Salamiya, al-Mahdī had given the impression that he was proceeding to the Yemen. See al-Yamānī, *Sīrat al-Ḥājib Jaʿfar*, pp. 110–111, 114 (tr. Ivanow, *Rise*, pp. 189–190, 195); al-Nuwayrī, *Nihāya*, p. 42; Shainool Jiwa, 'The Initial Destination of the Fatimid Caliphate: the Yemen or the Maghrib?' *British Society for Middle Eastern Studies Bulletin*, 13 (1986), pp. 15–26.

depravity.[200] When this became known, the man who had corrupted him disowned him, as happened with the cursed Devil as God says about him: '*Remember when he said to man, "Deny God", but when (man) denied God, (the evil one) said, "I am free of thee. I do fear God, the Lord of the worlds"*' (59:16). ('Alī b. al-Faḍl) waged war against Abū al-Qāsim. He had adventures which would be too long to relate.[201] He died in this state of sin and error. We seek refuge with God from disappointment, error and loss!

These events[202] came to the knowledge of the imam, who did not wish to proceed to the Yemen under these circumstances. He continued to reside in Egypt disguised as a merchant. Meanwhile, the ruler of Egypt[203] and the governor[204] there received letters from Baghdad, giving his description, with orders to look for him and arrest him. One of the members of the entourage of this governor was a faithful devotee [of al-Mahdī].[205] He hastened to inform al-Mahdī, advised him to hide, and intervened subtly on his behalf until he left Egypt

---

200. On the dissension of 'Alī b. al-Faḍl from the *da'wa* see Charles L. Geddes, 'The Apostasy of 'Alī b. al-Faḍl', in R. L. Bidwell and G. R. Smith ed., *Arabian and Islamic Studies: Articles Presented to R. B. Serjeant* (London, 1983), pp. 80–85.

201. These events are related in greater detail in Yemenite sources. See al-Ḥammādī, *Kashf*, pp. 35ff.; Kay, *Yaman*, Arabic text of al-Janadī, *Kitāb al-Sulūk*, pp. 146–147 (tr. pp. 201–203); and al-Hamdānī, *al-Ṣulayḥiyyūn*, pp. 41–48.

202. The term 'events' here applies only to the period when Fīrūz was in the Yemen with 'Alī b. al-Faḍl, while al-Mahdī was still in Egypt (where he stayed probably until the middle of the year 292/905). It does not cover 'Alī b. al-Faḍl publicly repudiating his allegiance to the Fatimid caliph, his war with Ibn Ḥawshab, and his death. These events occurred after the advent of al-Mahdī in Ifrīqiya in 297/910.

203. The Abbasid general Muḥammad b. Sulaymān al-Kātib who took al-Fusṭāṭ in Ṣafar 292/January 905 and put an end to Ṭūlūnid rule. See Ibn al-Athīr, *al-Kāmil*, vol. 6, pp. 110–111; Abū al-Maḥāsin Ibn Taghrī Birdī, *al-Nujūm al-zāhira fī mulūk Miṣr wa-al-Qāhira* (Cairo, n.d.), vol. 3, p. 144; and 'Arīb b. Sa'd al-Qurṭubī, *Ṣilat Ta'rīkh al-Ṭabarī*, ed. M. J. de Goeje (Leiden, 1897), pp. 1–8. According to 'Arīb, p. 51, Muḥammad b. Sulaymān arrested al-Mahdī, confiscated his money and later released him.

204 The governor at that time, 'Īsā al-Nūsharī, attempted to arrest al-Mahdī during his stay in Egypt. See Ibn al-Athīr, *al-Kāmil*, vol. 6, pp. 129, 137; al-Maqrīzī, *Itti'āẓ*, vol. 1, pp. 27, 60–61; *al-Muqaffā*, pp. 78, 83–84; and al-Nuwayrī, *Nihāya*, vol. 24, pp. 151–152 (tr. *Berbères*, vol. 1, pp. 445–446). On him see also note 332 below.

205. The devotee in question is named Ibn 'Ayyāsh in al-Yamānī, *Sīrat al-Ḥājib Ja'far*, p. 113 (tr. Ivanow, *Rise*, p. 194).

with his son al-Qā'im[206] and several of his slaves, carrying with him money in several loads. He bought goods there and put the money with the bales of goods, and set out on his way with a caravan in the guise of a merchant. When he arrived at al-Ṭāḥūna,[207] brigands attacked the caravan and robbed many travellers. In this some of al-Mahdī's belongings were lost. The most important was the loss of books of wisdom of the imams. Then when al-Qā'im bi-amr Allāh conducted his first expedition to Egypt, he forced those who had attacked and robbed the caravan to return what they had plundered, thus recovering the same books. About this al-Mahdī used to say, 'Even if this expedition had been undertaken only to recover the books, it would have been a great victory.' He felt wonderful joy at the return of these books.

On the day of this raid, Abū al-'Abbās Muḥammad b. Aḥmad b. Zakariyā,[208] brother of Abū 'Abd Allāh, who was accompanying al-Mahdī was wounded. He was among those who departed with al-Mahdī. When the caravan reached the city of Tripoli, (al-Mahdī) dispersed those who were with him and made the people think that they were merchants travelling in company. He dispatched Abū al-'Abbās to al-Qayrawān, together with some of what he had with him with orders to take it to Kutāma territory to which he was himself intending to go. There were with him some Kutāma tribesmen who had been sent to him before.[209] When Abū al-'Abbās arrived in al-Qayrawān, Ziyādat Allāh had already received letters asking to look for al-Mahdī, giving his description and ordering his arrest, because he had escaped search and left Egypt. Accordingly, Ziyādat Allāh gave orders to enquire about al-Mahdī. Some of those who were

206. On al-Qā'im see al-Maqrīzī, *al-Muqaffā*, pp. 113–129; Sobernheim, 'al-Ḳā'im', *EI*, vol. 4, p. 643; and Farhat Dachraoui, 'al-Ḳā'im bi-amr Allāh', *EI*², vol. 4, pp. 458–460.

207. A stopping place in the territory of the Banū Mudlij, four stages west of Alexandria. See al-Idrīsī, *Nuzha*, p. 137 (tr. p. 164).

208. On Abū al-'Abbās see also Ibn al-Haytham, *al-Munāẓarāt*, index; and al-Maqrīzī, *al-Muqaffā*, pp. 36–38.

209. Abū 'Abd Allāh sent Kutāma tribesmen to al-Mahdī in Salamiya to announce his conquest of Mīla in 289/902, and to keep him informed of the progress of the *da'wa* in the Maghrib. See Ibn al-Athīr, *al-Kāmil*, vol. 6, p. 129; al-Maqrīzī, *Itti'āẓ*, vol. 1, p. 60; and Ibn Khaldūn, *al-'Ibar*, vol. 4, p. 70 (tr. *Berbères*, vol. 2, p. 515).

in the caravan with (al-Mahdī) reported that he had remained in Tripoli and mentioned that Abū al-ʿAbbās was one of his associates. (Abū al-ʿAbbās) was arrested and pressed to confess, but he denied everything, affirming that he was only a merchant. Nevertheless he was imprisoned. This news reached al Mahdī while he was in Tripoli. He chanced upon a caravan leaving for Qasṭīliya, so he left with it. Meanwhile, the governor of Tripoli received Ziyādat Allāh's letter containing (al-Mahdī's) description and orders to search for him. However, al-Mahdī had gained the sympathy of the governor and given him gifts. The governor, therefore, replied that he had already left his jurisdiction and was heading for the region of Qasṭīliya.

Al-Mahdī arrived in Qasṭīliya and spent there a feast day. There were in the caravan with al-Mahdī people from the lands of the Maghrib, al-Zāb and Sijilmāsa. Al-Mahdī's intention was to join Abū ʿAbd Allāh. However, when he heard that Abū ʿAbd Allāh's brother had been arrested and that it was known that he was one of his associates, he feared that if he proceeded to join Abū ʿAbd Allāh it would confirm these suspicions and that (Abū al-ʿAbbās) would be put to death. Hence, he abandoned his intention of joining Abū ʿAbd Allāh and travelled to Sijilmāsa.[210] Having attended the *ʿīd* prayers in Qasṭīliya,[211] (al-Mahdī) called one of his slaves and said to him, 'Alas, by God, I have a presentiment that I am being searched for. Go to the leader of the caravan, greet him on my behalf and tell him that we have accomplished our *ʿīd* prayers. We are travelling and the more distance we cover the better, and if he wishes to give the signal to depart at once, then let him do so.'

Al-Mahdī had been gracious towards (the leader of the caravan), bestowing presents and gifts upon him. When his messenger reached him, he said, 'By God, this will be extremely arduous for

---

210. Cf. al-Qāḍī al-Nuʿmān, *Sharḥ al-akhbār*, (*juz*ʾ 15), vol. 3, p. 430. Apart from al-Mahdī's concern for the personal safety of Abū al-ʿAbbās, it is also likely that he did not consider Abū ʿAbd Allāh's position to be strong enough, in spite of his initial success. The fortresses around Kutāma territory, including Billizma, Bāghāya and Ṭubna, had not yet been subdued and the Aghlabid army was still intact.

211. Qasṭīliya here refers to Tūzar, the administrative centre of the district of Qasṭīliya. See al-Yamānī, *Sīrat al-Ḥājib Jaʿfar*, p. 116 (tr. Ivanow, *Rise*, p. 198), and note 63 above.

the travellers, but I feel that I cannot refuse the request of Abū Muḥammad.'

He beat the drum [signalling departure] and set out with the caravan. Next day the courier from Ziyādat Allāh came to the governor of Qasṭīliya with orders to search for al-Mahdī. It so happened that he had already left his jurisdiction. God protected him from them, diverting their efforts to harm him, because He willed to accomplish his cause and achieve what was written in his destiny.

He travelled on until he reached Sijilmāsa, where he stayed. Throughout the course of his journey, wherever he alighted or whichever city he entered, all eyes could see al-Mahdī and anyone with discernment and clairvoyance who saw him would say of him, 'By God, he is no merchant. Surely, he must be a king or a prince.' Many inhabitants of Sijilmāsa who saw him used to say the same thing about him. What indicated this was his superiority to those who accompanied him or came to see him, and the dignity and veneration which God had put into the eyes of those who saw him. At that time the ruler of Sijilmāsa was al-Yasaʿ b. Midrār. Al-Mahdī bestowed upon him gifts and presents. Therefore, he paid him due respect and reverence until when he received the letter sent by Ziyādat Allāh, who had learnt that (al-Mahdī) had arrived there, informing him that he was the person in whose favour Abū ʿAbd Allāh was preaching. This changed the ruler's attitude towards him. We shall narrate this in due course, God willing.

18

The conquest of the town of Saṭīf.

The ruler of the town of Saṭīf was ʿAlī b. Ḥafṣ, known as Ibn ʿUslūja after his mother. He was among the few brave men without equal in terms of bravery and fame in the entire region. His brother, Abū Ḥabīb,[212] was like him or almost like him. He was among those who denounced Abū ʿAbd Allāh. He had devised a stratagem to seize him

212. He is referred to thus only by his *kunya* in Ibn Khaldūn, *al-ʿIbar*, vol. 4, p. 72 (tr. *Berbères*, vol. 2, p. 516).

and twice participated in Abū Ḥawāl's expeditions against him. We have already related his account. He did everything he could and made every effort in this direction.

Now when Abū ʿAbd Allāh seized the town of Mīla, and established his authority over the Kutāma in its environs, he assembled troops from among them and advanced upon Saṭīf and attacked it with the army. ʿAlī b. ʿUslūja maintained close relations with many of the Kutāma tribesmen near to him. Some of their chiefs and protectors had found refuge with him. He fought Abū ʿAbd Allāh. He would set out with them as well as the inhabitants of Saṭīf to attack him. (ʿAlī b. ʿUslūja) inflicted such calamity as was unprecedented. It is related that in battle he killed thirteen horsemen in a single day, each with a single blow [of the sword]. When Abū ʿAbd Allāh witnessed this he said, 'This is the cursed one about whom God says, '*And when you exert your strong hand, do you do it cruelly, without restraint*?' (26:130).

Abū ʿAbd Allāh besieged Saṭīf for forty days, while (Ibn ʿUslūja) fought him coming out of the town. Then Abū ʿAbd Allāh returned to Īkjān where he remained for a month, gathering the followers and mobilising troops in large numbers. He then advanced upon Saṭīf with innumerable troops and surrounded the town. ʿAlī b. ʿUslūja came out with his troops to fight him. He fought (Abū ʿAbd Allāh) just like he did the first time coming forth from the town until (Abū ʿAbd Allāh) defeated him. (Ibn ʿUslūja) sought refuge inside the citadel. Both he and his brother Abū Ḥabīb died within a few days. After their death, authority in Saṭīf collapsed.[213]

Among the Kutāma tribesmen who had emigrated (to Saṭīf) was Dāwūd b. Ḥubāsa al-Lahīṣī. He was a knight and eminent chief of the Lahīṣa. He was handsome, virtuous and intelligent. Afterwards he became one of the *dāʿīs*. He restored the situation in Saṭīf. His brothers, who were with Abū ʿAbd Allāh, talked to (Dāwūd) to ask for guarantee of safety. He replied, 'If I can seek guarantee for the safety of all the inhabitants, I will do so.'

Abū ʿAbd Allāh was informed about this, and he granted him safety. (Dāwūd) came out to (Abū ʿAbd Allāh) and obtained protection

213. The fall of Saṭīf took place towards the end of 291/904. See Talbi, *L'émirat aghlabide*, pp. 648ff.

for the inhabitants of Saṭīf from him, excepting those who according to him deserved to die. (Dāwūd) then returned to them and they opened the gates of the town. The followers entered the town and those who deserved to die therein were executed. The walls of the town were demolished.[214] The family of ʿAlī b. ʿUslūja had buried him and his brother when they died but concealed their graves, fearing that if they were discovered they would be exhumed and crucified because the followers hated these two men for what they had done to them. Abū ʿAbd Allāh returned to Īkjān with all the troops, appointing a governor for the town of Saṭīf.

19

Ziyādat Allāh's dispatching Ibrāhīm b. Ḥabashī to Kutāma territory to fight Abū ʿAbd Allāh and his defeat.

Ziyādat Allāh came to know about Abū ʿAbd Allāh's exploits, his victory over the Kutāma, their rallying together to him, and his conquest of the towns of Mīla and Saṭīf. Some Kutāma who feared for their life and whose protectors had been killed emigrated to him. They incited him and frightened him saying that if he did not deal quickly with Abū ʿAbd Allāh, his power would grow and triumph. So (Ziyādat Allāh) began to mobilise troops and gave gifts abundantly. A large number of troops gathered under him. He entrusted their command to Ibrāhīm b. Ḥabashī[215] who was a member of his family. However, (Ibrāhīm b. Ḥabashī) was not an experienced warrior or someone who would inflict harm. He was mostly meek. (Ziyādat Allāh) dispatched the army with him and gathered troops numbering 40,000 men, among them cavalry and infantry. Such numerous and powerful army of the Aghlabids was unprecedented since their coming to Ifrīqiya.[216] He dispatched with him several loads of money,

---

214. According to al-Bakrī, *al-Masālik*, p. 76 (tr. p. 155), the Kutāma destroyed this ancient wall because the Arab conquerors had captured Saṭīf from them and forced them to pay tax every time they wanted to enter the town.

215. He is Ibrāhīm b. Ḥabashī b. ʿUmar al-Tamīmī. On him see Ibn ʿIdhārī, *al-Bayān*, vol. 1, pp. 137–138.

216. Such large number of troop involvement in the expedition is confirmed in other sources.

robes of honour and weapons The expedition was reinforced by all his defenders, the Kutāma who had sought refuge with him and the people of al-Zāb. He instructed Ibn Ḥabashī to lavish gifts upon the tribes on his way and win over their chiefs by presenting them the loads and the robes of honour.

The inhabitants of the regions advised him not to approach the Kutāma from the same region as Abū Ḥawāl had done. Thus, (Ibn Ḥabashī) proceeded to Quṣṭanṭīna (Constantine),[217] which is an ancient city on a rugged mountain on the edge of Kutāma territory. Here he took up his quarters. The Kutāma of the outskirts of the city submitted to him. He fought those of them near the city who were unyielding towards him and killed them. The Kutāma were overwhelmed by their attack, their large numbers and their weaponry. The distance between the place where they camped and Īkjān, where Abū ʿAbd Allāh stayed, was less than two stages. However, he was at the edge of Kutāma territory, so Abū ʿAbd Allāh did not proceed against him. Ibn Ḥabashī remained in Quṣṭanṭīna for six months.[218]

Meanwhile, Shayb b. Abī al-Shaddād[219] had the command of his army at Ṭubna.[220] Ziyādat Allāh ordered him to proceed towards Ibn Ḥabashī. (Shayb) came to him with his army. It is related that about 100,000 horsemen and foot-soldiers gathered under his command at Quṣṭanṭīna. Now when (Ibn Ḥabashī) saw Abū ʿAbd Allāh holding back, he advanced upon him with all the armies that were with him,

---

See Ibn al-Athīr, *al-Kāmil*, vol. 6. p. 130; al-Maqrīzī, *Ittiʿāẓ*, vol. 1, p. 62; Ibn Khaldūn, *al-ʿIbar*, vol. 4, p. 72 (tr. *Berbères*, vol. 2, p. 517); and Ibn ʿIdhārī, *al-Bayān*, vol. 1, p. 137, note 1.

217. On Quṣṭanṭīna, impregnable fortress-city, see Georges Yver, 'Ḳuṣṭanṭīna', *EI*², vol. 5, pp. 530–532; al-Bakrī, *al-Masālik*, p. 63 (tr. pp. 131–132); and al-Idrīsī, *Nuzha*, pp. 94–96 (tr. pp. 110–113).

218. Ibn Ḥabashī's prolonged stay in Quṣṭanṭīna can be explained by the difficulties which he had to face in attacking Īkjān in the middle of winter. This tactical error allowed Abū ʿAbd Allāh enough time to gather his forces and prepare for battle.

219. He is referred to as Shabīb b. Abī al-Shaddād al-Qammūdī in Ibn ʿIdhārī, *al-Bayān*, vol. 1, p. 140.

220. Ṭubna, ancient Thubunae, was the capital of al-Zāb and residence of the governors. See Georges Yver, 'Tobna', *EI*, vol. 8, p. 805; M. Côte, 'Ṭubna', *EI*², vol. 10, p. 580; Ibn Ḥawqal, *Ṣūrat al-arḍ*, p. 85; al-Bakrī, *al-Masālik*, pp. 50–51 (tr. pp. 108–110); and al-Idrīsī, *Nuzha*, p. 93 (tr. p. 109). On Abū ʿAbd Allāh's conquest of Ṭubna see below pp. 131ff.

until he reached Kabūna[221] in the territory of the Ijjāna. Abū ʿAbd Allāh sent a detachment of horsemen, whom he had picked and chosen, to gather information about Ibn Ḥabashī's encampment, where he had halted and where he was proceeding. The detachment of horsemen came across him at Kabūna. When the horsemen came into his view, (Ibn Ḥabashī) proceeded towards them by himself, acting like someone ignorant of warfare. He had not set up camp, nor had anyone of his companions. The supplies were still on the backs of the pack animals and camels when fighting broke out. The group whom they encountered were the best horsemen of the Kutāma. There was battle between them. They fought a fierce battle while the companions of Ibn Ḥabashī had not yet alighted, nor did they have a camp-site. Abū ʿAbd Allāh came to know of the battle, so he advanced with the armies towards them. Ibn Ḥabashī and his companions were routed. His draught-horse was hamstrung and he was injured. He was rescued only by his steed. Defeat was complete. They abandoned all the supplies and wealth and took the road to Bāghāya. The followers pursued them all that day and the following day, killing some of them and taking their property as booty. Only God reckons the number of them killed. Everybody seized incalculable booty from their possessions, including loads of property, robes and sheep.[222]

Ibn Ḥabashī and those who escaped with him arrived in Bāghāya. He wrote a letter to Ziyādat Allāh in his hand, stating therein, 'I am writing to the emir, may God prolong his life, from the town of Bāghāya, at a time when the victorious army has been defeated. Only a small group of it was saved. All the possessions, weapons and other supplies which I had with me are lost. Most of the soldiers of the victorious army have been slain.' He began to inform in his letter of what had happened. Every time he mentioned his army, he would say 'the victorious army', which shows his weakness and foolishness. Then, without waiting for Ziyādat Allāh's reply, he returned to Ifrīqiya with the remnants of those of its inhabitants who remained with him. All those who survived returned to their own regions. Shayb returned to

221. Ibn al-Athīr, *al-Kāmil*, vol. 6, p. 130, gives Karma; Ibn ʿIdhārī, *al-Bayān*, vol. 1, p. 138, gives Kaynūna and a variant reading Kabūna.

222. The battle took place probably in Rajab 292/May-June 905. See Talbi, *L'émirat aghlabide*, p. 651.

Ṭubna with the remaining soldiers. Ifrīqiya became disturbed and the matter of Abū ʿAbd Allāh staggered its people. The defeated remnant who returned there related to them what they had seen with their own eyes and what they had experienced.

Abū ʿAbd Allāh wrote to al-Mahdī at Sijilmāsa announcing the victory which God had granted him, as well as the riches and spoils which he had taken. He sent to him some of the booty with Kutāma tribesmen, his emissaries. This was the first victory for al-Mahdī. It was through his blessing and the blessing of the days of his emigration. This pleased him and he praised God for it.

20

The conquest of the town of Ṭubna.

Then Abū ʿAbd Allāh called the people to arms and they rallied around him. This is how he also enlisted volunteers, by calling to arms.[223] He advanced with a large number of troops upon Ṭubna. Previously he had attacked the town with army after army. Then he arrived there with all the armies and besieged the town from all sides. The inhabitants of the town saw that they were helpless, and unable to come out and attack him. They, therefore, barricaded themselves. Its governor at that time was Ḥasan b. Aḥmad b. Nāfidh, known by his *kunya* of Abū al-Muqāriʿ.[224] In the town the commander of the garrison was Shayb b. Abī al-Shaddād, called Shayb junior (Shayb al-Ṣaghīr), and Fatḥ b. Yaḥyā, commander of troops of his household and troops from the Berber tribes. He had been injured with a penetrating blow which weakened him. Muḥammad b. Qurhub,[225] superintendent of

223. Ibn ʿIdhārī, *al-Bayān*, vol. 1, p. 138, gives details of this procedure adopted by Abū ʿAbd Allāh.

224. He was formerly chamberlain (*ḥājib*) of Ziyādat Allāh. After the mutiny of his two commanders Mudlij b. Zakariyā and Aḥmad b. Masrūr al-Khāl, at the beginning of the year 293/906, the emir reinforced Ṭubna and entrusted its command to Abū al-Muqāriʿ together with Shayb (Shabīb) b. Abī Shaddād al-Qammūdī and Khafāja al-ʿAbshī (al-ʿAbsī) with orders to launch incursions against the Kutāma. See Ibn ʿIdhārī, *al-Bayān*, vol. 1, pp. 139–140.

225. He was a member of the Qurhub family which served the Aghlabids in Ifrīqiya and Sicily.

the intelligence service, and Yaḥyā b. al-Qasrī, superintendent of the pension department (*ʿaṭāʾ*), were inside the town. They barricaded themselves in the town, ascended the wall and fought from there. The followers moved against them from every side and advanced upon them with the help of a siege tower (*dabbāba*),[226] and breached one of the towers of the surrounding wall which collapsed. The followers launched an assault. All the troops, fighters and commanders fled and took cover inside an old fortified citadel built in stone inside the town. The followers took possession of the town whose inhabitants were mostly merchants.[227] Abū ʿAbd Allāh granted them safety and they were touched only by those troops who were disorderly.

Those who had sought refuge in the citadel barricaded themselves and ascended it and pursued fighting against (Abū ʿAbd Allāh). Abū al-Muqāriʿ ordered a mangonel (*manjanīq*)[228] which was there to be deployed. When it was set up and they were about to use it, its beam (*sahm*) broke. They looked at something to repair it with but they could not find it, so they skinned a dead pack animal and cut a strip of leather from it and tied the beam with it. Then they went to shoot with it. Then its axle (*khinzīra*) broke. Thereupon Abū al-Muqāriʿ said, 'Leave it! This is the decree of God which cannot be rejected.'

Shayb, commander of the army, said to him, 'O Abū al-Qāsim, what stratagem can be used?'

Abū al-Muqāriʿ asked him, 'What do you think?'

He replied, 'I think we should find a way to escape by night. Some people escaped from Mīla and they were saved.'

He said, 'Woe to you! We are not in the same situation as the people of Mīla. We are in the middle of a town which has already been taken by our enemy and surrounded by them from all sides. The nearest inhabited place to us is Bāghāya which is at a distance of three days' journey. Even if we escape from the town, we shall not escape from

---

226. A siege tower filled with armed troops placed near city walls. See Reinhart Dozy, *Supplément aux dictionnaires arabes* (Leiden-Paris, 1967), vol. 1, p. 421.

227. In Ibn ʿIdhārī, *al-Bayān*, vol. 1, pp. 141–142, the conquest of Ṭubna is mentioned under the year 293/906.

228. A stone-throwing siege-engine. See Donald R. Hill, 'Mandjanīḳ,' *EI²*, vol. 6, pp. 405–406. For a detailed description of siege-engines, see Ibn Aranbughā al-Zaradkāsh, *al-Anīq fī al-manājanīq*, ed. Iḥsān Hindī (Aleppo, 1985).

what surrounds it. If we escape and are pursued, we shall be caught. Giving up hope of escape from all this is more reasonable.'

He said, 'We can surrender to them without fighting them, because fighting would turn them and enrage them against us; or we can throw ourselves at their mercy. Then maybe they will spare us.'

Abū al-Muqāri' said, 'This will hasten death.'

Shayb said, 'Then what stratagem do you have?'

He replied, 'We shall ask to be granted safety, while they see us in a defensive position. Perhaps they will consider granting safety better for them than besieging [us].'

He said, 'Then do so!'

Abū al-Muqāri' cried out asking for safety. Abū Zākī, who was face to face with him, said, 'You have safety.'

Abū al-Muqāri' asked him, 'Who are you?'

He replied, 'I am Abū Zākī.'

He asked, 'Is this guarantee of safety from you or from the master?'

He replied, 'It is from me.'

He said, 'We shall only surrender if the master grants us safety.'

Abū Zākī said, 'If he does not do so, what will you do?'

He replied, 'It will be as the poet says:

He established his foot in the swamp of death
And said to (the foot), 'Beneath your sole is the gathering.'[229]

He asked, 'Is that so?'

He replied, 'Yes! We have no rest in hastening death; rather, noble dying after exerting effort is better.'

Abū Zākī went to Abū 'Abd Allāh and informed him what had happened. (Abū 'Abd Allāh) told him, 'Grant them safety.'

Abū Zākī went and informed (Abū al-Muqāri') to this effect, and he and those who were with him descended. He was attired and dressed. He came to Abū 'Abd Allāh who was in a tent (*fāza*). He greeted him

---

229. The lines are from Abū Tammām's elegy on Muḥammad b. Ḥumayd (d. 214/829), the Abbasid caliph al-Ma'mūn's commander, who was killed in an engagement with the rebel Bābak al-Khurramī. See Abū Bakr Muḥammad b. Yaḥyā al-Ṣūlī, *Akhbār Abī Tammām*, ed. Muḥammad 'Abduh 'Azzām et al. (3rd ed., Beirut, 1980), pp. 124–125.

and congratulated him on the victory. Abū ʿAbd Allāh asked him, 'What caused you to prolong this obstinacy and persistence?'

Abū al-Muqāriʿ replied, 'May God prolong your life! What we did benefited us without harming you. We have left behind family and children. We feared that if we surrendered without guarantee of safety for them, they would be made to suffer. Now that is protected on your account.'

He said, 'Indeed.'

He thanked him and invoked prayers. Abū ʿAbd Allāh liked his eloquence and fluency of speech. He instructed Abū Zākī to protect him and his companions. He executed Fatḥ b. Yaḥyā and some of the soldiers who were with him.

Then he appointed Yaḥyā b. Sulaymān governor of Ṭubna and returned with the army to Īkjān. He took Abū al-Muqāriʿ and his companions with him and lodged them in Īkjān. Abū al-Muqāriʿ attained a good status with him. He distinguished him, allowed him proximity and honoured him. He left him free to choose between staying with him or leaving. (Abū al-Muqāriʿ) said, 'I am not the one to withdraw from you. Nor will I enter Ifrīqiya except when you do. How can I choose to be with those from whom fortune has turned away, and leave you when fortune smiles upon you?'

Abū ʿAbd Allāh was pleased with his remark. (Abū al-Muqāriʿ) remained with him in Īkjān until Abū ʿAbd Allāh conquered Ifrīqiya and sent for him to come.

21

The conquest of the town of Billizma.

Abū ʿAbd Allāh made incursions upon Billizma, dispatching his troops there several times. (Its inhabitants) would fight him and repel him. He dispatched his troops to attack them at the time of harvests for three years until they ran out of food. Then he advanced upon them and besieged them. During the siege Ḥayy b. Tamīm[230] died. The

---

230. He was lord of Billizma and a member of the coalition against Abū ʿAbd Allāh. See above, p. 77.

inhabitants of Billizma were in desperation. Among them was a man called Abū ʿAbd Allāh who was originally from Majjāna.[231] He was outspoken, and incited them to revolt and persevere. He would make for them mangonels, stone-hurlers and implements of war. During the prolonged siege which was harsh for them, he descended to Abū ʿAbd Allāh who asked him as to why he was acting thus, and he began to argue before him. Abū ʿAbd Allāh ordered him to be killed and he was executed. This is the way to act with the obstinate agitator in war. If it were not obligatory to fight polytheists and rebels until they are defeated and the one who brings the irrefutable proof wins, there would never be fighting. Nor is it necessary that they be fought and killed until they have been defeated one by one, but the procedure is that they should be invited and pleaded with if the summons (*daʿwa*) has not already reached them. Then if they respond positively [well and good], if not they should be fought.

The inhabitants of Billizma fought a fierce battle and put up stiff resistance. Abū ʿAbd Allāh deployed against them siege towers (*dabbābāt, abrija*), but they burnt these. He could only subjugate them through enormous effort and by forcing them to starvation. He maintained the siege until they ran out of supplies and had eaten up all the animals which they had and eaten their hide. Then when all that was exhausted, they returned to their leather shields. They would cut these, moisten them, cook them and eat them until they were overcome with hunger and were captured. Abū ʿAbd Allāh conquered the town by force and killed the surviving defenders there.[232] He did not harm free women. The troops plundered whatever goods, possessions and other items that they found in the town. Abū ʿAbd Allāh gave orders to destroy its wall, and it was destroyed. Then he returned to Īkjān.

---

231. Majjāna was called Majjānat al-Maṭāḥin and Majjānat al-Maʿādin, because of its millstone (*maṭāḥin*) and mines (*maʿādin*). It was one stage north-west of Marmājanna. See Ibn Ḥawqal, *Ṣūrat al-arḍ*, p. 84; al-Idrīsī, *Nuzha*, p. 118 (tr. p. 138); and al-Bakrī, *al-Masālik*, pp. 49, 145 (tr. pp. 106, 278). On Abū ʿAbd Allāh's battles in the region of Majjāna see below pp. 153ff.

232. Billizma was conquered in 293/906. Abū ʿAbd Allāh entered the town at the end of Dhū al-Ḥijja of the same year. See Ibn ʿIdhārī, *al-Bayān*, vol. 1, p. 141; Ibn al-Athīr, *al-Kāmil*, vol. 6, p. 130; and Ibn Khaldūn, *al-ʿIbar*, vol. 4, p. 72 (tr. *Berbères*, vol. 2, p. 517).

22

The battle of Dār Maluwwal.

Ziyādat Allāh received the news of Abū ʿAbd Allāh's conquest of Ṭubna and Billizma. He was alarmed at this news and began to mobilise the people. He expended money and bestowed gifts to raise an army of 12,000 men, among them cavalry and infantry. He lavished gifts upon them, gave them mounts, and gave robes to their chiefs and commanders. He entrusted their command to Hārūn al-Ṭubnī,[233] whose brother Ziyādat Allāh [al-Ṭubnī] was his governor at Bāghāya. He dispatched (Hārūn) to him, ordering him to secure (Bāghāya). (Hārūn) arrived there and took up his quarters. He sent to Ziyādat Allāh with him loads of riches and robes and ordered him to bestow gifts upon the tribes that he came across. The people became amenable to him and came to him. He lavished gifts upon them. A large number of troops rallied to him at Bāghāya.

It came to (Hārūn's) knowledge that the inhabitants of Dār Maluwwal[234] had submitted to the authority of Abū ʿAbd Allāh. Therefore he advanced upon them with all his forces and killed them, razed its fortress, and withdrew. When (Hārūn) reached Faḥṣ al-Rimāḥ (Plain of Lances), Ghazwiyya was keeping a look-out from the mountain of Billizma. Abū ʿAbd Allāh had sent him at the head of 1,000 horsemen towards Billizma when he learned of Hārūn's presence at Bāghāya. However, Ghazwiyya and his companions were unaware of Hārūn's advance upon Dār Maluwwal. Now when they saw the troops in Faḥṣ al-Rimāḥ, they halted and lined up on horseback. Hārūn and his companions looked at them. They started fleeing, shouting at each other, 'The mountain! The mountain!' They meant thereby the Awrās (Aurès).[235] 'Let us keep our backs

233. On Hārūn al-Ṭubnī and his expedition see Ibn al-Athīr, *al-Kāmil*, vol. 6, p. 130; Ibn Khaldūn, *al-ʿIbar*, vol. 4, p. 72 (tr. *Berbères*, vol. 2, p. 517); and al-Maqrīzī, *Ittiʿāẓ*, vol. 1, p. 62.

234. Dār Maluwwal was situated at one long stage to the east of Ṭubna on the way to Bāghāya. Its old fortress served as an observatory over the whole of the region. See Ibn Ḥawqal, *Ṣūrat al-arḍ*, p. 85; and al-Idrīsī, *Nuzha*, p. 93 (tr. p. 109).

235. The Awrās (Aurès) mountain range in the south-east of Algeria forms part of the eastern Saharan Atlas. See Georges Yver, 'Awrās', *EI*, vol. 1, pp. 519–523, and 'Awrās', *EI*², vol. 1, pp. 770–771.

towards it.[236] If the matter turns against us we shall seek shelter in (the mountain), and if the matter turns to our advantage, we shall pursue the enemy through the length of the plain.' Hardly had they proceeded making their way towards the mountain, when a crier among them called out, 'The town! The town!'

Then every group proceeded towards their town. Ghazwiyya and his companions looked at the rising dust while the troops dispersed. They gave them hot pursuit on horseback and a multitude of them were killed, including Hārūn, commander of the troops. They plundered everything which they had and returned to Abū 'Abd Allāh with an unprecedented victory and incalculable spoils and riches. Only a few among the people of Ifrīqiya reached Bāghāya, most of them being killed. The tribesmen returned to their tribes. Ziyādat Allāh [al-Ṭubnī], governor of Bāghāya, wrote to Ziyādat Allāh announcing to him the news of the defeat and the death of his brother, for which he was deeply saddened.

23

The conquest of the town of Tījis.

A group of Hawwāra[237] and Banū Ma'ād[238] from Ra's al-Faḥṣayn[239] had joined Abū 'Abd Allāh. They had long been won over to Shi'ism. Among them was Ismā'īl b. Naṣr al-Ma'ādī, from the time of al-Ḥulwānī, who had received instruction from his companions. He came to Abū 'Abd Allāh who appointed him and some members of his family as *dā'īs*. Among the people of that region who came

236. On the significance of the mountain motif in battles fought by Muslim armies, see Albrecht Noth, *The Early Arabic Historical Tradition: A Source-critical Study* (Princeton, 1994), pp. 142–143.

237. Originally the Hawwāra settled in Tripolitania and adopted Ibāḍī Kharijite doctrines. On the several sections of the Hawwāra spread across the Maghrib see Tadeusz Lewicki and Peter M. Holt, 'Hawwāra', *EI*², vol. 3, pp. 295–300.

238. The Ma'ād are listed among the Kutāma clans. See Ibn Khaldūn, *al-'Ibar*, vol. 6, p. 302 (tr. *Berbères*, vol. 1, p. 292).

239. Apparently Ra's al-Faḥṣayn (the head of the two plains) was located in the region between Tījis and Bāghāya.

to see Abū ʿAbd Allāh was Ḥamza al-Malazzī, a strong and valiant horseman. He met with a group of his companions, and they agreed among themselves to set out in a detachment of cavalry to make incursions in the districts of their country where they were known. Ḥamza sought Abū ʿAbd Allāh's permission to do so. He gave him his approval. (Ḥamza's) companions, however, abandoned him. They changed their opinion about what they had agreed with him to do as they were afraid. Therefore, Ḥamza on his own with a servant of his slipped away. At Fajj al-ʿArʿār[240] (gorge of junipers) they came across a group of people proceeding by night from al-Qayrawān to Bāghāya. Among them was a courier bearing letters from Ziyādat Allāh. (Ḥamza and his servant) attacked the group and killed some of them, and took from them whatever money they found on them and whatever goods they could. The messenger was among those whom they killed. The two men seized his letters and came to Abū ʿAbd Allāh. (Abū ʿAbd Allāh) was pleased with that. He was most pleased with the letters and the contents thereof. When (Ḥamza's) companions, who had stayed away from him, saw this, they joined in and made incursions upon the regions between Bāghāya and Tījis.[241]

Ziyādat Allāh had stationed at Tījis a garrison of 500 horsemen under the command of Yaḥfūr, one of his black slaves whom he set up at the request of Ibn Rikāb, governor of this town. When the inhabitants of Tījis saw that these incursions were overrunning their country and their localities, and that the neighbouring towns had been conquered, they feared for their lives. Consequently Ibn Rikāb wrote to Abū ʿAbd Allāh, asking him to send troops to him to enable him to deal with the garrison which was stationed among them. Abū ʿAbd Allāh sent a detachment of troops under the command of Maknadās al-Jīmalī who attacked them, but the mounted troops of

240. Fajj al-ʿArʿar in Ibn Khaldūn, *al-ʿIbar*, vol. 4, p. 74 (tr. *Berbères*, vol. 2, p. 518). Apparently the gorge was located in the foothills of the Awrās to the east or north-east of Bāghāya.

241. Ancient Thigisis, identified with Aïn el-Bordj, to the south-east of Constantine and to the north of Bāghāya. See Tissot, *Géographie*, vol. 2, pp. 420–423; al-Yaʿqūbī, *Kitāb al-Buldān*, p. 11 (tr. p. 214); al-Bakrī, *al-Masālik*, pp. 53–54, 63 (tr. pp. 114–115, 131); and al-Idrīsī, *Nuzha*, p. 118 (tr. p. 137).

the garrison did not venture to fight them. Instead, they barricaded themselves in the impregnable fortress. Ibn Rikāb was unable to do anything to them. Maknadās maintained the siege for some days and then returned [to Īkjān]. Then Abū ʿAbd Allāh sent a second army under the command of Yūsuf b. Sakla al-Ghashmī[242] who attacked Tījis and besieged it. The inhabitants of the town sought to surrender peacefully on the condition that the garrison of troops stationed among them would not be harmed saying, 'They are our guests. We cannot deceive them.'

Yūsuf accepted their request. The mounted troops of the garrison came out with all their belongings and returned to Ziyādat Allāh, without anyone of them being harmed in any way. The followers entered Tījis on the basis of a peace treaty, without causing any harm to any of its inhabitants, and they withdrew.[243] Ibn Rikāb and a group of notables of the town proceeded to Abū ʿAbd Allāh. They adhered to the *daʿwa* and returned to their country.

The mounted troops of the garrison arrived at the court of Ziyādat Allāh and reported their story and how the guarantee of safety granted to them was fulfilled. This news spread among the inhabitants of Ifrīqiya. Abū ʿAbd Allāh and his companions had been vilified among them for deception and killing. It had been said that they would grant safety to the population only to kill them when they came out to them, and that they would conclude treaties with them only to deceive them without fulfilling them. However, the way they dealt with the mounted troops of the garrison who were stationed at Tījis laid bare the slander which had been said about them. This was widely reported and, as a result, favourable reports about Abū ʿAbd Allāh and his companions spread among the commonalty of Ifrīqiya. They were placated and their hearts leaned towards them after having been fearful of them because of what had been said about them. Ifrīqiya became agitated and people began to talk much, expecting the arrival of Abū ʿAbd Allāh to them.

---

242. He was a Kutāma tribesman of the Ghashmān of Tāzrūt who were staunch supporters of the *daʿwa* from the very beginning. Ibn Khaldūn, *al-ʿIbar*, vol. 4, p. 72 (tr. *Berbères*, vol. 2, p. 517) gives 'al-Ghassānī' for 'al-Ghashmī'.

243. The town was taken probably at the end of 293/906.

24

Ziyādat Allāh's proclamation addressed to the provinces to pacify them and calm down the fright which he learnt had spread therein.

Ziyādat Allāh came to know of the situation of the towns in the regions of Ifrīqiya, that its inhabitants were overcome with fear, and that false rumours were spreading among them. Fearing that this would cause him disaster, he ordered a letter to be written and copies of it made, and a copy sent to each of the regions of Ifrīqiya. He ordered these to be read from the pulpits of the mosques to pacify the people. The following is an exemplar of it:

> In the name of God, the Compassionate, the Merciful. From the emir Ziyādat Allāh b. ʿAbd Allāh, helper of God's religion, upholder of the sunna of the Messenger of God, may God's blessings be upon him and his progeny, fighter against the enemies of God, to the community of Muslims in such-and-such town and its nomads. Peace be with you! The emir praises God. There is no deity except Him. He implores God to bless Muḥammad, His servant and Messenger. May God's blessings be upon him and his progeny. Now then! God, blessed and sublime is His name, the Mighty, the Glorious, has guaranteed victory and honour to adherents of His religion and defenders of the sunna of His Messenger against those who are hostile to them. He has given them strength against those who stand against them, who show enmity towards them, who oppose Him, who plot against Him, who change His religion and who alter the norms (*sunan*) of His prophets.
>
> Assembly of Muslims! This disbeliever from Ṣanʿāʾ[244] who alters God's religion and distorts His book, considers it proper to shed the blood of Muslims without reason. He considers illicit sexual relations allowable. He plunders their wealth as you know from what you have come to know about him. He has sought refuge with the ignorant, lowly Kutāma Berbers of unintelligible speech, seeking to beguile them. He has attracted them and seduced them, inviting them to alter the religion of God, and they have responded to him. He has invited them to distort the sunna of His

244. Abū ʿAbd Allāh had maintained among the Kutāma that he was from Ṣanʿāʾ. See p. 47 above.

Messenger, may God's blessings be upon him and his progeny, and they have submitted to his authority out of their ignorance of religion and the sunna. God willed for them misery and misfortune because they are like bolting donkeys and livestock, accepting and following whatever he has embellished before them. However, those of them with intelligence and some knowledge of the Book and the sunna fled from him to us with their religion, and rose to fight him, fulfilling the promise of God to destroy and eradicate him as is His custom with him and those like him. The least which shows his infidelity and spreads his disgraceful arrogation and cause, which is known and divulged about him, and upon which those who follow him agree, is openly cursing Abū Bakr and ʿUmar, the two companions of the Messenger of God, may God's blessings be upon him and his progeny, his two in-laws and successors who are resting with him,[245] ʿUthmān, the one bestowed with two lights, the spouse of (the Prophet's) two daughters,[246] and Ṭalḥa and al-Zubayr, (the Prophet's) two disciples, and a group of his excellent companions, may God have mercy on them. He claims that ʿAlī, may God have mercy on him, thought of them in these terms. However, God has absolved (ʿAlī) from this through his good companionship with them and his pleasant association with them during his lifetime and their lifetime, and through his agreement with them on what was pleasing to God. Furthermore, the sinner alleges that those who do not profess this teaching, adhere to it, express it, believe in it and dissociate from the foremost companions of the Messenger of God, may God's blessings be upon him, are outside the community of Muslims. He alleges that it is permissible to shed their blood, seize their wealth and imprison their descendants. Then he enacted a law which is different from the law (*sharīʿa*) of Islam, and followed a way (*sunna*) different from the sunna of Muḥammad, may God's blessings be upon him and his progeny. He kept it secret and hidden, exacting pledges and oaths from those to whom he divulged it to keep it secret and avoid talking about it, and not to disclose it so that it would not become apparent

---

245. On the burial-place of the Prophet and the first two caliphs see ʿAlī b. ʿAbd Allāh al-Samhūdī, *Wafāʾ al-wafā bi-akhbār Dār al-Muṣṭafā*, ed. Qāsim al-Sāmarrāʾī (London, 2001), vol. 2, pp. 309–320.

246. ʿUthmān (d. 35/655), the third caliph, married Ruqayya and after her death Umm Kulthūm. This is one reason, according to some sources, for his being known as 'the one bestowed with two lights' (*dhū al-nūrayn*). Aḥmad b. ʿAlī Ibn Ḥajar al-ʿAsqalānī, *al-Iṣāba fī tamyīz al-ṣaḥāba* (Cairo, 1939), vol. 1, p. 477.

to Muslims who would then deem it permissible to fight (*jihād*) them on its account. He imposed on anyone who adhered to his cause one dinar called *dīnār al-hijra*, and one dirham which he claimed was the *dirham al-fiṭra*.[247] He established to his own account an obligatory due on the wealth of the community.[248] He destroyed mosques, abolished the prayer, derided reverence for religion and distanced himself from the community of Muslims.

The emir Ziyādat Allāh b. ʿAbd Allāh has resolved to seek the reward of God, his lord, by fighting (*jihād*) personally against this offender, and proceed towards him with his champions and the supporters of his dominion, seizing the opportunity to attack him before he does. It has come to the notice of the emir that when the Commander of the Faithful al-Muktafī bi-llāh,[249] may God prolong his reign, came to know of his resolve, ordered the dispatch of his troops to support the emir Ziyādat Allāh b. ʿAbd Allāh and provide him with reinforcements. The emir hopes that God will grant him victory over the offender without these (troops), that He will make him an instrument for defeating him, and grant him glory and reward, and that He will make this something that pleases (the Commander of the Faithful). May He combine (Ziyādat Allāh's) renown with his glory for the Commander of the Faithful with his good intention. The emir Ziyādat Allāh b. ʿAbd Allāh is one of his arrows and one of his shooting stars, so whatever victory God grants him or causes him to triumph, is ascribed to the Commander of the Faithful and is due to him.

The emir is aware of the slander which is spread among you by those who spread lies and the false reports of those who slander, and those who spread alarm regarding the cursed offender when they heard that

---

247. In fact Abū ʿAbd Allāh refused to accept any dues which had no basis in the Qurʾan and the sunna. See, for example, Ibn ʿIdhārī, *al-Bayān*, vol. 1, pp. 141–142. The contributions of *dīnār al-hijra* and *dirham al-fiṭra* were instituted by the Qarmatian leader Ḥamdān Qarmaṭ in Iraq. The former was paid by every adult devotee for covering the cost of founding the abode of emigration (*dār al-hijra*) and fulfilling the needs of the emigrant believers. The latter tax was paid by every member of the community, men, women and children. See al-Maqrīzī, *Ittiʿāẓ*, vol. 1, p. 156, and *al-Muqaffā*, pp. 257–258.

248. Funds entrusted to Kutāma Berber chiefs from spoils of war were set aside for the imam and not for Abū ʿAbd Allāh. Thus when al-Mahdī was in transit at Īkjān, he took over the possession of these funds. See p. 203 below. See also al-Yamānī, *Sīrat al-Ḥājib Jaʿfar*, p. 131 (tr. Ivanow, *Rise*, p. 220).

249. The Abbasid caliph al-Muktafī bi-llāh (r. 289–295/902–908). On him see Karl V. Zetterstéen, 'al-Muktafī', *EI*², vol. 7, pp. 542–543.

> the troops had withdrawn from him, and that he overran places close to him. This enhanced the one who spreads lies and alarm, and the liar and negator slandered because of it. However, whatever they said, or spread lies or alarm, is not the case. It is unavoidable in war that there will be attacks, audacity, defeats and retreats. It is said that 'Victory in war goes by turns',[250] sometimes you win, sometimes you lose. The companions of the Messenger of God, may God bless him and grant him salvation, were defeated on more than one battlefield, and they retreated in more than one place. Then the outcome was in favour of the believers, just as God, the Mighty, the Glorious, had promised them in His elucidating book. Therefore, keep your faith in God and let your hearts be confident of what He has promised. Let your lack of concern about this offender be an indication of your confidence in your Lord! So go forth to fight him, '*whether it be easy or difficult*', as God has commanded you, '*and strive hard with your wealth and your lives*', (9:41) as He has enjoined upon you. Put an end to the shedding of your blood and the violation of your womenfolk! Do not be subjected to temptation in your religion; fight for it anyone who alters it, and dissociate yourselves from anyone who introduces innovation into it and changes it. May God grant you success in achieving what He wishes, what pleases Him and what brings near unto Him. Peace be with you, and God's mercy and His blessings!

This proclamation was read out from the pulpit of the mosque of al-Qayrawān as well as in all other towns. It only increased people's fear and rumouring, and their disdain and contempt for (Ziyādat Allāh). They began to talk about his circumstances and enumerate his deeds: he had shed the blood of his father, brothers and paternal uncles; he committed forbidden acts; he drank wine; and he was preoccupied with entertainment and musical instruments. They would talk about reports which came to their knowledge about Abū 'Abd Allāh and his companions. They would exchange news about their piety, faith, integrity, honesty and virtue, and their diligence in observing the ritual prayer and fasting, and their abstaining

250. Arabic proverb *al-ḥarb sijāl*, explained in al-Maydānī, *Majma' al-amthāl*, vol. 1, p. 214. Abū Sufyān used this expression after the Muslim defeat at the Battle of Uḥud. See Muḥammad b. 'Umar al-Wāqidī, *Kitāb al-Maghāzī*, ed. M. Jones (London, 1966), vol. 1, pp. 296–297; Ibn Hishām, *al-Sīra al-nabawiyya*, vol. 3, p. 56 (tr. p. 386); and al-Bukhārī, *Ṣaḥīḥ*, vol. 4, p. 172.

from forbidden and sinful acts. Now the slander which (Ziyādat Allāh) had said about Abū ʿAbd Allāh and his companions, and the allegations which he had made against them, began to be imputed to him. This came to his knowledge, and the fact that people knew that these were lies concocted by him through which he meant to put an end to what was being said about him. This was hard for him to bear. He employed an envoy seemingly coming to him from Baghdad bringing robes of honour, flags, swords, coats of mail and copies of a letter which he wrote and were circulated.[251] This letter was also read from the pulpits of mosques. The exemplar of the letter is as follows:

> In the name of God, the Compassionate, the Merciful. From the Servant of God, Abū Muḥammad the Imam al-Muktafī bi-llāh, Commander of the Faithful, to the Muslim inhabitants of Ifrīqiya. Peace be with you! The Commander of the Faithful praises God. There is no deity except Him. He implores God to bless Muḥammad, His servant and Messenger, may God's blessings be upon him and his progeny. Now then! Truly God established Islam as a path which guides to His satisfaction, a shield which protects from His anger, a place of refuge and protection for anyone who seeks refuge in it, and a means for salvation. He made Muslims brothers and brought their hearts together. He enjoined upon them to help each other and work together. He withholds protection from anyone who leaves their community, deviates from their assembly, renounces their religion and adopts a faith other than theirs. (Such a person) is absolved from the covenant, exchanging ingratitude for favour. (God) has enjoined upon them to unite against others and treat as enemies those who show enmity to them, and to gather together against those who rebel against them, to wage war against those who are hostile to them, and live in peace with those who treat them as friends. They are agreed upon this matter in word and deed, so that the enemy of God is their enemy, intended by their stratagem, defeated at their hands, overthrown by their cooperation, and defeated by their mutual support. (The rebels) will not find a confidant among them, nor a way to bring disharmony among them. Those who act thus are treading the exemplary path. They have grasped '*the firm hand-*

251. The fact that Ziyādat Allāh received a letter from al-Muktafī is reported in Ibn ʿIdhārī, *al-Bayān* vol. 1, p. 140, under the year 293.

hold' (2:256)[252] and deserve the best of this world and the Hereafter. They obey God and follow His command. Those who avoid Him, opposing Him, deviating from Him, turning away from His way, have corrupted His religion. They have betrayed His trust and covenant, thereby incurring the wrath of their Lord. They have gathered firewood on their backs, and sinned against themselves. God says, '*Thou wilt not find any people who believe in God and the Last Day, loving those who oppose God and His Messenger, even though they be their fathers or their sons, or their brothers, or their kindred*' (58:22). God will help whom He loves with His guidance and good fortune, and will entrust those from whom He dissociates to themselves and their choice. '*He whom God sends astray, for him there is no guide. And he whom God guides, for him there can be no misleader. Is not God Mighty, Lord of Retribution?*' (39:36–37).

The Commander of the Faithful has heard about the enemy of God, the dissenter having appeared in the outermost regions of the Maghrib, attracting to himself followers of error and ignorant riffraff, and those determined to sow dissension. They believe in casting off the bond of Islam and putting on the garment of infidelity, displaying dissent, hypocrisy and deviation from religion and the community. They are freely committing atrocities, shedding blood, perpetrating forbidden acts, committing sins and spreading wickedness among them. His officials have received reports about them, and that the emir Ziyādat Allāh b. 'Abd Allāh despatched armies against them on several occasions, and that these infidels persist in resisting him and coveting his regions. They are deceived by the respite which God has set as an argument against them. He tolerates them so that they commit more offences to add to their offences, and bear more burdens with their burdens. The people of prudence, good sense, discernment and discretion know very well the position of obedience and the extent of excellence it brings about for those who abide by it in terms of integrity of religion and this world, and the safety of the beginning and the end. For God, exalted be His praise, has linked obedience to His government and to His caliphs on earth with obedience to Him and obedience to His Messenger. He has enjoined it on the believers among His creation, saying, '*O ye who believe! Obey God, and obey the messenger and those of you who are in authority*' (4:59). Therefore, the fortunate one with plenty of good fortune, the rightly-guided, the winner some day

252. The same Qur'anic expression, '*al-'urwa al-wuthqā*', is used by Abū 'Abd Allāh (p. 193 below), and al-Mahdī (p. 207 below) in their letters.

is the one who holds fast to its rope (*ḥabl*)[253] and seeks refuge under its shade; and the miserable one, the loser, the one who stumbles is the one who swerves from it and seeks another path.

You are aware of the situation of Ziyādat Allāh b. ʿAbd Allāh with regard to friendship, loyalty and adherence to the Commander of the Faithful, and his following his path, guided by his example, following his obligation, obeying his command, his good conduct, kindness to the subjects, establishing justice, defending the border towns in whose route he is, fighting infiltrators into them as well as those who covet them, who attempt to seize opportunities there. [You are aware of] what his ancestors accomplished one after another. Whoever follows this conduct of Ziyādat Allāh, his means is certain, and his tie is close with the Commander of the Faithful. He is worthy of being chosen, being treated kindly and being relied upon. The Commander of the Faithful is pleased with him. He praises his manner, trusts his sincerity and relies upon him in the spot where he is. He has confronted these infidels and acted against them with God's help, being alone in his action in this, and encouraging the Commander of the Faithful to his most excellent practice in his view with the likes of him. The Commander of the Faithful is about to dispatch the armies and provide reinforcements to him to help and strengthen his cause, and to strengthen his hands in his course of action.

The Commander of the Faithful considered proper to write to you to let you know the position of Ziyādat Allāh before him and his status in his view, and to inform you of the respect he has for him, and the bond he preserves for him on account of himself and his ancestors, so that you will choose to hold fast to obeying him, abandon opposition to him, and abide by what he commands and forbids, and assist him in fighting and waging war against the infidels, enemies of God. Respond to his call when he calls upon you. Join him and abandon reluctance towards him. Honour him so that his letters [to the Commander of the Faithful] relate this description of you and inform this about you. May he testify favourably for you, and you assume the position of friends and people who hear and obey, who must be protected and trusted. May this bring for you benefits which will delight you and commend your choice with him. Know this to be the view of the Commander of the Faithful, and act accordingly. Stand by him. Do not oppose him for someone else. Respond positively to the letter of the

253. Cf. the expression 'the rope of God' in Qur'an 3:103; also 'the rope of al-Mahdī', p. 217 below.

Commander of the Faithful, accept it, and comply with what he has set out therein, God willing. Peace!

When this proclamation was also read out from the pulpit of the mosque of al-Qayrawān and in all the towns, people talked more about Ziyādat Allāh, slandering him. They said, 'Nothing has come about from his rule but lies. What can the subjects possibly do for him? The subjects are only under the one who conquers. If he has power and wealth, let him fight. As for the subjects, they do not know how to resist, nor are they accustomed to waging war.'

People began to say such things openly in the markets, in the streets, in the towns and in the country. (Ziyādat Allāh) demanded of them explanation for this, giving orders to the elders of al-Qayrawān and others of the towns whom he held responsible. They procrastinated, proceeded reluctantly and did not agree with him. He, therefore, refrained from asking them about the matter. He saw no advantage in proceeding with what he had demanded and wished. On the contrary, he considered that it contributed to the slander and became a means of revealing what the masses thought. He regretted his action and was upset.

25
Ziyādat Allāh's setting out at the head of troops for al-Urbus and his withdrawal from there.

When Ziyādat Allāh saw the disturbance of the people of the country against him and the lot of defamation of him, he expressed the intention to march personally against Abū 'Abd Allāh. He proceeded to prepare the implements of war, armament and funds. He appealed to the towns by giving gifts generously to the infantry and the cavalry. He dispatched recruiting agents to the chief towns and garrisons. He instructed the members of his family, all his courtiers and his men to set out with him. A large number of troops rallied to him. People came to him from everywhere to seek pay. He began to sit under a dome in Raqqāda known as the Dome of Parade (*qubbat al-ʿarḍ*). Dinars were poured out in front of him. The inhabitants of the towns were reviewed before him and he would present the pay to them. If he was pleased with someone passing before him, he would scoop a handful of dinars with a large plate, which was in front of him, and which was large enough to hold about fifty dinars. He would give these to him. It became known about him that he was presenting gifts with a large plate, so people came to him from all directions. Numerous volunteers complied with him and this put an end to people spreading false reports and alarm about him. The most they would say was, 'This is the decisive blow; it will belong to whomever.'

The commanders from his family formerly took pride in bravery and generosity. They belittled and disparaged those of them who lacked these qualities. Each one of them was well prepared and had gathered around him a number of his slaves, clients and those devoted to him, who would do what was needed in terms of riding animals, apparel, weapons and so forth. Ziyādat Allāh brought out the well-guarded contents of his store houses, including his treasures and the treasures of his ancestors, which included equipment, ornaments and robes of honour. He displayed them and gave thereof to each one of his commanders, dignitaries and members of his family according to what he thought each deserved. There appeared because of this a style of costume not seen by the people of that time. Large embroidered banners and pavilions were made the like of which had not been made before.

At the beginning of the year 295/October 907, Ziyādat Allāh left for al-Urbus, accompanied by some jurists (*shuyūkh*) from al-Qayrawān. Upon his arrival in al-Urbus he appointed to the judgeship Abū al-ʿAbbās Muḥammad b. ʿAbd Allāh b. Jīmāl[254] who adhered to the school of the ʿIrāqīs.[255] This met with the satisfaction of members of his family and the dignitaries of his entourage. He did this when he saw that there was no advantage in flattering the inhabitants of al-Qayrawān. (Ziyādat Allāh) authorised (the *qāḍī*) to hear pleas from litigants of al-Qayrawān who wished to refer to him as well as from all the towns and to invest with authority whoever he wished. He

254. He was appointed at the request of the *wazīr* Ibn al-Ṣāʾigh. See al-Khushanī, *'Ulamāʾ Ifrīqiya*, pp. 254, 309; and Ibn ʿIdhārī, *al-Bayān*, vol. 1, pp. 140, 143. The appointment of this Ḥanafī was unpopular with the Mālikī inhabitants of al-Qayrawān.

255. The Ḥanafī school of jurisprudence.

granted him proximity, and raised his status. He turned away from Ḥimās,[256] and rejected him.

(Ziyādat Allāh) stayed in the town of al-Urbus where the troops arrived in large numbers. He intended to command them personally against Abū ʿAbd Allāh, and sought the advice of his courtiers and dignitaries, but they advised, 'This is risky! If you encounter him yourself together with all your weapons, it will be decisive and we do not know what the outcome will be. He has up to now attacked several armies without weakening the kingdom, since you were its support and its shade. We advise that you remain in the capital of your kingdom, for we are not sure what might happen after you leave. Retain strong troops here with one of your officers. Then if [Abū ʿAbd Allāh] al-Shīʿī attacks any place, (the officer) here will march against him, and you will support him.'

(Ziyādat Allāh) accepted their advice. He entrusted the command of the army to Ibrāhīm b. Abī al-Aghlab.[257] He was brave, and one of the most prominent members of his family. (Ziyādat Allāh) left with him all the troops, and withdrew to Raqqāda with his family and intimate courtiers.

When he arrived, he supported Ibn Jīmāl, and his crier proclaimed in al-Qayrawān that if litigants brought disputes before him and before Ḥimās, the one whom he summoned had to respond to him. People inclined with their litigation to him. When Ḥimās saw this, he vacated his office and closed its door. Thus, the function of judgeship was exercised exclusively by Ibn Jīmāl. The inhabitants of al-Qayrawān began to buy desert tents and pitched them in the area of Bāb Salm, and remained in them day and night with arms and supplies. (Ziyādat Allāh) enlisted from each of its guard posts a fixed number of their young men. He sent them out for this task under compulsion to show that the inhabitants of al-Qayrawān were joining him for battle. He mobilised the inhabitants of the towns and remained in Raqqāda, while Ibn Abī al-Aghlab remained in al-Urbus.

---

256. On this Mālikī *qāḍī* see note 192 above.

257. Ibrāhīm b. Abī al-Aghlab was Ziyādat Allāh's cousin. Ibrāhīm's father, known for his asceticism, had renounced the commandership in Sicily in favour of his nephew Ziyādat Allāh. See p. 117 above.

26

The conquest of the town of Bāghāya.

Abū ʿAbd Allāh came to know the truth of these events. Some inhabitants of Bāghāya had joined him, among them Ibrāhīm known as Ibn al-Mazīlī, ʿAbd Allāh al-Radm and Ḥammūd al-Qaṣīr, and others. They corresponded with the inhabitants of the town and encouraged Abū ʿAbd Allāh to go there. They brought him letters of those of their associates with whom they had corresponded and in which they wished him to come, stating that if he did so they would submit to his authority. Accordingly (Abū ʿAbd Allāh) advanced at the head of numerous troops. When he approached the town, the governor came to know of the correspondence of those of their associates in the town. Fearing that they might seize him, he fled to al-Urbus. Some leading inhabitants of Bāghāya came out to receive Abū ʿAbd Allāh and asked him to grant safety. He granted them safety and stayed there.[258] His troops entered the town, traded in the market and stayed there for a few days. (Abū ʿAbd Allāh) appointed as the town's governor Abū Yūsuf Māknūn b. Ḍubāra al-Ijjānī, paternal uncle of Abū Zākī. He stationed with him there a garrison and returned to Īkjān. Abū Yūsuf remained in Bāghāya with 500 horsemen. When Ziyādat Allāh came to know about this, he was distressed. The people of Ifrīqiya talked about him and slander became widespread.

Ziyādat Allāh gathered around him his advisors and sought their advice on how to deal with the matter. Some of them said to him, 'Write to Ibn Abī al-Aghlab, asking him to attack Bāghāya and besiege them. Perhaps they will surrender to him those [supporters of Abū ʿAbd Allāh] who are there.'

ʿAbd Allāh b. al-Ṣāʾigh,[259] who was his chief adviser and most

---

258. Bāghāya was conquered in Shaʿbān 294/May-June 907 according to Ibn ʿIdhārī, *al-Bayān*, vol. 1, p. 143.

259. ʿAbd Allāh b. al-Ṣāʾigh, before becoming *wazīr* and chief advisor of Ziyādat Allāh, had been secretary of Abū Muslim Manṣūr b. Ismāʿīl b. Yūnus, a dignitary under Ibrāhīm b. Aḥmad. He was accused of having supported Ziyādat Allāh in his attempted revolt against his father Abū al-ʿAbbās ʿAbd Allāh. He was imprisoned and then released after the

senior of his men, said, 'This is not a good idea, for if Ibn Abī al-Aghlab attacks Bāghāya, Abū ʿAbd Allāh will rush towards him with all the Kutāma. Then if he resists him he would not be safe, and if he withdraws from him it would be a defeat. It is not certain that (Abū ʿAbd Allāh) would pursue him, and if he pursues him it is not certain that the army would disintegrate. Rather, Ibn Abī al-Aghlab should remain where he is. Then if al-Shīʿī, that is Abū ʿAbd Allāh, advances to a place other than Bāghāya, he should forestall him before he reaches his intended destination. If he had done this before he arrived at Bāghāya or he had arrived there before him, it would have been a sound view. But since the inhabitants of Bāghāya have supported him, and the town has his governor and his army, and the town is a fortified stronghold, and since he is near to it, then it is not appropriate for Ibn Abī al-Aghlab to advance to it.'

Ibn al-Shamīm, who was one of (Ziyādat Allāh's) boon companions and accompanied him in jest and wantonness which he used to engage in, said, 'What is Bāghāya? May God strengthen the emir! And who are the inhabitants of Bāghāya? By God! They were merely a burden, drawing sustenance from your wealth and taking [it] for their suckling children. They were not useful to you, nor did they fight your enemy. They bore no hardship and no advantage. God has relieved you from them and removed from you the burden to provide for them. I have improvised a verse of poetry for the moment. So may the emir order the musicians to render it with a style of singing, to relax him from this anxiety and burden which is affecting his heart. Let him do so.'

This is because whenever he gathered them, he would ask the table to be served and they would eat. Then he would ask date wine to be served and they would drink. Then, while drinking with them, he would say to them whatever he wanted. This was as they had drunk several goblets, while the entertainers and singers were at a distance outside the sitting area. Ziyādat Allāh asked, 'What is this verse?'

He replied, 'We shall tell it to the musicians so that they choose

---

assassination of the latter. See Ibn ʿIdhārī, *al-Bayān*, vol. 1, pp. 135–137, 143, 145; al-Nuwayrī, *Nihāya*, vol. 24, p. 147 (tr. *Berbères*, vol. 1, pp. 441–442); Ibn al-Abbār, *al-Ḥulla*, vol. 1, p. 189; and Ibn al-Khaṭīb, *Aʿmāl*, pp. 37–38.

a tune for it. Then the emir will hear it from them as a song which is better.'

He said, 'Let it be so.'

Then he went to the musicians and told them, 'Sing, play your wind instruments and move your instruments. Say at the end of every verse of the ode that you are singing, "Drink! Serve us drinks! Spare us nearness (to the enemy)." Prepare for it a *ḥalla* tune.'[260] And they did so. When Ziyādat Allāh heard this, he smiled and took a glass and drank it. He said to Ibn al-Shamīm, 'O 'Abd Allāh, it is as you say. We can spare us nearness.'

He said, 'O my master, was is not from al-Qayrawān that we defeated the troops of Mudlij[261] and killed him?'

He replied, 'Yes.'

He said, 'What is Bāghāya compared to al-Qayrawān, and what causes you sadness so quickly?'

He replied, 'Nothing.'

When Ibn al-Ṣā'igh and those who were speaking about this with reflection and discernment saw that Ziyādat Allāh was pleased with what Ibn al-Shamīm was saying, that he was accepting this nonsense from him, and that he inclined to him, they agreed with him in his idea and engaged in drinking until they were drunk and dispersed. This happened with him after every change of fortune brought about by Abū 'Abd Allāh. Ziyādat Allāh immersed himself in drinking, music and amusement as if he were making the most of his days and satisfying his desires. However, he would supply Ibn Abī al-Aghlab with money and troops, ordering him to lavish pay to his troops and not to move from his station except for any important matter which needed his attention, while he continued with his pleasures.

---

260. Apparently *ḥalla* is a rhythmic mode of Tunisian origin. See Herman Rechberger, *The Rhythm in Arabian Music* (Helsinki, 2004), p. 100.

261. Mudlij b. Zakariyā was Ziyādat Allāh's commander who, together with Aḥmad b. Masrūr al-Khāl, revolted against him in Jumādā II 293/April 906. The two men had been put in command by the emir to fight Abū 'Abd Allāh. See Ibn 'Idhārī, *al-Bayān*, vol. 1, p. 139.

27

Abū ʿAbd Allāh's battles at Majjāna and in its region adjacent to al-Urbus.

When Abū ʿAbd Allāh came to know that Ziyādat Allāh had stationed troops in al-Urbus, he wished to visit him. Khafāja al-ʿAbshī,[262] Ziyādat Allāh's governor in Majjāna, was one of his elite horsemen and companions. He had become afflicted with leprosy. There was a garrison with him stationed in Majjāna. Abū ʿAbd Allāh dispatched a detachment of about 1,000 of his selected horsemen under the command of Abū Madīnī, ordering them to reach Majjāna. They took the road leading to Bāghāya and from there set out to proceed to Majjāna. As they approached Majjāna, Khafāja led the men of the garrison and the inhabitants of Majjāna to resist him. He fought them near the town until they were interrupted by nightfall. (Khafāja) withdrew inside the town, and the followers encamped in the valley of Majjāna and spent the night. Next morning they approached the town. Khafāja barricaded himself and did not come out to fight them. They advanced to the fortress of Majjāna (Qalʿat Majjāna), plundered those settlements and returned to Abū ʿAbd Allāh at Īkjān.

He remained for a while. Then he sent again a detachment of cavalry under the command of Abū Madīnī with orders to proceed to Majjāna. When they arrived at Bāghāya they learned that the inhabitants of Majjāna had taken up position in Qalʿat Busr.[263] Abū Madīnī commanding the troops took the road leading to Tebessa[264] and then through the region of Majjāna. Khafāja was in Majjāna together with the horsemen who were stationed with him at Majjāna,

---

262. He had previously been in command in Ṭubna. See Ibn ʿIdhārī, *al-Bayān*, vol. 1, p. 140 (where he is referred to as Khafāja al-ʿAbsī).

263. The fortress owes its name to the Arab general Busr b. Abī Arṭāt who conquered it in the 1st/7th century. See al-Bakrī, *al-Masālik*, p. 145 (tr. p. 278); Yāqūt, *Muʿjam*, vol. 4, p. 390, and vol. 5, p. 56.

264. Ancient Thevesta, Tabassā/Tabassa in Arabic sources, located in the north-east of what is now Algeria. This fortified town commanded the road to al-Zāb. See Albert Charles Maitrot, 'Theveste. Étude militaire d'une cité romano-byzantine, 70 à 705', *Recueils des notices et mémoires de la Société archéologique du Département de Constantine*, 45 (1912), pp. 37–263; and Mohamed Talbi, 'Tebessa', *EI*², vol. 10, pp. 410–411.

while the foot-soldiers were on their horses in Majjāna. He took the road leading to the mountain of al-Maṭāḥin and proceeded towards the Malzūza,[265] a branch of the Nafza, near Majjāna who were on their horses. They removed the possessions, the household and the weak to the fortress. The battle cry reached their ears, and (Khafāja) came out together with those who were with him. Abū Madīnī came out and met them in the mountain of al-Maṭāḥin and they fought a fierce battle. Khafāja al-ʿAbshī and some of his companions were killed. The remainder sought refuge in the fortress. Many of them were killed before reaching it. Their heads were cut off together with the head of Khafāja. The troops returned to Abū ʿAbd Allāh and reached Īkjān.

There was a battle between the Karnāya[266] and the inhabitants of Qaṣr al-Ifrīqī,[267] in which one of their (Karnāya) leaders named ʿAbbalū was killed. He had a brother called Fūnās who came to Abū ʿAbd Allāh to seek his help for his companions. He described to him their weapons. (Abū ʿAbd Allāh) ordered the dispatch of a detachment led by Abū Jaʿfar al-Saktānī Aḥmad b. Sulaymān. They reached Qaṣr al-Ifrīqī and fought them. (Its inhabitants) fled. He pursued them with killing until they retired to Ṭabarshiq.[268] He plundered the settlements of the Miklāta[269] and the Banū ʿUmar, killing several of them and returned to Īkjān.

---

265. The Malzūza belonged to the Butr branch of the Berbers. In fact, they shared the same origin as the Nafza, having descended from Tamzīt. See Ibn Ḥazm, *Jamhara*, p. 496; Ibn Khaldūn, *al-ʿIbar*, vol. 6, pp. 246, 254 (tr. *Berbères*, vol. 1, pp. 172, 236, 248); and Tadeusz Lewicki, 'Malzūza', *EI*², vol. 6, pp. 310–311.

266. According to Ibn Ḥawqal, *Ṣūrat al-arḍ*, p. 102, the Karnāya (Karntāya) descended from the Zanāta.

267. Qaṣr al-Ifrīqī, which was not surrounded by a wall, was one day's march to the south-west of Tīfāsh. See Ibn Ḥawqal, *Ṣūrat al-arḍ*, p. 87; al-Bakrī, *al-Masālik*, p. 53 (tr. p. 114); and al-Idrīsī, *Nuzha*, p. 120 (tr. p. 140).

268. Ṭabarshiq here is Roman Thubursicum Numidarum, modern Khamissa, in Algeria, near where the Medjerda takes its source. On it see Tissot, *Géographie*, vol. 1, p. 57, and vol. 2, pp. 387–390; Ch. Al. Joly, 'Thubursicum Numidarum (Khemissa)', *Recueils des notices et mémoires de la Société archéologique du Département de Constantine*, 39 (1906), pp. 165–192; and Samuel M. Stern, 'Three North-African Topographical Notes (Islamic-Roman)', *Arabica*, 1 (1954), pp. 343–344.

269. The Miklāta, according to Ibn Ḥawqal, *Ṣūrat al-arḍ*, p. 102, descend from the Zanāta, but according to Ibn Khaldūn, *al-ʿIbar*, vol. 6, pp. 192, 231 (tr. *Berbères*, vol. 1, pp. 172, 227), they were a branch of the Nafzāwa settled in Kutāma territory.

Isḥāq b. Abī Salās was Ziyādat Allāh's governor of Tīfāsh.[270] When he saw Abū ʿAbd Allāh's troops reaching him while Ibn Abī al-Aghlab did not move from his place, he feared he would turn towards him. He therefore joined Abū ʿAbd Allāh and abandoned Tīfāsh. This came to the knowledge of Ziyādat Allāh who dispatched some troops to (the town) to take charge of it, and they regained control. (Ziyādat Allāh) was told of a [notable] inhabitant of (Tīfāsh), named Ḥabīb b. Līfa. He invested him with the governorship and sent him a gift and a robe of honour. (Ḥabīb b. Līfa) accepted the appointment and assumed the governorship of Tīfāsh.

In the town there was a man from Majjāna named ʿAbd Allāh b. Kulayb, a Shiʿi who had long adhered to Shiʿism. He had gone to Abū ʿAbd Allāh who summoned him to the *daʿwa* (*daʿʿāhu*). He used to send him to the region to bring him news. He had a mother in Tīfāsh. He sought Abū ʿAbd Allāh's permission to bring her to Īkjān. (Abū ʿAbd Allāh) allowed him to do so, and he brought her as well as two men who were among the notable inhabitants of Tīfāsh. One of them was named Muḥammad b. Zunbūr and the other Abū Zaʿbal. Abū ʿAbd Allāh summoned them both to the *daʿwa*. The two men informed him on the town and urged him to dispatch troops to take Tīfāsh. So he dispatched troops with them under the command of one of the *dāʿīs*, Ṣūlāt b. al-Qāsim al-Saktānī. The number of troops sent under him was 500 horsemen. This came to the knowledge of Ḥabīb b. Līfa who fled to al-Urbus to Ibn Abī al-Aghlab. Ṣūlāt arrived in Tīfāsh. He was received by its inhabitants who asked him for protection. He granted them protection, and entered the town and stayed there.

Then Khalfūn b. Mahdī, commander of Qālama,[271] came to (Ṣūlāt) and asked to adhere to the *daʿwa* and obtain protection for the inhabitants of the town. (Ṣūlāt) accepted him in the *daʿwa* and granted them protection. He ordered him to bring back from the town men, among them Murābiṭ b. ʿĪsā, ʿAbd Allāh b. Maymūn and Ibrāhīm al-Burūj.

270. Also called Tīfāsh al-Ẓālima, ancient Tipasa, located to the south-east of Ṭabarshiq. Its impregnable fortress rose not far from the source of the Medjerda. On Tīfāsh see Tissot, *Géographie*, vol. 2, pp. 387–390; Ibn Ḥawqal, *Ṣūrat al-arḍ*, p. 87; al-Bakrī, *al-Masālik*, p. 53 (tr. p. 114); al-Idrīsī, *Nuzha*, p. 120 (tr. p. 140); and Yāqūt, *Muʿjam*, vol. 2, pp. 66–67.

271. Ancient Calama, Guelma in present Algeria. See al-Idrīsī, *Nuzha*, pp. 91, 96 (tr. pp. 106, 113).

The latter used to mint coins there. So he set out for this purpose. Ṣūlāt dispatched with him 300 horsemen led by Wāklīd b. Sunbul. Ṣūlāt remained in Tīfāsh with 200 horsemen. Then a group of the Banū Wardīm led by Jābir b. Mūsā, Faraḥ b. Ḥayya and Yūsuf b. Ayyūb came to Ṣūlāt asking to adhere to the *daʿwa* and be granted protection. (Abū ʿAbd Allāh) accepted them in the *daʿwa* and granted them protection. Then Ṣūlāt b. Bāzil, ʿAdī b. Dhikr, Ḥabīb b. Bakr and Ḥammūd b. Ḥafṣ of the Banū Hurāsh[272] came to him and asked the same and he granted them the same, and ordered all of them to move their families to Īkjān, and he consolidated his position in the region.

When Ibn Abī al-Aghlab came to know that only 200 horsemen remained stationed at Tīfāsh, he advanced against the town at the head of 12,000 horsemen and innumerable foot-soldiers. It was at the instigation of Ḥabīb b. Līfa and others that he took this action. Ṣūlāt and the followers who were with him in Tīfāsh were not aware of this until the troops came very close. Then Ṣūlāt ordered them to leave the town for he was afraid of its inhabitants. They left except for a few who did not have a riding animal. They remained in the town. Ṣūlāt and those who were with him remained near the gate of the town until the vanguards of Ibn Abī al-Aghlab encountered them, and they fought them. They put the vanguards to flight until they caught up with them with the main body of the army and killed some of them. Then Ibn Abī al-Aghlab and his troops withdrew and placed the weak horsemen to the front of them and the rest remained behind them until they reached the town and bypassed it. When they reached the town, they remained there and did not pursue the followers. Ṣūlāt and those who were with him travelled to Qālama, and met with Wāklīd and the horsemen who had been dispatched with him there. They conveyed to Abū ʿAbd Allāh the news. He ordered them to withdraw, so they withdrew to Īkjān. Ibn Abī al-Aghlab's army entered Tīfāsh and killed the followers who had remained there. Among those killed

272. Apparently the Banū Hurāsh were settled in the region of Tīfāsh on the eastern edge of Kutāma territory. Later, they sought refuge with the Kutāma after a punitive expedition by the first Zīrid ruler against them following their rebellion of 364/975. See al-Nuwayrī, *Nihāya*, vol. 24, pp. 183–184; al-Maqrīzī, *Ittiʿāẓ*, vol. 1, p. 218; Hady Roger Idris, *La Berbérie orientale sous les Zīrides, Xe-XIIe siècles* (Paris, 1962), p. 50, and 'Glanes sur les Zīrides d'Ifrīqiya dans le manuscrit d'Istanbul de l'*Ittiʿāẓ al-ḥunafā*', *Arabica*, 11 (1964), pp. 286, 295.

by them was ʿAbd Allāh b. Kulayb. He was killed by Ḥabīb b. Līfa. When Abū ʿAbd Allāh arrived in Raqqāda, the mother of ʿAbd Allāh b. Kulayb, who was a pious believer, came to him and said to him, 'Let me retaliate against Ḥabīb b. Līfa for my son.'

So [when Ḥabīb was captured, Abū ʿAbd Allāh] ordered him to be sent to her. She said, 'I do not wish to kill him with a sword or a lance, but let him be fettered and left to die.' Accordingly, this was done for her.

Then Manṣūr b. Khalīl al-Awrabī came to Abū ʿAbd Allāh and related that the Awraba[273] had killed his father and were acting with hypocrisy. Earlier, his father had been appointed as *dāʿī* and a chief over them. Abū ʿAbd Allāh ordered an army to be dispatched. He appointed for each tribe in the army a leader from among their own tribe. They set out with Manṣūr until they arrived at Būna.[274] They halted at Majāz al-Marākib and divided the army into three columns. One column took the road to the coast, another took the road to Sandīnī and Īzān,[275] and a third marched in the middle of the plain. They launched raids against the Awraba, killing all those that they came across and plundering their belongings. They gathered at Bāb Zāna and returned to Īkjān with the booty.

28

The battle of Dār Madyan.

Abū ʿAbd Allāh himself set out with a large army, passing through Bāghāya, and marched until he reached Miskiyāna.[276] He then pro-

273. The Awraba, like the Kutāma, belonged to the Burnus branch of the Berbers. They lived particularly in the region of Būna. See al-Bakrī, *al-Masālik*, p. 55 (tr. p. 117); Ibn Khaldūn, *al-ʿIbar*, vol. 6, pp. 296–300 (tr. *Berbères*, vol. 1, pp. 286–290); Gaston Deverdun, 'Awraba', *EI*², *Supplement*, pp. 102–103; and P. Morizot, 'Awerba', *Encyclopédie berbère* (Aix-en-Provence, 1984–), vol. 8, pp. 1192–1196.

274. Būna (Bône), ancient Hippona or Hippo Regius, now ʿAnnāba on the Algerian coast. See Georges Marçais, 'al-ʿAnnāba', *EI*², vol. 1, pp. 511–512.

275. Reading from Beirut MS/297.8: N 97 aAC. 2. Other variants: Īrān in MS 79, p. 211; MS 254, fol. 101a; MS 1147, p. 147, and Īrwān in MS 934, fol. 110b; MS 1001, p. 347.

276. The fortified town of Miskiyāna (present day Meskiana in eastern Algeria), to the west

ceeded to Tebessa and from there he reached Maydara,[277] which is a fortress where he found remnants of the inhabitants of Qaṣr al-Ifrīqī, Majjāna, al-Qalʿa,[278] Tebessa and Marmājanna, and various other people who had sought refuge in it and had barricaded themselves. (Abū ʿAbd Allāh) camped before it. He had a chronic illness of a stone which used to afflict him. He was occupied with himself. The inhabitants of Maydara closed their gates and stood on the walls. The army surrounded them from all sides. They asked for safety. Some troops granted them safety and they opened the gates to them. When (the troops) were among (the inhabitants) and in the centre of the town, they attacked with swords those who were inside and plundered (the town). Abū ʿAbd Allāh came to know of this and he was saddened by this [behaviour]. He himself came out in spite of his condition. The elders came to see him, bringing what they had found. He made all possible amends and spared all those whom he came across and returned everything he found in the possession of the troops. He was extremely saddened at this [misdeed] and looked for the perpetrators, but they were not to be found. When Ziyādat Allāh came to know of what had happened at Maydara, he defamed Abū ʿAbd Allāh, accusing him of treachery and breaking the covenant and trust.

Abū ʿAbd Allāh set out from Maydara and camped before al-Qaṣrayn,[279] in Qammūda.[280] Its inhabitants barricaded themselves and sought protection. Abū ʿAbd Allāh granted them protection, but

---

of Marmājanna, was on the Bāghāya to Tebessa route. Ibn Ḥawqal, *Ṣūrat al-arḍ*, p. 84; al-Bakrī, *al-Masālik*, pp. 50, 145 (tr. pp. 106, 278); and al-Idrīsī, *Nuzha*, p. 119 (tr. pp. 139–140).

277. Maydara here is the Roman citadel of Ammaedara, present Haïdra, whose ruins lie on the Oued Haïdra in Tunisia. See Tissot, *Géographie*, vol. 2, pp. 459–462; Stern, 'Three North-African Topographical Notes (Islamic-Roman)', p. 344; and François Baratte and Noël Duval, *Haïdra: les ruines d'Ammaedara* (Tunis, 1974).

278. The citadel near Majjāna, also called Qalʿat Busr. See p. 153 above.

279. The fortress of al-Qaṣrayn is the Roman Cillium and modern Kasserine in Tunisia. See al-Idrīsī, *Nuzha*, pp. 91, 96 (tr. pp. 106, 113); and Stern, 'Three North-African Topographical Notes (Islamic-Roman)', p. 344.

280. The territory of Qamūda/Qammūda, ancient Thacamuda, lies roughly between al-Qayrawān and Qafṣa, and between Sabība and Sfax. On it see Hassen Husni Abdul-Wahab, 'Les steppes tunisiennes (région de Gammouda) pendant le Moyen-Age', *Les cahiers de Tunisie*, 2 (1954), pp. 5–16; al-Yaʿqūbī, *Kitāb al-Buldān*, p. 10 (tr. pp. 211–212); and al-Idrīsī, *Nuzha*, p. 103 (tr. p. 120).

ordered them not to open the gate to their town because of abuses committed at Maydara. They pledged allegiance to the troops from above the fortress. Abū ʿAbd Allāh showed anger at his companions and disapproved of their treatment of the inhabitants of Maydara. His sadness about it increased and he came to know of what was being said about this in Ifrīqiya, and the fact that Ziyādat Allāh wrote letters to this effect which were read from the pulpits of mosques. He gathered the elders of the Kutāma and informed them about this and censured them for this. They apologised to him for this [saying] that they did not know who had done this, that they had spared no effort in restoring whatever they could, and that they had executed some of those who were caught with plundered goods in their possession who were known to have been offenders. They sought to satisfy him by punishing them and he was satisfied with them.

Ibn Abī al-Aghlab came to know that Abū ʿAbd Allāh wanted to attack Ziyādat Allāh in Raqqāda, that he had arrived at al-Qaṣrayn, and that Ziyādat Allāh did not have a large army. Ibn Abī al-Aghlab, therefore, set out from al-Urbus with his entire army and moved to Dār Madyan.[281] Abū ʿAbd Allāh learnt of this [move] while he was at al-Qaṣrayn. He ordered the dispatch of a detachment of 2,000 horsemen towards Dār Madyan to gather intelligence about Ibn Abī al-Aghlab. They arrived there, encountered him there and engaged him in battle. A group of followers were killed. Abū ʿAbd Allāh found news of them was long overdue. He therefore led all his troops towards them. Their messenger met him, informing him that they had already engaged in battle. He therefore disposed his troops and set out towards them. While he was travelling, suddenly he encountered them. They were fleeing, dispersed in rough terrain and woodland at the approach of night. When they saw (Abū ʿAbd Allāh), they as well as the vanguard turned around and attacked. Ibn Abī al-Aghlab fled before them and they killed a group of his companions. They stopped fighting at nightfall. Abū ʿAbd Allāh withdrew to al-Qaṣrayn and Ibn Abī al-Aghlab withdrew to Dār Madyan. He wrote to Ziyādat

281. Dār (or Dūr) Madyan has been identified with ancient Althiburos, present Medeïna or Henchir Medeïna, in Tunisia. See Mongi Ennaïfer, *La cité d'Althiburos et l'édifice des Asclepieia* (Tunis, 1976), pp. 39–40. Dār Madyan was one day's march to the east of Tīfāsh. See al-Idrīsī, *Nuzha*, pp. 57, 91, 96 (tr. pp. 65, 106, 113).

Allāh about what had happened, exaggerating that he had defeated Abū ʿAbd Allāh and killed his troops. Ziyādat Allāh added to this and wrote proclamations to the towns to this effect which were read out from the pulpits of mosques. This calmed the slandering against him and put an end to a lot of what people were saying about him. Abū ʿAbd Allāh returned to Īkjān and Ibn Abī al-Aghlab returned to al-Urbus.

The Banū Washnū and the Banū Ṣadghāyān[282] of the Banū Hurāsh rallied to (Ibn Abī al-Aghlab) after having submitted to the authority of Abū ʿAbd Allāh. When Abū ʿAbd Allāh came to know of this, he dispatched troops under the command of Ghazwiyya b. Yūsuf and Abū Makdūl[283] to fight them. They both marched with the troops until they arrived at Qaṣr al-Ifrīqī, but found it deserted. They got eventually to Ṭabarshiq and spent the night there, while the Banū Washnū were hidden near them. (Ghazwiyya b. Yūsuf, Abū Makdūl and their troops) concealed themselves without lighting a fire. The next morning they encountered the (Banū Washnū) and killed them, except for a few. Then they proceeded to the Banū Ṣadghāyān and killed them quickly, burnt their settlements, plundered their belongings, and returned to the halting place where they were and encamped there.

Ibn Abī al-Aghlab had set out, heading for the Banū Wardīm to kill them for having accepted the authority of Abū ʿAbd Allāh. Abū ʿAbd Allāh came to know of his departure, so he sent a messenger to Ghazwiyya b. Yūsuf and Abū Makdūl to warn them about him. When his messenger reached them both, Ibn Abī al-Aghlab was already near to them, there being only a distance of one resting place between them. None of them was aware of this until Abū ʿAbd Allāh's messenger came to them. They immediately rose and marched day and night until they halted at Qālama. Abū ʿAbd Allāh dispatched 500 mounted troops in the region of the Banū Wardīm, ordering them to go to them, and should they reach them when they had engaged in hostilities against Ibn Abī al-Aghlab, they should help them; and if

282. Ibn Khaldūn, *al-ʿIbar*, vol. 6, p. 848 (tr. *Berbères*, vol. 3, p. 63), notes the presence of the Ṣadghayān along with the Kutāma on the island of Djerba (Jarba).

283. Abū Makdūl belonged to the Kutāma clan of Jīmla. See Ibn Khaldūn, *al-ʿIbar*, vol. 4, p. 73 (tr. *Berbères*, vol. 2, p. 518).

they reached them when they had surrendered to him, they should withdraw from them. They met Ghazwiyya and a group of those who were with him in Qālama. Ghazwiyya and Abū Makdūl and those who were with them withdrew to Īkjān. The mounted troops marched to where Abū ʿAbd Allāh had directed them. A group of companions of Ghazwiyya b. Yūsuf withdrew with them, reached the mountain of Bānūrāt and set up camp there. They found the troops of Ibn Abī al-Aghlab had already set up camp on the mountain of al-Sāṭūr. The Banū Wardīm were positioned between the two mountains. The troops of Ibn Abī al-Aghlab led by Ibn al-Hamdānī were heavily-laden with supplies. The following morning they advanced upon the Banū Wardīm. The 500 mounted troops [of Abū ʿAbd Allāh], as well as the accompanying foot-soldiers and troops of Ghazwiyya who had joined them on the mountain, stood watching the movement of the Banū Wardīm in their position as Abū ʿAbd Allāh had ordered them. As the Banū Wardīm were aware of their presence, their resolve was strengthened, for they feared that if they surrendered to the troops of Ibn Abī al-Aghlab, they might have to bear unpleasant consequences from Abū ʿAbd Allāh. Hence they opened hostilities against the troops of Ibn Abī al-Aghlab and defeated them, killing a number of them. The mounted troops sent by Abū ʿAbd Allāh descended and helped them, and stayed with them for some days. Then they returned to Abū ʿAbd Allāh.

Then the Banū Mājin, a branch of the Hawwāra of Kādrān, defected to Ibn Abī al-Aghlab. When Abū ʿAbd Allāh came to know about this, he sent troops made up of the Jīmla and the Ijjāna to [attack] them. He appointed Abū Makdūl to command the Jīmla troops, and Abū Yūsuf Māknūn b. Ḍubāra to command the Ijjāna troops. The troops reached them, killed them and plundered their belongings.

29

The conquest of Qasṭīliya and Qafṣa.

Then Abū ʿAbd Allāh gathered the followers and a large number of troops and set out in the direction of Qasṭīliya. When he reached Bāghāya, he was met there by Yaḥyā b. Sulaymān, governor of

Ṭubna, who informed him about fourteen men from among the followers whom Abū ʿAbd Allāh had sent with money to al-Mahdī in Sijilmāsa. They had delivered (the money) and left to return to him with the reply. While they were on their way back from (Sijilmāsa), they were ambushed by a group of Zanāta.[284] When they saw (the Zanāta) approaching towards them in multitude, they gathered together and buried the letters which they had at a spot saying, 'If anyone of us survives, he shall recover them.' Then they stood for the enemy until they reached them. They fought them and kept on fighting them and killing them, while they fell one after another until the last of them fell. The Zanāta carried away their dead and withdrew, leaving them fallen on the ground. Then they were caught up in a heavy downpour and water penetrated into the wounds of one of their men. There was a spark of life left in him. He revived himself and stood up by his own strength. He kept walking until he reached Ṭubna and informed Yaḥyā b. Sulaymān of what had happened. He described to him the spot where the letters were. Having accomplished this, he died. May God have mercy upon him and his companions. God, the Mighty, the Glorious, willed this message of His friend should reach its destination. He had written to Abū ʿAbd Allāh in those letters important matters. Yaḥyā b. Sulaymān went to the place which the man had described to him. He found [the bodies of] the men lying and buried them. He recovered the letters and delivered them to Abū ʿAbd Allāh in Bāghāya. (Abū ʿAbd Allāh) was overcome with grief at the murder of these men, for they were among the best of believers. He was about to lead an expedition against the Zanāta to attack them. He gathered the elders and consulted them on this matter. They said, 'The land is far and this army is near to us. We cannot be sure that it would not come to our country in our absence, whereas the matter of the Zanāta will not escape us, God willing. Whoever of us is killed is in paradise. He will die while obeying his lord.' They consoled him over them and eased him regarding them. He was pleased to receive the letter

284. The powerful tribes of the Zanāta group, spread across the central Maghrib, belong to the Butr branch of the Berbers. On their origin and history see Ibn Ḥazm, *Jamhara*, pp. 495–496, 498–499; Ibn Khaldūn, *al-ʿIbar*, vol. 7, pp. 3–16 (tr. *Berbères*, vol. 3, pp. 179–192); and C. Hamès, 'Zanāta', *EI*², vol. 11, pp. 442–443.

of al-Mahdī, and praised God, the Exalted, that the Zanāta did not become acquainted with its contents.

(Abū ʿAbd Allāh) led the army to Qasṭīliya. (The inhabitants) came out and fought him for some time during the day. Then they surrendered to him, and asked him for protection. Abu ʿAbd Allāh granted them protection. During the battle and before the [granting of] protection, the followers gathered a lot of booty from them. Abū ʿAbd Allāh seized the wealth of Ziyādat Allāh and his men which he found there.[285]

(Abū ʿAbd Allāh) marched and camped before Qafṣa. (Its inhabitants) asked him for protection which he granted them. He also seized the property of Ziyādat Allāh which was held with them. He withdrew and came to Bāghāya where he left a garrison of 500 horsemen under the command of Abū Makdūl. Muḥammad b. Ghazwiyya died in (Bāghāya), so his father Ghazwiyya tarried there with fifty horsemen of the Malūsa. Abū ʿAbd Allāh continued marching at the head of the army until he arrived in Īkjān.

When Abū ʿAbd Allāh was heading for Qasṭīliya, Ibn Abī al-Aghlab had feared that he was proceeding to Ifrīqiya. He had been expecting this and determined that if he received information to this effect, he would march to Ifrīqiya. However, when he learnt that he had returned to Īkjān and that only 500 horsemen remained in Bāghāya, he advanced with all his troops from al-Urbus and camped before Bāghāya. Abū Makdūl sent emissaries to Abū ʿAbd Allāh. When they reached him, he immediately ordered drums to be beaten. The Kutāma alerted each other and then emerged from all sides. They spread over the plain and rough terrain, rushing towards Bāghāya. When Abū ʿAbd Allāh saw that, he preceded them to the Saktān and held back the people. He picked 12,000 horsemen under the command of Abū Madīnī. He instructed him saying, 'If you catch up with the enemy at Bāghāya and they fight you before reaching (the town), then ride yourself even though you might have to ride on top of the lances and let no one prevent you from reaching Bāghāya. However,

285. The conquest of Qasṭīliya followed by that of Qafṣa took place probably at the beginning of the autumn of 296/908. See Ibn ʿIdhārī, *al-Bayān*, vol. 1, p. 145; and Ibn al-Athīr, *al-Kāmil*, vol. 6, p. 131. It allowed Abū ʿAbd Allāh to gain a foothold in a region inclined to Kharijism.

if you find that they have already withdrawn, or if you fight them and they flee, then do not go beyond Fajj al-ʿArʿār.'

Abū Madīnī proceeded towards Bāghāya, and Abū ʿAbd Allāh returned with the bulk to Īkjān.

There were at that time in Bāghāya a group of its inhabitants, among whom was Ḥārith al-Madgharī at the head of 300 horsemen of the Madghara.[286] When Ibn Abī al-Aghlab attacked them, they came out and fought a fierce battle. On that day Ghazwiyya made an astounding stand and Ḥārith al-Madgharī fought a fierce battle. Ibn Abī al-Aghlab told him, 'O Ḥārith! God will punish you for our benevolence towards you.' This is because Ziyādat Allāh had given him gifts and had been generous towards him.

Ḥārith replied, 'Abū ʿAbd Allāh's generosity towards me is greater than your generosity. He saved me from blindness and delivered me from ignorance.'

Among the followers at that time in Bāghāya also was Rajā' b. Abī Qitta. He fought a fierce battle and stood a severe test. The companions of Ibn Abī al-Aghlab looked at the resistance of the followers in Bāghāya in spite of their small number, and realised that they were powerless. They feared that help would come to them and they were agitated. The battle on that day lasted throughout the day. Then with the approach of evening, the companions of Ibn Abī al-Aghlab were put to flight. The followers, being few in numbers, did not pursue them. The halting place of their army was based at al-Qirbāt where they spent the night.

Meanwhile, Abū Madīnī spent the same night at Kursha. The following morning he arranged his troops and marched at their head. When he approached Bāghāya, those who were in (the town) came out towards him. They marched in this formation towards the halting place of Ibn Abī al-Aghlab, but found that he had departed during the night. They found remnants of the army and possessions. They killed those whom they found and seized whatever they found. They pursued the [Aghlabid] army until they reached Fajj al-ʿArʿār.

---

286. The Madghara or Maṭghara tribe were descended from the Butr branch of the Berbers. See Ibn Ḥazm, *Jamhara*, p. 496; Ibn Khaldūn, *al-ʿIbar*, vol. 6, pp. 239–245 (tr. *Berbères*, vol. 1, pp. 236–241); al-Idrīsī, *Nuzha*, p. 85 (tr. p. 98); and Georges S. Colin, 'Maṭghara', *EI*², vol. 6, p. 815.

Then Abū Madīnī stopped, saying, 'This is the limit set upon us by the shaykh. He had instructed us not to go beyond it.' He withdrew to Bāghāya and Ibn Abī al-Aghlab reached al-Urbus. Abū Madīnī returned to Īkjān together with the troops who had come from there. Abū Makdūl and Ghazwiyya returned with him. Abū Yūsuf remained in Bāghāya with the mounted troops who were with him.

30

The conquest of the town of al-Urbus and Ibn Abī al-Aghlab's defeat.

At the beginning of spring, when the weather was pleasant, Abū 'Abd Allāh amassed troops in large numbers and made preparations. Then he marched against Ibn Abī al-Aghlab in al-Urbus. He set out from Īkjān on 1 Jumādā II 296/25 February 909, and camped at Bāghāya where he reviewed those with him and assembled them. The size of the army reached 200,000 men, including mounted troops and foot-soldiers. Ziyādat Allāh had (also) concentrated troops and distributed gifts. He sent reinforcements to Ibn Abī al-Aghlab. Hence, innumerable troops gathered in al-Urbus. God alone knows their number. Abū 'Abd Allāh marched from Bāghāya and reached Miskiyāna. He then went up along the river valley (*al-wādī*)[287] up to Wādī Majjāna,[288] then crossed [*wādī*] Marmājanna to reach Wādī al-Raml,[289] where he set up camp. He dispatched a detachment of horsemen on Thursday 21 Jumādā II 296/17 March 909 to Manyūla. They pillaged Manyūla. On the following day, Friday, he dispatched another detachment of horsemen to Shaqbanāriya,[290] which they reached before midday. (Its inhabitants) fought them until after-

287. That is Wādī Miskiyāna, a tributary of the Mellègue (Wādī Mallāq).

288. Wādī Majjāna is apparently a section of Wādī Mallāq which al-Bakrī, *al-Masālik*, pp. 49, 145 (tr. pp. 106, 278), mentions farther to the west of Majjāna.

289. Wādī al-Raml (Oued Rmel) is a tributary of the Mellègue to the west of al-Urbus and south-west of Shaqbanāriya.

290. Shaqbanāriya, ancient Sicca Veneria, today Chicca Bénar (Shiqqa Banāriya) or al-Kef, in north-western Tunisia. See Mohamed Talbi, 'al-Kāf', *EI*^{2}, vol. 4, pp. 402–404; and al-Bakrī, *al-Masālik*, p. 33 (tr. p. 74).

noon. Then, after being granted safety, they surrendered and came to Abū ʿAbd Allāh with their notables. That day Abū ʿAbd Allāh had dispatched detachments of horsemen. One of them proceeded to [attack] the Banū Jūdān. These horsemen were intercepted by numerous horsemen of Ibn Abī al-Aghlab who fought them. A Kutāma tribesman was taken prisoner and brought to Ibn Abī al-Aghlab while Maḥbūb b. ʿAbdūn[291] was with him. (Maḥbūb) asked him to be spared, but Ibn Abī al-Aghlab refused to spare him. Maḥbūb was enraged and turned away from him. Ibn Abī al-Aghlab gave orders to execute the man, and he was executed.

Then the following morning, on Saturday 23 Jumādā II [296]/19 March 909, Abū ʿAbd Allāh set apart the troops and disposed them for battle. He placed the Banū Nabṭāsh at the right flank, the Banū Yanāwa at the left flank, and the Malūsa and the Masālta in the centre. He chose 10,000 horsemen, among them *dāʿīs*, chiefs of tribes and the elite of the troops. He placed them with him and advanced upon al-Urbus. He encountered Ibn Abī al-Aghlab who had already mobilised his army. There was fighting in close combat. Abū ʿAbd Allāh positioned himself with the 10,000 horsemen on a hill overlooking the town.[292] Fighting spread in the plain and people beat each other. The battle was violent with many dead on both sides. Fighting between them continued from the beginning of daylight until the time for the afternoon prayer. The companions of Ibn Abī al-Aghlab frowned. All the worthy troops of Ziyādat Allāh, Arabs or Berbers, of the regions and outskirts of Ifrīqiya accompanied Ibn Abī al-Aghlab.

Abū ʿAbd Allāh saw that (Ibn Abī al-Aghlab's troops) were disconcerting for his companions. He sensed some desperation among his companions and feared their defeat. He told the elders who were around him, 'Select from among the infantry those whom you consider to be superior, and send them to occupy the gorge, a gorge called al-Maḍāra, and hide in it to ambush the horsemen. Then perhaps they will provoke them.'

---

291. He was a chief of the Hawwāra camping in the region. Ibn ʿIdhārī, *al-Bayān*, vol. 1, p. 149, refers to him as Maḥbūb b. ʿAbd Rabbih al-Hawwārī.

292. The hill is situated on the site of al-Urbus to the north-west near Djebel Zafrane. Ibn Ḥawqal, *Ṣūrat al-arḍ*, p. 87, and al-Bakrī, *al-Masālik*, p. 46 (tr. p. 99), refer to excellent saffron produced in the territory to which the mountain owes its name.

(The elders) selected 575 men whom they considered to be the strongest. They stripped and each one of them took two lances and a shield, and walked to that gorge. It so happened that Ibn Abī al-Aghlab had thought and planned of doing the same. He had dispatched foot-soldiers from him to that gorge. They confronted each other at a place called al-Ghurra al-Bayḍā' near to a plantation of almonds on the route from al-Urbus to Shaqbanāriya. The first man to emerge from the Kutāma tribesmen confronted the first man to emerge from the companions of Ibn Abī al-Aghlab. The two then fought a duel with lances, each one of them attacking the other. The Kutāma tribesman killed the companion of Ibn Abī al-Aghlab who had attacked him. His companions attacked the foot-soldiers of Ibn Abī al-Aghlab, who fled. The battle cry was raised among them and the troops of Ibn Abī al-Aghlab fled. The foot-soldiers of Abū ʿAbd Allāh engaged their cavalry and his cavalry attacked them. They turned away fleeing, each side proceeding to its own locality. Ibn Abī al-Aghlab and the accompanying foot-soldiers of Ziyādat Allāh and the inhabitants of Ifrīqiya withdrew to the mountain of al-Ḥarrāqīn. The Lawāta,[293] the Karnāya and the Miklāta took the road to Jathīr Mas.[294] All the black guards with diverse elements of the inhabitants of Ifrīqiya took the road to al-Qayrawān. Maḥbūb b. ʿAbdūn together with the Hawwāra and the Nafza took the route in the direction of the Banū Bashīr. The followers pursued them from all directions, killing them, taking them prisoners and plundering what they were carrying. Some of them proceeded to the town, where they killed those that they came across and plundered whatever they could until sunset. At nightfall they withdrew to their halting place and spent the night there. The following morning Abū ʿAbd Allāh gave orders to proceed to the town of al-Urbus. This is because its inhabitants kindled fire and persisted

293. The Lawāta belong to the Butr branch of the Berbers. They were dispersed in several regions of North Africa and Egypt. Ibn Ḥawqal, *Ṣūrat al-arḍ*, p. 102, relates them to the Zanāta and the Mazāta. On them see Tadeusz Lewicki, 'Lawāta', *EI*², vol. 5, pp. 694–697; and Ibn Khaldūn, *al-ʿIbar*, vol. 6, pp. 234–239 (tr. *Berbères*, vol. 1, pp. 231–236).

294. Jathīr Mas (variants: Ḥashīr Mas, Ḥasīr Mar, Ḥashīr Mammas) is probably Sāqiyat Mams which al-Bakrī, *al-Masālik*, p. 146 (tr. p. 280), mentions on the route approaching al-Qayrawān from the west, and where Abū ʿAbd Allāh halted before entering Raqqāda. See Ibn ʿIdhārī, *al-Bayān*, vol. 1, p. 149.

with Ibn Abī al-Aghlab. The followers took (the town) by force and killed countless in it.[295] They plundered whatever was there and stayed on Sunday. On Monday Abū ʿAbd Allāh departed with all the troops and took the route to Duqqa[296] heading for Qammūda while people were saying that he was heading for Qasṭīliya.[297]

31

Ziyādat Allāh's flight from Raqqāda.

Ziyādat Allāh received the news of the defeat on Sunday after the noon prayer.[298] He knew for certain that if the army of al-Urbus was defeated, then he would have nothing left, because it was the last stratagem and the hardest effort that he was able to make. He had already gathered all his belongings and made preparations to flee. Now when he received the news of the defeat, he proclaimed that he had gained victory. He gave orders to execute and decapitate some men who had been detained in the prison. He ordered their heads to be paraded in al-Qayrawān and al-Qaṣr al-Qadīm. He began to gather his possessions and carried his valuables and belongings. He warned the dignitaries of his entourage and members of his family to leave with him, giving them the news which he had received. Ibn al-Ṣāʾigh advised him to stay, saying, 'The soldiers will rally to you. If you bestow gifts, the people will come to you; [Abū ʿAbd Allāh] al-Shīʿī will dare not attack you. Do not abandon your kingdom, for your grandfather Ziyādat Allāh[299]

---

295. A description of this conquest is found in al-Bakrī, *al-Masālik*, p. 46 (tr. p. 99); Ibn ʿIdhārī, *al-Bayān*, vol. 1, pp. 146–147; Ibn al-Athīr, *al-Kāmil*, vol. 6, pp. 131–132; al-Maqrīzī, *Ittiʿāẓ*, vol. 1, pp. 62–63; and Ibn Khaldūn, *al-ʿIbar*, vol. 4, pp. 73–74 (tr. *Berbères*, vol. 2, pp. 518–519).

296. Apparently Duqqa here is Henchir Dougga, ancient Tucca Terebenthina, located twenty-five miles north-north-west of Sabība and twelve miles south of Zanfour (Assuras), hence south-east of al-Urbus on El Kef to Sbeitla route. See Tissot, *Géographie*, vol. 2, p. 619.

297. Ibn ʿIdhārī, *al-Bayān*, vol. 1, p. 147, states that Abū ʿAbd Allāh headed for Bāghāya after the battle.

298. 24 Jumādā II 296/20 March 909.

299. Ziyādat Allāh b. Ibrāhīm b. al-Aghlab (r. 201–223/817–838).

waged war throughout Ifrīqiya, gathering its inhabitants from al-Qaṣr al-Qadīm for twelve years. You have strength from the members of your family and your dignitaries. Therefore, do not disperse your community. Do not lose your kingdom. Resist them.'

(Ziyādat Allāh) did not agree with him. (Ibn al-Ṣā'igh) urged him in this matter. Thereupon Ziyādat Allāh said, 'This proves what is being said about you, that you corresponded with al-Shī'ī and wanted him to seize me.'

(Ibn al-Ṣā'igh) apologised to him. He denied having anything to do with what was being said about him, and kept away from him.[300]

Ziyādat Allāh began to pack his belongings, precious robes, jewels, weapons and light luggage. He arranged to meet by night with those of his entourage who were present. Each one of them departed, carrying with him whatever he wanted. They feared that they would be killed if they remained behind. He took the slave-girls, maid servants who had borne him children (*ummāhāt al-awlād*), his sons and daughters whom he wanted to take with him. He chose 1,000 Slavs (*ṣaqāliba*) from among his personal slaves. He placed on each one of them a belt containing 1,000 dinars, fearing that the loads of his (own) belongings would be followed. He gathered the rest of his belongings in loads. Then when the muezzin called to the evening prayer, he left Raqqāda, followed by successive groups of his entourage led by torches. He took the route to Qalshāna[301] on the main highway for Egypt.

Ibn al-Ṣā'igh also left soon after him with his valuables, load and servants. He headed for the citadel of Sousse (Qaṣr Sūsa)[302] where he had prepared a sailing vessel for himself to take him to Sicily.[303]

---

300. The wording of the account of the *Iftitāḥ* is closely followed by al-Nuwayrī, *Nihāya*, vol. 24, pp. 146–147 (tr. *Berbères*, vol. 1, pp. 441–442).

301. Qalshāna was twelve miles south-east of al-Qayrawān. See al-Bakrī, *al-Masālik*, p. 29 (tr. p. 65).

302. Sousse (Sūsa) lies in the heart of the Sāḥil in the east central coastal region of Tunisia. See Mohamed Jedidi, 'Sūsa', *EI*², vol. 9, pp. 901–902. The citadel of Sousse was founded by Ziyādat Allāh b. Ibrāhīm b. al-Aghlab in 206/821. On it see Alexandre Lézine, *Le ribat de Sousse: suivi de notes sur le ribat de Monastir* (Tunis, 1956); and Marçais, *L'architecture musulmane*, pp. 30–31.

303. According to al-Nuwayrī, *Nihāya*, vol. 24, p. 148 (tr. *Berbères*, vol. 1, p. 442), Ibn al-Ṣā'igh

He parted from Ziyādat Allāh because he feared for his life from his dignitaries who were accompanying him. He feared that they would encourage him to kill him. He had been hostile to most of them, and they treated him as an enemy because of his precedence at the court of Ziyādat Allāh and his predominance with him. He did not feel safe from their slandering of him to (Ziyādat Allāh), for he had heard that they had accused him of corresponding with Abū ʿAbd Allāh, and also what Ziyādat Allāh told him when he advised him to stay. Ibn al-Ṣāʾigh left Raqqāda with torches when (Ziyādat Allāh) left, and he took the road to al-Qaṣr al-Qadīm. Thirty loads of luggage containing valuables which had been delayed followed him. Those who were conveying the luggage saw Ibn al-Ṣāʾigh's torches and thought that they were Ziyādat Allāh's torches and followed them. Ibn al-Ṣāʾigh arrived at Sousse and immediately set out to sea. The loads of luggage containing the riches arrived at Sousse after him. Ibn al-Hamdānī[304] seized them and deposited them.[305] Then when Abū ʿAbd Allāh entered Raqqāda, he seized them.[306]

The remaining inhabitants of Raqqāda fled by night on their way to al-Qaṣr al-Qadīm, to al-Qayrawān, to Sousse, and in all directions, taking with them their light luggage and whatever they could carry. On Monday morning the inhabitants of al-Qayrawān and people arriving from everywhere rushed to Raqqāda, looting whatever they found there. They seized each other, the strong looting the weak. After the inhabitants of al-Qayrawān left, malicious people engaged in plundering Raqqāda. They looted what Ziyādat Allāh had left in its palaces, and what was found in the homes of his dignitaries as

---

embarked for Sicily from farther south at Lamṭa.

304. He was governor of Sousse at that time. See Ibn ʿIdhārī, *al-Bayān*, vol. 1, p. 148.

305. Ibn ʿIdhārī, *al-Bayān*, vol. 1, p. 148, accuses Ibn al-Ṣāʾigh of treason and theft. He tried to divert the thirty loads of 16,000 *mithqāls* each with the complicity of the treasurers. However, these treasurers missed the appointed place of meeting and proceeded to Sousse, where the governor seized these funds and deposited them in the citadel of Sousse (Qaṣr al-Ribāṭ). This is plausible if one admits al-Nuwayrī's account that the *wazīr* embarked at Lamṭa.

306. Abū ʿAbd Allāh sent Ghazwiyya b. Yūsuf to Sousse to grant protection to its inhabitants. Ghazwiyya returned with twenty-eight of the loads which had been deposited in the citadel of Sousse (Qaṣr al-Ribāṭ). See Ibn ʿIdhārī, *al-Bayān*, vol. 1, p. 150.

well as whatever was found in the homes of other people, including the most precious and exquisite things, without leaving anything. They went to search the underground granaries, pulling out the iron of the gates and carrying away the thrones and heavy furniture. They continued looting in this manner until the cavalry of Abū ʿAbd Allāh arrived.

Then members of the Aghlabid aristocracy who had stayed behind were overcome with fear. There were a large number of them, most of whom were in a state of poverty and misery. Many of their notables stayed behind after Ziyādat Allāh's departure, including some of his slaves and dignitaries, warriors and officials of the administration. Most of them were in Raqqāda. They dispersed, as we mentioned, on the night of Ziyādat Allāh's flight. Most of them were also in al-Qaṣr al-Qadīm and in its suburbs. Those that were in the suburbs converged on (al-Qaṣr al-Qadīm). Then the notables who had remained there were alarmed, and broke the locks of its gates on the eve of Tuesday. The bulk of them left for al-Qayrawān and other towns and hid therein. When the rest saw this the next day, they all set out for al-Qayrawān, and nobody remained in al-Qaṣr al-Qadīm. They took their belongings from there and dispersed in al-Qayrawān, in the desert, in Sousse and wherever each one of them chose to go. Every criminal engaged in plundering Raqqāda, for nobody ventured on the highway or elsewhere. There was no killing or anything among the people apart from what occurred in Raqqāda. They snatched away the plundered goods from the hands of each other.

32

Ibrāhīm b. Abī al-Aghlab's arrival in al-Qayrawān and his designs over the city.

Ibrāhīm b. Abī al-Aghlab reached the city of al-Qayrawān on the morning of Tuesday at the head of those who had joined him at the time of the defeat of his companions [at al-Urbus]. When they learnt of Ziyādat Allāh's flight, they dispersed from him, each group proceeding in the direction of its locality. Ibrāhīm b. Abī al-Aghlab entered the city of al-Qayrawān and proceeded to the emir's palace (*dār al-imāra*) and took up residence there. His crier proclaimed the order to calm the people. He summoned the jurists and notables of al-Qayrawān who came before him. People heard from each other about their going to him, so they came to the emir's palace and a crowd gathered in front of its gate. It was time for the midday prayer. The muezzin called to prayer and they greeted (Ibrāhīm) as the ruler. He asked the jurists and the notables to enter and denounced before them the evil conduct of Ziyādat Allāh which brought about the decadence of his dominion, strengthened his enemy against him, and his plundering of his kingdom. He condemned Abū ʿAbd Allāh and the Kutāma, slandering them in the most repulsive terms and frightened them, saying, 'I have only come to you to fight them away from your womenfolk, your blood and your property. Therefore, support me with your allegiance, and extend assistance to me with your property and men. Defend your lives, your womenfolk and your property.'

They replied, 'As for hearing and obeying, we owe that to you and to whoever governs us. However, you will not get the help that you want from our property and our hands, for we are shopkeepers, merchants and vendors. Our possessions are insufficient for what you want and we are unable and powerless to fight. You have fought these people, while you had with you the valiant professional warriors and the notables. The public treasury from which you draw [funds] was behind you, and yet you were unable to defeat them. Then how will you be able to do that with our help and our wealth?'

They kept on discussing the matter until eventually he told them, 'See what reserves you have in the endowments and deposits, and give these reserves to me as a loan so that I can announce the pay and rally people around me.'

They said to him, 'What could possibly be in the endowments and deposits? If you stretched your hand to these funds, the people would reject it and resist it.'

When (Ibrāhīm b. Abī al-Aghlab) despaired of them, he dismissed them and they left. People had gathered at the gate of the emir's palace, not knowing what was being discussed. However, when they came out and informed them about it, they shouted at him, 'Go away! We shall not suffer for your sake.'

The mob threatened and insulted him, and shouted, 'You will be seized and shackled!'

When (Ibrāhīm) heard this, he and those who were with him rode their mounts, drew their weapons and stormed the gate. Those who were at the gate ran away and let them go. They were pelted with stones from the tops of houses. They shielded themselves and urged their mounts until they left the city. Ibrāhīm b. Abī al-Aghlab and his companions were joined by Ziyādat Allāh's men who had remained behind, fearing for their lives, and he reached Ziyādat Allāh.

Predictions were being related that the first ruler of the Aghlabids was named Ibrāhīm,[307] and the last of them would also be named Ibrāhīm. Therefore on that day when Ibrāhīm became ruler in al-Qayrawān, people said, 'He is the one about whom it has been related that the last of them would be Ibrāhīm.'[308] Similarly, it was being related about the Marwānids that the first of them was named Marwān, and the last of them would be named Marwān,[309] and it so happened. Similarly it was being related that the first of (the Marwānids) in Andalusia was ʿAbd al-Raḥmān,[310] and the last of them would also be named ʿAbd al-Raḥmān.[311]

---

307. Ibrāhīm b. al-Aghlab (r. 184–196/800–812).

308. On Ibrāhīm b. Abī al-Aghlab's attempt to secure the emirate after the flight of Ziyādat Allāh, see Talbi, *L'émirat aghlabide*, pp. 684–686.

309. The Umayyad caliphs Abū ʿAbd al-Malik Marwān b. al-Ḥakam (r. 64–65/684–685) and Abū ʿAbd al-Malik Marwān b. Muḥammad (r. 127–132/744–750).

310. ʿAbd al-Raḥmān b. Muʿāwiya (r. 138–172/756–788).

311. In fact the last Umayyad caliph of Spain was Hishām b. Muḥammad (r. 418–422/1027–1031) (d. 428/1036). The Andalusian rival of the Fatimid caliph-imam al-Muʿizz, under whose reign the *Iftitāḥ* was completed, was ʿAbd al-Raḥmān al-Nāṣir. See al-Qāḍī al-Nuʿmān, *Kitāb al-Majālis wa-al-musāyarāt*, ed. al-Ḥabīb al-Faqī et al. (Tunis, 1978), pp. 115–116, 164–170, 173ff., 217, 234–236, 363–364. Also Farhat Dachraoui, 'Tentative d'infiltration šiʿite en Espagne musulmane sous le regne d'al-Ḥakam II', *al-Andalus*, 23 (1958), pp. 97–106.

33

Abū ʿAbd Allāh's arrival in Ifrīqiya, his stay in Raqqāda and the consolidation of his position there.

The news of Ziyādat Allāh's flight reached Abū ʿAbd Allāh after his departure from Duqqa before his arrival at Sabība.[312] He took the road to Saktāna,[313] and halted at Wādī al-Raml[314] where he spent the night. The following morning he dispatched an advance guard of 1,000 mounted troops under Ghazwiyya b. Yūsuf and Ḥasan b. Abī Khinzīr to Raqqāda, ordering them not to harm anyone. They arrived in Raqqāda and came across people there looting food and junk. When they saw them they dispersed, for they were afraid of them. However, they granted them protection without harming anyone and let each one of them retain what they were already carrying, but stopped them from taking the rest. Those who were in Raqqāda came to al-Qayrawān and related the news. The people were happy with this and satisfied.

The notables and the jurists of al-Qayrawān come out to meet Abū ʿAbd Allāh. They met with him, greeted him and congratulated him on the victory.[315] He turned his face towards them, responded to them most favourably and ordered them to ride their mounts. He summoned them and asked them to accompany him. He talked to them and granted them safety for their lives and property. They were pleased with his humility and familiarity which they could see. They informed him about Ibn Abī al-Aghlab and how he had treated them. They expressed to him their wish to turn towards him and support

---

312. Sabība (S'biba), ancient Sufes, lies on the route from al-Qayrawān to Majjāna. See Ibn Ḥawqal, *Ṣūrat al-arḍ*, p. 84; al-Bakrī, *al-Masālik*, pp. 49, 146 (tr. pp. 106, 279); al-Idrīsī, *Nuzha*, p. 119 (tr. p. 139); and Yāqūt, *Muʿjam*, vol. 3, p. 186.

313. Thus in MS 934, fol. 124b, and in the Hamdani manuscript used in both editions. Variants: Saksāna in MS 78, p. 345; MS 79, p. 237; MS 1147, p. 195, and both copies of the Beirut manuscripts; Saknāriya in MS 254, fol. 114a, and Sakāna in MS 1001, p. 389. Dachraoui in his edition, Arabic text p. 243 and French summary p. 112, suggests Silyāna, since the Oued Siliana takes its source to the south-east of Henchir Dougga.

314. al-Bakrī, *al-Masālik*, p. 49 (tr. p. 106)mentions a Wādī al-Raml to the west of al-Qayrawān.

315. The meeting took place on Saturday 1 Rajab 296/25 March 909 at Sāqiyat Mams to the west of al-Qayrawān. See Ibn ʿIdhārī, *al-Bayān*, vol. 1, p. 149.

him. He told them, 'You have received your good fortune, have looked after your best interest and have acted in accordance with where your deliverance and your well-being lie, and what will bring you advantage in the near and distant future.'

Then they began to relate to him about Ziyādat Allāh, describing his wickedness and his evil deeds, while Abū 'Abd Allāh remained silent about the matter. Eventually, when they talked at length about it, he said, 'His imams who appointed him and gave him authority, his ancestors before him and their ancestors before them, were worse than him. If you knew and saw the immoral and wicked circumstances of the Abbasids, you would not find appalling what you think of this [man], his ineptitude and the weakness of his authority that you have described. (Ziyādat Allāh) continued to resist and fight with the power and ability which he had. He did have power and dominion that you saw. However, the decree of God cannot be opposed. No one can fight it, for the friends of God are the victorious and His soldiers are the victorious. His prudence and the strength of His condition brought about his flight away from us when he realised that he had no power over us.'

Then they realised that they had been mistaken in their description of Ziyādat Allāh's ineptitude, because it has been said that whoever belittles the matter of the one murdered, belittles the matter of his murderer. Thus they refrained from what they were saying and began to thank and praise Abū 'Abd Allāh. They wished him well and requested him to treat them well and pardon their disrespect. During all this he reassured them and promised (to pardon) them until he arrived in Raqqāda, with them walking around him. He halted there and allowed them to depart. They returned to the city of al-Qayrawān. He appointed over them Ḥasan b. Aḥmad b. Abī Khinzīr as governor.

Abū 'Abd Allāh entered (Raqqāda) on Saturday 1 Rajab 296/25 March 909. This is the year and the month about which predictions and reports have preceded stating what would happen in them, and which we have already mentioned at the beginning of the book. Abū 'Abd Allāh lodged at one of the castles[316] of Raqqāda. He distributed

316. It was Qaṣr al-Ṣaḥn, according to Ibn 'Idhārī, *al-Bayān*, vol. 1, p. 150, and Ibn Ḥammād,

to the Kutāma quarters there which had been abandoned. All the Kutāma lodged in them. They also lodged in al-Qaṣr al-Qadīm in the quarters of those who fled with Ziyādat Allāh, in the suburbs around it and around Raqqāda. They were like widespread locusts. When the people saw their numerous assembly, they could not imagine that anything like it would gather among any people. The people saw their good discipline, modesty and tranquillity, which led them to believe what had been said among them about them, that none of them stretched his hand on anything, or transgressed what he had been told, or disobeyed what he had been commanded to do, as if they were standing in prayer, or there were guards over them who controlled their hands and prevented them from transgressing.

34

Safety granted by Abū ʿAbd Allāh to the populace and his administrative and political measures.

When Abū ʿAbd Allāh had settled down in Raqqāda, he ordered a herald to proclaim in al-Qayrawān the granting of safety to the common people, allowing those who had moved away from their homeland to return. Hence people returned to their homeland and settled in their residence. He dispatched governors to the towns to proclaim the granting of amnesty there, and seek out malicious and wicked people, and punished them. Then the turmoil of the common people subsided and roads became safe. Travellers proceeded and criminals were frightened, for they were killed wherever they were seized, and they were sought out wherever they went. (Abū ʿAbd Allāh) banned the drinking of intoxicants as well as everything reprehensive that appeared in public. He spread justice and proclaimed it. The situation became stable and calm. The kingdom became strong and powerful. Anyone who had been fearful because of having assumed some responsibility in the service of Ziyādat Allāh now felt secure. Members of his family who had remained behind,

---

Akhbār, p. 8 (tr. p. 20). On Aghlabid palaces see Vonderheyden, *La Berbérie orientale*, pp. 191–197.

his slaves, clients, the clients of his ancestors as well as those who depended on them, felt secure and appeared in public and became dispersed. They joined (Abū ʿAbd Allāh) and his men, and entered his service and activities.

(Abū ʿAbd Allāh) appointed Muḥammad b. ʿUmar al-Marwadhī[317] to the office of *qāḍī* of the city of al-Qayrawān. He had adhered to Shiʿism for long and based himself on matters of jurisprudence on the sayings of the imams. (Abū ʿAbd Allāh) granted him the power to appoint judges and arbitrators in the other towns. At the head of his letters and decrees it was inscribed: 'From Muḥammad b. ʿUmar, Chief Judge (*qāḍī al-quḍāt*).' He was appointed by him on the 1 Ramaḍān 296/24 May 909.[318] (Abū ʿAbd Allāh) gave orders to gather everything which came to light belonging to Ziyādat Allāh, his wealth, slaves, weapons, riding animals and his remaining slave-girls without prosecuting anyone for this.[319] A group of Ziyādat Allāh's slave-girls of beauty and prestige were gathered before (Abū ʿAbd Allāh). He asked as to who was responsible for providing for them and protecting them. He was told that there was a woman called Rawand at the court of Ziyādat Allāh who cared for them. He had her brought before him and gave her gifts and was charitable to her. He instructed her to protect them, look after them and do what was required for them, and that she should submit to him [details of] this matter so that he could order for them the provision of everything useful for them. She said, 'O master! May God strengthen you. You have commanded and set up a condition of looking after them and submit what they need. What is useful for them is what they are accustomed to, and what is customary and nourishes and sustains them.'

---

317. He is Muḥammad b. ʿUmar b. Yaḥyā b. ʿAbd al-Aʿlā al-Marwadhī (d. 303/915–916), whose harshness is well documented. He was eventually dismissed and executed under the reign of al-Mahdī. See Ibn al-Haytham, *Kitāb al-Munāẓarāt*, index; al-Khushanī, *ʿUlamāʾ Ifrīqiya*, pp. 298, 302, 309; al-Mālikī, *Riyāḍ al-nufūs*, vol. 2, pp. 41, 48, 54–55, 60, 155; ʿIyāḍ, *Madārik*, pp. 375, 383, 379, 412; Ibn ʿIdhārī, *al-Bayān*, vol. 1, pp. 151–152, 159, 169, 173, 189; and Ibn Nājī, *Maʿālim*, vol. 2, pp. 262–265, 268–269, 289–292, 331, 348, vol. 3, pp. 10–11, 57.

318. According to Ibn ʿIdhārī, *al-Bayān*, vol. 1, p. 151, the investiture of al-Marwadhī took place on Thursday 18 Shaʿbān 296/12 May 909.

319. The assessor of Ziyādat Allāh's wealth was Aḥmad b. Farrūkh al-Tubnī al-Aḥdab. See Ibn ʿIdhārī, *al-Bayān*, vol. 1, p. 151.

He asked, 'And what is that?'

She replied, 'Good food.'

He said, 'They will be provided the best food that they have ever savoured.'

She said, 'Then there is fine clothing, cushions, blankets and soft bedding.'

He said, 'They will be provided what they are used to, and better than that.'

She said, 'There are two other things, if the master allows me to mention them.'

He said, 'Mention whatever seems appropriate to you.'

She said, 'They are accustomed to drinking.'

He said, 'They will not obtain this thing with us. Give them something else in abundance instead.'

She said, 'They want from men that which men want from them.'

He said, 'That is reserved for their master who will come to them soon, God willing. So exercise kind speech in this matter and the promise of it, and take care of them.'

He ordered for her everything which she wanted for them in terms of food, clothing, cushions, blankets and expenditure, the best of these which they had known. He did not cast his eye on anyone of them and knew their description only by word of mouth. Then, when al-Mahdī, peace be upon him, arrived, they went to him, and he found them in the best condition and under the best care.

Then on Friday, (Abū ʿAbd Allāh) ordered the observance of the communal prayer. He appointed a preacher for the mosque of Raqqāda and another for the mosque of al-Qayrawān. He addressed for the same purpose letters to the [other] towns. He prescribed in the sermon to invoke blessings upon Muḥammad and his family, upon ʿAlī, the Commander of the Faithful, upon al-Ḥasan and al-Ḥusayn, and upon Fāṭima al-Zahrāʾ. May the blessings of God be upon them all.[320] On the day he entered [Raqqāda], he ordered the introduction in the call to the prayer the expression, 'Come to the best of works'

320. Upon entering Raqqāda, al-Mahdī added his own name after this invocation. On the religious policy of the Fatimids in the Maghrib see Wilferd Madelung, 'The Religious Policy of the Fatimids toward their Sunnī Subjects in the Maghrib', in Barrucand, ed., *L'Égypte fatimide*, pp. 97–104.

(*ḥayya ʿalā khayr al-ʿamal*).[321] He ordered that coinage be struck, but without inscribing anyone's name on it. However, on the obverse in the place where names are inscribed, he ordered to be inscribed the formula, 'The Proof of God has been accomplished' (*balaghat ḥujjat Allāh*) and on the reverse the formula, 'The enemies of God have dispersed' (*tafarraqa aʿdāʾ Allāh*).[322] On another coin instead of this formula, he inscribed the formula, 'Praise be to God, Lord of the worlds' (*al-ḥamd li-llāh rabb al-ʿālamīn*).[323] He engraved on weapons, 'Implement dedicated in the way of God' (*ʿudda fī sabīl Allāh*). He inscribed on [the thighs of] horses, 'Sovereignty belongs to God' (*al-mulk li-llāh*). He [ordered to be] engraved on the stone of his finger ring, '*Confide in God! Indeed, you are following the manifest truth*' (27:79). On the seal with which he sealed his letters was engraved the formula, '*The word of your Lord has been fulfilled, in truth and justice. None can change His words. He is all-hearing, all-knowing*' (6:115).[324]

(Abū ʿAbd Allāh) remained with whatever meagre clothing he had, made of coarse cloth. He did not change this and nor did anyone of his men. If they were told to dress, they said, 'We shall not wear the garment of the tyrants.'

They remained with what they had been accustomed to, in spite of having affluence in their world. They acquired and benefited from

321. On the changes introduced in religious ritual see Ibn ʿIdhārī, *al-Bayān*, vol. 1, pp. 151–152; Idris, 'Contribution', pp. 144–145; and Robert Brunschvig, 'Fiqh fatimide et histoire de l'Ifriqiya', in *Mélanges Georges Marçais*, pp. 13–20, reprinted in his *Études d'islamologie*, ed. A. M. Turki (Paris, 1976), vol. 1, pp. 63–70.

322. A specimen of this dinar, minted in the year 297, is described by Henri Lavoix, *Catalogue des monnaies musulmanes de la Bibliothèque nationale: Espagne et Afrique* (Paris,1891), p. 339. Another specimen, minted in 297 at al-Qayrawān, is described by J. Farrugia de Candia, 'Monnaies fatimites du Musée du Bardo', *Revue tunisienne*, 27–28 (1936), pp. 334, 343–344.

323. This coin was named *al-Sayyidiyya*, after Abū ʿAbd Allāh who was styled *al-Sayyid* by the Kutāma. A specimen of this dinar, minted in 296, and found in the collection of Henri Sauvaire, is mentioned by Lavoix, *Catalogue*, p. 400. The charge of the mint was entrusted to Abū Bakr al-Faylasūf, known under the name of Ibn al-Qammūdī, who was maintained in his office by al-Mahdī. See Ibn ʿIdhārī, *al-Bayān*, vol. 1, pp. 151, 159.

324. Cf. legends and inscriptions given in Ibn Ḥammād, *Akhbār*, pp. 7–8 (tr. p. 19); Ibn al-Athīr, *al-Kāmil*, vol. 6, p. 132; Ibn ʿIdhārī, *al-Bayān*, vol. 1, p. 151; al-Nuwayrī, *Nihāya*, p. 40; al-Maqrīzī, *Ittiʿāẓ*, vol. 1, p. 64; Ibn Khaldūn, *al-ʿIbar*, vol. 4, p. 75 (tr. *Berbères*, vol. 2, p. 520); Idrīs ʿImād al-Dīn, *ʿUyūn al-akhbār*, ed. al-Yaʿlāwī, p. 139, ed. Ghālib, vol. 5, p. 87.

abundant bounties and wide worldly affluence which God granted them, and yet in spite of this they continued to be characterised by humility and sufficiency, except for horses, weapons and implements which enabled them to conduct war (*jihād*). Indeed, they had in this domain that the like of which no one else had. This is because everything pertaining to this which was found in the treasures of the Aghlabids and all their notables passed on to them and became their property which God granted to them. They had horses the likes of which had not been seen in terms of excellence, breed, agility and quality, none of them having any disease or blemish.

(Abū ʿAbd Allāh) had left behind at Īkjān the person known as Abū al-Muqāriʿ Abū al-Qāsim al-Ḥasan b. Aḥmad b. Nāfidh[325] and those who were with him at Ṭubna. Now he wrote to him asking him to come [to Raqqāda]. When he arrived and called upon him, he rose for him and greeted him. This was his custom with anyone who came to see him and who had been away from him for a long time. Whenever anyone calling upon him greeted him and kissed his hand, he also would kiss the person's hand. He continued like this as he used to act with the Kutāma. While he was still in Īkjān, Abū al-Muqāriʿ would say to him when he saw him acting thus, 'When God grants you victory over Ifrīqiya and you go there, you must cease this custom and refrain from practising it, because the people of Ifrīqiya are not familiar with this conduct from their emirs and will not adopt this.'

He would reply to him, 'If this is so, we shall practise with them what is suitable for them, God willing.'

So when (Abū al-Muqāriʿ) called upon (Abū ʿAbd Allāh) and he rose for him, he said, 'O master! Did we not agree between us to drop this custom for it is inappropriate in this place?'

He replied, 'O Abū al-Qāsim! Indeed, it is appropriate in every place.'

Here is the text of the letter which (Abū ʿAbd Allāh) wrote granting safety to all the towns:

> In the name of God, the Compassionate, the Merciful. May God bless His Messenger Muḥammad the Prophet and the pure members of his household. Now then! All praise is due to God. He helps His friends according

325. On him see note 224 above.

to His promise to them, and forsakes His enemies after having warned them of His punishment. He brings together helpers of the truth and followers of falsehood in one place to seek judgment, only to grant victory to helpers of His religion, strengthen them with glory, and bring upon His enemies misery, misfortune, ruin and perdition, so as to manifest the excellence of truth in His sight, and humiliate those who deviate from His way and turn away from His truth; a praise which will satisfy Him and which He will accept, bestowing upon them His favour in abundance. Indeed, with the praise and grace of God, I have not ceased since I accomplished for God the duty of His right to defend His religion, seeking revenge of His friends, enjoining what is right and summoning to Him, and forbidding what is wrong and warning against it, reviving the marks of the truth which the unjust caused to die, combating the enemies of God, the defectors, the usurpers of the right of the progeny of the Messenger of God, may God bless him and grant him salvation, presenting admonition to the Aghlabids and warning them of the shrinking of their borders and penetration of their towns, wishing them to revert to the truth, and return to Him, and their acknowledgement of Him, and their entry under His banner, abstaining from attacking them, hoping to prevent shedding the blood of Muslims. The more determined I was to be kind to them, the more they persisted in error. They conspired to oppress the servants of God, and persisted in sins with courage and boldness in transgression, filled with conceit because of the delay of their punishment. They have taken over the property of God in turns and His worshippers as servants among themselves. They will not return to piety and will not respect covenant and obligation to God. When I gave up hope that they would turn to contrition and when I ceased to wish that they might repent, I saw that it was not possible for me to give up fighting them. So I proceeded with some of my victorious armies and supported troops at the meeting place of their armies at al-Urbus, trusting God and relying upon Him, to seek fulfilment of what He has promised His friends regarding those who wage war against them and treat them as enemies, and who assume power in their place. God granted the adherents (*awliyāʾ*) of His religion their support. They killed them most violently in every valley, cave and hiding place. Those of them who were unharmed became dispersed and isolated. God exterminated them, broke their valour and destroyed their dissent. Their defeated remnant came to Ziyādat Allāh, the forsaken who gave up his dominion, and came out fleeing. His sins and transgression

> humiliated him. He abandoned his people, wealth, children and household. In his flight was the greatest good for Muslims. It spared their blood and brought an end to his injustice and oppression of them. I cast upon his womenfolk the veil of modesty and preserved their blood as he did not preserve it, taking into account God's reward, and following His word, may His mention be exalted, '*No bearer of burdens shall bear the burden of another*' (6:164; 17:15; 35:18; 39:7; 53:38). After having decided to depart to alleviate the violence against the inhabitants of al-Qayrawān, out of kindness towards them and forgiveness for them until their messenger came to me, and their ulema and notables met me and requested from me safety and protection for them and asked me for that, I granted their request, fulfilled their hopes, and averted calamity. I included in the guarantee of safety the innocent as well as the corrupt, the pious as well as the dissolute among them, and others after the victorious troops and the divinely supported armies had surrounded them. I prevented the flight of the fearful, accepted the return of the returnee and pardoned whoever asked for pardon, seeking the generous reward of God. And you, all the inhabitants of such and such town, are included in whatever I included them and will be treated in respect to safety, protection and preservation as I have treated them, as long as you accept that and as long as you seek it, and as long as you recognise the overflow of favour upon you in it. So listen and obey, and be firm and respond. Praise your Lord for what He has granted you and defended you. Be helpers of the truth and supporters of eradicating falsehood and you will win your portion. Thank God for His favours to you and He will continue to grant them to you and grant you more. Do not be ungrateful, lest His punishment should fall upon you. He, the most truthful sayer, says, '*If you give thanks, I will give you more; but if you are thankless, lo! My punishment is dire*' (14:7).

In the copy of this letter addressed to the inhabitants of Sicily, (Abū 'Abd Allāh) added:

> And you, gathering of the inhabitants of the island of Sicily, are most worthy of the kindness and benevolence which I have applied to you and have granted you. You are the most deserving and closest to them, because of the proximity of your abode to the abode of the polytheists and the fact that you are carrying out warfare (*jihād*) against the disbelievers, the unjust. I shall fill your island, God willing, with cavalry and infantry of believers who will truly fight for God. Indeed, God will honour the

religion and the Muslims, and by them He will subdue polytheism and polytheists. Power and strength belong to God, the Mighty. He is sufficient for us and how excellent a guardian is He!

When his letters were read out in the country, its inhabitants felt secure. They became confident and calmed down. They gave thanks and stopped being fearful. Delegations came to him from every town to thank him and congratulate him. They saw his justice, kindness and sound governance. This gave them much joy and they were satisfied with him.

35

Ziyādat Allāh's journey, his arrival in the east, and events relating to him until his death.

When Ziyādat Allāh left Raqqāda, he was accompanied by his notables, his slaves and his guards who had arrived at the time of his departure and whom he ordered to leave with him. Later he was joined by those who were not present [in Raqqāda, but] were recognised and feared for their lives. Ibn Abī al-Aghlab also joined (Ziyādat Allāh) together with those who fled from the city of al-Urbus after their defeat. Thus, many people gathered with (Ziyādat Allāh). He travelled with them until he reached the city of Tripoli and entered it. He proceeded to the residence of the governor and lodged there. Its governor at that time was Ibn Qurhub. (Ziyādat Allāh) did not see ʿAbd Allāh b. al-Ṣāʾigh leaving with them. He became certain of the accusations levelled against (Ibn al-Ṣāʾigh) of having corresponded with Abū ʿAbd Allāh.

Ibn al-Ṣāʾigh hated some of Ziyādat Allāh's notables and treated them as enemies. They envied him because of his proximity to (Ziyādat Allāh) and his influence with him. They had all conspired against him and testified before Ziyādat Allāh that he had corresponded with Abū ʿAbd Allāh, whereas he had not corresponded with him. At that time (Ziyādat Allāh) had not believed what they were alleging about him. [In Tripoli] they brought before him a man who had adhered to Abū ʿAbd Allāh who testified against (Ibn al-Ṣāʾigh) regarding this matter. He rejected his testimony, turned him over to (Ibn Qurhub) and the man was killed. (The notables) despaired of wronging before (Ziyādat Allāh), but they continued to bear hostility towards (Ibn al-Ṣāʾigh) and hate him. This was the reason for his delaying the departure with Ziyādat Allāh, and he feared them for his life. Now when he did not leave with (Ziyādat Allāh), they talked much about (Ibn al-Ṣāʾigh) and assured (Ziyādat Allāh) and he believed them and regretted that he had let (Ibn al-Ṣāʾigh) go.

ʿAbd Allāh b. al-Ṣāʾigh had embarked at sea from Sousse in a ship which he had there bound for Sicily, but adverse winds diverted it to Tripoli. While Ziyādat Allāh was there, the ship arrived and anchored. Ibn al-Ṣāʾigh disembarked and when he learnt that Ziyādat Allāh was there, he came to him and made it appear to him that he had come to see him. (Ziyādat Allāh) received him and asked him to come near him and granted him proximity. He reprimanded him for his delay. (Ibn al-Ṣāʾigh) apologised to him, saying that he had a load which he could not transport by land. It seemed that this removed from (Ziyādat Allāh) much of his suspicion about him. His notables were dismayed at this. They were incensed that he granted him proximity. They said that he was lying and brought forward someone who was on the ship. He informed (Ziyādat Allāh) that (Ibn al-Ṣāʾigh) had been aiming only for Sicily. (Ziyādat Allāh) realised that (Ibn al-Ṣāʾigh) had not corresponded with Abū ʿAbd Allāh because if he had done so, he would have remained in Ifrīqiya. He realised that he had been proceeding to Sicily only because he feared for his life from the notables, and he saw that they were jealous of him. He realised that they would not be useful to him with (Ibn al-Ṣāʾigh) being there. He feared that misfortune would befall him from them because of this. So he became somewhat withdrawn from (Ibn al-Ṣāʾigh) and told him, 'You wanted to deliver me in the hands of (Abū ʿAbd Allāh) al-Shīʿī, and you conspired against me.'

(Ibn al-Ṣāʾigh) replied, 'O my master, how is that?'

(Ziyādat Allāh) said, 'On the day I wanted to leave, did you not tell me to stay? You advised me so even when my troops had disintegrated and my companions had dispersed. You only intended to drive me out.'

He replied. 'God forbid! By God, I only wished to do you good so that you follow in the footsteps of your ancestors. Your grandfather Ziyādat Allāh was besieged in al-Qaṣr al-Qadīm for twelve years. Then he achieved victory.'

However, (Ziyādat Allāh) did not accept his pleas. He kept him at a distant and away from him. His notables who were around him pestered him about (Ibn al-Ṣā'igh) until he feared that his position might crumble because of him. So he ordered him to be executed.[326] Ziyādat Allāh remained in Tripoli many days.[327]

When Abū al-'Abbās, brother of Abū 'Abd Allāh, escaped from prison, he travelled secretly and reached Tripoli. Ziyādat Allāh arrived there soon after him. Previously, when he was brought before Ziyādat Allāh in Raqqāda, he imprisoned him. Then on the day when Mudlij rebelled against him, he broke out with the group of prisoners. He remained in hiding in the city of al-Qayrawān for some time. He was searched for and security patrols were on the look out for him. He feared that if he set out to travel to Abū 'Abd Allāh, he would be captured. So he travelled secretly until he reached Tripoli. Then, when Ziyādat Allāh arrived there he was informed about him and (Abū al-'Abbās) was brought before him. (Ziyādat Allāh) told him, 'God has enabled us to overpower you.'

He then pressed him to confess whether he was the brother of Abū 'Abd Allāh, but he denied this, saying, 'May God protect the emir! I am only a merchant. I have come from the east with goods. I transgressed in your land, so I was arrested and imprisoned and deprived of comfort. If I were the man to whom I have been linked, I would have gone to him and travelled towards him, but when I escaped from the prison, I set out for my country.'

(Ziyādat Allāh) told him, 'If this is the case, then travel with us until we make you reach your country and ascertain what you are saying and confirm that the allegations against you are false.'

(Abū al-'Abbās) said, 'May God ennoble the emir! You have already branded me with this mark and I have been gravely accused

---

326. The execution was carried out by Rāshid al-Aswad, one of the black guards of the emir. See Ibn 'Idhārī, *al-Bayān*, vol. 1, p. 149.

327. According to Ibn al-Athīr, *al-Kāmil*, vol. 6, p. 123, Ziyādat Allāh remained in Tripoli for nineteen days.

before you. You will arrive at a place ruled by someone else. I fear that I will be blamed. I will be imprisoned and perish without the matter becoming clear. The east is wide and my country is remote. So fear God for my sake and do not expose me to destruction.'

(Ziyādat Allāh) said, 'Your case is either as has been alleged against you or as you are asserting. We shall therefore spare you. Then if the matter is as is alleged against you, you will willingly protect for us those whom we have left behind. If you are what you say, we will not commit a crime against you.' Having said this, he set him free.[328]

Al-Mahdī had given orders about the womenfolk and the eunuchs whom he had left behind [in Salamiya] that they should join him. An old man from among his trusted men and followers called Abū Jaʿfar al-Khazarī[329] escorted them. He also encountered Ziyādat Allāh in Tripoli while they were with him. He used to meet with Abū al-ʿAbbās inside the congregational mosque before and after the arrival of Ziyādat Allāh. The two would debate about [the merits of] knowledge (*ʿilm*) in the presence of the congregation. Each one of them would pretend that he opposed the other, criticised him, dissociated from him and considered him to be a disbeliever. No one suspected who al-Khazarī was or that he was collaborating with him. He came before Ziyādat Allāh and greeted him. He displayed sadness and pain at his plight. On the day when Ziyādat Allāh set out from Tripoli, he walked under his stirrup. He was crying, shedding his tears on his beard, saying, 'For whom are you leaving us behind, O master of the Arabs?'

Ziyādat Allāh praised him and turned towards him. Afterwards he was asked, 'Talk may be pretence. From where did you have tears and how were you able to cry?'

---

328. According to Ibn Khaldūn, *al-ʿIbar*, vol. 4, p. 74 (tr. *Berbères*, vol. 2, p. 519), Abū al-ʿAbbās was in prison in Raqqāda from where Abū ʿAbd Allāh freed him. According to Ibn ʿIdhārī, *al-Bayān*, vol. 1, p. 150, and Ibn Ḥammād, *Akhbār*, p. 9 (tr. p. 21), Abū ʿAbd Allāh summoned him to Raqqāda from Tripoli where he had been imprisoned.

329. Abū Jaʿfar al-Khazarī (or al-Jazarī), a senior *dāʿī*, was entrusted with the task together with Abū Aḥmad Ṣuʿlūk, one of the first two chamberlains of al-Mahdī. The womenfolk escorted by them comprised al-Mahdī's mother, his two daughters, the two daughters of his brother, Umm Ḥabīb, who was the wife of al-Qāʾim, and Umm ʿAlī, the housekeeper. See al-Yamānī, *Sīrat al-Ḥājib Jaʿfar*, pp. 110–111 (tr. p. 190); Canard, 'L'autobiographie', pp. 286–287; and Ibn ʿIdhārī, *al-Bayān*, vol. 1, pp. 150, 159.

He replied, 'By God! It was only out of sadness for his escape and his rescue [from vengeance].'

When Ziyādat Allāh set out from the city of Tripoli, its seniors and notables walked with him. Then, when he came to the gate of the city, he dismissed them saying, 'Lock the gate of your city behind yourselves. Do not open (the city) to anyone who returns from behind me to you.' And he left. When he had gone far, he changed his mind about Abū al-ʿAbbās and wanted to kill him. So he sent back Ibn Qurhub to look for him and bring him back. Ibn Qurhub reached the city of Tripoli. He had been its governor, yet they did not let him in saying, 'The emir has ordered us not to let anyone in.'

He said, 'Then send out the man to me.'

They said, 'We do not know where he is.'

When he lost hope with them, he went away and caught up with Ziyādat Allāh, and informed him of what had happened, but he turned away from (Ibn Qurhub) and journeyed on.

Ziyādat Allāh was resentful of Ibrāhīm b. Abī al-Aghlab because he wished to be invested with the governorship of the city of al-Qayrawān. What he had been saying to its inhabitants about him came to his knowledge. Therefore, he cast him aside and shunned him. Abū al-Muṣʿab b. Zurāra[330] was favourably inclined to Ibn Abī al-Aghlab, so Ziyādat Allāh avoided him also. It happened that the two were slandering him and discrediting him. They were denounced before him and it was said, 'This is what the two are saying about you. They are with you and in your grasp. How will they be when they reach Miṣr?[331] They will discredit you and openly denounce your wickedness, and ascribe to you every vile act.'

Therefore, he decided to kill both of them. This happened when they had already approached Miṣr. They came to know about this, so they fled by night to Alexandria and sought asylum with its governor. (The governor) granted them asylum and then immediately

---

330. Abū al-Muṣʿab b. Zurāra, a companion in arms of Ibn Abī al-Aghlab during the campaign of al-Urbus, supported him in his attempt to seize power after Ziyādat Allāh's flight. See al-Nuwayrī, *Nihāya*, vol. 24, p. 151 (tr. *Berbères*, vol. 1, p. 445); Ibn al-Athīr, *al-Kāmil*, vol. 6, p. 124; and Ibn al-Dawādārī, *Kanz al-durar*, vol. 6, pp. 41–42.

331. Miṣr denotes Egypt as a country and also its capital situated south-west of later Cairo. Arent J. Wensinck, 'Miṣr,' *EI*, vol. 5, pp. 520–521.

sent them to Miṣr. They arrived there before Ziyādat Allāh. When this news reached (Ziyādat Allāh), he knew that they would slander him before the governor of Miṣr. Its governor at that time was ʿĪsā al-Nūsharī.[332] The two came to him and discredited Ziyādat Allāh before him. They informed him of his wickedness, which had caused his downfall in Ifrīqiya, and that he had designs over Miṣr. Al-Nūsharī was impressed with what they said. He decided to prevent Ziyādat Allāh from entering Miṣr until he had written to Baghdad and received a reply about him.

Ziyādat Allāh had sent word to those with whom he corresponded secretly, seeking information about Ibn Abī al-Aghlab and Abū al-Muṣʿab. He received the news of them both, as well as al-Nūsharī's resolve to prevent him entering Miṣr. He sent Ibn al-Qadīm[333] with a letter to al-Nūsharī in which he asked him permission to enter and requested him to consider a dwelling for him to stay.[334] He informed (al-Nūsharī) that he would wait there until his messenger returned to him. However, when he dispatched Ibn al-Qadīm with the letter, he followed him immediately. Ibn al-Qadīm arrived at the end of the day. When al-Nūsharī read the letter, he thought that (Ziyādat Allāh) would wait until his messenger returned to him. He decided to send to him the following day instructions to stay, informing him that he could not let him enter Miṣr until after he had received orders.

At the end of the night Ziyādat Allāh arrived at the bridge [of al-Jazīra].[335] The guards barred his way. He attacked them, removed

---

332. ʿĪsā al-Nūsharī (d. 297/909) governed Miṣr for five years, 292–297/905–909. On his reign see Muḥammad b. Yūsuf al-Kindī, *Wulāt Miṣr*, ed. Ḥusayn Naṣṣār (Beirut, 1959), pp. 278–286; Ibn Taghrī Birdī, *al-Nujūm al-zāhira*, vol. 3, pp. 145–171.

333. Abū al-Qāsim ʿAbd Allāh b. Muḥammad, well known as Ibn al-Qadīm, was a dignitary under the reign of Ziyādat Allāh. He administered the emir's wealth and misappropriated his funds. He returned to Ifrīqiya and obtained pardon from al-Mahdī, who entrusted to him the directorship of land tax. He was implicated in the plot against al-Mahdī, and executed. See p. 220 below; al-Yamānī, *Sīrat al-Ḥājib Jaʿfar*, p. 132 (tr. Ivanow, *Rise*, p. 222); and Ibn ʿIdhārī, *al-Bayān*, vol. 1, pp. 159, 167.

334. Ibn Taghrī Birdī, *al-Nujūm al-zāhira*, vol. 3, p. 156, dates Ziyādat Allāh's arrival in Ramaḍān 296/May-June 909.

335. Jazīrat Miṣr or Jazīrat al-Rawḍa is the island formed by the two branches of the Nile which divides Miṣr. Approaching from the west, Ziyādat Allāh would have entered the town on the west bank in the quarter of al-Jīza and crossed the first branch of the river on

them from the bridge and crossed over to al-Jazīra with all his troops. The alarm was raised in al-Jazīra and the second bridge ahead of him was cut off. When al-Nūsharī learned about this fact, he was angry with Ibn al-Qadīm. However, (Ibn al-Qadīm) swore before him that he had no knowledge of this, and that when he left (Ziyādat Allāh) he had resolved to stay put until he returned to him with (al-Nūsharī's) letter. The following morning Ziyādat Allāh was stationed with his troops at the second bridge which had been cut off before him. Meanwhile al-Nūsharī met with Abū al-ʿAbbās b. Bisṭām, who at that time was director of the land tax (*kharāj*) of Miṣr, and sought his advice to deal with the matter. Ibn Bisṭām told him, 'This man has already overrun al-Jazīra and is stationed there with a large army. If you oppose him, he will wage war against you from there, and you will become besieged with him and he will cross al-Jazīra without you. However, I shall use subtle means with him on your behalf.'

He boarded a boat and reached Ziyādat Allāh and reproached him for what he had done saying, 'While you are aspiring to gain the satisfaction and assistance of the Commander of the Faithful,[336] guard against invading his provinces, for he will come to know of such action on your part.' He admonished him, making him understand that al-Nūsharī had been alienated from him.

Ziyādat Allāh apologised to him saying, 'It was not something that I had intended, but I rose from the place by night to approach the town and arrive at daybreak, so the vanguard of the army preceded me and they did what happened.'

He withdrew from there until repairs were done for him. All his men took up quarters in al-Jazīra. The bridge was brought back and he was allowed to enter. He lodged in the house of Ibn al-Jaṣṣāṣ, while his men dispersed in Miṣr and took up residence in its environs. After a stay of eight days in (Miṣr), Ziyādat Allāh left for Baghdad. Most

---

a bridge, supported by some sixty boats, to reach the island. He would then have to cross another bridge, supported by thirty boats, to reach the east bank where the palace of the government was located. See Ibn Ḥawqal, *Ṣūrat al-arḍ*, p. 137; al-Idrīsī, *Nuzha*, pp. 142–143 (tr. pp. 170–171). For historical and topographical details see Carl H. Becker, 'Cairo', *EI*, vol. 2, pp. 815–826; Jacques Jomier, 'al-Ḳāhira', *EI*², vol. 4, pp. 424–444, and 'al-Fusṭāṭ', *EI*², vol. 2, pp. 957–959.

336. The Abbasid caliph al-Muqtadir bi-llāh (r. 295–320/908–932).

of those who had accompanied him remained behind. When he arrived at al-Ramla he wrote to Baghdad about them. Then al-Nūsharī received instructions [from Baghdad] to allow them to follow him, and they joined him.

(Ziyādat Allāh) had eunuchs with him. Some men of the Banū al-ʿAbbās coveted them. They asked him to sell them to them, but he refused to do so. He arrived in al-Raqqa.[337] Those whom he had refused to sell the eunuchs wrote about the matter. Therefore, he was forced to stay in al-Raqqa and not allowed to proceed to Baghdad. While he stayed there, his men abandoned him and dispersed. He was addicted to drinking wine and pursuing amusements. They incited a market inspector against him who summoned him before the judge of al-Raqqa about the eunuchs which they had asked him to sell. They testified against him that he was indulging in debauchery with them. So the judge of al-Raqqa ruled that he should sell them and his circumstances became humble. Ibn al-Qadīm was the caretaker of his wealth and in charge of his expenditure. He retained much of (Ziyādat Allāh's) wealth, dispossessed him and moved away from him. (Ziyādat Allāh) demanded back what he had retained. Ibn al-Qadīm sought refuge with someone who protected him from (Ziyādat Allāh), saying that if he had a claim against him, then let him sue him before a judge.

(Ziyādat Allāh) remained in al-Raqqa for sometime using subtle means to obtain permission to enter Baghdad, but he was unable to do so.[338] Some slandered him and conspired to dismiss him. It was said that he should be sent back to the Maghrib to seek his own revenge and fight those who had fought him. He was sent written instructions to this effect and was dismissed. Instructions were sent to al-Nūsharī and Ibn Bisṭām to support him by providing men and money.

When (Ziyādat Allāh) returned to Miṣr, al-Nūsharī relocated him

---

337. An important town on the left bank of the Middle Euphrates in Northern Mesopotamia. See M. Meinecke, 'al-Raḳḳa', *EI*², vol. 8, pp. 410–414.

338. Ziyādat Allāh wrote to Ibn al-Furāt, *wazīr* of al-Muqtadir, to obtain the caliph's permission to enter Baghdad. He remained in al-Raqqa for a year, only to be ordered to return to Ifrīqiya. See Ibn al-Athīr, *al-Kāmil*, vol. 6, p. 124; Ibn Khaldūn, *al-ʿIbar*, vol. 4, p. 441.

to Dhāt al-Ḥumām,[339] and told him, 'You will set off and then money and men will come to you.' He dispatched to him some of his men. A group of inhabitants of Ifrīqiya who had come with him gathered around him. Al-Nūsharī kept delaying sending him the money and the men. However, he sent him gifts and presents, and loads of wine. (Ziyādat Allāh) was addicted to it and indulged in drinking. He spent what he had until it was exhausted and those who had come to him abandoned him. Al-Nūsharī wrote to Baghdad relating (Ziyādat Allāh's) wickedness and shamelessness. He was instructed to dismiss him. The reply to this effect did not come until (Ziyādat Allāh) had sold most of what he possessed and had spent it. When he arrived from al-Raqqa, he had brought with him attire and supplies. He passed through Egypt with two swords and displayed the weapons and supplies which were still with him. He sold all these during his stay at Dhāt al-Ḥumām. He was struck with illness which, it was said, resulted from having been poisoned. His body became flabby and he lost most of his hair on his head and his beard. He went to Miṣr and from there to Jerusalem, where he died[340]. It is said that when he was buried, his grave collapsed. This is because it happened to be on the place of an old latrine and it fell. His corpse could not be retrieved. It was left like that and buried.

339. Dhāt al-Ḥumām was on the route to the Maghrib, at the edge of the territory of the Banū Mudlij in the district of Alexandria. See al-Ya'qūbī, *Kitāb al-Buldān*, p. 2 (tr. p. 201); and al-Idrīsī, *Nuzha*, p. 137 (tr. p. 164). According to al-Bakrī, *al-Masālik*, p. 3 (tr. pp. 10–11), Dhāt al-Ḥumām was so called because anyone drinking its water caught fever.

340. Ziyādat Allāh died either in al-Ramla or Jerusalem. The date of his death is variously given in the sources between 299/911 and 304/916. Ibn al-Athīr, *al-Kāmil*, vol. 6, p. 124 (al-Ramla); al-Nuwayrī, *Nihāya*, vol. 24, p. 153 (tr. *Berbères*, vol. 1, p. 447) (Jerusalem); Ibn Khaldūn, *al-'Ibar*, vol. 4, p. 441 (Jerusalem); Ibn 'Idhārī, *al-Bayān*, vol. 1, p. 167 (in 299 at Jerusalem), and p. 173 (in 303 at al-Ramla). Ibn Taghrī Birdī, *al-Nujūm al-zāhira*, vol. 3, p. 191 (in 304 at Barqa or al-Ramla).

36

Abū ʿAbd Allāh's march to Sijilmāsa, his conquest of that town and al-Mahdī's departure from there.

When Abū ʿAbd Allāh was firmly established in Raqqāda, his brother Muḥammad Abū al-ʿAbbās b. Aḥmad came to him. Abū ʿAbd Allāh was pleased with his arrival. Muḥammad was older than him, with more penetrating and acute intelligence. He was better versed in scholarship and had greater precedence than him, while Abū ʿAbd Allāh was more judicious and pious than Abū al-ʿAbbās. Abū ʿAbd Allāh honoured him. When (Abū al-ʿAbbās) visited him, he would rise to honour him and remain standing until he permitted him to sit; and when he in turn visited him, he would kiss his hand and stand until he asked him to sit. When Abū al-ʿAbbās arrived, the scholars (*shuyūkh*) of the inhabitants of al-Qayrawān came to visit him and greeted him. They congratulated Abū ʿAbd Allāh on his arrival and saw him honouring (Abū al-ʿAbbās). Therefore he gained importance in their eyes. He conducted discussions, summoning the people and gathering the jurists of the inhabitants of al-Qayrawān. He debated with them on the imamate and on judicial opinions in which they opposed the *ahl al-bayt*, and he silenced them. They were amazed at his proficiency. Abū ʿAbd Allāh began to make preparations to leave for Sijilmāsa. When he was ready and had fulfilled his needs, he wrote a letter and made several copies of it. He sent a copy to every pulpit of Ifrīqiya to be proclaimed. Here is the content thereof:

> In the name of God, the Compassionate, the Merciful. Through Him I get help and I rely upon Him. Now then! Indeed all praise is due to God, who has honoured the status of justice, raised its esteem and stature. He has chosen it for Himself and approved it, making it a means to guidance and a means of attaining piety. He has established it as a balance among His creation by which He has ordained integrity for everything, His order, basis and completeness. His justice is such that He assigned reward for those who obey Him and punishment for those who disobey Him. He has not assigned to the evil-doer the reward of the one who does good. Nor has He assigned to the one who does good the punishment of the evil-doer. Indeed, He rewards all according to their effort, and grants

to everyone the reward of their deeds in accordance with His justice, for He, the Praiseworthy, says in His clear book which '*no falsehood can approach from before or behind*' (41:42), '*that man can have nothing but what he strives for, and that (the fruit of) his striving will soon come in sight; then will he be rewarded with a reward complete*' (53:39–41). God has enjoined upon those whom He has granted power in His land and over His servants to proclaim the way of justice and abolish the customs of oppression and injustice. He granted me victory, assistance, glory and power against His enemies and the enemies of the Messenger of God, may God's blessings be upon him and his progeny, until the reins of affairs came to me and their reins became obedient. Indeed, the most worthy person to promote justice and defend it is the one to whom God has granted the understanding of the knowledge of His Book, the positions of His promise and His threat, just as He has granted the understanding to me. This person must know that he is responsible for his subjects, and has been commanded to treat them with justice and to do good to them. God, the Blessed and Sublime, says, '*Behold, God enjoins justice, the doing of good, and generosity to kinsfolk; and He forbids lewdness, injustice and wickedness. He exhorts you in order that you may take heed*' (16:90). The Blessed and Sublime established governing with equity as a general principle which applies to the noble as well as the lowly, the young as well as the old. Then the Messenger of God, may God's blessings be upon him and his progeny, indicated to his community the two things which deliver from error and guide to integrity of conduct. He instructed his community to adhere to them both, saying, '*I am leaving amongst you two precious things. As long as you hold fast to them you will not err after me. They are the Book of God and my family, members of the household*.'[341] Hence those who adhere to the Book of God act in accordance with it and conform to its commands and restraints, have indeed adhered to the supreme proof. Those who adhere to the sunna of the Messenger of God, may God bless him and grant him salvation, and the manners of the members of his household, '*have indeed grasped the firm hand-hold*' (2:256). The two things together will lead them to salvation, and halt with them at the way of justice with which God commanded His prophet David, peace be upon him, to judge, saying, '*O David! We have indeed*

---

341. Cf. Muslim b. al-Ḥajjāj al-Qushayrī, *Ṣaḥīḥ Muslim*, ed. Muḥammad Fu'ād 'Abd al-Bāqī (Cairo, 1955), vol. 4, p. 1873, English tr. Abdul Hamid Siddiqi (Lahore, 1976), vol. 4, pp. 1286–1287.

made you a vicegerent on earth. Therefore, judge between mankind with justice, and do not follow vain desire, lest it lead you astray from the path of God. Verily, for those who go astray from the path of God there is an awful doom for having forgotten the Day of Reckoning' (38:26). He thus commanded His prophet David, peace be upon him, to judge with justice which is the most virtuous action, the most noble provision, the most weighty of all that is weighed, and the most excellent of all that is stored with Him. Then the Messenger of God, may God bless him and grant him salvation, gave information about the ranks of the people of equity and justice in the Hereafter, saying, '*The dispensers of justice will be on pulpits of light on the Day of Judgement*.'[342] God knows, and He suffices as witness and knower, that my intention, my innermost thought, and my wish is to establish justice among the subjects, to do good to them and treat them with kindness. Now if displaying this and carrying it through become difficult because of the disorder of the cavalry and the transference of authority, and crimes were committed inadvertently by the foolish and the mob, I do not permit myself to utter a word about it, even if their deed weighs heavily upon me. I will not punish the innocent with the corrupt, nor the gentle with the imprudent, for God, the Blessed and Sublime, says, '*No bearer of burdens shall bear the burden of another*' (6:164; 17:15; 35:18; 39:7; 53:38). So do not regard what has been difficult as too troublesome. May God have mercy upon you. Every outburst will weaken, everything that flows will settle, everyone who enters causes a surprise, everyone who lights a fire produces smoke, and every demolition throws up dust. Thereafter matters calm down and become stable, steady and orderly. Do not be upset by my rapid departure from your town and my disappearance from you. Indeed, I have preferred to give up a life of ease and abundance. I have migrated from the resting place of a carefree and comfortable life to seek the reward of God and proximity with Him, and to gather your dispersion and bring together your spread, and that which will bring you benefit today and tomorrow, now and in future. Therefore, be reassured by this and feel secure. Be supporters of promoting the truth and helpers of abating falsehood. I pray that God will enable me to display equity and promote justice to such an extent that the wolf and the sheep will drink from the same watering place,[343] that the enemy will meet with his enemy in a place out of satisfaction with the justice and be reconciled with it, that

342. Cf. Muslim, *Ṣaḥīḥ*, vol. 3, p. 1458 (tr. vol. 3, p. 1016).

343. Cf. Isaiah, 11:6; 65:25.

> travellers and caravans will travel without a guard or an envoy from the land of Egypt to the farthest outposts in the Maghrib, God willing. I have instructed Tammām b. Muʿārik to govern the subjects with kindness He should do good to them, and spread justice and benevolence among them. He should seize the hand of oppression and eliminate injustice from them. He should send a copy of this letter of mine to all the provincial governors in all the provinces of Ifrīqiya so that they comply with it, are made aware of my order contained in it, and abide by it without disregarding it, God willing. Salutation!

Abū ʿAbd Allāh appointed Abū Zākī Tammām b. Muʿārik as deputy to govern Ifrīqiya together with his brother Abū al-ʿAbbās, before leaving with the bulk of his army and other warriors from the men of Ifrīqiya. He stationed garrisons with Abū Zākī as well as in all the towns.

(Abū ʿAbd Allāh) left for Sijilmāsa in Ramaḍān 296/June 909, taking the main highway,[344] without passing through Kutāma territory. The people of the Maghrib were shaken at his advance. The tribes deserted the area and moved out of his way. The Zanāta feared that he would attack them because he had threatened them that he would do so for his troops killed by them. The chief of all the Zanāta and the entire tribes of the Berbers at that time, Muḥammad b. Khazar,[345] offered his submission. He came to meet (Abū ʿAbd Allāh) at Ṭubna, and sought pardon, imploring him, and extending his hands towards

---

344. This was the route from al-Qayrawān to Fās. A link road from this route led to Sijilmāsa. See al-Bakrī, *al-Masālik*, pp. 141–146 (tr. pp. 271–280). For routes to Sijilmāsa see Ibn Ḥawqal, *Ṣūrat al-arḍ*, pp. 84–90. According to al-Bakrī, *al-Masālik*, pp. 151–152 (tr. pp. 289–290), the journey between Sijilmāsa and al-Qayrawān took forty-six or fifty-three days of march.

345. He was chief of the Maghrāwa, a large confederation of Berber tribes belonging to the Zanāta group of the central Maghrib. Soon after Abū ʿAbd Allāh's conquest of Tāhart, Muḥammad b. Khazar rebelled and sought to capture it. See Ibn ʿIdhārī, *al-Bayān*, vol. 1, pp. 155–156; Idrīs ʿImād al-Dīn, *ʿUyūn al-akhbār*, ed. al-Yaʿlāwī, pp. 178–180, ed. Ghālib, vol. 5, p. 116. Later, under the reign of al-Mahdī, he rallied to the cause of the Umayyads of Spain. See Ibn Khaldūn, *al-ʿIbar*, vol. 4, pp. 81–82, and vol. 6, pp. 52–54 (tr. *Berbères*, vol. 2, p. 527, 549, and vol. 3, pp. 229–231); Evariste Lévi-Provençal, *Histoire de l'Espagne musulmane* (Paris, 1950–1953), vol. 2, pp. 94–95. Subsequently the chief repudiated Umayyad suzerainty and submitted to the Fatimid caliph-imam al-Muʿizz who granted him pardon. See Lévi-Provençal, *Histoire*, vol. 2, p. 107; also p. 234 below.

him. (Abū ʿAbd Allāh) granted him and his people safety, and exacted allegiance from him. Before letting him go, (Abū ʿAbd Allāh) made him take an oath that he would not kill, betray or oppress any of the followers during his lifetime and after his death.

(Abū ʿAbd Allāh) continued his march, proceeding to Sijilmāsa. He attacked tribes that he came across on his way about whose wickedness he had received intelligence.[346] As he approached Sijilmāsa, its ruler, al-Yasaʿ b. Midrār, received the news of his advance and that he was proceeding towards him. Ziyādat Allāh had already written to him to inform him about al-Mahdī, peace be upon him, giving his description and stating that he was the person in whose favour Abū ʿAbd Allāh was preaching, but he had not shown any aversion to this. However, when Abū ʿAbd Allāh advanced towards him, he sent someone to ask (al-Mahdī) about his descent, his position and whether it was towards him that Abū ʿAbd Allāh was proceeding. (Al-Mahdī) acknowledged his descent because he could not deny it, but responded ambiguously concerning Abū ʿAbd Allāh, saying that he had never seen him or known him. It is true that he had not seen him.[347] We have already narrated the story of (Abū ʿAbd Allāh's) early career. He stated to him that he was only a merchant because he feared for his safety and saw that (al-Yasaʿ) disapproved of Abū ʿAbd Allāh's coming and showed displeasure at his entering his town. (Al-Yasaʿ) spoke to him harshly about this matter, but (al-Mahdī) persisted in saying what he had said before. God put awe for (al-Mahdī) into his heart, and respect into his eyes. Hence he did not subject him to more ordeal than confining him to a residence and placing him under guard. Likewise, he placed his son al-Qāʾim bi-amr Allāh in another residence to keep them apart and investigate both of them, but their accounts were identical. He did not dare to cause them harm because of their standing in relation to the Messenger of God, may God bless

346. This would include the tribes of Tāhart and their Rustamid rulers. See Ibn ʿIdhārī, *al-Bayān*, vol. 1, p. 153. On the Rustamids see Mohamed Talbi, 'Rustamids', *EI*², vol. 8, pp. 638–640; and Chikh Bekri, 'Le kharijisme berbère: quelques aspects du royaume rustumide', *Annales de l'Institut d'études orientales*, 15 (1957), pp. 55–109.

347. The fact that Abū ʿAbd Allāh had not personally seen al-Mahdī is confirmed in the sources. See al-Yamānī, *Sīrat al-Ḥājib Jaʿfar*, pp. 121–122 (tr. Ivanow, *Rise*, p. 206); and Ibn ʿIdhārī, *al-Bayān*, vol. 1, p. 128.

him and grant him salvation, of which he had been informed and which he acknowledged to be correct. God left (al-Yasaʿ) in the lurch and deprived him of their wealth of which he had the greatest need and which was nearest to him. (Al-Yasaʿ) subjected men[348] who were with them to torture to obtain confession regarding them, but they only affirmed what the two had already said.

The news reached Abū ʿAbd Allāh who was greatly concerned by it. He had been telling those whom he initiated in the *daʿwa*, 'God shall cause the cause of al-Mahdī to triumph, granting him a great victory.' He sent to al-Yasaʿ b. Midrār messengers from among his servants and wrote a letter to him in which he guaranteed him safety and kind treatment, stating that he was advancing only for a certain need, not for waging war. He promised him his personal favour, righteousness and honour, giving his firm and utmost assurances. However, when the messengers arrived with his letter, (al-Yasaʿ) threw it away after having learnt its contents. He ordered the execution of the messengers, and they were put to death. When this came to Abū ʿAbd Allāh's knowledge, he reiterated his benevolence, fearing that al-Mahdī might be subjected to mistreatment. However, he avoided referring to him out of precaution. But this time the same thing happened as before. (Al-Yasaʿ) persisted in his tyranny. (Abū ʿAbd Allāh) reiterated his message for the third time, while (al-Yasaʿ) remained obstinate and persisted in his error. Then (Abū ʿAbd Allāh) implored God's help and prepared his troops and approached the town. Al-Yasaʿ b. Midrār came out to confront him leading his force, but before long the cavalry charged him into the city, killing a number of his companions after he engaged it in a skirmish for a while. This happened as evening was approaching and dusk had fallen. The troops therefore withdrew and camped where they stopped.

When night fell, Ibn Midrār fled with his cousins and members of his family. Abū ʿAbd Allāh and his men spent the night in great anxiety, not knowing what he might have done to al-Mahdī and unable to enter the town at night. They did not know about the flight

348. These men included Jaʿfar al-Ḥājib, Abū Yaʿqūb al-Qahramānī, and Ṭayyib, previously named Burkān. After some time Abū Yaʿqūb al-Qahramānī was unable to endure the torture and betrayed al-Mahdī. See al-Yamānī, *Sīrat al-Ḥājib Jaʿfar*, pp. 122–123 (tr. Ivanow, *Rise*, p. 208).

of the villain until the morning when the notables of the town came out to them and informed them of what had happened. Then they entered with them the place where al-Mahdī was held and released him. They also released al-Qā'im. There was great rejoicing amongst the people, which caused them almost to lose their wits. Two horses were brought for (al-Mahdī and al-Qā'im) who mounted them. The believers surrounded them, while the *dā'īs* walked around (al-Mahdī and al-Qā'im). Abū 'Abd Allāh walked in front of the imam, saying, 'This is my lord and your lord, O believers!' He praised God, the Mighty, the Glorious, and offered Him thanks, weeping from intense joy. Eventually the imam arrived at a tent (*fāza*) where carpets had been spread out for him. He went inside and ordered a search for al-Yasa' b. Midrār. The troops set out in search of him. (Al-Mahdī) remained there until past noon. Then he went out to the believers. Carpets had been spread out for him in front of the tent. The people surrounded him and listened with tears to what he was saying. They praised God for having granted them the favour of seeing him, while al-Mahdī praised them.[349] He recognised their merit, saying that God had prepared for them a great reward, promised them favour and gave them glad tidings that they would attain prosperity in this world and the Hereafter. When the muezzin called to the sunset prayer, he stood up and led them in prayer, reciting the *Fātiḥa* and the chapter (*sūra*) *al-Qadr* in the first [*rak'a*], and the *Fātiḥa* and the chapter '*Say, He is God the One*' (112:1)[350] in the second [*rak'a*]. Having completed the prayer, he entered the tent and the people dispersed.

The troops caught up with al-Yasa' b. Midrār and the members of his family who had fled with him. They seized them and brought them to (al-Mahdī) who ordered al-Yasa' b. Midrār to be whipped. He was given forty lashes and paraded in the camp and in the town of Sijilmāsa. (Al-Mahdī) confiscated his wealth as well as the wealth of members of his family who had supported him and fled with him. Thereafter he killed him and them.[351] He granted safety to the rest

349. Cf. in al-Yamānī, *Sīrat al-Ḥājib Ja'far*, pp. 125–131 (tr. Ivanow, *Rise*, pp. 211–220).

350. *Sūrat al-Ikhlāṣ* (no. 112) which begins with these words.

351. On the intervention of al-Qā'im, the life al-Yasa' b. Midrār was spared, but he died afer a few days because of the flogging. See al-Yamānī, *Sīrat al-Ḥājib Ja'far*, p. 131 (tr. Ivanow, *Rise*, p. 220).

of the people and the inhabitants of the districts, and appointed a governor over them. The tribes from the outlying regions came to him, offering submission and he also (granted safety) to them. He stayed in Sijilmāsa for forty days, and then set off with all the troops for Ifrīqiya.

Ifrīqiya had been cut off from information about Abū ʿAbd Allāh. People spread rumours about him and he was increasingly slandered. It was not long before the courier came to them, bringing the news of the conquest of Sijilmāsa, of what had become of al-Mahdī, and a letter from Abū ʿAbd Allāh as follows:

> In the name of God, the Compassionate, the Merciful. Through Him I get help and I rely upon Him. Now then! Praise be to God who guides to His unity through the signs in His creation, and summons to His knowledge through proofs of His argument (*ḥujja*). His will preceded and His decree was to make triumphant His friends who supported His religion and carried out His right, and to humiliate those who rebelled against Him and rejected His favour. His friends were opposed only by those who attack His religion which they support, and who were enemies of the right which they establish. This is because they present the proof (*ḥujja*) in front of their swords, and the summon (*duʿā'*) before they fight, with deliberation and without rushing, confident that the one overcome in argument will be the one who has parted from their way, and the one defeated will be the one who has forsaken their community. Deliberation demonstrates their right and reveals the falsehood of their enemies. They will accept the repentance of those who return to the truth, but will fight those who persist in their error after establishing proof against them. Indeed, God does not grant remission to the one who persists, nor does He accept the repentance of the one who is stubborn and remains in sin. Rather, He releases His might and His revenge against him, '*for God is stronger in might and stronger in inflicting punishment*' (4:84). I had proceeded to Sijilmāsa in spite of the long and difficult journey, the remoteness of its visit and its rough terrain. I did this in order to fulfil the right of God, may His mention be exalted, to discharge one of His obligations, manifest one of His arguments on His earth, and rescue the son of the Messenger of God from the riff-raff and lowly, seeking to please (God) and gain proximity with Him. As I approached (Sijilmāsa), I offered safety to the traitor al-Yasaʿ b. Midrār, just as had been my practice with the towns. I

had intended to fulfil my need there and withdraw from there without provoking sedition or raising dust. So I wrote to him a letter, as a brother would write to his brother. In it I sought his sympathy. I granted him safety and invited him to establish a pact of brotherhood between myself and him with a view to releasing the son of the Messenger of God, may God's blessings be upon him and his progeny. I wished to retain him and his associates to protect what they had lost. However, the traitor refused and frowned, showing contempt when my envoys came to see him. He ordered them to be killed, contrary to the sunna of the Messenger of God, may God bless him and grant him salvation, and the practice prevalent among the people of all the communities of not causing harm to envoys. Then I set forth the argument against him and again sent him envoys, hoping that he would respond favourably and come back to what is safer for him and more advantageous to him. However, he detained the envoys in dungeons and weighted them down with iron. He imprisoned the son of the Messenger of God, may God bless him and grant him salvation, in the narrowest cell and placed him under guard, refusing to let through any food to him, but he survived–by my father and my mother–in the cell for days, fasting continuously through lack of food. Then he considered his own act in confining him in that cell as trifling. So he moved him to a narrower cell and threatened to kill him for falsely claiming descent from the Messenger of God, may God bless him and grant him salvation. I sent envoys to him, promising him that I would refrain from fighting and withdraw from him without even drinking any water from his town, but the more I insisted upon seeking (al-Mahdī), the more he persisted in refusing what I was trying to obtain from him. He acted thus out of arrogance towards God, persisting in major offences out of haughtiness, ignorance and viciousness. '*He loses both this world and the Hereafter. That is the sheer loss*' (22:11). I saw that the traitor had resolved to wage war against God, the Mighty, the Glorious, regarding the descendants of the Messenger of God. He entertained fallacious hopes, whereas God's promise on this matter is truthful. He had futile thoughts about it, whereas God's judgement on the matter is effective. He willed to persist in his ignorance and remain in his error. He chose to unleash war and arouse its dust. Therefore, I shook the supporters of the truth to fight him. I found their intentions with God becoming firm and their discernment effective in waging war against him. I advanced with them towards him, seeking the fulfilment of what God had promised His friends with regard

> to their enemies. The cavalry did a warm-up and then launched attack after attack against them, piercing with lances, striking with swords and shooting arrows. When the sinners felt the agony of death and wounds, and when the war turned against them and its fangs injured them, and they realised they had no protector from God and no refuge from His friends, they turned back and took to their heels. The treacherous offender released reluctantly what I had been seeking from him voluntarily, and darkness interrupted fighting between us. The following day, the supporters of the truth resumed attacking them and dislodged them. The followers took control of their town and kindled the fire of war (*nār al-ḥarb*) in it. They searched their houses. The traitor took advantage of the night and fled under cover of darkness on his way to the land of the blacks (*balad al-sūdān*), disregarding [his] family and children. I saved his wife and protected her. I cast upon her the veil of modesty, taking into account God's reward. Then I went in pursuit of the traitor myself for ten days until God subdued him without any truce or treaty. I brought him in fetters to the friend of God [al-Mahdī] so that he serve as a warning to dissenters and hypocrites, and an example to everybody. Praise be to God, cherisher of His religion, who ennobles those who uphold His right and joins the means of felicity to His obedience. He set quick success and victory, and delayed the reward and victory for His friends. If they argue they will win the argument, and if they wage war victory will accompany them. May His praise fulfil His right and further abundance of His bounty. The Commander of the Faithful, the friend of God and son of His Messenger is in the best state, in accordance with God's customs, as regards himself, his sons and the supporters of his realm. He is arriving soon with the blessings, success, help and assistance of God. Salutation!

When this letter reached Abū Zākī and he read it, he ordered it to be read from the pulpit. The followers rejoiced immensely. God put an end to the calumnies spread by the calumniators and gave the lie to the sayings of the agitators. The news spread throughout the country and the glad tidings of the advent of al-Mahdī spread. The friend was filled with joy at this and the enemy was subdued. The whole population looked out for him, anticipating his coming, with their eyes longing for him.

37

Al-Mahdī's coming from Sijilmāsa and his arrival in Ifrīqiya.

Then al-Mahdī arrived accompanied by al-Qā'im. At that time al-Mahdī was in the prime of his youth without any grey hair, while al-Qā'im was at an age when his moustaches sprouted. Abū ʿAbd Allāh returned from the expedition with him together with all his troops. He handed over the command to (al-Mahdī) and informed the *dāʿī*s that he was the imam in whose favour he had been carrying out the mission. He presented him to all the believers, saying, 'He is my lord and your lord, the guardian of your destiny, your guide in the straight path, your awaited Mahdī whose glad tidings I had announced. God, the Mighty, the Glorious, has caused him to triumph, just as He had promised. He granted assistance to his followers and his soldiers.'[352]

The first of his proofs and portents which the followers saw with their own eyes was that they observed that God, the Mighty, the Glorious, had willed to accomplish (al-Mahdī's) cause; that God, the Blessed and Sublime, protected him from his enemy by putting fear of him in his heart, in spite of the fact that he was in his dominion and swords were sharpened against him. His followers and helpers were being killed for him, but (the enemy) was unable to inflict any harm upon him. Nor could (al-Yasaʿ b. Midrār) stretch his hand to do any misdeed, in spite of the fact that one of his courtiers had advised him to kill him saying, 'These people have only flocked to him, but when they are disappointed with him, they will disperse. So if you kill him, it will give a lie to what his companion is preaching about him among them, that he would reign and triumph. Kill him because that will certainly give a lie to what his companion is preaching about him among them. That will create discord among them and divide them.'

However, God, the Mighty, the Glorious, abandoned him so that he did not accept this advice from the one who gave it and the one who advised him to do so. God killed the one who gave this advice at the hands of His friend and enabled (al-Mahdī) to be protected from his enemy.

---

352. Cf. al-Yamānī, *Sīrat al-Ḥājib Jaʿfar*, p. 130–131 (tr. Ivanow, *Rise*, pp. 217–219).

Al-Mahdī, peace be upon him, approached. When he was alongside Kutāma territory, he turned towards it and arrived in Īkjān. He ordered funds to be brought forth. These had been under the custody of the *dāʿīs* and the elders who had buried them there. They submitted (the funds) to him. He ordered that the custody of the funds be taken over from them. He packed them in loads and proceeded with them. This was the first matter which changed the corrupt hearts.[353] They had imagined that they would be as Abū ʿAbd Allāh had accustomed them: commanding, forbidding, collecting taxes and disbursing.

When al-Mahdī arrived in Īkjān, he instructed Abū ʿAbd Allāh to write a letter to Abū Zākī informing of his arrival. Abū ʿAbd Allāh wrote the letter and sent it with a courier. The letter was read out from the pulpit of the mosque. Here is its copy:

> In the name of God, the Compassionate, the Merciful. Now then! Praise be to God, protector of His religion and cherisher of His friend. He caused His religion to triumph over all religions, and His friend over oppressors and aggressors who were hostile to him. This letter of mine to you is from Īkjān, the abode of emigration and the established home of the faith. The imam, our lord and master, al-Mahdī bi-llāh, may God's blessings be upon him, has arrived together with his son, may God fulfil through him his best hopes, at the head of all the supporters of religion (*awliyāʾ al-dīn*) and the believers who were accompanying him. The arrival was excellent, most auspicious, joyous and satisfying. He has illuminated with his arrival the abode of emigration of his followers and gladdened the believers, men as well as women, who had remained behind, being excused from fighting (*jihād*), as well as those whom we had stationed there to secure the place. They approached from all sides to reach him and from every horizon hastened towards him, seeking to be blessed by looking at him and to be healed by his glance, praising God for having conveyed to them the accomplishment of His promise and the manifestation of His cause. They hastened to deliver to him the deposits of God which they had held in trust and delivered to him what God has enjoined upon them.[354] The

353. A reference to those who plotted with Abū al-ʿAbbās and Abū Zākī against al-Mahdī. See p. 105 above, and p. 215 below.

354. These deposits held in trust (*amānāt*) included monies due to the imam from the wealth of the believers, in accordance with Shīʿī practice. See al-Qāḍī al-Nuʿmān, *Kitāb al-Himma*, pp. 41–44.

> war is over by the grace of God. God extinguished its fire, and destroyed those who provoked it and scattered and divided those who thereby intrigued against the religion of God. The Commander of the Faithful is coming straight to Ifrīqiya. With success, capacity, help and facilitation granted by God, he will be able to arrive on Thursday 20 Rabīʿ II 297/6 January 910, God willing. Let this be known. Be ready for him with those who are with you. Praise God for having entrusted you that favour and that He has your appointed time of death until you reached him. Solicit from him that this be completed for you by glancing at your lord and his satisfaction with you. Salutation!

When the letter bearing this statement arrived, it was read out. The news spread and the followers were overjoyed. It put an end to the slander and rumours which had spread. The people got ready and prepared themselves to meet him. Their eyes aspired towards him and their souls looked up to him and to his coming. (Al-Mahdī), may God's blessings be upon him, arrived on the appointed Thursday as stated in the letter. The people met him according to their rank. The inhabitants of al-Qayrawān received him in their multitude. Among them on that day were elders, notables and jurists who had perception, intelligence, forbearance and eloquence. Those who lived before that time were also like them, but all that vanished from them with the manifestation of the friends of God among them and from all those like them who opposed their authority. God eclipsed their light, abated their splendour and took away their joy, because this can only reside in the friends of God and those who follow them. Glory, brilliance, beauty, perfection and splendour appertain to them alone, just as the sun, when it rises, takes away the light of the stars and their shapes, overcomes the light of the lamps and eclipses their rays, so that doubt does not accompany the truth, nor should there be any obscurity which could cause doubt about those who are its rightful owners.

Al-Mahdī, peace be upon him, approached, leading the supporters of his realm and multitudes of troops of his followers, like the full moon of completeness and the lamp of darkness. Abū ʿAbd Allāh led the group of *dāʿīs*, while the elders and the followers marched in front of him. Al-Qāʾim followed behind him, while the cortege and the troops marched along the length and breadth of the plain of al-Qayrawān. The jurists (*shuyūkh*) of the people of al-Qayrawān greeted (al-Mahdī) as caliph and imam. They congratulated him on his victory and safety. He reciprocated towards them kindly and agreeably. He asked them to retire and they left. He told Abū 'Abd Allāh and those accompanying him, 'It is as if we have seen a people who resemble the inhabitants of towns of the east. The inhabitants of the Maghrib that we have seen [so far] are only like the Bedouins.' He settled in his palace in Raqqāda. The followers settled in their quarters and dispersed to their regions. Every group of the people of Ifrīqiya went to their place, and went by his order and permission to their towns.

38

Political measures taken by al-Mahdī as imam and applied publicly amongst the people.

On Friday morning, the day after his arrival, (al-Mahdī) issued a decree, ordering it to be invoked from the pulpits of mosques. He addressed it to the two preachers of Raqqāda and al-Qayrawān, prescribing invocation of blessings upon himself after the invocation of blessings of God upon the Prophet, ʿAlī, Fāṭima, al-Ḥasan, al-Ḥusayn and the imams from his posterity, which had been put into practice by Abū ʿAbd Allāh.[355] The decree contained the following invocation:

> O Lord! Bless your servant and vicegerent who presides in Your lands upon the destiny of Your servants, the Servant of God, Abū Muḥammad al-Imām al-Mahdī bi-llāh, Commander of the Faithful, just as You blessed his ancestors, Your rightly-guided vicegerents led on the right path, who ruled and rendered justice, observing the truth. O Lord! Just as You have designated him for Your guardianship and chosen him for Your vicegerency, and have made him a protection and pillar for Your religion, as well as an asylum and refuge for Your subjects, may You also cause him to triumph over Your enemies in rebellion, heal through him the hearts of the believers, and cause him to conquer the earth, the east as well as

355. See p. 178 above.

the west, just as You promised him. Grant him Your support against the unjust rebels. God of all the beings, Lord of the worlds.

He ordered the transcription of another decree which was read from the pulpit in al-Qayrawān. Copies of the decree were sent to the towns and read from the pulpits. Here is its exemplar:

In the name of God, the Compassionate, the Merciful. We seek His help. From the Servant of God, Abū Muḥammad al-Imām al-Mahdī bi-llāh, Commander of the Faithful, to his followers among the believers and all the Muslims. Peace be with you. The Commander of the Faithful praises God before you. There is no god except Him. He prays to Him that He may bless Muḥammad, His servant and Messenger. May God bless him and his progeny. Now then! All praise is due to God who raised the flag of truth and honoured its adherents. He overturned the banners of falsehood and humiliated its party. The Powerful who cannot be opposed in His power, the Exalted in might whose decree cannot be resisted. The Protector of His religion which He chose for Himself and which He honoured with the most noble of His prophets, the highest in rank among them before Him, the most noble among them in status, the nearest of them as intermediary before Him, Muḥammad, may God bless him, bearer of His wisdom and depository of His mystery. After him there will be no deception of the deceivers, no treason of the traitors, no oppression of the oppressors for the members of his household, for He promised him help, assistance, glory and authority concerning them, just as He says in His clear Book and revelation that '*no falsehood can approach from before or behind*' (41:42), '*And We wished to show favour unto those who were oppressed in the earth, and to make them examples and to make them the inheritors, and to establish them in the earth, and to show Pharaoh and Hāmān and their hosts that which they feared from them*' (28:5–6). And He says, '*And verily we have written in the Scripture, after the Reminder: My righteous servants will inherit the earth. Behold! This is a plain statement for folk who are devout*' (21:105–106). (God), may His praise be exalted and His names sanctified, fulfilled His promise to His Messenger, may God bless him and his progeny, by restoring the inheritance of prophethood and the keys of the imamate to the family of His Prophet. He honoured religion and the believers, saving them from disaster in every situation with the advent of the Servant of God, Abū Muḥammad al-Imām al-Mahdī bi-llāh, Commander of the Faithful. (God) manifested the splendour and beauty of Islam with his advent. He secured the heritage of his ancestor the Prophet, and his forefather (ʿAlī), the legatee (*waṣī*). May the blessings of God be upon them both. (God) endowed His friends and the supporters of His right, Arab chiefs and valiant Kutāma, with perspicacity. The imamate cast its staff in its house with delight; its solitude became tamed, and its basis became firm.[356] The Commander of the Faithful became a high, lofty mountain, a firm mountain on earth and a sheltering shadow for its inhabitants. The foothold of guidance became firm and the fright of piety was calmed by him. He straightened its support which had become crooked, and strengthened its foundations which had become loose. He reinforced its rope (*ḥabl*) which had dissolved, restoring its unity which had been dispersed. What was scattered was repaired by the blessing of the Commander of the Faithful, the good fortune of his nature, the good omen of his star and the breeze of his zephyr. He treated Islam from incurable disease and repaired its fissures. He mended cracks in it which could not be mended, and reconciled splits in it which could not be reconciled. He is the key of mercy and the guide of the good, defending the truth, protecting religion, taking care of the affairs of Muslims, and watchful of that which thwarts the aspirations of the peddlers of falsehood. Praise be to God, Lord of the worlds. By the grace of God, whenever the Commander of the Faithful attempted a great and difficult feat, God facilitated it. When he met any hardship, (God) subdued it. When he came to any rough terrain, (God) made it smooth. Unity was established through him, harmony was continuous and calamity was averted. The farthest and closest regions of the earth are secure through him. His friend is powerful and protected, while his enemy is humble and restrained. Whoever strikes fire with his flint and gathers firewood in his rope (*ḥabl*) is assured help and ordained for him is victory. Whoever breaks his oath to him, betrays his trust, violates his treaty and breaks his commitment will incur the wrath of God for opposing him and causing sedition. War will burn with its fire whoever kindles against him the fire of war (*nār al-ḥarb*) and will wound him with its claws, and whoever holds on to obedience to him grasps '*the firm hand-hold*' (2:256), and will be victorious in the Hereafter and in this world. Whoever solicits a confidant other than it, '*he loses both this world and the Hereafter. That is the sheer loss*' (22:11). Therefore, praise

356. The wording is reminiscent of a poet's words in which the expression 'to cast one's staff' (*alqā ʿaṣāhu*) is used of a traveller who settles down at the end of a long journey. See al-Qurṭubī, *al-Jāmiʿ*, vol. 1, p. 419.

God who has let you attain the time of the Commander of the Faithful, and distinguished you with the blessing of his reign and good fortune of his dominion. May your hopes be high and your optimism grow with confidence in his justice. May your expectation rise to recognise the excellence of his attention. May your adherence to the rope of obedience to him and the bonds of loyalty to him become strong, for indeed, no bond connects God and His servants except through their love for the family of Muḥammad, may God bless him and grant him salvation. God, exalted be His mention, has said, '*Say: "No reward do I ask of you for this except the love of those near of kin"*' (26:23). The Messenger of God says, '*My family among you are like Noah's ark. He who sails in it will be safe, but he who holds back from it will drown.*' So renew thanks to God for having granted you the compassion and mercy of the Commander of the Faithful, and his constant care for your affairs, compensating for your shortcomings. Indeed, giving thanks is the surest preserver for the one benefiting from His bounties, and the surest custodian for His abundant kindness, and the most effective means derived for the beginning of His benefit and the provision of its abundance. The Commander of the Faithful prays to God, possessor of benevolence and bounties, and bestower of favours and graces, that He may bless Muḥammad, the key of His mercy and conveyor of His message, to whom He granted all His virtues and nobility. May He cause (the Commander of the Faithful) to be filled with His fear and regard. May he carry out with good fortune His precepts. May He grant him the best inspiration in fulfilling the leadership which He has granted him and carrying out the affairs of His servants that He has entrusted to him, just as He inspired His rightly-guided vicegerents. May He support him in his good intention and grant him the best trial. May He grant him success to act in obedience to Him and to uphold His right so that he can restrain infidelity and heresy, and subjugate the outlying regions of the land. May He make him the best leader who is kind to his subjects. May He make his subjects the best subjects who discharge the right of their leader. Indeed, success lies with Him and abundance proceeds from Him. Salutation!

(Al-Mahdī) was proclaimed caliph on Friday 21 Rabīʿ II 297/7 January 910 at Raqqāda, al-Qayrawān and al-Qaṣr al-Qadīm. This letter was read out from the pulpit of al-Qayrawān and was dispatched to the provinces with the *dāʿīs*. He was proclaimed thereafter and it was read out from the pulpits when it reached there. The people were happy and pleased with this and invoked blessings upon him profusely. Delegations of the towns came from every region and place in proportion to the proximity of their settlements. (Al-Mahdī) continued to sit in assembly for the people. Abū Jaʿfar al-Khazarī arrived with the womenfolk from the city of Tripoli in the best manner.

Whenever (al-Mahdī) sat for his assembly, he allowed his close followers to come in his presence. When he had satisfied their needs, he allowed those who were below them in rank, and often allowed the common people to come in his presence to greet him. Poets composed verses about him and eulogised him. The first poet of Ifrīqiya to eulogise him was Saʿdūn al-Warjīnī. He was a poet who had eulogised the Aghlabids and held their functions. He had been taken prisoner in Byzantium and had been ransomed. He was permitted to come before (al-Mahdī) and recite to him what he had composed about him. This happened immediately after the arrival of the womenfolk, while (al-Mahdī) was seated and the followers congratulated him on their safe arrival. (The poet) came in his presence and recited the poem[357] in which he says:

> Stop with the mounts on the pastures of regions.
> Their features are wearing garments of dust,
> Two winds play with them until their traces are erased,
> An easterly and a westerly wind.

Then he reached these verses:

> The agile she-camel ran turning away from the destination,
> While the hand of destination ruled the rein of my journey.
> She feared that mishap might befall me because I
> Previously had been absent then returned after a long time.

---

357. Some verses of the poem are reproduced in al-Maqrīzī, *Ittiʿāẓ*, vol. 1, p. 73; al-Maqrīzī, *al-Muqaffā*, p. 95; Ibn al-Dawādārī, *Kanz al-durar*, vol. 6, p. 115; Idrīs ʿImād al-Dīn, *ʿUyūn al-akhbār*, ed. al-Yaʿlāwī, p. 175, ed. Ghālib, vol. 5, pp. 112–114; al-Yaʿlāwī, *al-Adab bi-Ifrīqiya*, pp 36–38. See also Pieter Smoor, 'Al-Mahdī's Tears: Impressions of Faṭimid Court Poetry', in U. Vermeulen and D. de Smet, eds., *Egypt and Syria in the Fatimid, Ayyubid and Mamluk Eras II*. Leuven, 1998, pp. 35–36.

Then after that we met, re-united.
O what a captive was united with a captive!

When he had recited these verses, al-Mahdī shed tears. His tears fell on his sleeve. Saʿdūn became silent. (Al-Mahdī) gestured to him to recite. (The poet) continued until he came to the verses:

Will you deter a man from the son of Fāṭima,
Daughter of the Prophet and the family of purification?
Abstain from distracting, I shall visit
The best one visited from the members of the household
of the revelation.

Abū ʿAbd Allāh, who was standing before al-Mahdī, told (Saʿdūn), 'You have spoken the truth. Indeed, he is the best of creatures!' Thereupon, Saʿdūn kissed the ground in front of al-Mahdī and continued to recite the verses until he reached these verses:

This is the Commander of the Faithful with whose coming
The supports of every commander were demolished.
This is the Fatimid imam through whom feel secure from threat.
The western lands of (the earth)
And the east, in spite of its Syria and Iraq, is no
Refuge from his victorious army,
Until he attains what he desires of the caliphate
And is obtained from him his extended justice.

The Commander of the Faithful said, 'Whatever God wills (*mā shā'a llāh*)!' He continued to recite the poem until he referred to Abū ʿAbd Allāh saying:

O chosen one from his finest *dāʿīs*.
The one most hoped for by them in difficulty and in ease,
Until he won over every tribe for (al-Mahdī)
And he threw to him the reins of every persistent stumbler,
You (al-Mahdī) resemble Moses and he (Abū ʿAbd Allāh)
is your serpent
Which is cast and snatches every falsehood of the magician.[358]

358. Cf. Qur'an 7:117; 26:45.

At this al-Mahdī looked at Abū ʿAbd Allāh and smiled. Abū ʿAbd Allāh kissed the ground in front of (al-Mahdī) and said to al-Warjīnī, 'I am beneath that (praise), as much as the distance between the sky and the earth!'

The Commander of the Faithful ordered (the poet) to be granted plentiful recompense and that it should be bestowed upon him every year. Abū ʿAbd Allāh also offered (the poet) a gift. It would be too long to mention the poets who have eulogised al-Mahdī. The elegies they have composed are so many that they are outside the scope of this book.

Through (al-Mahdī), stability came to reign the realm, and through him the turmoil of the common people subsided. Roads became safe and the situation became normal, secure and regular. When those slave-girls were presented to him, he picked some of them for himself and gave some to al-Qā'im, but he distributed most of them to the Kutāma chiefs, to whom he also assigned the provinces of Ifrīqiya. He assigned to every Kutāma contingent a district of (Ifrīqiya) and other towns which fell under his jurisdiction and where his authority extended. He appointed their chiefs as governors over its towns. He commanded them to adorn themselves and display splendour, so they dressed in the finest garments, adorned their saddles and bridles, and displayed exquisite attire.[359] They abandoned the attire which used to be their custom. Their possessions became vast and their wealth increased because of the provinces allotted to them and the towns which they ruled. Moreover, he bestowed upon them gifts and lavished upon them grants.

(Al-Mahdī) organised the administrative departments and gave orders to levy taxes. The land register was burnt when Ziyādat Allāh fled. He ordered it to be restored.[360] He set up an intelligence service, a department for real estate and a department for property which belonged to those who fled with Ziyādat Allāh. He confiscated their

---

359. See Jawdhar's account of al-Mahdī distributing garments preserved in Abū ʿAlī Manṣūr al-ʿAzīzī al-Jawdharī, *Sīrat al-Ustādh Jawdhar*, ed. M. Kāmil Ḥusayn and M. ʿAbd al-Hādī Shaʿīra (Cairo, 1954), pp. 35–36; tr. Marius Canard, *Vie de l'Ustadh Jawdhar* (Algiers, 1958), pp. 45–47.

360. Al-Mahdī entrusted this task to Ibn al-Qadīm, who had held the same functions under the reign of Ziyādat Allāh. See p. 188 above.

property, leaving alone what was due to their wives, whose safeguard and protection he guaranteed. He took in his service black slaves and white slaves of Christian origin (*al-rūm*), and established a department for pensions where he ordered the registration of freed slaves and sons of slaves and applicants who had hastened to be registered for maintenance. Many offices were thus established. He gave order to recover the pillage of Raqqāda, of which a great deal was recovered from the hands of people who were prosecuted and from whom large sums were gathered. He instituted a public treasury for which a department was set in place. It is said that the director of the public treasury[361] presented to him an account of allowances for the month of Ramaḍān amounting to 100,000 dinars, and which the director of the treasury had considered enormous. However, al-Mahdī replied, 'If I would attain my dues by the grace of God and realise my hopes, I would not be satisfied with all this as the pay for a single one of my followers.'

He was very generous with money which is a characteristic of the Mahdī, peace be upon him, as reported of old in traditions. Nevertheless he would neither waste nor neglect the least sum, and he would not get involved in expenses which could not be justified. Such are the characteristics of the imams. It has been reported that a man came to al-Ḥasan b. 'Alī, peace be upon him, to beg from him without recognising who he was, for he had been led to him. He saw (al-Ḥasan) asking someone for something trivial which was due to him of his right. So he refrained from begging from him and thought of giving up. Then he dared to approach him and begged from him. (Al-Ḥasan) gave him many times more than he had expected. He told him, 'By God! I don't know at what to marvel. Should I marvel at your giving this or at your asking for what I saw you previously demanding?'

(The beggar) related to him what had caused him to lose hope. (Al-Ḥasan) said, 'O man! The one whom you saw us asking for the paltry thing you saw wanted to deceive our intelligence, so we declined, while you appealed to our generosity and we donated to you.'

---

361. The first holder of this office was Abū Ja'far al-Khazarī. On officials appointed to various administrative functions see Ibn 'Idhārī, *al-Bayān*, vol. 1, p. 159.

Members of the Aghlabid family, their clients, troops and servants who had remained behind feared (al-Mahdī), even though Abū ʿAbd Allāh had granted them a guarantee of safety. So al-Mahdī confirmed it to them. Their dignitaries and chiefs entered before him when he sat for audience together with others who did. (Al-Mahdī) granted them proximity and was friendly with them. He was kind to them and employed some of them. He sent on missions and military campaigns all those who were suitable for that, and granted them the status of followers. Hence they felt secure and became confident, and their fear calmed down. People observed his discipline, resolve, sound administration, kindness and generosity to the extent which they had not expected of him. He spread justice, established it and ordered it to be enforced in places distant and remote as well as near and close. He redressed injustices and would hear such cases himself. He accepted written petitions from complainants while riding or sitting. He would hear from them their complaints and would redress their grievances on the basis of justice and equity. Consequently he gained the sympathy of the elite as well as the commonalty who regarded him highly. Abū ʿAbd Allāh was disregarded and his light was eclipsed by the light of al-Mahdī. People turned away from (Abū ʿAbd Allāh) and turned towards (al-Mahdī). In spite of this, (Abū ʿAbd Allāh) showed humility, self-abasement, reverence and submission, and acknowledged (al-Mahdī's) kindness, confirmed his authority and wished him well, much more than he used to do before. This showed sincere intention, purity of innermost thought and commitment to duty, until something happened to him which we shall relate in the next chapter, God, the Most High, willing.

39

Events relating to the hypocrites against al-Mahdī and the outcome of their affair.

When God arranged for His friend what we have reported, and supported him with good fortune and assistance which we have described, Abū al-ʿAbbās, brother of Abū ʿAbd Allāh, became resentful. This is because when he arrived from Tripoli at the court of Abū

ʿAbd Allāh, he tasted leadership because (Abū ʿAbd Allāh) gave him precedence, ennobled him and openly honoured him, as we have previously reported. Abū ʿAbd Allāh treated him with good manners and good intention as (Abū al-ʿAbbās) was older than him and had precedence. He respected him for this and protected him and accorded him for this reason what he needed. Then, when (Abū ʿAbd Allāh) left for Sijilmāsa, (Abū al-ʿAbbās) governed the people and they looked up to him. Authority to command and forbid was vested in him. When he lost this (power), his intention became corrupted and he became filled with envy. Satan incited him and led him astray, deluding him. He began to disapprove this, and revile and slander al-Mahdī before his brother Abū ʿAbd Allāh. Abū ʿAbd Allāh found this awful and dissociated from him on this matter, while honouring him and without being unpleasant to him. Abū al-ʿAbbās intensified this matter and became arrogant, confirming the means of hypocrisy, making allusions and criticising.[362] Then he encountered Abū ʿAbd Allāh, speaking to him openly. He negotiated with him publicly and told him, 'You possessed a dominion which submitted to you. Then you brought someone who took it away from you and excluded you from it, belittled you and oppressed you. The least requirement towards you would be that he should have allowed you to remain as you were so that you would command and prohibit, and he would occupy himself, if he wished, with his own business without doing you wrong by humiliating you in such role.'

(Abū al-ʿAbbās) continued to reproach (Abū ʿAbd Allāh) with such speech repeatedly and blamed him until eventually he influenced him and forced him to speak face to face with al-Mahdī on some of the concerns.[363] (Abū ʿAbd Allāh) expressed these in the form of advice to (al-Mahdī) saying, 'O our lord! The Kutāma are a people whom I

---

362. Among other things, Abū al-ʿAbbās raised doubts about al-Mahdī's right to the imamate. See Ibn al-Athīr, *al-Kāmil*, vol. 6, p. 134; al-Maqrīzī, *Ittiʿāẓ*, vol. 1, p. 67; and Ibn Khaldūn, *al-ʿIbar*, vol. 4, p. 77 (tr. *Berbères*, vol. 2, p. 522).

363. According to Ibn ʿIdhārī, *al-Bayān*, vol. 1, pp. 161–162 it was Abū ʿAbd Allāh himself who, during an expedition against the Ṣadīna and the Zanāta in 297/910–1, hatched the plot by colluding with the Kutāma chiefs to overthrow al-Mahdī. However, Ghazwiyya who accompanied Abū ʿAbd Allāh on the expedition, betrayed him on his return to Raqqāda and informed al-Mahdī about the conspiracy.

set aright, organised and instructed in a particular way. Having done this, I was able to achieve with them what I aspired to do with them, and attained what I had aimed to do with them. But that which you have done with them, by giving them money and appointing them over provinces, and commanding them to wear [fine] clothing and ornaments, is spoiling them, because it turns them away from that to which they are accustomed. Leave them as they were before, so that I might, in your place, assume the task of commanding them and prohibiting them, of directing them as they are accustomed to being directed by me, of treating them in the manner in which I did up until now, and of carrying on your wars and conducting the affairs in your place, with them and with others. Then you might stay in peace in your palace, without being disturbed by any of them or by anyone else. If you do so, it will create much more respect for you, reinforce your authority, and bring about complete success and order which you wish.'

When al-Mahdī heard this from him, he knew for certain what was on his mind and where it came from. He gave a courteous reply about the matter, without showing him that he knew of his situation, and caused him to despair of what his self had enticed him to do.

When Abū al-ʿAbbās came to know of this, he caused more corruption. (Abū ʿAbd Allāh) listened to him and he exercised his spell on him. Then he swayed the *dāʿī*s and the elders. They honoured him since they saw Abū ʿAbd Allāh honouring him, and heard his eloquence, knowledge and expertise in various talents. Many of them supported him and he would insinuate before them, making allusion after allusion, until eventually he spoke openly to those whom he saw had been affected by what he was saying. (Abū al-ʿAbbās) refuted the imamate before them, casting doubts upon it. He approached them from the object of their aspiration and addressed them from what they wanted, stating that what was rightly due to them and must be under their control was several times more than what had been granted them. He reminded them of the removal of funds from their custody, the introduction of black guards, people of Ifrīqiya, and others among the troops together with them. He told them various things which would be too long to relate and have implications, for which this book is too short to deal exhaustively.

Al-Mahdī was aware of all this but pretended not to take notice while Abū ʿAbd Allāh was nevertheless wavering. His unbelief had not reached to the extent of denial and hypocrisy. Abū al-ʿAbbās went to see Abū ʿAbd Allāh and those of his companions whom he had sought to corrupt. He warned them and caused them fear for themselves, stating that if they did not act quickly they would be apprehended. This became firm in their hearts and increased their treachery. All this time he confirmed what he wanted and reinforced his cause by various tricks and methods of deception, until eventually he forced those *dāʿīs* whom he incited to separate with hypocrisy and declare dissension.

He deluded Hārūn b. Yūnus al-Azāyī, who was called 'chief of elders' (*shaykh al-mashāyikh*), so that he confronted al-Mahdī with speech which (Abū al-ʿAbbās) embellished for him, and through which he sought to corrupt him. He told al-Mahdī to his face, 'We have doubts about you, so bring forth a miraculous sign if you are the Mahdī as you have asserted.'

Al-Mahdī found what he said impertinent. He let him know of the viciousness of his speech on the basis of the Book of God, may His mention be exalted, which rebukes peoples who asked their prophets to produce miraculous signs. It would be too long to relate what he said to him on this matter. There are indeed proofs concerning al-Mahdī for this scoundrel and for those whom he incited, such that if they considered carefully they would be satisfied with them. Because God, the Mighty, the Glorious, says in His book to those like him who asked His Prophet, may God bless him and grant him salvation: '*They say, "Why does he not bring us a sign from his Lord?" Has not a clear sign come to them of all that was in the former scriptures?*' (20:133). And He, exalted be His praise, replies: '*Is it not enough for them that We have sent down unto thee the Book which is read unto them?*' (29:51).

He instituted His revelation as the miracle of His Prophet, and its esoteric interpretation as the miracle of the imams from his posterity, and He instructed in His Book and through the tongue of His Prophet, bestowing guidance on this matter whose significance is beyond the scope of this book, and which is not our intention to investigate.

Al-Mahdī told Hārūn, referring to his 'words we have doubts about you', 'Woe unto you! You had been full of conviction, and doubt cannot remove conviction.'

What (al-Mahdī) said is a basis of religion, while the scoundrel Hārūn was unaware of it. He failed before it and persisted in his infidelity and hypocrisy until eventually he deserved to be executed and '*the decree of punishment was carried out against him*' (39:19), because of the evidence and persisting in infidelity and sin. He proceeded to the wrath and curse of God. When Abū al-'Abbās and those whom he had sought to corrupt found out about his death, he used this as a reason for dissent. They were overcome with fear because of it. He instigated them to abandon courtesy and magnified the matter to Abū 'Abd Allāh who became bold. His distrust of al-Mahdī became firm. They withdrew to conclude a pact. They gathered to this end at the house of Abū Zākī Tammām b. Mu'ārik and devised a plot. They agreed to assassinate al-Mahdī and remove the right of God from his hand. They sought to extinguish the light which God, the Mighty, the Glorious, has placed in him, defying God, the Mighty, the Glorious, being devoid of faith and outside the community of believers, '*but God will perfect His light however much the disbelievers are averse*' (61:8).

Most of the Kutāma sided with the suggestions of the accursed. Ghazwiyya b. Yūsuf was among those who opposed (Abū al-'Abbās), and held fast to the rope (*ḥabl*)[364] of al-Mahdī. He kept (al-Mahdī) informed about (the conspirators). Al-Mahdī appointed him to take command of the black guards who stood prepared. Believers who were free from hypocrisy rallied around him. They stood prepared for the hypocrites even though they were greater in number while the believers were few among them. Abū Ḥalīfa was also among those who stood firm in a group of elders. The others separated through hypocrisy and gathered crowds. They surrounded al-Mahdī's palace to attack him, while he remained upright, sitting and patient. He was unconcerned, having confidence in God's promise. (God), exalted be His praise, assisted him and protected him, dispersing the crowd which had joined forces against him, and striking terror in their

364. Cf. the expression 'the rope of God' in Qur'an 3:103.

hearts. Hence they dispersed. It would be too long to relate these events in this book.[365] We have based it on brevity and arranged it on succinctness. In this connection al-Mahdī had proofs, miracles, portents and miraculous signs. God caused him to triumph. He granted him His protection and assistance, putting fear in the hearts of his enemies and those who had joined forces against him to attack him, in spite of their large number and the small number of those who supported him, just as He, the Mighty, the Glorious, protected through fear his ancestor, Muḥammad, and assisted him with His protection. He provided him reinforcements with His angels.

Al-Mahdī would receive the news of those Kutāma notables who had contracted that hypocrisy with Abū al-ʿAbbās and who approached him and collaborated with him. Meanwhile they would come to see (al-Mahdī), believing every time they entered his chamber that they would attack him and seize him. However, when they came before him their hearts were filled with fear and reverence. God restrained their hands, preventing them from harming him. In spite of this, al-Mahdī took no precautions against them. He disregarded what he had come to know about them, having confidence in God's promise to him. He entrusted his fate to Him, having complete trust in Him. When they withdrew from him, they regretted having left him unharmed and assured each other that they would carry out what they had agreed to do when they next went to meet him. However, when they went to him, it happened to them as before. Then at night they gathered at the house of Abū Zākī. Abū ʿAbd Allāh and Abū al-ʿAbbās were also there among them. Then, during one of those days, al-Mahdī looked at Abū ʿAbd Allāh who was wearing his attire inside out. He came to see him thus for three days. On the third day (al-Mahdī) asked him, 'O Abū ʿAbd Allāh! What concern is causing you to neglect yourself?'

He replied, 'O my lord! What do you mean?'

He said, 'I see you wearing your shirt inside out for three days without being aware of it or changing it.'

---

365. On the events leading to the execution of Abū ʿAbd Allāh, see al-Nuwayrī, *Nihāya*, p. 48; Ibn Khaldūn, *al-ʿIbar*, vol. 4, pp. 76–78 (tr. *Berbères*, vol. 2, pp. 521–523); al-Maqrīzī, *Ittiʿāẓ*, vol. 1, pp. 67–68; and Ibn al-Athīr, *al-Kāmil*, vol. 6, pp. 134–151.

He looked and said, 'By God! O my lord, I was unaware of it.'

He said, 'It must indeed be a great concern. And where did you spend the nights since such and such nights?'

(Abū 'Abd Allāh) remained silent.

He said, 'Was it not at the house of Abū Zākī?'

He replied, 'Yes, my lord.'

He asked, 'What caused you to leave your house, which we allocated to you, and go to the house of Abū Zākī?'

He replied, 'O my lord, I feared for my life.'

He asked, 'Who are you afraid of?'

He remained silent.

He asked, 'Of me?'

He replied, 'You frightened me, so I was afraid.'

He asked, 'Does one fear anyone except one's enemy?'

He said, 'I seek refuge with God.'

Al-Mahdī said, 'The believer does not fear his protector.'

Abū 'Abd Allāh remained silent and realised that his secret lay bare before the friend of God. He lost the argument and (al-Mahdī) was free of him. It became permissible to kill him for his having waged war against him. He retired.

The conspirators learnt what the Commander of the Faithful had said. They refrained from going to see him and feared for their lives. Ibn al-Qadīm had taken hold of them, making wicked suggestions to them. He corrupted them and won them over by offering Ziyādat Allāh's wealth which was under his charge. He feared that the Commander of the Faithful would confiscate it from him. (Al-Mahdī) had already appointed him director of the courier (*dīwān al-barīd*),[366] and was charitable to him, while he paid him back by causing discord and plotting against him. (Al-Mahdī) was aware of his situation. One day while (Ibn al-Qadīm) was before him, al-Mahdī remarked that the conspirators were staying away from him. (Ibn al-Qadīm) said, 'O my lord, if you wish, I can bring them before you.'

(Al-Mahdī) asked, 'Are you able to do so?'

---

366. According to Ibn 'Idhārī, *al-Bayān*, vol. 1, p. 159, Ibn al-Qadīm was appointed director of the land tax (*dīwān al-kharāj*). In al-Yamānī, *Sīrat al-Ḥājib Ja'far*, 132 (tr. Ivanow, *Rise*, p. 221), he had supervision of all the departments. See also note 333 above.

He replied, 'Yes, right away.'

He left and returned with them. Hence al-Mahdī knew that he was indeed with them and was one of their companions. They declared their innocence of what was being alleged about them and defended themselves from what had reached him concerning them. He responded to them politely on this matter, and dispatched some of their leaders to various provinces to disperse them. Among them he dispatched Abū Zākī to Tripoli, whose governor was his paternal uncle Abū Yūsuf. When (Abū Zākī) arrived there, (al-Mahdī) wrote to (the governor) to execute him.[367] Accordingly Abū Yūsuf, his paternal uncle, killed him in captivity and sent his head to al-Mahdī. Several conspirators were also executed in the provinces and in Raqqāda in various ways.[368] Ibn al-Qadīm fled and went into hiding, but was caught after a search and was executed.

One day, while Abū 'Abd Allāh and Abū al-'Abbās were on their way to al-Mahdī's palace as usual, Ghazwiyya b. Yūsuf attacked Abū 'Abd Allāh with a lance and Ḥabr b. Tumāshit[369] attacked Abū al-'Abbās also with a lance. Ghazwiyya killed Abū 'Abd Allāh, and Ḥabr killed Abū al-'Abbās between the palaces.[370] They were both killed on Monday around midday 15 Jumādā II 298/18 February 911.[371]

---

367. Before his execution, Abū Zākī had played a leading role in defeating the rebelling tribes of Zanāta, Hawwāra and Lamāya in Tripoli. See Ibn 'Idhārī, *al-Bayān*, vol. 1, pp. 163–164.

368. Ibn 'Idhārī, *al-Bayān*, vol. 1, pp. 167, 169, gives the names of some conspirators who were executed: Muḥammad b. Abī Sa'īd al-Mīlī, inspector of the markets; Muḥammad b. Abī Rajjāl al-Baghā'ī and Abū al-Wahb b. 'Amr b. Zurāra al-'Abdarī executed in 299/912 at the same time as Ibn al-Qadīm; and Muḥammad b. Abī Ayyūb executed in 300/913.

369. In Ibn 'Idhārī, *al-Bayān*, vol. 1, p. 164, he is called Jabr b. Numāsib al-Mīlī; al-Nuwayrī, *Nihāya*, p. 49: Khayr b. Māshīt; Idrīs 'Imād al-Dīn, *'Uyūn al-akhbār*, ed. al-Ya'lāwī, pp. 186: Jabr b. Tumāshit al-Jīmalī, ed. Ghālib, vol. 5, p. 121: Jabr b. Tumāshit al-Jamīlī. According to Ibn Khaldūn, *al-'Ibar*, vol. 4, p. 77 (tr. *Berbères*, vol. 2, p. 522), Ghazwiyya's brother, Ḥubāsa, helped him to assassinate the two brothers.

370. In Ibn 'Idhārī, *al-Bayān*, vol. 1, p. 164: *behind Qaṣr al-Ṣaḥn*. Later, in 302/914–5, Ghazwiyya led a Kutāma revolt against al-Mahdī in al-Qayrawān. Al-Mahdī dispatched a large army under the command of his client Ghālib. In the ensuing battle Ghazwiyya was killed and his head was sent to al-Mahdī. See Ibn 'Idhārī, *al-Bayān*, vol. 1, p. 172; al-Maqrīzī, *Itti'āẓ*, vol. 1, p. 69.

371. Ibn 'Idhārī, *al-Bayān*, vol. 1, p. 164, dates the execution of the two brothers on 1st Dhū al-Ḥijja 298/31 July 911. The *Iftitāḥ*'s account of the conspiracy and the killing of Abū 'Abd

Coincidentally, Abū Zākī was killed on the same day. Al-Mahdī gave orders for the two [brothers] to be buried in the cemetery. He invoked mercy upon Abū ʿAbd Allāh and spoke well of him, but he cursed Abū al-ʿAbbās and spoke ill of him. God destroyed the hypocrites and erased their traces after giving them warning, and the cogency of the proof against them from God and His friend.

It is said that after warning them personally and seeing their persistence and insistence, (al-Mahdī) sent surreptitiously to everyone [of the conspirators] someone whom he trusted, and to whom he inclined in order that he would advise him sincerely. Abū ʿAbd Allāh was wavering. He would advance, delay, hide and show forth. Abū al-ʿAbbās said to someone who blamed him concerning that, 'By God, we shall not allow anyone else to live in a building which we built with our hands, for which we toiled and where our lives were spent, while we remain behind its doors. Rather, we shall stay in its high points or make him join its lowest [places].'

Someone else told Abū Zākī similar things. He replied, 'No, by God, I will not spend days in which the son of the herdsman, meaning Ghazwiyya b. Yūsuf, precedes me and rises above me.'

Someone else said to one of them on this matter, and (that person) replied, 'We shall not leave him, meaning al-Mahdī, until he shares with us these palaces where he resides, and the gardens which are around them liberally, and we shall command and rule as we used to do. We are not satisfied to take from under his hand like slaves do. Rather, what we have taken by our swords will remain with us and under our hands just as it was, and we have merit in that which we give him from it.' They said a lot of things out of foolishness, stupidity, infidelity and hypocrisy as has been reported from them, until eventually '*the decree of punishment was carried out against him*' (39:19), so that God destroyed them all and made them like '*a field mown down, still and silent as ashes*' (21:15). God, the Mighty, the Glorious, protected His friend from their harm, and made him victorious over them just as He protected his ancestor Muḥammad, may God bless

Allāh and Abū al-ʿAbbās is closely followed by Jamāl al-Dīn ʿAlī Ibn Ẓāfir, *Akhbār al-duwal al-munqaṭiʿa*, ed. A. Ferré (Cairo, 1972), pp. 8–10; and al-Nuwayrī, *Nihāya*, pp. 47–49. Details on Abū ʿAbd Allāh's role in crushing various revolts of the tribes omitted by al-Qāḍī al-Nuʿmān are to be found in Ibn ʿIdhārī, *al-Bayān*, vol. 1, pp. 160–162.

him and grant him salvation, from the harm of the idolaters of the Quraysh when they joined forces against him and plotted to kill him, in spite of their large number and strength and the small number and weakness of his supporters. Exactly the same thing happened with al-Mahdī.

God protected the believers who were with His friend, and who remained firm in their loyalty to him, in spite of having been called to do what others agreed to do out of hypocrisy, and in spite of what was said to them about this matter to mislead them and what they were led to believe. They would tell Abū al-ʿAbbās in the presence of Abū ʿAbd Allāh when he told them anything on this matter, 'This [man] informed us and declared to us that he is our imam and our lord, and he expressed this in his presence. You also summoned to him for sometime and you said what he said. We have remained faithful to what we have pledged and what we know. Now what will alienate us from him?'

When Abū ʿAbd Allāh heard this he would lower his head and remain silent, while Abū al-ʿAbbās would debate with falsehood, misrepresent and insist stubbornly on his opinions. He deserved the curse of God and His friends, while Abū ʿAbd Allāh earned punishment for having doubts because of him, and which the friend imposed upon him swiftly in this world. He asked forgiveness for him in the Hereafter because of his previous pious deeds and good intention. This conforms to God's words, '*Whoever works evil, will be requited accordingly*' (4:123), and also His words, '*Whatever calamity may befall you, is because of what your own hands have wrought*' (42:30). When debasement affects gold, it must be dissolved so that fire might burn away the debasement in it and make it pure. The easiest punishment is that which is swift in this world, while the most severe punishment is that of the Hereafter. We seek refuge with God from His punishment and agony, and implore Him for safety and protection in this world and in the Hereafter. He is the Giver, the Generous.

40

Inhabitants of Ifrīqiya who betrayed the clemency granted to them and their punishment for treason and hostility.

We have already reported that when Abū ʿAbd Allāh arrived, he initially granted safety to the inhabitants of al-Qayrawān and all the other towns, to the members of the Aghlabid family who remained behind after the departure of the forsaken one,[372] to those who had been under the service of the forsaken one, to his clients and his servants. We also reported that subsequently al-Mahdī granted benevolence and favour to those who submitted to his authority and remained faithful to the covenant.

Now the first instance of their antagonism emerged when some members of the Aghlabid family were at the house of Abū al-Ḥasan b. Abī Ḥajar.[373] He was one of their dignitaries, leaders and wealthy men. While his food was ready and they were dining with him, one of his attendants came to him and said, 'Abū ʿAbd Allāh and Abū al-ʿAbbās have just been killed.' Thereupon he withdrew his hands from the food, kicked the dining table and said to the members of his family who were with him, 'By God, all of you will be killed!'

They asked, 'What is our fault?'

He replied, 'The one who granted you safety has been killed. He was the master of this realm and the cause of this dominion. Who are you then, you who are considered as enemies? He who kills his friend would kill his enemy more swiftly.'

Their hearts were overcome with hypocrisy. They slandered (al-Mahdī) among themselves and became apprehensive of him. They were all at al-Qaṣr al-Qadīm where trouble broke out between a commoner and a Kutāma tribesman. (The Aghlabids) attacked the Kutāma tribesmen, expelled them from al-Qaṣr and closed its gates. They came across a group of followers and displayed hostility. This happened just after the incident of hypocrisy about which we have fully reported. The Kutāma who were around al-Qaṣr al-Qadīm shouted to one another. They marched to it and surrounded it. They

---

372. Reference to Ziyādat Allāh b. ʿAbd Allāh.

373. He was a former governor of Qafṣa. On him see note 86 above.

set fire to the minaret so that the inhabitants of al-Qayrawān would come to their help. A group of them did come to their help, but before they could reach them the Aghlabids unpacked what weapons and supplies they had, and distributed them to their ruffians. They rode their mounts and mobilised the horsemen and the foot soldiers inside al-Qaṣr at a place called 'the arena' (*al-maydān*) where there was a large public square. They opened the Gate of Happiness (Bāb al-Sa'āda) near this arena and all at once they attacked the Kutāma who were there, killing some of them. Then (the Kutāma) closed ranks against them for some time and overcame them. On that day Abū Ḥalīfa came out [from al-Qayrawān to rescue the Kutāma]. When al-Mahdī came to know about this, he sent someone to prevent the Kutāma from attacking (the Aghlabids). He expressed to them his disapproval and they withdrew.

Then the Aghlabids unpacked their tents (*fāzāt*) and desert tents (*akhbiya*), and pitched them outside al-Qaṣr al-Qadīm towards Raqqāda, at a place called al-Hadaf, in a state of open insurrection and war against the friend of God, but he avoided them. They remained thus for a few days and then dispersed and returned to their homes. They deserved to be killed for their betrayal and desertion. Al-Mahdī left them alone for a while. Then he ordered the arrest of some of their leaders. They were arrested and executed in captivity at the gate of Raqqāda where their heads were displayed. Those who survived thought that the ones who were executed were the ones wanted. Then after sometime, a second group of them was arrested and executed. Then (al-Mahdī) ordered a search for them throughout the land and they were executed everywhere. Those (Aghlabids) who did not get involved in the conspiracy were pursued and imprisoned. They remained in prison until al-Manṣūr,[374] out of favour to them, released them after his victory.[375] He gave them presents and sent them to Egypt.[376] This happened when he released prisoners.

---

374. The Fatimid caliph-imam al-Manṣūr bi-llāh Ismā'īl (r. 334–341/946–953). On him see al-Maqrīzī, *al-Muqaffā*, pp. 142–192; Georges Marçais, 'al-Manṣūr Ismā'īl', *EI*, vol. 5, p. 257; and Farhat Dachraoui, 'al-Manṣūr bi'llāh', *EI*², vol. 6, pp. 434–435.

375. This was his victory over the Kharijite rebel Abū Yazīd in 336/947.

376. Ibn Ḥammād, *Akhbār*, pp. 37–38 (tr. p. 59), reports: 'There (in al-Mahdiyya) he set free twenty surviving members the Aghlabid family. He gave to each of them 20 *mithqāls*

Then there was also a quarrel between an inhabitant of al-Qayrawān and a Kutāma tribesman in (the town). The populace turned against (the Kutāma) who were in the town, and killed about 700 of them at the same time.[377] This news came to the knowledge of al-Mahdī at that time. He asked, 'Have they any cohesion or a leader in this matter?'

He was told, 'No. This was done by the mob and people who are unknown. They cannot be identified and have no importance.' Thereupon (al-Mahdī) quoted the poet's verse:

Throw moist earth on Daysam,
God's decree refused everything but what has happened.[378]

The jurists of al-Qayrawān came to him led by the *qāḍī* al-Marwadhī.[379] They apologised for this matter, but he ignored them. He did not punish them immediately. Afterwards, he punished them as appropriate for the like of them, by seizing the wealth of (some jurists) since the perpetrators among them were not known, and he executed some of them in their city and among their community. It was not clear that those whom he punished was because of [their complicity in] what had been done. However, this is what was being said, and God knows best.

According to another version, some of those who killed on that day and massacred the followers were known to (al-Mahdī). However, he did not touch them because there was no evidence against them and they could not be executed according to the letter of the law. Eventually they all rebelled with the accursed Deceiver (*al-dajjāl*) Makhlad b. Kaydād during his rebellion outside al-Mahdiyya to lend

---

and exiled them to Egypt.'

377. On this disturbance and subsequent Kutāma revolts, see Ibn 'Idhārī, *al-Bayān*, vol. 1, p. 166; Ibn al-Athīr, *al-Kāmil*, vol. 6, p. 135; Ibn Khaldūn, *al-'Ibar*, vol. 4, pp. 77–78 (tr. *Berbères*, vol. 2, p. 523); and al-Maqrīzī, *Itti'āẓ*, vol. 1, p. 68.

378. These lines were uttered by the poet Abū al-Baydā' al-Riyāḥī (2nd/8th c.) at the burial of his son Daysam. See Abū 'Abd Allāh Muḥammad b. Dāwud Ibn al-Jarrāḥ, *al-Waraqa* (2nd ed., Cairo, 1967), p. 70. Apparently al-Mahdi was giving instructions to bury the Kutama who were killed.

379. On him see note 317 above.

him support.[380] He placed them at the head with all the inhabitants of al-Qayrawān in the battle called the Battle of Lulyāna[381] when he launched his offensive in that locality. God defeated them and they were all exterminated. None of them remained alive on that day. God punished them and brought upon them His vengeance swiftly. He inflicted upon them the might of His power.

41

General events relating to al-Mahdī until his death.

When God, the Mighty, the Glorious, dispersed the host of wrongdoers, eradicated the hypocrites, while He sustained, strengthened and manifested the cause of His friend, (al-Mahdī) designated his son, Muḥammad Abū al-Qāsim al-Qā'im, as heir apparent. He decreed his letters to be written in his name, and styled him 'Heir Apparent of the Muslims' (*walī 'ahd al-muslimīn*). He showed happiness with him whenever he saw him and often cited poetry when he appeared before him. He would recite:

> Blessed and fortunate appearance,
> He is suitable for the world and religion.

The remaining hypocrites left and arrived in Kutāma territory where they installed a little boy from the most despicable family among

---

380. The Kharijite rebel Abū Yazīd Makhlad b. Kaydād acquired a large following among the Ibāḍī Berbers of the Awrās and began his rebellion against the Fatimids in 332/943 during the reign of al-Qā'im. He conquered all of southern Ifrāqiya, including al-Qayrawān, and laid siege to al-Mahdiyya. He was eventually defeated by al-Manṣūr in 336/947. Samuel M. Stern, 'Abū Yazīd al-Nukkārī', *EI²*, vol. 1, pp. 163–164; Roger Le Tourneau, 'La révolte d'Abû Yazîd au Xme siècle', *Les cahiers de Tunisie*, 1 (1953), pp. 103–125; Abū Zakarīyā Yaḥyā b. Abī Bakr al-Warjalānī, *Kitāb Siyar al-a'imma wa-akhbārihim*, ed. Ismā'īl al-'Arabī (Algiers, 1979), pp. 116–123; Ibn al-Athīr, *al-Kāmil*, vol. 6, pp. 302–311; Ibn Ḥammād, *Akhbār*, pp. 18–37 (tr. pp. 33–58); al-Jawdharī, *Sīrat al-Ustādh Jawdhar*, pp. 44–46, 48–50, 53–55 (tr. Canard, *Vie*, pp. 62–66, 68–73, 78–80); al-Qāḍī al-Nu'mān, *al-Majālis wa-al-musāyarāt,* Index; and Idrīs 'Imād al-Dīn, '*Uyūn al-akhbār*, ed. al-Ya'lāwī, Index, ed. Ghālib, vol. 5, Index.

381. A village in the suburbs of al-Mahdiyya. See al-Tijānī, *Riḥla*, p. 371; Djelloul, 'Histoire topographique', pp. 72, 93.

them called the Banū Māwaṭnat[382] of the Ūrissa and claimed that he was the Mahdī.[383] Then they falsely attributed prophethood to him and claimed that he received revelation and that books from God descended upon him. They appointed *dāʿīs* for him just like the *dāʿīs* of Abū ʿAbd Allāh, who spoke in terms like they did and who were organised in their manner. They said that Abū ʿAbd Allāh was still alive; he was not dead. They permitted fornication and forbidden acts, and perpetrated great confusion. Some of the common people of Kutāma territory adopted this creed. They marched to Mīla and captured it. All this happened in a short time. Al-Mahdī dispatched al-Qā'im at the head of troops to fight them. They fought him, but he defeated them and eventually drove them towards the sea, killing many of them. Then most of them relented. He granted them safety and captured the boy they had set up. He was brought before al-Mahdī who executed him.

Then the inhabitants of the city of Tripoli revolted. Al-Mahdī dispatched al-Qā'im to (the city), who after having laid siege to (the city) for sometime conquered it by force. He granted pardon to most of the population of (the city), but he executed those of the notables who had organised the uprising and he confiscated their possessions.[384] (Al-Mahdī) sent a contingent of troops to Barqa who conquered it. Then the town having revolted, he sent another contingent to conquer it and gave orders to execute the notables who had organised the uprising.[385] (Al-Mahdī) did the same with the inhabitants of Sicily who had also revolted and brought to power

382. The Māwaṭnat are listed among the Kutāma clans. See Ibn Khaldūn, *al-ʿIbar*, vol. 6, p. 302 (tr. *Berbères*, vol. 1, p. 292).

383. Ibn ʿIdhārī, *al-Bayān*, vol. 1, pp. 166–167 gives details on this Kutāma uprising and their Mahdī, Kādū b. Muʿārik, known under the name of al-Māriṭī (al-Māwaṭnatī). See also Ibn al-Athīr, *al-Kāmil*, vol. 6, p. 135; Ibn Khaldūn, *al-ʿIbar*, vol. 4, p. 78 (tr. *Berbères*, vol. 2, pp. 523–524); and al-Maqrīzī, *Ittiʿāẓ*, vol. 1, p. 68.

384. The inhabitants of Tripoli were also forced to pay a heavy tribute. Their uprising against the governor Abū Yūsuf Māknūn b. Ḍubāra, and the reconquest of the city took place in 300/912–3. See Ibn ʿIdhārī, *al-Bayān*, vol. 1, pp. 168–169; and Ibn Khaldūn, *al-ʿIbar*, vol. 4, p. 78 (tr. *Berbères*, vol. 2, p. 524).

385. Barqa was first conquered for the Fatimids in 301/913–4 by Ḥubāsa b. Yūsuf, brother of Ghazwiyya. It was reconquered in 304/916–7 by Abū Madīnī after a long siege lasting eighteen months. See Ibn ʿIdhārī, *al-Bayān*, vol. 1, pp. 170, 175.

Ibn Qurhub.[386] The latter was brought before him and he executed him.

Al-Qā'im raided Egypt twice. He seized al-Fayyūm and Upper Egypt (al-Ṣa'īd), and was prevented from reaching Miṣr only because of the Nile, and God willed this conquest to be achieved through one of his descendants.[387] He conquered many Byzantine towns.[388] The inhabitants of Tāhart revolted against him. He attacked (this town) and conquered it and executed those of the notables who had incited the revolt there.[389]

(Al-Mahdī) founded the proverbial city of al-Mahdiyya,[390] which was announced in the books under the name of al-Bayḍā', and about which it was said that the Deceiver (*al-dajjāl*) would never be able to reach or enter it. And it came to pass as had been foretold in the accounts about it. (The city) was one of the most wonderful construction. He had it constructed from stone and provided it with gates of

386. He is named Aḥmad b. Ziyādat Allāh b. Qurhub who rose in 300–304/913–916 together with his son Muḥammad. He defeated the Fatimid fleet, but was overthrown and delivered to al-Mahdī by the Sicilians themselves. See Yaḥyā b. Sa'īd, *Ta'rīkh*, p. 762; Ibn al-Athīr, *al-Kāmil*, vol. 6, pp. 142–143; Ibn Khaldūn, *al-'Ibar*, vol. 4, p. 79 (tr. *Berbères*, vol. 2, pp. 524–525); and Ibn 'Idhārī, *al-Bayān*, vol. 1, pp. 168, 171, 174.

387. The first Fatimid expedition against Egypt was launched in 301/913–4 with the support of the fleet commanded by Ḥubāsa b. Yūsuf who seized Alexandria in 302/914 but retreated before the Abbasid general Mu'nis. In the second expedition, in 306/918, al-Qā'im was forced to retreat before the same Mu'nis, and the Fatimid fleet was destroyed at Rosetta by a fleet despatched from Tarsus. See Ibn al-Athīr, *al-Kāmil*, vol. 6, pp. 147, 149–150, 161; Ibn Khaldūn, *al-'Ibar*, vol. 4, pp. 78–79 (tr. *Berbères*, vol. 2, p. 524); al-Maqrīzī, *Itti'āẓ*, vol. 1, pp. 68–69, 71–72; Ibn 'Idhārī, *al-Bayān*, vol. 1, pp. 171–172, 181; and Ibn Ḥammād, *Akhbār*, pp. 11–12 (tr. pp. 24–25).

388. Reference to conquests in Sicily and in Calabria in 313/925, 316/928, and 317/929 see Ibn 'Idhārī, *al-Bayān*, vol. 1, pp. 190, 193–194; and Ibn al-Athīr, *al-Kāmil*; vol. 6, p. 182.

389. The uprising of Tāhart was suppressed at the beginning of Ṣafar 299/September 911. On these events see Ibn 'Idhārī, *al-Bayān*, vol. 1, pp. 165–166; Ibn al-Athīr, *al-Kāmil*, vol. 6, p. 135, Ibn Khaldūn, *al-'Ibar*, vol. 4, p. 78 (tr. *Berbères*, vol. 2, p. 523); and al-Maqrīzī, *Itti'āẓ*, vol. 1, p. 68.

390. The construction of al-Mahdiyya began on Saturday 5 Dhū al-Qa'da, 303/11 May 916 and was completed in 306/918–9. However, al-Mahdī settled there only two years later. On al-Mahdiyya see Mohamed Talbi, 'al-Mahdiyya', *EI*², vol. 5, pp. 1246–1247; Marçais, *L'architecture musulmane*, pp. 89–92; and Lucien Golvin, 'Mahdiya à l'époque fātimide', *Revue de l'Occident musulman et de la Méditerranée*, 27 (1979), pp. 75–98.

solid iron. He moved to it in Shawwāl 308/February-March 921 and took up residence there. People could then contemplate the miracles through which God willed to accomplish the founding of (the city), and facilitate the task before him in carrying out such an enterprise. (Al-Mahdī) ordered to advance the construction into the sea, dig into the rock a harbour which would penetrate (the city) and link it to the sea through a passage provided with a chain to lock it. When he looked at its fortification and gates and observed the marvel of the people before such an enterprise, he would exclaim, 'All this is a provision for only one moment of a day.' And it came to pass what he had predicted, because when the accursed Makhlad reached (al-Mahdiyya) and stopped a moment before it, that was his last glimpse of (this city) until the day when his body was hung from the top of its wall. The cause of al-Mahdī was reinforced there and it served him as the base for many conquests. He installed [the headquarters of] the *daʿwa* there.

The Maghrib fell into a state of turmoil. (Al-Mahdī) dispatched al-Qāʾim there who restored order and crushed those who caused dissent there.[391] He withdrew after achieving his objectives.

It was brought to (al-Mahdī's) attention that a group of people who had adhered to his *daʿwa* had renegaded, considered as lawful what is prohibited and denied the exoteric (*ẓāhir*).[392] He punished them according to the seriousness of their sins, executing some of them and imprisoning others. He detained them in cells for life in fetters until they all perished. He tested the believers by closing the doors of his mercy for sometime through the years. Then he showed his mercy to those who sought [it] and he raised the obedient ones to the ranks of the righteous. God, the Mighty, the Glorious, continued to grant him success, integrity and grant him help and assistance which he is worthy of before Him and entitled to before Him, and in

391. This refers to the expedition led by al-Qāʾim in Ṣafar 315/April-May 927 to punish the Maghrāwa chief Muḥammad b. Khazar, emir of the Zanāta, and subdue the central Maghrib. See details in Ibn al-Athīr, *al-Kāmil*, vol. 6, p. 190; Ibn Khaldūn, *al-ʿIbar*, vol. 4, pp. 82–83 (tr. *Berbères*, vol. 2, pp. 527–528); *Ittiʿāẓ*, vol. 1, p. 82; and Ibn ʿIdhārī, *al-Bayān*, vol. 1, pp. 191–192.

392. Ibn ʿIdhārī, *al-Bayān*, vol. 1, pp. 185–186, locates this situation in al-Qayrawān, Bāja (Béja) and Tunis under the year 309/921–22.

accordance with His promise to him until God took him to Himself to the nobility He had prepared for him. May the most excellent, cleanest, purest and highest blessings of God be upon him. His death was announced on the morning of Tuesday 10 Jumādā II 322/27 May 934.[393] The duration of the manifestation of his imamate since his arrival in Raqqāda until his death was twenty-four years, one month and twenty days.

42

Summary account of the period from the death of al-Mahdī, peace be upon him, until the time this book was composed.

Then al-Qā'im bi-amr Allāh, may God's blessings be upon him, succeeded al-Mahdī. He followed his example, continued his legacy and pursued his policies. He allowed mourning to be observed for him, while he continued to grieve at his bereavement thereafter for the rest of his life. He did not sleep on a bed, nor ride on an animal, nor prepare a resting place, nor emerge from the gate of his palace out of sorrow for him, and remembering him frequently. It was God's doing for him that, like al-Mahdī, his father, may God's blessings be upon them, he conquered towns of the Byzantines and raided them in the region of Andalusia, returning with booty, captives and plunder.[394]

More than one rebel rebelled against him, but God, the Mighty, the Glorious, enabled him to subdue them. Among those who rebelled against him was a scoundrel called Ibn Ṭālūt, who traced his descent to the Quraysh. He was a scribe from Iraq. He went to the region of Tripoli and claimed to the Berbers that he was the son of al-Mahdī.[395] So they rose with him and followed him. He marched

393. Al-Mahdī's death occurred two months earlier on 14 Rabīʿ I 322/4 March 934, but was kept secret, which explains the conflicting dates in the sources. See Ibn al-Athīr, *al-Kāmil*, vol. 6, p. 238; Ibn Khaldūn, *al-ʿIbar*, vol. 4, p. 83 (tr. *Berbères*, vol. 2, p. 528); al-Maqrīzī, *Ittiʿāẓ*, vol. 1, p. 73; Ibn ʿIdhārī, *al-Bayān*, vol. 1, p. 208; and Ibn Ḥammād, *Akhbār*, p. 15 (tr. p. 28).

394. The Fatimid fleet commanded by Yaʿqūb b. Isḥāq undertook in 324/925–6 a vast expedition against Calabria, Genoa, Sardinia and the coasts of Christian Spain. See Ibn al-Athīr, *al-Kāmil*, vol. 6, p. 249.

395. On this pretender see Ibn ʿIdhārī, *al-Bayān*, vol. 1, p. 209; Ibn al-Athīr, *al-Kāmil*, vol.

on the city of Tripoli in great numbers to capture it. (The inhabitants of Tripoli) fought him and defeated him, killing some of his companions. Then the Berbers found out about him and killed him, and brought his head to al-Qā'im.

Then the Deceiver (*al dajjāl*) whom (al-Qā'im) had been expecting, and who had been foretold in the prophetic tales, led a rebellion against him. (Abū Yazīd) Makhlad b. Kaydād rose in the Awrās mountains at the head of his followers. He invaded the country, attracting towards himself people of corruption and aggression until he seized al-Qayrawān from him and put to death Khalīl b. Isḥāq[396] who had been stationed there at the head of troops. Then between al-Mahdiyya and al-Qayrawān he killed Maysūr al-Ṣaqlabī,[397] who had marched to fight him at the head of an army. Then he arrived before al-Mahdiyya, reached its gate and stopped for a moment in front of the gate which had been closed to him. However, his supporters were defeated while they were fighting a battle with the Kutāma from behind Jamma.[398] When this news reached him he withdrew. That is the time of which al-Mahdī had foretold. He would say that it was only for this hour that he had founded al-Mahdiyya. The cursed one set up camp near Sūq al-Aḥad,[399] from where he blockaded the city and its surroundings.

6, p. 238; al-Maqrīzī, *Itti'āẓ*, vol. 1, p. 74; and Ibn Khaldūn, *al-'Ibar*, vol. 4, p. 83 (tr. *Berbères*, vol. 2, p. 528).

396. He is Abū al-'Abbās Khalīl b. Isḥāq b. Ward, poet and Fatimid general. He devoted himself to the service of the Fatimids during al-Qā'im's conquest of Tripoli. Later he accompanied al-Qā'im on the second expedition to Egypt of 306/918. He governed Sicily during 325–329/936–940 where he was noted for his excesses. See Ibn 'Idhārī, *al-Bayān*, vol. 1, p. 215; Ibn al-Athīr, *al-Kāmil*, vol. 6, pp. 261–262; and Ibn al-Abbār, *al-Ḥulla*, vol. 1, pp. 302–304.

397. He was a eunuch of al-Qā'im who commanded an expedition in 323/935 against Mūsā b. Abī al-'Āfiya al-Miknāsī, governor of Fās, to restore Fatimid rule. He was defeated and killed in 333/945 by the Banū Kamlān, a branch of the Hawwāra, who defected from his ranks and joined the forces of Abū Yazīd. See al-Bakrī, *al-Masālik*, pp. 31, 97–98, 128, 142, 155 (tr. pp. 70, 194, 249, 272, 295); and Ibn Khaldūn, *al-'Ibar*, vol. 4, pp. 83, 86 (tr. *Berbères*, vol. 2, pp. 529, 532), vol. 6, pp. 276–277 (tr. *Berbères*, vol. 1, 269).

398. More exactly to the north-west of the peninsula. See Djelloul, 'Histoire topographique', p. 72. On Jamma see note 119 above.

399. Sūq al-Aḥad was located six miles from al-Mahdiyya. See Canard, *Vie*, p. 128, note

The followers among the Kutāma and others fought him in disarray without being led by anyone. Al-Qā'im had predicted his days, the duration of his revolt and his time. Then (Abū Yazīd) retreated from the region where he had set up his camp and reached al-Qayrawān. Later, he came back to Sousse and besieged it. When al-Qā'im felt that the hour of his end had approached, he chose as his heir apparent his son the Imam al-Manṣūr[400] and instructed him to fight him. (Al-Manṣūr) set out to march against him at the head of a handful of troops and supporters. (Abū Yazīd) raised the siege of Sousse. (Al-Manṣūr) pursued him to al-Qayrawān. After some days of hesitation, (Abū Yazīd) retreated from there. Al-Manṣūr pursued him while he was fleeing at his advance. Every time he caught up with him, he attacked his supporters, but (Abū Yazīd) escaped until he reached the citadel of Kiyāna,[401] in the region of al-Zāb, where he remained retrenched. Al-Manṣūr besieged him there until when God delivered (Abū Yazīd) to him as prisoner, seriously wounded. Before long he died in captivity and God dispatched him quickly to hellfire. His rebellion lasted for twenty months from the time he arrived in al-Qayrawān until the day he came out of it. I have given an exhaustive account of his adventures in a voluminous book where I have gathered all the information.[402]

263; al-Tijānī, *Riḥla*, p. 325; and Djelloul, 'Histoire topographique', pp. 72, 94.

400. This public designation took place in Ramaḍān 334/April 946, shortly before the death of al-Qā'im. See Ibn 'Idhārī, *al-Bayān*, vol. 1, p. 218; Ibn Ḥammād, *Akhbār*, p. 21 (tr. p. 37); and Ibn Khaldūn, *al-'Ibar*, vol. 4, p. 89 (tr. *Berbères*, vol. 2, p. 535). However, al-Qā'im had designated his heir secretly much earlier, and on more than one occasion. In two passages of his *al-Majālis wa-al-musāyarāt*, al-Qāḍī al-Nu'mān affirms that al-Qā'im had designated al-Manṣūr secretly twelve or thirteen years earlier: *al-Majālis wa-al-musāyarāt*, pp. 468–469 (twelve years), p. 448 (thirteen years). Furthermore, according to Jawdhar's testimony, before burying al-Mahdī's body, al-Qā'im confided to him that his son Ismā'īl, the future al-Manṣūr, was his proof (*ḥujja*) and heir apparent. Jawdhar kept this designation secret for seven years. See al-Jawdharī, *Sīrat al-Ustādh Jawdhar*, p. 40 (tr. Canard, *Vie*, p. 55).

401. Kiyāna denotes the citadel and also the mountain which dominates al-Masīla. See Ibn Ḥammād, *Akhbār*, pp. 30ff. (tr. pp. 50ff.). Later it became Qal'at Abī Ṭāwil. See al-Bakrī, *al-Masālik*, p. 49 (tr. p. 105). Then, on the same massif, Qal'at Banī Ḥammād was built. Lucien Golvin, 'Ḳal'at Banī Ḥammād', *EI*², vol. 4, pp. 478–481.

402. This work is now lost. See Poonawala, *Biobibliography*, p. 58.

Al-Qā'im died in Shawwāl 334/May 946,[403] and proceeded to the bountiful grace of God which He had prepared for him. It was through al-Manṣūr that God extinguished the dissension and delivered the community. He followed a policy of granting pardon and forgiveness to those who came under his rule, and who had waged war against him and participated in the dissension against him.[404] He raided the land of the Byzantines and conquered most of the land of Calabria, returning with booty and captives from there.[405] He did not announce the death of al-Qā'im until God, the Mighty, the Glorious, enabled him to defeat the accursed Deceiver (*al-dajjāl*).[406] Only then did he announce his death publicly, and showed patience at his bereavement and endurance at this tragedy, anticipating God's reward for bearing the burden and the pain of his grief. Then (al-Manṣūr) died at the end of Shawwāl 341/19 March 953,[407] after appointing his son al-Muʿizz li-dīn Allāh to the imamate and designating him to the caliphate.[408]

(Al-Muʿizz) assumed the imamate after him, following in his footsteps and in the footsteps of his forefathers. Just like al-Manṣūr, he showed patience at his bereavement and endured his loss which he continued to bear thereafter. He assumed the burdens of the caliphate in the aftermath of general dissension, at a time when the outlying regions of the kingdom were in a state of revolt and routes were insecure. Darkness had not yet dispelled, nor had the flames of the fire of dissension subsided. The chiefs of the tribes who had

403. More exactly on Sunday 13 Shawwāl 334/18 May 946. See Ibn ʿIdhārī, *al-Bayān*, vol. 1, p. 218; al-Maqrīzī, *Ittiʿāẓ*, vol. 1, p. 86.

404. See the letter of al-Manṣūr on this subject in al-Jawdharī, *Sīrat al-Ustādh Jawdhar*, pp. 69–70 (tr. Canard, *Vie*, pp. 100–101).

405. The Fatimid fleet commanded by Faraḥ and supported by reinforcements from the governor of Sicily, al-Ḥasan b. ʿAlī al-Kalbī, was victorious in Calabria in 340/951–2. See Umberto Rizzitano, 'Ḳillawriya (Calabria)', *EI²*, vol. 5, p. 105; Ibn al-Athīr, *al-Kāmil*, vol. 6, pp. 327–328; and Ibn Khaldūn, *al-ʿIbar*, vol. 4, pp. 94–95 (tr. *Berbères*, vol. 2, pp. 540–541).

406. See al-Manṣūr's sermon in which he announced the death of al-Qā'im in al-Jawdharī, *Sīrat al-Ustādh Jawdhar*, pp. 55–60 (tr. Canard, *Vie*, pp. 80–87).

407. See the letter of al-Muʿizz announcing the death of his father to Jawdhar and asking him to keep it secret, as well as the sermon in which he announced the death, in al-Jawdharī, *Sīrat al-Ustādh Jawdhar*, pp. 72–74 and 76–84 (tr. Canard, *Vie*, pp. 106–108 and 111–122).

408. This designation took place in 340/951–2. See Ibn ʿIdhārī, *al-Bayān*, vol. 1, p. 221.

provoked the war and kindled its fire remained entrenched in their hideouts in the mountains and the outlying regions. Al-Muʿizz li-dīn Allāh set out to fight them immediately after God conveyed to him the caliphate. God caused them to descend from their fortresses and struck terror in their hearts. They came to him seeking his arbitration over themselves, entrusting their affairs to him. He pardoned them, following the policy of his father, and brought them all the stability of his dominion. The war was over, its smoke abated and its fire was extinguished. Routes became safe and fear subsided. People calmed down and felt secure. God reconciled the hearts of His servants through him and put an end to the causes of corruption. The outlying regions and the tribes all submitted to him, whether close or far away and near or remote. Muḥammad b. Khazar,[409] chief of the Berbers, came to him to offer his submission and entrust his affairs to him. He sought forgiveness and pardon, which (al-Muʿizz) granted him out of his grace. He stayed at his court at his request to stay with him, and moved his family and members of his house to him. Formerly his ancestors had been chiefs and commanders of the Berbers until he submitted to al-Muʿizz and abandoned his ways. Neither he nor any of his ancestors had submitted to anyone before that time. Their leadership of them did not cease, nor did the Berbers abandon submission to their authority until God brought him back and caused him to see the path of his righteousness and guided him to the integrity of his soul.

Al-Muʿizz raided the Umayyads of Andalusia and set their fleet and shipyard on fire. He captured Almeria[410] and its goods with a few ships which he had dispatched for some purpose. They transgressed at sea and ventured on the route to the east without his order.

---

409. On him see note 345 above.

410. A strategic town in the most easterly part of Andalusia on the Mediterranean coast established in 344/955 by ʿAbd al-Raḥmān al-Nāṣir. See C. F. Seybold, 'Almeria', *EI*, vol. 1, pp. 313–314; Jacinto Bosch-Vila, 'al-Mariyya (Almeria)', *EI*², vol. 6, pp. 575–577. The daring raid on Almeria was carried out in 344/955 by the governor of Sicily, al-Hasan b. ʿAlī al-Kalbī, to avenge an attack on a Fatimid ship heading for al-Mahdiyya. See al-Qāḍī al-Nuʿmān, *al-Majālis wa-al-musāyarāt*, pp. 164–165; Ibn al-Athīr, *al-Kāmil*, vol. 6, p. 349; and Lévi-Provençal, *Histoire*, vol. 2, p. 108.

He raided Byzantine territory and captured Calabria. He demolished its churches and despoiled its towns after his fleet encountered the fleet of the tyrant[411] near it and engaged it. He defeated him and arrived in Byzantine territory. Then the admiral of the fleet of the tyrant and commander of his army submitted tribute (*jizya*) to him on behalf of the people of his community. He came reluctantly to the court of (al-Muʿizz).[412] This was as a victory and favour from God, the Mighty, the Glorious, which He bestowed upon him, just as He bestowed favours upon his forefathers before him. He conquered his dominion with good fortune and felicity. He mitigated difficulties for him, extended assistance to him, and bestowed upon him favour, good fortune and integrity.

(Al-Muʿizz) conducted the work of his *daʿwa* himself, hoping thereby to gain reward from God, his lord, without being haughty or disdainful in dealing with the strong who sought that, nor the lowly, nor nobleman, nor commoner. God granted him wisdom, eloquence, sound argument and proof. He performed the prayers of the festivals and many Friday congregational prayers during which he himself delivered the sermon with the greatest eloquence and awe. It was clear through this that he had received God's assistance in accomplishing this, since he was quite young and had little experience and tutoring. He was not known to have had a teacher to teach him, nor an instructor to instruct him other than the friend of God [al-Manṣūr] who had transmitted to him whatever knowledge he had received from God. God, the Mighty, the Glorious, gave him more of it, distinguishing him with His grace. He guided him ever more constantly, inspired him and assisted him. He bestowed favours upon him, through which He chose him for noble traits and distinguished him with their miracles. He indicated thereby that he had inherited the imamate, which would continue to be transmitted in the worthy descendants of his posterity, as a favour which God established for

411. The emperor of Byzantium.

412. On this embassy which crowned the Fatimid military success over the Byzantines in Sicily and Calabria see al-Qāḍī al-Nuʿmān, *al-Majālis wa-al-musāyarāt*, pp. 366–370; Samuel M. Stern, 'An Embassy of the Byzantine Emperor to the Fāṭimid Caliph al-Muʿizz', *Byzantion*, 20 (1950), pp. 239–258; and Farhat Dachraoui, 'La Crète dans le conflit entre Byzance et al-Muʿizz,' *Les cahiers de Tunisie*, 7 (1959), pp. 307–318.

them, a mark of nobility which He has preserved in their offspring from Muḥammad, seal of the prophets, until the end of the world. Praise be to God, Lord of the worlds.

We have recorded the biography of al-Muʿizz, detailing the favours which God bestowed upon him, and the nobility which He granted him, from the time He granted him the caliphate until the time I completed this book, hour by hour and day by day. I shall continue to gather material and add to it the favours which God grants him, and bestows upon him until the end of his life, and the end of my term during the continuation of his long reign, under his obedience and attaining his satisfaction, God willing. We have already gathered to this effect several chapters whose meanings I have set forth at length and in which I have fully reported what I intended to report, so I must not deplete this book of anecdotes which I have mentioned in it. This is according to the condition of conciseness that I had set at the beginning of it and on which basis I had designed it. I completed it in al-Muḥarram 346/April 957. Abundant praise be to God, which meets with His satisfaction, and which may bring us near to Him. May God bless His Prophet and his pure posterity from his descendants, and may He grant them all salvation.

Bibliography

Abdul-Wahab, Hassen Husni. 'Les steppes tunisiennes (région de Gammouda) pendant le Moyen-Age', *Les cahiers de Tunisie*, 2 (1954), pp. 5–16.

Abou El Fadl, Khaled. *Rebellion and Violence in Islamic Law*. Cambridge, 2001.

Abū al-ʿArab Muḥammad b. Aḥmad b. Tamīm al-Qayrawānī. *Ṭabaqāt ʿulamāʾ Ifrīqiya wa-Tūnis*, ed. ʿAlī al-Shabbī and Naʿīm Ḥasan al-Yāfī. Tunis, 1968.

Abū al-Aswad al-Duʾalī. *Dīwān Abī al-Aswad al-Duʾalī sanʿat Abī Saʿīd al-Ḥasan al-Sukkarī*, ed. Muḥammad Ḥasan Āl Yāsīn. Beirut, 1974.

Abū Dāwūd Sulaymān b. al-Ashʿath al-Sijistānī. *Sunan Abī Dāwūd*, ed. Muḥammad Muḥyī al-Dīn ʿAbd al-Ḥamīd. Beirut, n.d. English tr. Ahmad Hasan, New Delhi, 1985.

Abū al-Fidāʾ ʿImād al-Dīn Ismāʿīl b. ʿAlī. *Kitāb Taqwīm al-buldān*, ed. J. T. Reinaud and W. Mac Guckin de Slane. Paris, 1840.

al-ʿAjlūnī al-Jarrāḥī, Ismāʿīl b. Muḥammad. *Kashf al-khafāʾ wa-muzīl al-ilbās ʿammā ishtahara min al-aḥādīth ʿalā alsinat al-nās*, ed. Aḥmad al-Qalāsh. Aleppo, n.d.

ʿArīb b. Saʿd al-Qurṭubī. *Ṣilat Taʾrīkh al-Ṭabarī*, ed. M. J. de Goeje. Leiden, 1897.

al-Bakrī, Abū ʿUbayd ʿAbd Allāh b. ʿAbd al-ʿAzīz. *al-Masālik wa-al-mamālik = Description de l'Afrique septentrionale*, ed. and French tr. W. Mac Guckin de Slane. Paris, 1965.

Baratte, François and Noël Duval. *Haïdra: les ruines d'Ammaedara*. Tunis, 1974.

Bekri, Chikh. 'Le kharijisme berbère: quelques aspects du royaume rustumide', *Annales de l'Institut d'études orientales*, 15 (1957), pp. 55–109.

Bosworth, Clifford E. *The New Islamic Dynasties: A Chronological and Genealogical Manual*. Edinburgh, 1996.

Brett, Michael. *The Rise of the Fatimids: The World of the Mediterranean and the Middle East in the Fourth Century of the Hijra, Tenth Century* CE. Leiden, 2001.

Brocklemann, Carl. *Geschichte der arabischen Litteratur (GAL)*. Leiden, 1996.

Brunschvig, Robert. 'Fiqh fatimide et histoire de l'Ifriqiya', in *Mélanges d'histoire et d'archéologie de l'Occident musulman II: Hommage à Georges Marçais*. Algiers, 1957, pp. 13–20, reprinted in his *Études d'islamologie*, ed. A. M. Turki. Paris, 1976, vol. 1, pp. 63–70.

al-Bukhārī, Abū ʿAbd Allāh Muḥammad b. Ismāʿīl. *Ṣaḥīḥ al-Bukhārī: Translation of the meanings of Sahih al-Bukhari, Arabic-English*, tr. M. M. Khan. New Delhi, 1987.

Canard, Marius. 'L'autobiographie d'un chambellan du Mahdî ʿObeidallâh le Fâṭimide', *Hespéris*, 39 (1952), pp. 279–329, reprinted in his *Miscellanea Orientalia*, London, 1973, article V.

——'Une famille de partisans, puis d'adversaires, des Fatimides en Afrique du Nord', in *Mélanges d'histoire et d'archéologie de l'Occident musulman II: Hommage à Georges Marçais*. Algiers, 1957, pp. 33–49, reprinted in his *L'expansion arabo-islamique et ses repércussions*, London, 1974, article V.

Cortese, Delia. *Ismaili and Other Arabic Manuscripts: A Descriptive Catalogue of Manuscripts in the Library of The Institute of Ismaili Studies*. London, 2000.

——*Arabic Ismaili Manuscripts: The Zāhid ʿAlī Collection in the Library of The Institute of Ismaili Studies*. London, 2003.

Dachraoui, Farhat. 'Tentative d'infiltration šiʿite en Espagne musulmane sous le regne d'al-Ḥakam II,' *al-Andalus*, 23 (1958), pp. 97–106.

——'La Crète dans le conflit entre Byzance et al-Muʿizz,' *Les cahiers de Tunisie*, 7 (1959), pp. 307–318.

——'Contribution à l'histoire des Fāṭimides en Ifrīqiya', *Arabica*, 8 (1961), pp. 189–203.

——'Les commencements de la prédication ismaʿilienne en Ifriqiya', *Studia Islamica*, 20 (1964), pp. 89–102.

——*Le califat fatimide au Maghreb (295–365 H./909–975 JC.): histoire politique et institutions*. Tunis, 1981.

Daftary, Farhad. *The Ismāʿīlis: Their History and Doctrines*. Cambridge, 1990.

——'The Ismaili *daʿwa* outside the Fatimid *dawla*', in M. Barrucand, ed., *L'Égypte fatimide: son art et son histoire*. Paris, 1999, pp. 29–43.

——'A Major Schism in the Early Ismaʿili Movement', *Studia Islamica*, 77 (1993), pp. 123–139.

——ed., *Mediaeval Isma'ili History and Thought*. Cambridge, 1996.

Djelloul, Néji. 'Histoire topographique de Mahdia et de ses environs au Moyen Âge', *Les cahiers de Tunisie*, 162–163 (1992–1993), pp. 71–103 + 5 plates.

Dozy, Reinhart. *Supplément aux dictionnaires arabes*. Leiden-Paris, 1967.

E. J. Brill's First Encyclopaedia of Islam 1913–1936. Leiden, 1987.

Encyclopaedia of Islam. New ed., Leiden, 1960–2006.

Encyclopédie berbère. Aix-en-Provence, 1984–.

Ennaïfer, Mongi. *La cité d'Althiburos et l'édifice des Asclepieia*. Tunis, 1976.

Fagnan, Edmond. 'Nouveaux textes historiques relatif à l'Afrique du Nord et à la Sicile', in *Centenario della nascita di Michele Amari*. Palermo, 1910, vol. 2, pp. 35–114.

——*Additions aux dictionnaires arabes*. Algiers, 1923.

Fahd, Toufic. *La divination arabe*. Paris, 1987.

Farrugia de Candia, J. 'Monnaies fâṭimites du Musée du Bardo', *Revue tunisienne*, 27–28 (1936), pp. 333–372; 29 (1937), pp. 89–136.

Féki, Habib. *Les idées religieuses et philosophiques de l'ismaélisme fatimide*. Tunis, 1978.

Gacek, Adam. *Catalogue of Arabic Manuscripts in the Library of The Institute of Ismaili Studies*. London, 1984–1985.

Gateau, Albert. 'La Sīrat Ja'far al-Ḥājib: contribution à l'histoire des Fatimides', *Hespéris*, 34 (1947), pp. 375–396.

Geddes, Charles L. 'The Apostasy of 'Alī b. al-Faḍl', in R. L. Bidwell and G. R. Smith ed., *Arabian and Islamic Studies: Articles Presented to R. B. Serjeant*. London, 1983, pp. 80–85.

Golvin, Lucien. 'Mahdiya à l'époque fātimide', *Revue de l'Occident musulman et de la Méditerranée*, 27 (1979), pp. 75–98.

Halm, Heinz. 'Die *Sīrat Ibn Ḥaušab*: Die ismailitische *da'wa* im Jemen und die Fatimiden', *Die Welt des Orients*, 12 (1981), pp. 107–135.

——*The Empire of the Mahdi: The Rise of the Fatimids*, tr. M. Bonner. Leiden, 1996.

——'The Isma'ili Oath of Allegiance (*'ahd*) and the 'Sessions of Wisdom' (*majālis al-ḥikma*) in Fatimid Times', in F. Daftary, ed., *Mediaeval Isma'ili History and Thought*. Cambridge, 1996, pp. 91–115.

Hamdani, Abbas and François de Blois. 'A Re-examination of al-Mahdī's Letter to the Yemenites on the Genealogy of the Fatimid Caliphs', *Journal of the Royal Asiatic Society*, (1983), pp. 173–207.

al-Hamdānī, Abū Muḥammad al-Ḥasan b. Aḥmad. *Ṣifat Jazīrat al-'Arab*, ed. Muḥammad b. 'Alī al-Akwa'. 3rd ed., Ṣan'ā', 1403/1983.

al-Hamdānī, Ḥusayn b. Fayḍ Allāh. *al-Ṣulayḥiyyūn wa-al-ḥaraka al-Fāṭimiyya fī al-Yaman (min sanat 268 h ilā sanat 626 h)*. Cairo, 1955.

——*On the Genealogy of Fatimid Caliphs*. Cairo, 1958.

Ḥasan Ibrāhīm Ḥasan and Ṭāhā Aḥmad Sharaf, *'Ubayd Allāh al-Mahdī: Imām al-Shī'a al-Ismā'iliyya wa-mu'assis al-dawla al-Fāṭimiyya fī bilād al-Maghrib*. Cairo, 1366/1947.

al-Ḥammādī al-Yamānī, Muḥammad b. Mālik b. Abī al-Faḍā'il. *Kashf asrār al-Bāṭiniyya wa-akhbār al-Qarāmiṭa*, ed. Muḥammad Zāhid b. al-Ḥasan al-Kawtharī. Cairo,1357/1939.

Higgins, A. J. 'Common Ectoparasites of the Camel and their Control', in A. Higgins, ed., *The Camel in Health and Disease*. London, 1986, pp. 72–91.

Hussain, Jasim M. *The Occultation of the Twelfth Imam: A Historical Background*. London, 1982.

Ibn al-Abbār, Abū 'Abd Allāh Muḥammad b. 'Abd Allāh b. Abī Bakr al-Quḍā'ī. *Kitāb al-Ḥulla al-siyarā'*, ed. Ḥusayn Mu'nis (Hussain Monès). Cairo, 1963–1964.

Ibn al-Anbārī, Muḥammad b. al-Qāsim. *Kitāb al-Aḍdād*, ed. Muḥammad Abū al-Faḍl Ibrāhīm. Kuwait, 1960.

Ibn Aranbughā al-Zaradkāsh. *al-Anīq fī al-manājanīq*, ed. Iḥsān Hindī. Aleppo, 1405/1985.

Ibn al-Athīr al-Jazarī, 'Izz al-Dīn Abū al-Ḥasan 'Alī b. Muḥammad. *al-Kāmil fī al-ta'rīkh*. Beirut, 1387/1967.

Ibn al-Dawādārī, Abū Bakr b. 'Abd Allāh. *Kanz al-durar wa-jāmi' al-ghurar*, vol. 6, ed. Ṣalāḥ al-Dīn al-Munajjid. Cairo, 1380/1961.

Ibn Ḥajar al-'Asqalānī, Aḥmad b. 'Alī. *al-Iṣāba fī tamyīz al-ṣaḥāba*. Cairo, 1939.

Ibn Ḥammād, Abū 'Abd Allāh Muḥammad b. 'Alī. *Akhbār mulūk Banī 'Ubayd wa-sīratuhum = Histoire des rois 'obaïdides*, ed. and tr. M. Vonderheyden. Algiers-Paris, 1346/1927.

Ibn Ḥawqal al-Naṣībī, Abū al-Qāsim Muḥammad. *Kitāb Ṣūrat al-arḍ*. Beirut, 1979.

Ibn al-Haytham, Abū 'Abd Allāh Ja'far b. Aḥmad. *Kitāb al-Munāẓarāt*, ed. and tr. W. Madelung and P. E. Walker as *The Advent of the Fatimids: A Contemporary Shi'i Witness*. London, 2000.

Ibn Ḥazm, Abū Muḥammad 'Alī b. Aḥmad. *Jamharat ansāb al-'Arab*, ed. 'Abd al-Salām Muḥammad Hārūn. Cairo, 1391/1971.

Ibn Hishām, 'Abd al-Malik. *al-Sīra al-nabawiyya*, ed. 'Umar 'Abd al-Salām Tadmurī. Beirut, 1413/1993. English tr. A. Guillaume, *The Life of*

Muhammad: A Translation of Isḥāq's Sīrat Rasūl Allāh. Karachi, 1982.

Ibn ʿIdhārī al-Marrākushī, Abū al-ʿAbbās Aḥmad b. Muḥammad. *Kitāb al-Bayān al-mughrib fī akhbār al-Andalus wa-al-Maghrib*, vol. 1, ed. G. S. Colin and E. Lévi-Provençal. Leiden, 1948.

Ibn al-Jarrāḥ, Abū ʿAbd Allāh Muḥammad b. Dāwud. *al-Waraqa*, ed. Farrāj ʿAbd al-Sattār Aḥmad Farrāj and ʿAbd al-Wahhāb ʿAzzām, 2nd ed., Cairo, 1967.

Ibn Kathīr, ʿImād al-Dīn Ismāʿīl b. ʿUmar. *al-Bidāya wa-al-nihāya*. Beirut, 1974–1977.

Ibn Khaldūn, ʿAbd Al-Raḥmān b. Muḥammad. *Kitāb al-ʿIbar wa-al-dīwān al-mubtadaʾ wa-al-khabar fī ayyām al-ʿarab wa-al-ʿajam wa-al-barbar wa-man ʿāṣarahum min dhawī al-ṣulṭān al-akbar*. Beirut, 1956–1961. Partial French tr. W. Mac Guckin de Slane as *Histoire des Berères et les dynasties musulmanes de l'Afrique septentrionale*. Paris, 1978.

Ibn al-Khaṭīb, Lisān al-Dīn Abū ʿAbd Allāh Muḥammad. *Aʿmāl al-aʿlām*, part 3 ed. Aḥmad Mukhtār al-ʿAbbādī and Muḥammad Ibrāhīm al-Kattānī as *Tārīkh al-Maghrib al-ʿArabī fī al-ʿaṣr al-wasīṭ: al-qism al-thālith min kitāb Aʿmāl al-aʿlām*. Casablanca, 1964.

Ibn Manẓūr, Abū al-Faḍl Muḥammad b. Mukarram al-Anṣārī. *Lisān al-ʿArab*. Beirut, 1374–1376/1955–1957.

Ibn Nājī al-Tanūkhī, Abū al-Qāsim b. ʿĪsā. *Maʿālim al-īmān fī maʿrifat ahl al-Qayrawān*, ed. Ibrāhīm Shabbūḥ. Cairo, 1968–1972.

Ibn Rashīq al-Qayrawānī, al-Ḥasan. *Unmūdhaj al-zamān fī shuʿarāʾ al-Qayrawān*, ed. Muḥammad al-ʿArūsī al-Maṭwī and Bashīr al-Bakkūsh. Tunis, 1406/1986.

Ibn Shākir al-Kutubī, Muḥammad. *Fawāt al-wafayāt wa-al-dhayl ʿalayhā*, ed. Iḥsān ʿAbbās. Beirut, 1973–1974.

Ibn Taghrī Birdī, Jamāl al-Dīn Abū al-Maḥāsin Yūsuf. *al-Nujūm al-zāhira fī mulūk Miṣr wa-al-Qāhira*. Cairo, 1932–1950.

Ibn Ẓāfir al-Azdī, Jamāl al-Dīn ʿAlī. *Akhbār al-duwal al-munqaṭiʿa*, ed. A. Ferré. Cairo, 1972.

Ibn al-Zubayr, Muḥammad et al. *Muʿjam asmāʾ al-ʿArab*. Muscat, 1991.

Idris, Hady Roger. *La Berbérie orientale sous les Zīrīdes, Xᵉ-XIIᵉ siècles*. Paris, 1962.

——'Contribution à l'histoire de l'Ifriḳiya. Tableau littéraire de la vie intellectuelle et administrative à Kairouan sous les Aglabites et les Fatimites (4 premiers siècle de l'Hégire), d'après le Riyāḍ En nufūs de Abū Bakr El Mālikī', *Revue des études islamiques*, 9 (1935), pp. 105–178, 273–305; 10 (1936), pp. 45–104.

——'Glanes sur les Zīrides d'Ifrīqiya dans le manuscrit d'Istanbul de l'*Itti'āẓ al-ḥunafā*', *Arabica*, 11 (1964), pp. 286–305.

Idrīs 'Imād al-Dīn al-Qurashī. *'Uyūn al-akhbār wa-funūn al-āthār fī faḍā'il al-a'imma al-aṭhār*, vols. 4–6 ed. Muṣṭafā Ghālib. Beirut, 1973–1984; vol. 5 and part of vol. 6, ed. Muḥammad al-Ya'lāwī as *Ta'rīkh al-khulafā' al-Fāṭimiyyīn bi-al-Maghrib: al-qism al-khāṣṣ min kitāb 'Uyūn al-akhbār*. Beirut, 1985.

al-Idrīsī, Abū 'Abd Allāh Muḥammad. *Kitāb Nuzhat al-mushtāq fī ikhtirāq al-āfāq*, ed. and tr. R. Dozy and M. J. de Goeje as *Ṣifat al-Maghrib wa-arḍ al-Sūdān wa-Miṣr wa-al-Andalus ma'khūdh min Kitāb Nuzhat al-mushtāq fī ikhtirāq al-āfāq = Description de l'Afrique et de l'Espagne par Edrîsî*. Leiden, 1986.

Ivanow, Wladimir. 'The Organization of the Fatimid Propaganda', *Journal of the Bombay Branch of the Royal Asiatic Society*, new series, 15 (1939), pp. 1–35.

——'Ismailis and Qarmatians', *Journal of the Bombay Branch of the Royal Asiatic Society*, new series, 16 (1940), pp. 43–85.

——*Ismaili Tradition Concerning the Rise of the Fatimids*. London, etc., 1942.

——*Ismaili Literature: A Bibliographical Survey*. Tehran, 1963.

'Iyāḍ, al-Qāḍī Abū al-Faḍl. *Tartīb al-madārik wa-taqrīb al-masālik li-ma'rifat a'lām madhhab Mālik*, selections ed. Muḥammad al-Ṭālibī as *Tarājim Aghlabiyya mustakhraja min Madārik al-Qāḍī 'Iyāḍ*. Tunis, 1968.

Ja'far b. Manṣūr al-Yaman. *Asrār al-nuṭaqā'*, ed. Muṣṭafā Ghālib as *Sarā'ir wa-asrār al-nuṭaqā'*. Beirut, 1404/1984.

——*Kitāb al-'ālim wa-al-ghulām*, ed. and tr. James W. Morris as *The Master and the Disciple: An Early Islamic Spiritual Dialogue*. London, 2001.

al-Jawdharī, Abū 'Alī Manṣūr al-'Azīzī. *Sīrat al-Ustādh Jawdhar*, ed. Muḥammad Kāmil Ḥusayn and Muḥammad 'Abd al-Hādī Sha'īra. Cairo, 1954. French tr. M. Canard, *Vie de l'Ustadh Jawdhar*. Algiers, 1958.

Jiwa, Shainool. 'The Initial Destination of the Fatimid Caliphate: the Yemen or the Maghrib?' *British Society for Middle Eastern Studies Bulletin*, 13 (1986), pp. 15–26.

Joly, Ch. Al. 'Thubursicum Numidarum (Khemissa)', *Recueils des notices et mémoires de la Société archéologique du Département de Constantine*, 39 (1906), pp. 165–192.

Kay, Henry Cassels, ed. and tr. *Yaman: Its Early Mediaeval History: also the abridged history of its dynasties, and an account of the Karmathians of Yaman*. London, 1892.

Kazimirski, Albin de Biberstein. *Dictionnaire arabe-français*. Cairo, 1875.

Kennedy, Hugh. ed. *An Historical Atlas of Islam*. 2nd rev. ed., Leiden, 2002.

Khūrī, Yūsuf Q. *al-Makhṭūṭāt al-ʿArabiyya al-mawjūda fī Maktabat al-Jāmiʿa al-Amrīkiyya fī Bayrūt*. Beirut, 1985.

al-Khushanī, Abū ʿAbd Allāh Muḥammad b. Ḥārith b. Asad. *Quḍāt Qurṭuba wa-ʿUlamāʾ Ifrīqiya*, ed. ʿIzzat al-ʿAṭṭār al-Ḥusaynī. [Cairo-Baghdad], 1372/[1953].

al-Kindī, Muḥammad b. Yūsuf. *Wulāt Miṣr*, ed. Ḥusayn Naṣṣār. Beirut, 1379/1959.

Kuthayyir ʿAzza. *Dīwān Kuthayyir ʿAzza*, ed. Iḥsān ʿAbbās. Beirut, 1391/1971.

Lane, Edward William. *Arabic-English Lexicon*. London, 1863–1893.

Lavoix, Henri. *Catalogue des monnaies musulmanes de la Bibliothèque nationale*. Paris, 1887–1896: [1] *Khalifes orientaux*, 1887, [2] *Espagne et Afrique*, 1891, [3] *Egypte et Syrie*, 1896.

Le Tourneau, Roger, 'La révolte d'Abû Yazîd au Xme siècle', *Les cahiers de Tunisie*, 1 (1953), pp. 103–125.

Lévi-Provençal, Evariste. *Histoire de l'Espagne musulmane*. Paris, 1950–1953.

Lézine, Alexandre. *Mahdiya: recherches d'archéologie islamique*. [Paris], 1965.

——*Le ribat de Sousse: suivi de notes sur le ribat de Monastir*. Tunis, 1956.

Lindsay, James E. 'Kitāb Iftitāḥ al-daʿwa by al-Qāḍī al-Nuʿmān: Section II, Chapters VIII and IX', *Al-ʿArabiyya*, 22 (1989), pp. 157–168.

——'Prophetic Parallels in Abu ʿAbd Allah al-Shiʿi's Mission among the Kutama Berbers, 893–910', *International Journal of Middle East Studies*, 24 (1992), pp. 39–56.

Luqbāl, Mūsā. *Dawr Kutāma fī tārīkh al-khilāfa al-Fāṭimiyya mundh taʾsīsihā ilā muntaṣaf al-qarn al-khāmis al-hijrī (11m)*. Algiers, 1979.

Madelung, Wilferd. 'The Religious Policy of the Fatimids toward their Sunnī Subjects in the Maghrib', in M. Barrucand, ed., *L'Égypte fatimide, son art et son histoire*. Paris, 1999, pp. 97–104.

——'Some Notes on Non-Ismāʿīlī Shiism in the Maghrib', *Studia Islamica*, 44 (1976), pp. 87–97.

——'The Sufyānī between Tradition and History', *Studia Islamica*, 63 (1986), pp. 5–48.

——"al-Mahdī', *EI*², vol. 5, pp. 1230–1238.

——"Manṣūr al-Yaman", *EI²*, vol. 6, pp. 438–439.

Maitrot, Albert Charles. 'Theveste. Étude militaire d'une cité romano-byzantine, 70 à 705', *Recueils des notices et mémoires de la Société archéologique du Département de Constantine*, 45 (1912), pp. 37–263.

al-Majdūʿ, Ismāʿīl b. ʿAbd al-Rasūl. *Fahrasat al-kutub wa-al-rasāʾil*, ed. Alinaqi Monzavi. Tehran, 1966.

al-Mālikī, Abū Bakr ʿAbd Allāh b. Muḥammad. *Kitāb Riyāḍ al-nufūs fī ṭabaqāt ʿulamāʾ al-Qayrawān wa-Ifrīqiya*, ed. Bashīr al-Bakkūsh, rev. Muḥammad al-ʿArūsī al-Maṭwī. 2nd ed., Beirut, 1414/1994.

al-Maqrīzī, Taqī al-Dīn Abū al-ʿAbbās Aḥmad b. ʿAlī. *Ittiʿāẓ al-ḥunafā bi-akhbār al-aʾimma al-Fāṭimiyyīn al-khulafā*, ed. J. al-Shayyāl and M. Ḥ. M. Aḥmad, Cairo, 1967–1973.

——*Kitāb al-Muqaffā al-kabīr (tarājim Maghribiyya wa-sharqiyya min al-fatra al-ʿUbaydiyya)*, ed. Muḥammad al-Yaʿlāwī. Beirut, 1407/1987. Biography of al-Mahdī tr. E. Fagnan as 'Traduction de la biographie d'ʿObeyd Allâh contenue dans le « Moḳaffa » de Maḳrīzī', in *Centenario della nascita di Michele Amari*. Palermo, 1910, vol. 2, pp. 35–85.

Marçais, Georges. *L'architecture musulmane d'Occident: Tunisie, Algérie, Maroc, Espagne et Sicile*. Paris, 1954.

Marçais, Georges. *La Berbérie musulmane et l'Orient au Moyen Age*. Paris, 1946.

al-Maydānī, Abū al-Faḍl Aḥmad b. Muḥammad b. Aḥmad b. Ibrāhīm al-Naysābūrī. *Majmaʿ al-amthāl*, ed. Muḥammad Muḥyī al-Dīn ʿAbd al-Ḥamīd. Cairo, 1374/1955.

Monès, Hussain. 'Le malékisme et l'échec des Fatimides en Ifriqiya', in *Etudes d'orientalisme dédiées à la mémoire de Lévi-Provençal*. Paris, 1962, vol. 1, pp. 197–220.

Muslim b. al-Ḥajjāj al-Qushayrī al-Nīsābūrī, Abū al-Ḥusayn. *Ṣaḥīḥ Muslim*, ed. Muḥammad Fuʾād ʿAbd al-Bāqī. [Cairo], 1374–1375/1955–1956. English tr. ʿAbdul Ḥamīd Ṣiddīqī. Lahore, 1976.

Nagel, Tilman. *Frühe Ismailiya und Fatimiden im Lichte der Risālat Iftitāḥ ad-daʿwa: eine religionsgeschichtliche Studie*. Bonn, 1972.

Nanji, Azim. 'An Ismāʿīlī Theory of *Walāyah* in the *Daʿāʾim al-Islām* of Qāḍī al-Nuʿmān', in *Essays on Islamic Civilization Presented to Niyazi Berkes*, ed. D. P. Little. Leiden, 1976, pp. 260–273.

al-Naysābūrī, Aḥmad b. Ibrāhīm. *Istitār al-imām*, ed. W. Ivanow, in *Bulletin of the Faculty of Arts*, University of Egypt, vol. 4 (1936), pp. 93–107. English tr. W. Ivanow, in his *Ismaili Tradition Concerning the Rise of the Fatimids*, pp. 157–183.

Noth, Albrecht. *The Early Arabic Historical Tradition: A Source-critical Study.* 2nd ed., tr. M. Bonner. Princeton, 1994.

al-Nuwayrī, Shihāb al-Dīn Aḥmad b. ʿAbd al-Wahhāb. *Nihāyat al-arab fī funūn al-adab*, vol. 24, ed. Ḥusayn Naṣṣār. Cairo, 1403/1983; selections ed. Muṣṭafā Abū Ḍayf Aḥmad as *Nihāyat al-arab fī funūn al-adab: al-dawla al-Fāṭimiyya bi-bilād al-Maghrib (296–361h/909–972m).* Casablanca, 1408/1988. Partial French tr. W. Mac Guckin de Slane: *Histoire des Berères et les dynasties musulmanes de l'Afrique septentrionale.* Paris, 1978.

Pellegrin, Arthur. *Essai sur les noms de lieux d'Algérie et de Tunisie: etymologie, signification.* Tunis, 1949.

Poonawala, Ismail K. *Biobibliography of Ismāʿīlī Literature.* Malibu, Calif., 1977.

——'Al-Qāḍī al-Nuʿmān and Ismaʿili Jurisprudence', in F. Daftary, ed., *Mediaeval Ismaʿili History and Thought.* Cambridge, 1996, pp. 117–143.

——'The Beginnings of the Ismaili *Daʿwa* and the Establishment of the Fatimid Dynasty as Commemorated by al-Qaḍī al-Nuʿmān', in Farhad Daftary and Josef W. Meri, ed., *Culture and Memory in Medieval Islam: Essays in Honour of Wilferd Madelung.* London, 2003, pp. 338–363.

al-Qāḍī al-Nuʿmān b. Muḥammad, Abū Ḥanīfa. *Daʿāʾim al-islām*, ed. A. A. A. Fyzee. Cairo, 1951–1960, English tr. A. A. A. Fyzee, rev. I. K. Poonawala, *The Pillars of Islam.* New Delhi, 2002–2004.

——*Kitāb al-Himma fī ādāb atbāʿ al-aʾimma*, ed. Muḥammad Kāmil Ḥusayn. Cairo, [1948].

——*Iftitāḥ al-daʿwa*, ed. Wadād al-Qādī. Beirut, 1970; ed. F. Dachraoui. Tunis, 1975.

——*al-Majālis wa-al-musāyarāt*, ed. al-Ḥabīb al-Faqī et al. Tunis, 1978.

——*Sharḥ al-akhbār fī faḍāʾil al-aʾimma al-aṭhār*, ed. al-Sayyid Muḥammad al-Ḥusaynī al-Jalālī. Qumm, n.d.

——*al-Urjūza al-mukhtāra*, ed. Ismail K. Poonawala. Montreal, 1970.

al-Qurṭubī, Abū ʿAbd Allāh Muḥammad b. Aḥmad. *al-Jāmiʿ li-aḥkām al-qurʾān.* Beirut, [1952]-1967.

Rechberger, Herman. *The Rhythm in Arabian Music.* Helsinki, 2004.

Reinach, Salomon. *Atlas de la province romaine d'Afrique, pour servir à l'ouvrage de M. Ch. Tissot.* Paris, 1888.

Sachedina, Abdulaziz A. *Islamic Messianism: The Idea of Mahdi in Twelver Shiʿism.* Albany, 1981.

al-Ṣafadi, Ṣalāḥ al-Dīn Khalīl b. Aybak. *al-Wāfī bi-al-wafayāt*, vol. 15 ed. B. Radtke, Wiesbaden, 1979.

Salama, Pierre. *Les voies romaines de l'Afrique du Nord*. Algiers, 1951.
al-Samhūdī, Alī b. ʿAbd Allāh, *Wafā' al-wafā bi-akhbār Dār al-Muṣṭafā*, ed. Qāsim al-Sāmarrāʾī. London, 2001.
Smoor, Pieter. 'Al-Mahdī's Tears: Impressions of Faṭimid Court Poetry', in U. Vermeulen and D. de Smet eds, *Egypt and Syria in the Fatimid, Ayyubid and Mamluk Eras II. Proceedings of the 4th, and 5th International Colloquium organized at the Katholieke Universiteit Leuven in May 1995 and 1996*. Leuven, 1998, pp.132–162.
Stern, Samuel M. 'Ismāʿīlī propaganda and Fatimid rule in Sind', *Islamic Culture*, 23 (1949), pp. 298–307, reprinted in his *Studies in Early Ismāʿīlism*, pp. 177–188.
——'An Embassy of the Byzantine Emperor to the Fatimid Caliph al-Muʿizz', *Byzantion*, 20 (1950), pp. 239–258.
——'Three North-African Topographical Notes (Islamic-Roman)', *Arabica*, 1 (1954), pp. 343–345.
——'Abū ʿAbd Allāh al-Shīʿī', *EI*², vol. 1, pp. 103–104.
——'Abū Yazīd al-Nukkārī', *EI*², vol. 1, pp. 163–164.
——*Studies in Early Ismāʿīlism*. Jerusalem-Leiden, 1983.
al-Ṣūlī, Abū Bakr Muḥammad b. Yaḥyā, *Akhbār Abī Tammām*, ed. Muḥammad ʿAbduh ʿAzzām et al. 3rd ed., Beirut, 1400/1980.
Talbi, Mohamed. *L'émirat aghlabide 184–296/800–909, histoire politique*. Paris, 1966.
al-Tijānī, ʿAbd Allāh b. Muḥammad. *Riḥlat al-Tijānī*, ed. Ḥasan Ḥusnī ʿAbd al-Wahhāb. Tunis, 1378/1958.
Tissot, Charles Joseph. *Géographie comparée de la province romaine d'Afrique*. Paris, 1884–1888.
van Arendonk, Cornelis. *Les débuts de l'imāmat zaidite au Yémen*, tr. J. Ryckmans. Leiden, 1960.
Vonderheyden, Madeleine. *La Berbérie orientale sous la dynastie de Benoû'l-Aṛlab 800–909*. Paris, 1927.
al-Wāqidī, Muḥammad b. ʿUmar. *Kitāb al-Maghāzī*, ed. M. Jones. London, 1966.
al-Warjalānī, Abū Zakarīyā Yaḥyā b. Abī Bakr. *Kitāb Siyar al-a'imma wa-akhbārihim*, ed. Ismāʿīl al-ʿArabī. Algiers, 1399/1979.
Yaḥyā b. Saʿīd al-Anṭākī. *Ta'rīkh al-Dhayl*, ed. and French tr. I. Kratchkovsky and A. Vasiliev as *Histoire de Yahya-ibn-Saʿïd d'Antioche: continuateur de Saʿïd-ibn-Bitriq* in *Patrologia Orientalis*, 18 (1924), pp. 705–833; 23 (1932), pp. 349–520.
al-Yaʿlāwī, Muḥammad. *al-Adab bi-Ifrīqiya fi al-ʿahd al-Fāṭimī, (296–365 h)*

= *La littérature en Ifriqiya sous les Fatimides (296–365/909–976)*. Beirut, 1986.

al-Yamānī, Muḥammad b. Muḥammad. *Sīrat al-Ḥājib Jaʿfar b. ʿAlī*, ed. W. Ivanow, in *Bulletin of the Faculty of Arts*, University of Egypt, vol. 4 (1936), pp. 107–133. English tr. W. Ivanow in his *Ismaili Tradition Concerning the Rise of the Fatimids*, pp. 184–223.

al-Yaʿqūbī, Aḥmad b. Abī Yaʿqūb. *Kitāb al-Buldān*, ed. A. W. T. Juynboll, Leiden, 1861. French tr. G. Wiet. *Les pays*. Cairo, 1937.

Yāqūt b. ʿAbd Allāh al-Ḥamawī al-Rūmī al-Baghdādī, Shihāb al-Dīn Abū ʿAbd Allāh. *Muʿjam al-buldān*. Beirut, 1374–1376/1955–1957.

al-Ziriklī, Khayr al-Dīn. *al-Aʿlām: qāmūs tarājim li-ashhar al-rijāl wa-al-nisāʾ min al-ʿarab wa-al-mustaʿribīn wa-al-mustashriqīn*. 10th ed., Beirut, 1992.

Index